Chapter 13 Blacksmith (Part 1)

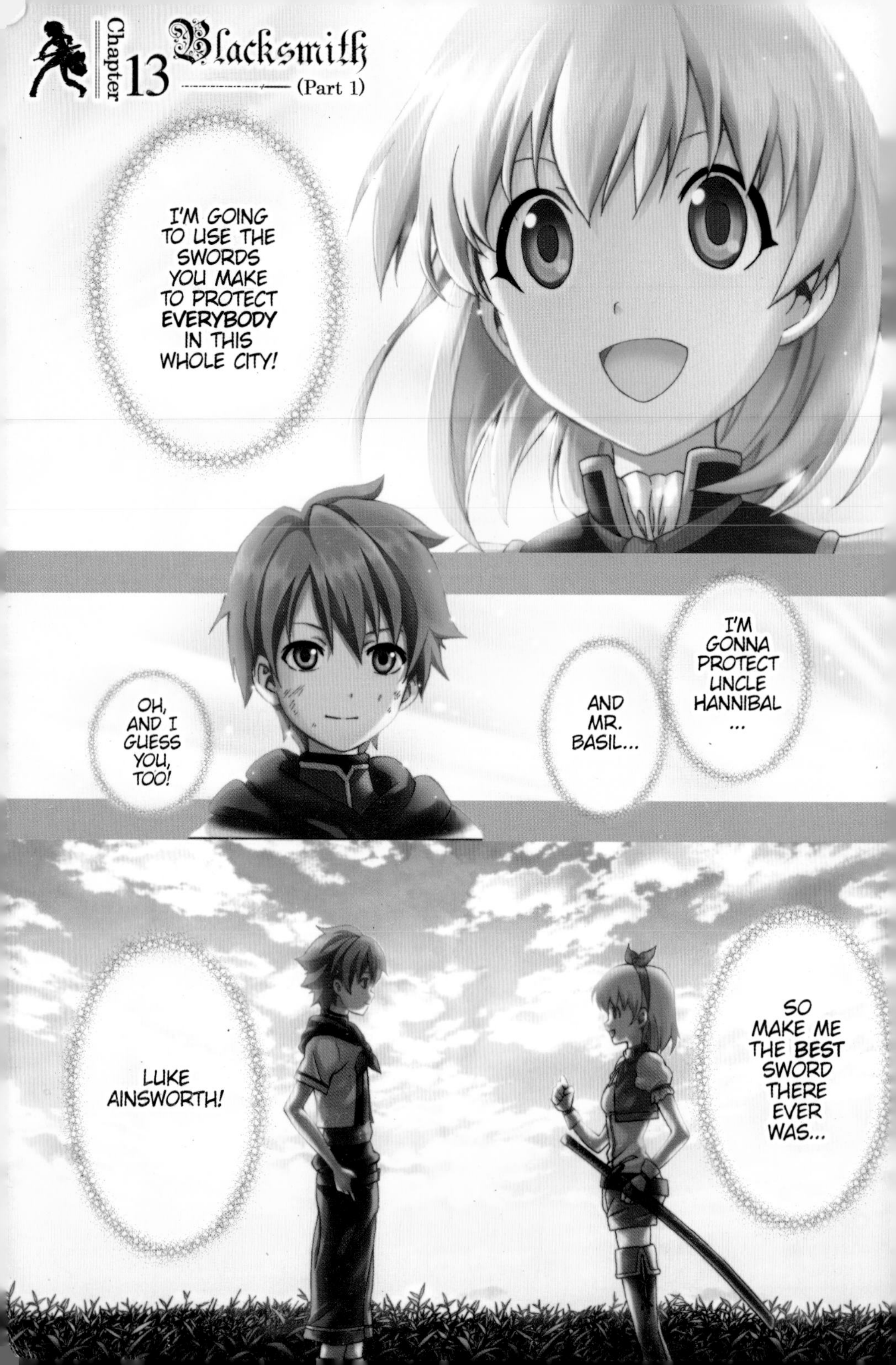
I'M GOING TO USE THE SWORDS YOU MAKE TO PROTECT **EVERYBODY** IN THIS WHOLE CITY!
I'M GONNA PROTECT UNCLE HANNIBAL ...
AND MR. BASIL...
OH, AND I GUESS YOU, TOO!
SO MAKE ME THE BEST SWORD THERE EVER WAS...
LUKE AINSWORTH!

Sacred Blacksmith

の刀鍛冶

ブラックスミス

4

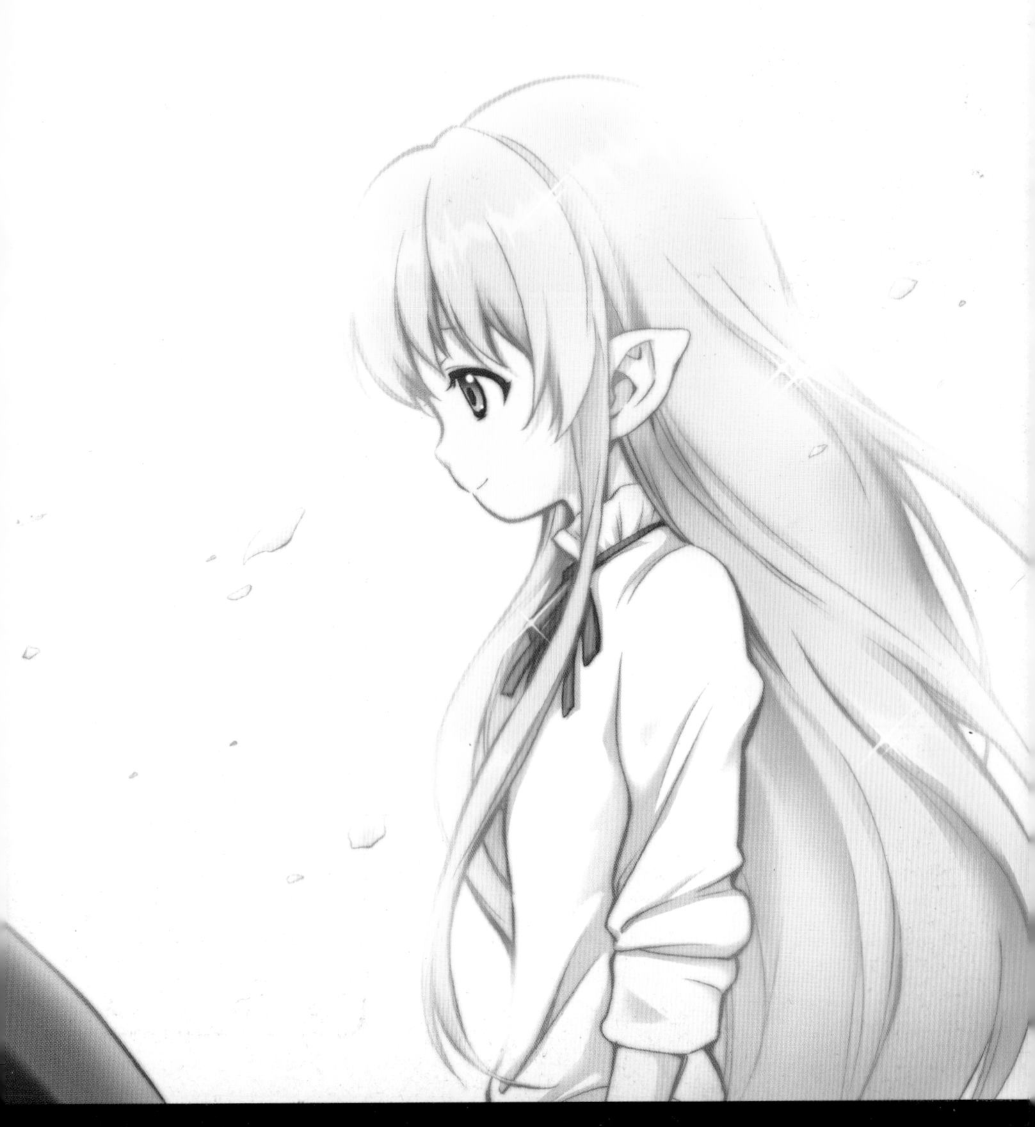

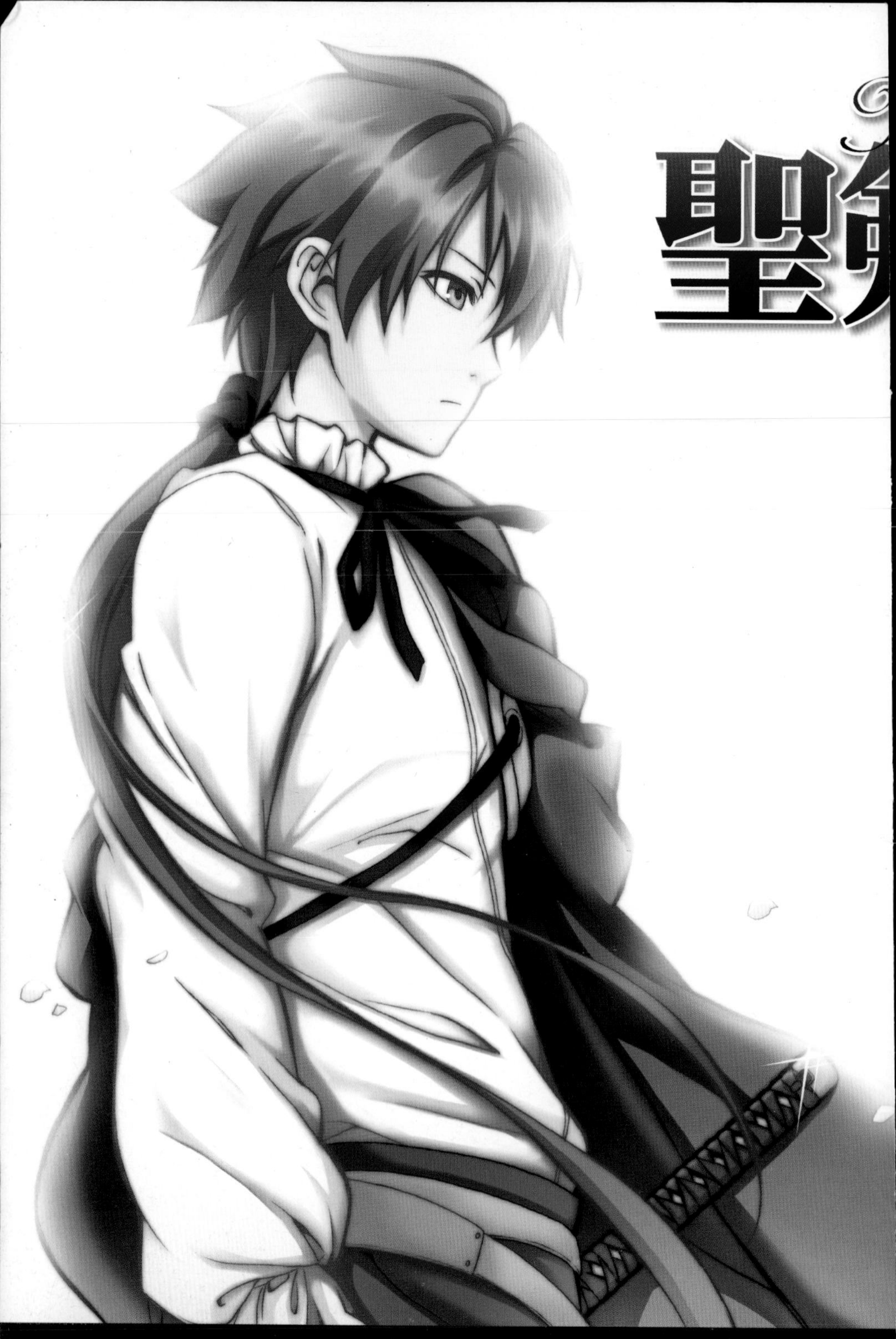
聖

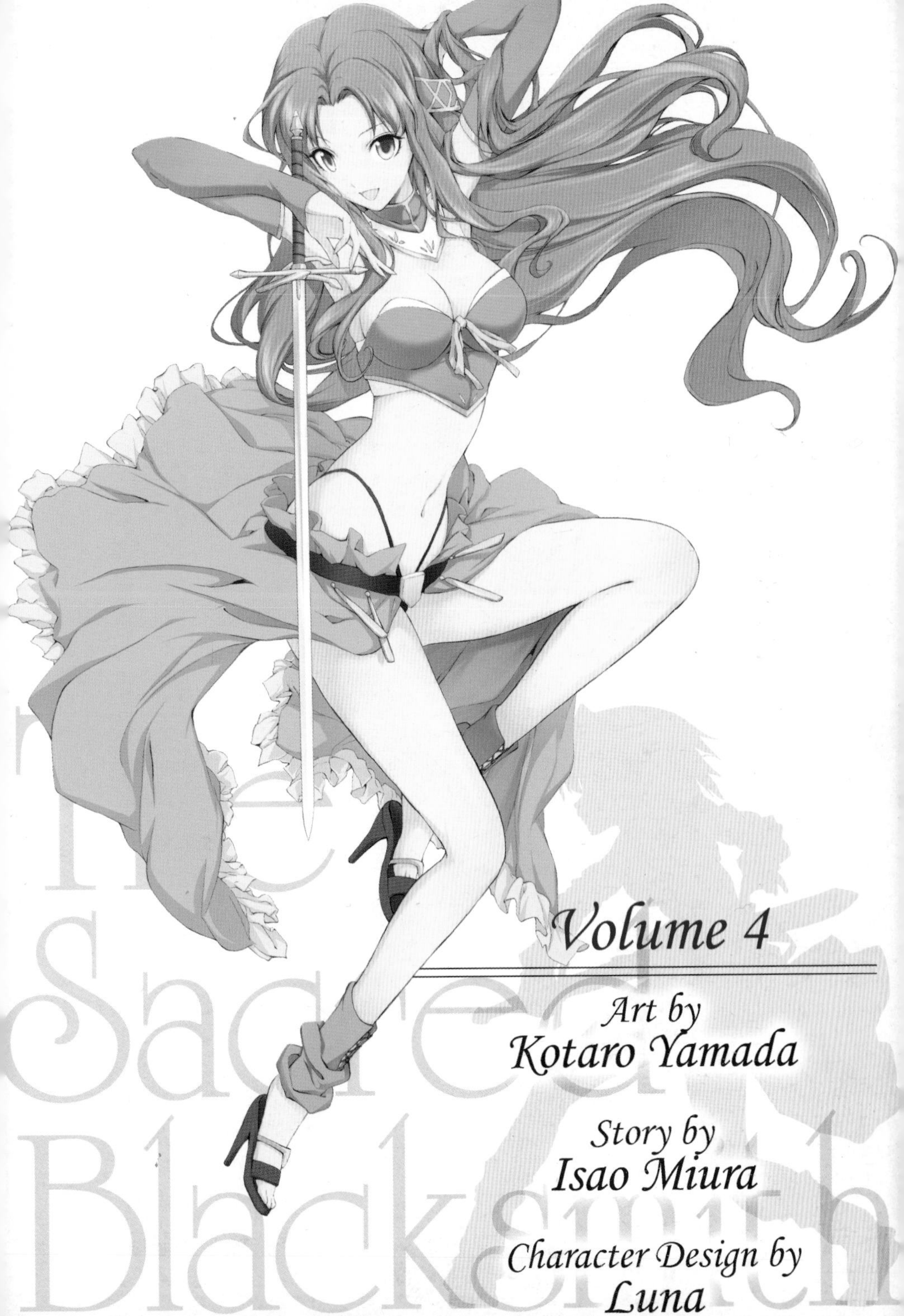

The Sacred Blacksmith

Volume 4

Art by
Kotaro Yamada

Story by
Isao Miura

Character Design by
Luna

登場人物紹介 Character

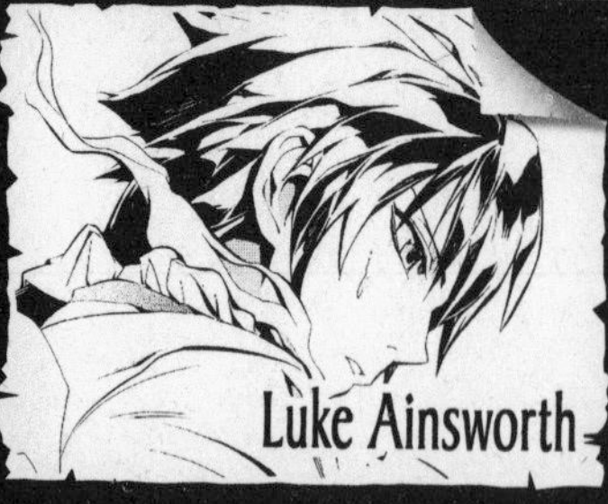

Luke Ainsworth

A proficient swordsman who uses an unusual blade called a "katana." Pessimistic and world-weary, he runs his own smithy.

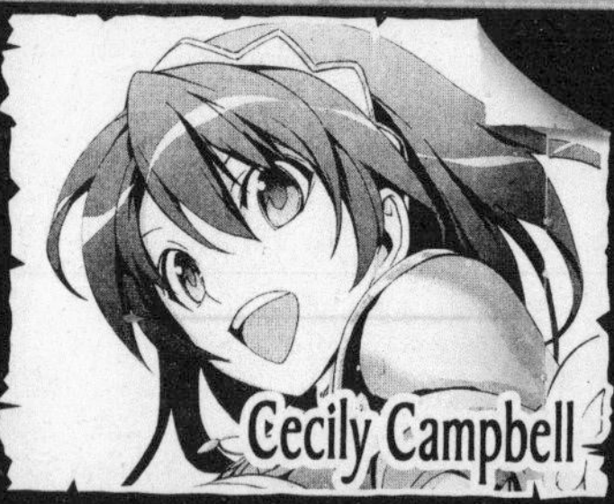

Cecily Campbell

A young lady knight who is part of the Knight Guard, charged with defending the independent trade city of Housman. Ex-nobility, she has a strong sense of justice.

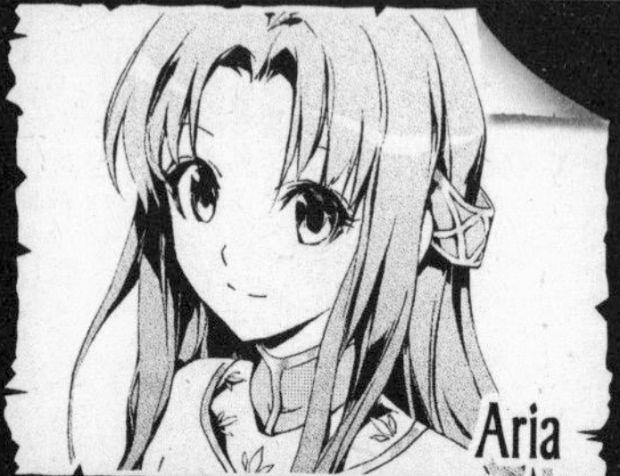

Aria

The "Demon Blade" of wind. A demon "born" at the end of the Valbanill War, she normally walks about as a human woman. However, she can turn into a rapier at will.

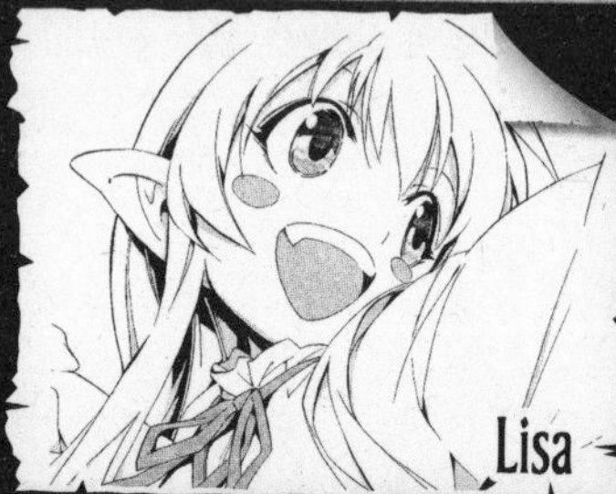

Lisa

The assistant who lives and works at Luke's smithy. Innocent and carefree, she loves talking with everyone. She says she is only three years old.

Other Characters

Hannibal Quasar

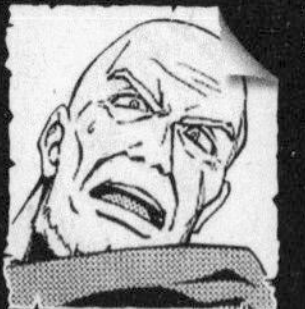

Captain of the Third District Knight Guard, and Cecily's commander.

Hugo Housman

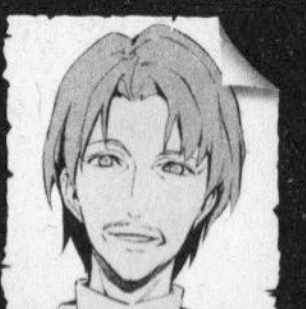

The elected mayor of the independent trade city of Housman, where Cecily and Luke live.

Charlotte E. Firobisher

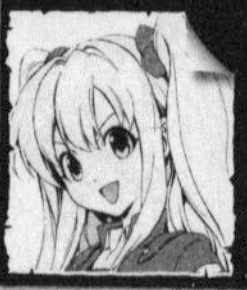

A princess of the Empire, who came looking for Demon Blades. Is now a fugitive from the Empire.

Evadne

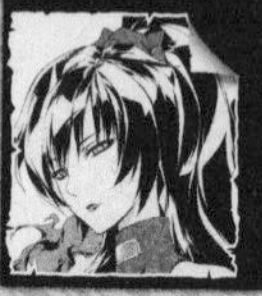

A Demon Blade who traveled with Charlotte. She can create black flame and turn into a flamberge.

Margot / Doris / Penelope

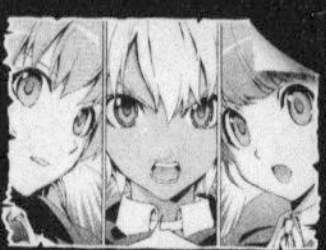

Charlotte's three retainers and Demon Blade wielders. They went with their mistress into exile.

Decades ago, a great war raged across the continent. Called the "Valbanill War," it saw the widespread use of powerful Demon Pacts.
Forty-four years later, a young lady knight named Cecily Campbell meets a mysterious blacksmith named Luke Ainsworth, and asks him to forge for her a sword.

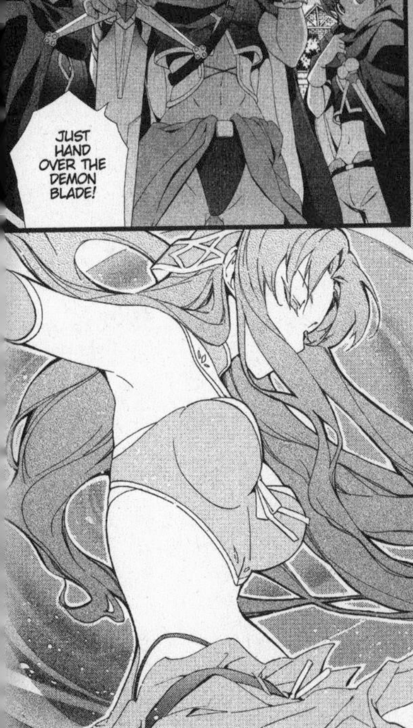
WE'VE GOT NO BUSINESS WITH YOU, KNIGHT.
JUST HAND OVER THE DEMON BLADE!

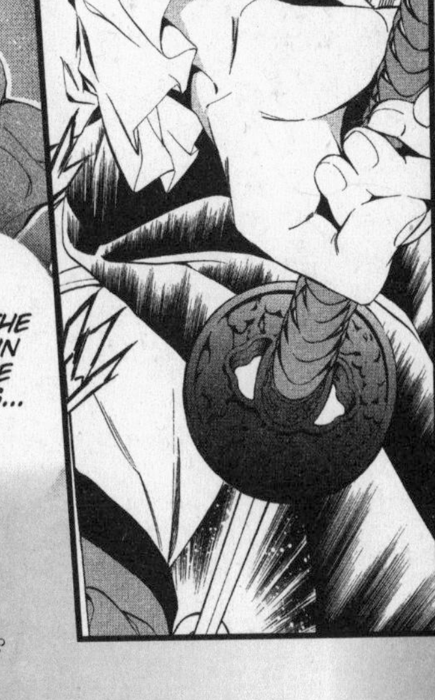
I DON'T THINK I LIKE YOU.

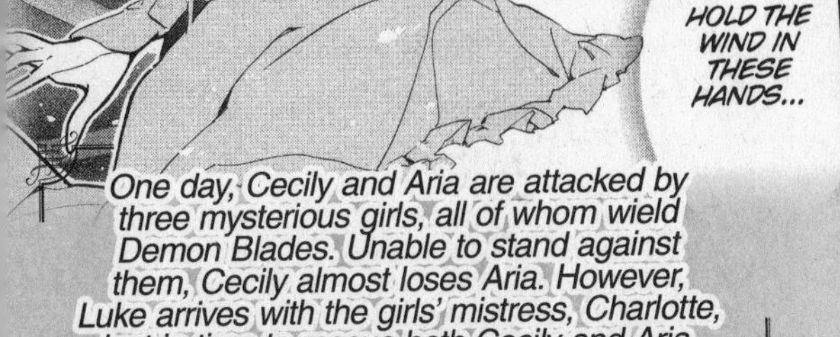
REACH FOR THE TRUTH.
HOLD THE WIND IN THESE HANDS...

One day, Cecily and Aria are attacked by three mysterious girls, all of whom wield Demon Blades. Unable to stand against them, Cecily almost loses Aria. However, Luke arrives with the girls' mistress, Charlotte, just in time to rescue both Cecily and Aria.

あらすじ Story

Charlotte, a princess of the Empire, bears Evadne, another Demon Blade like Aria. Charlotte declares that she came to Housman to collect other Demon Blades. However, she and her three retainers wind up spending time at Cecily's house, while the Mayor sends a message to the Empire to confirm whether she really is who she claims to be.

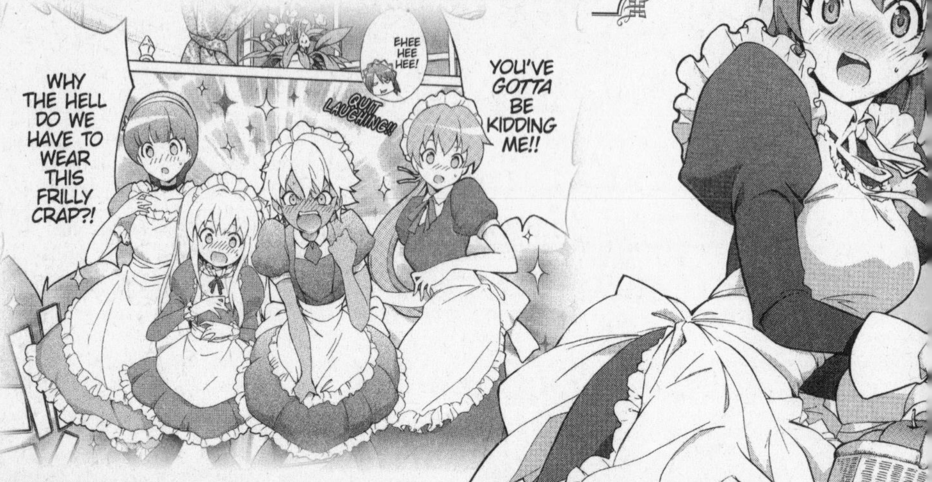
YOU'VE GOTTA BE KIDDING ME!!
EHEE HEE HEE!
QUIT LAUGHING!!
WHY THE HELL DO WE HAVE TO WEAR THIS FRILLY CRAP?!

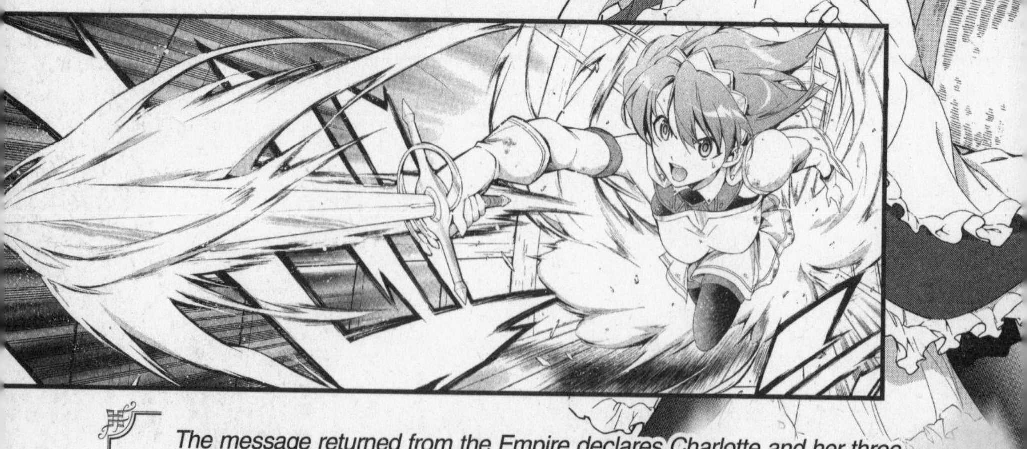

The message returned from the Empire declares Charlotte and her three companions to be traitors and demands for them to be turned over to Imperial forces for punishment. The Mayor suggests that the four girls seek asylum in the Militant Nation. Charlotte wavers, but after a battle-filled "consultation," Cecily forcibly convinces her to escape, giving up any claim to Imperial blood.

The Sacred Blacksmith

聖剣の刀鍛冶

ATELIER LIZA

KLONG

TMP

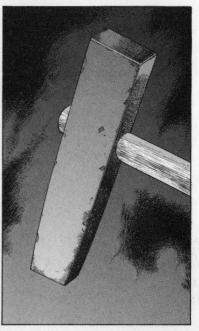

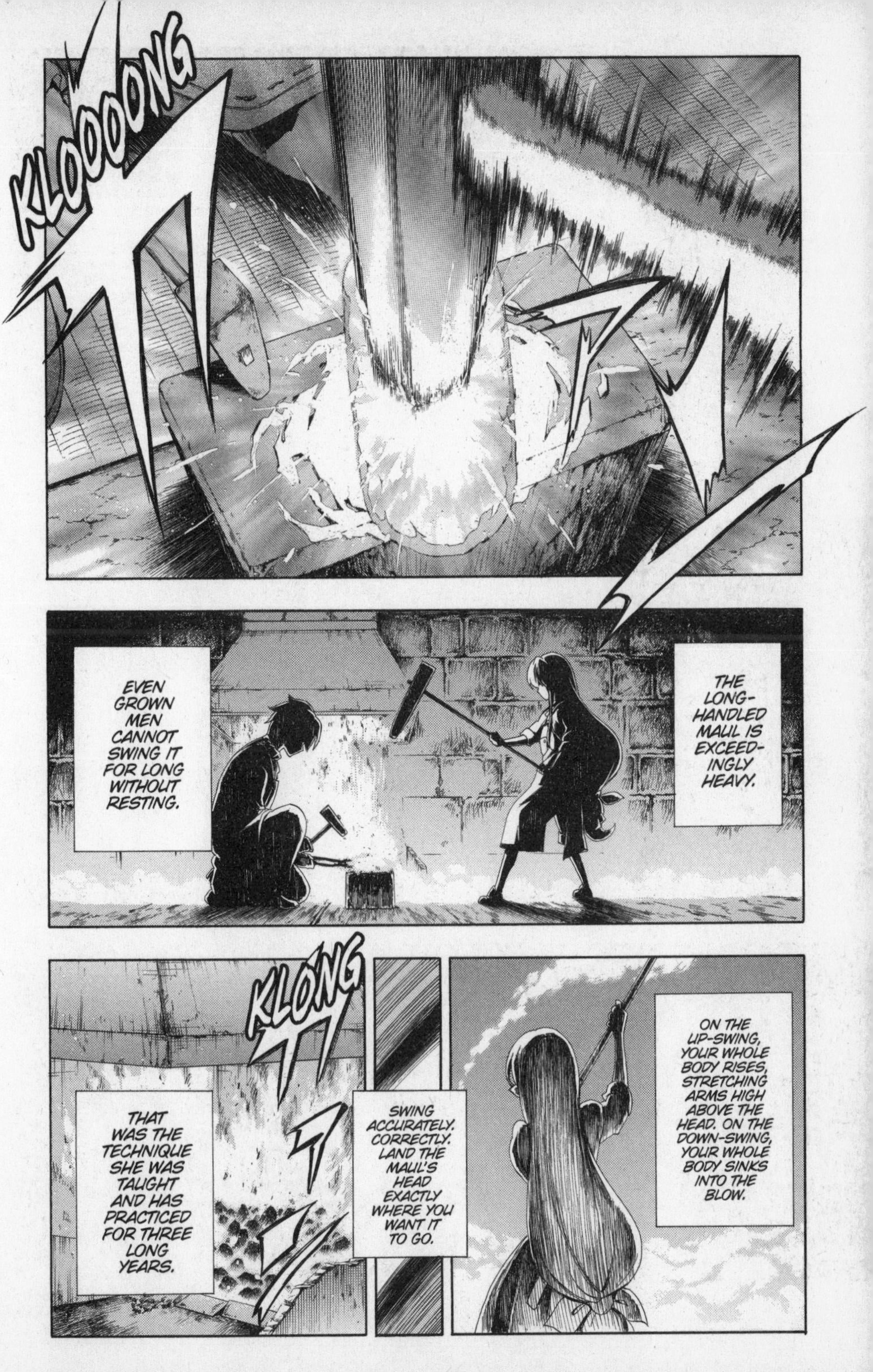
KLOOONG
THE LONG-HANDLED MAUL IS EXCEEDINGLY HEAVY.
EVEN GROWN MEN CANNOT SWING IT FOR LONG WITHOUT RESTING.
ON THE UP-SWING, YOUR WHOLE BODY RISES, STRETCHING ARMS HIGH ABOVE THE HEAD. ON THE DOWN-SWING, YOUR WHOLE BODY SINKS INTO THE BLOW.
SWING ACCURATELY. CORRECTLY. LAND THE MAUL'S HEAD EXACTLY WHERE YOU WANT IT TO GO.
KLONG
THAT WAS THE TECHNIQUE SHE WAS TAUGHT AND HAS PRACTICED FOR THREE LONG YEARS.

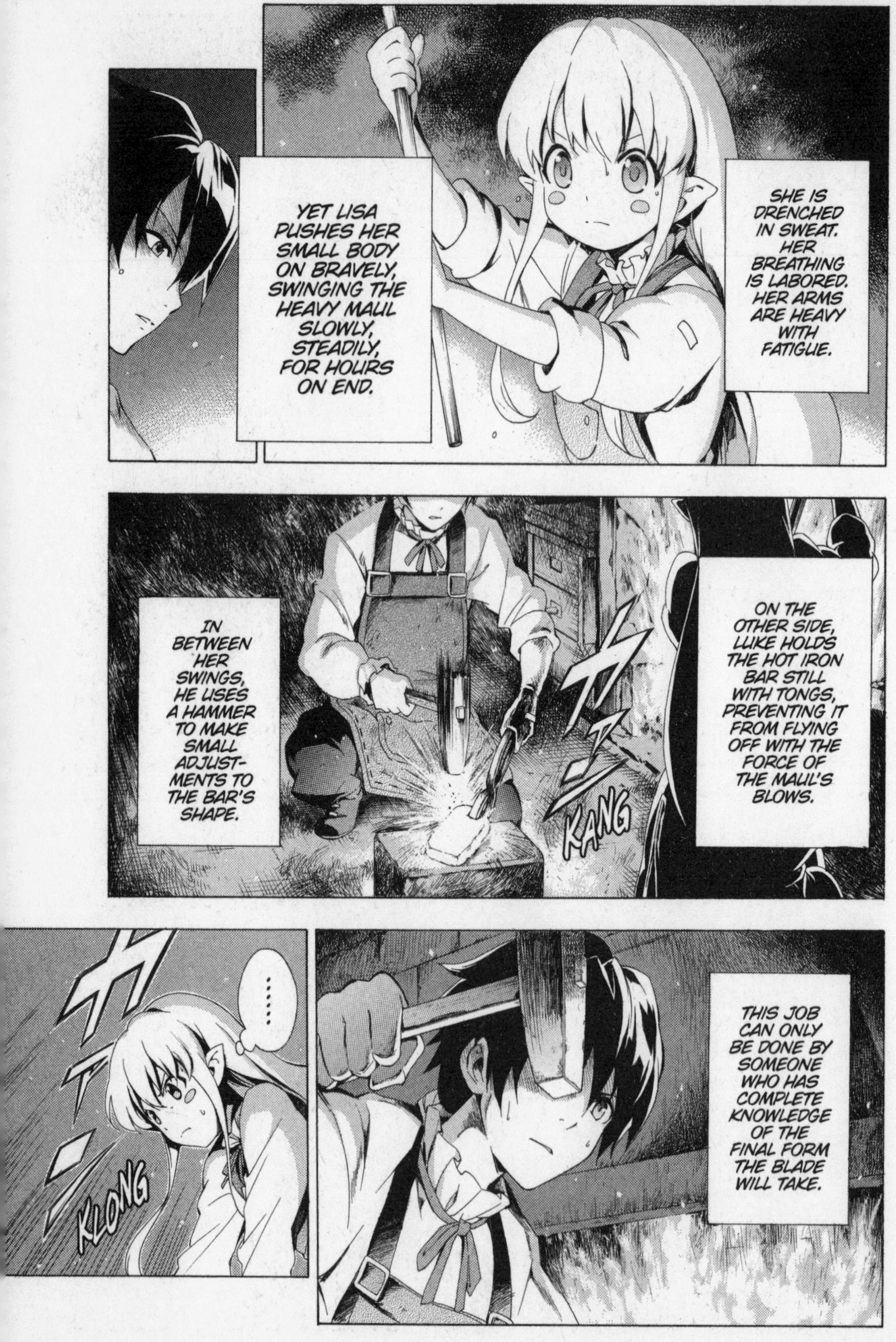
SHE IS DRENCHED IN SWEAT. HER BREATHING IS LABORED. HER ARMS ARE HEAVY WITH FATIGUE.
YET LISA PUSHES HER SMALL BODY ON BRAVELY, SWINGING THE HEAVY MAUL SLOWLY, STEADILY, FOR HOURS ON END.
ON THE OTHER SIDE, LUKE HOLDS THE HOT IRON BAR STILL WITH TONGS, PREVENTING IT FROM FLYING OFF WITH THE FORCE OF THE MAUL'S BLOWS.
KANG
IN BETWEEN HER SWINGS, HE USES A HAMMER TO MAKE SMALL ADJUST-MENTS TO THE BAR'S SHAPE.
THIS JOB CAN ONLY BE DONE BY SOMEONE WHO HAS COMPLETE KNOWLEDGE OF THE FINAL FORM THE BLADE WILL TAKE.
......
KLONG

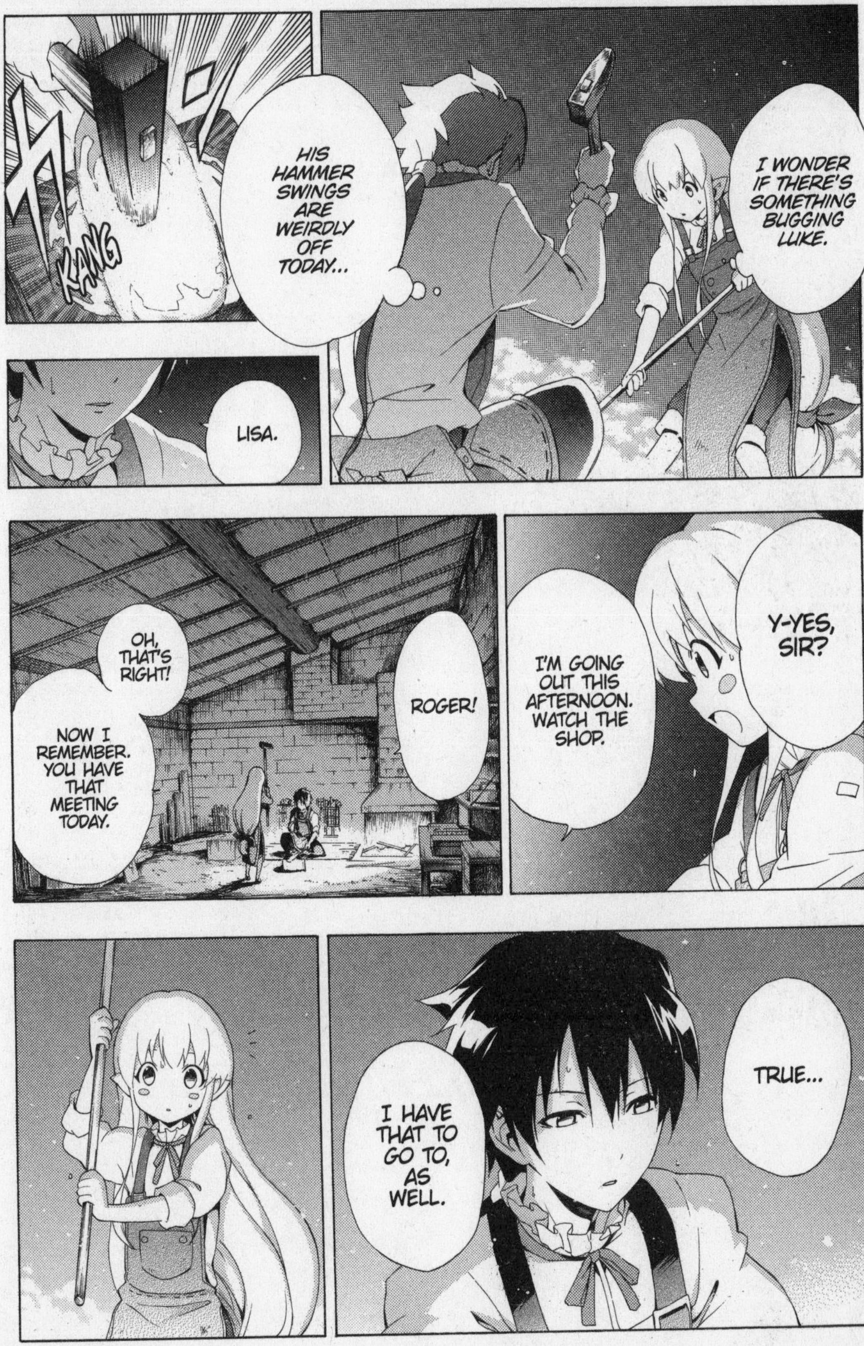
I WONDER IF THERE'S SOMETHING BUGGING LUKE.
HIS HAMMER SWINGS ARE WEIRDLY OFF TODAY...
KANG
LISA.
Y-YES, SIR?
I'M GOING OUT THIS AFTERNOON. WATCH THE SHOP.
ROGER!
OH, THAT'S RIGHT!
NOW I REMEMBER. YOU HAVE THAT MEETING TODAY.
TRUE...
I HAVE THAT TO GO TO, AS WELL.

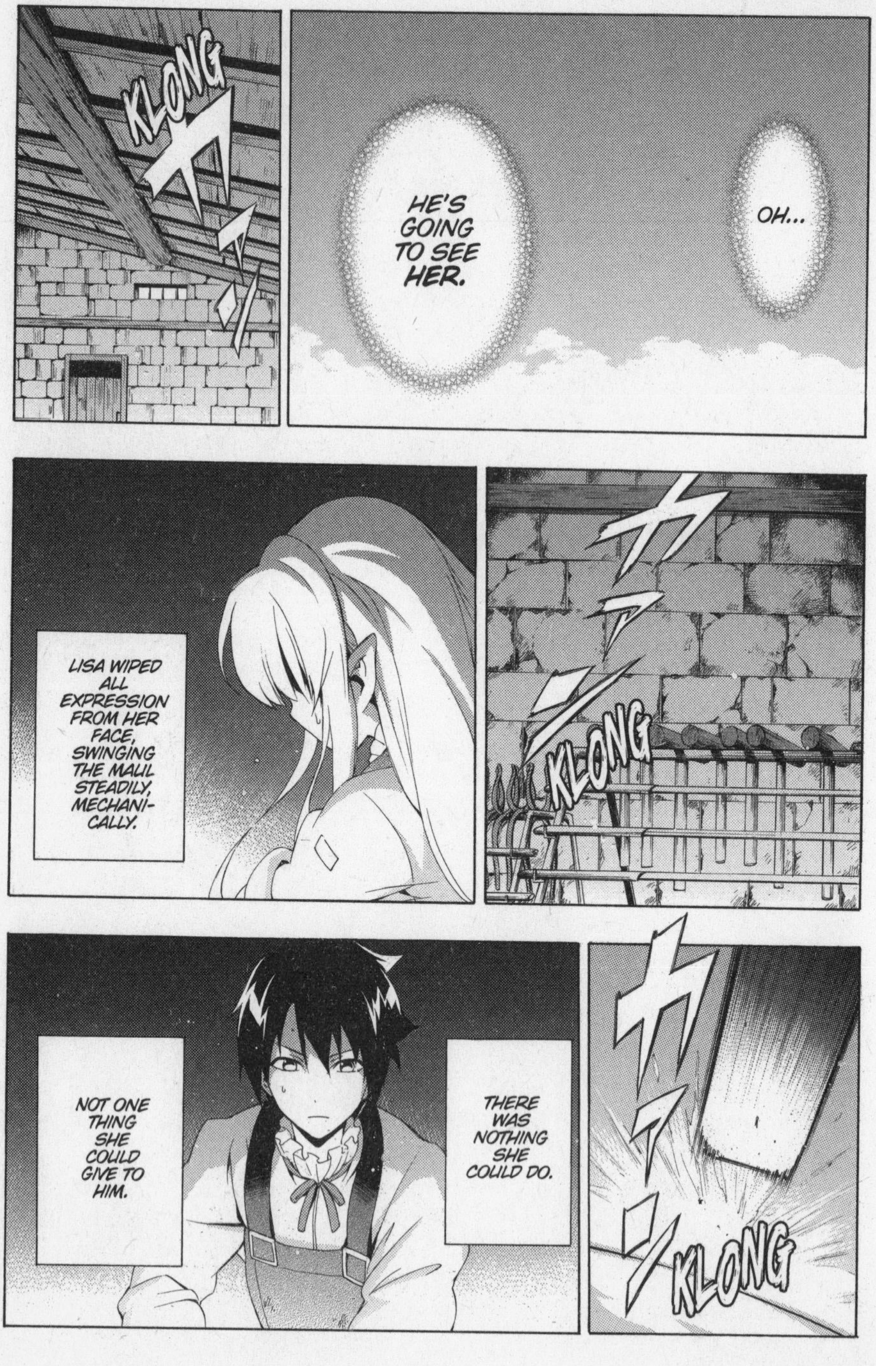
OH...
HE'S GOING TO SEE HER.
KLONG
KLONG
LISA WIPED ALL EXPRESSION FROM HER FACE, SWINGING THE MAUL STEADILY, MECHANI-CALLY.
KLONG
THERE WAS NOTHING SHE COULD DO.
NOT ONE THING SHE COULD GIVE TO HIM.

I MEAN, I'M NOT HER.

I'M NOT EVEN HUMAN.

I'M JUST A DEMON...

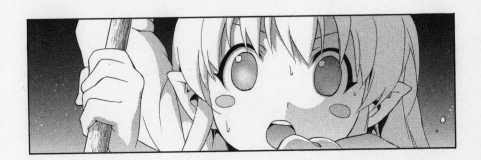

A POOR COPY OF HER.

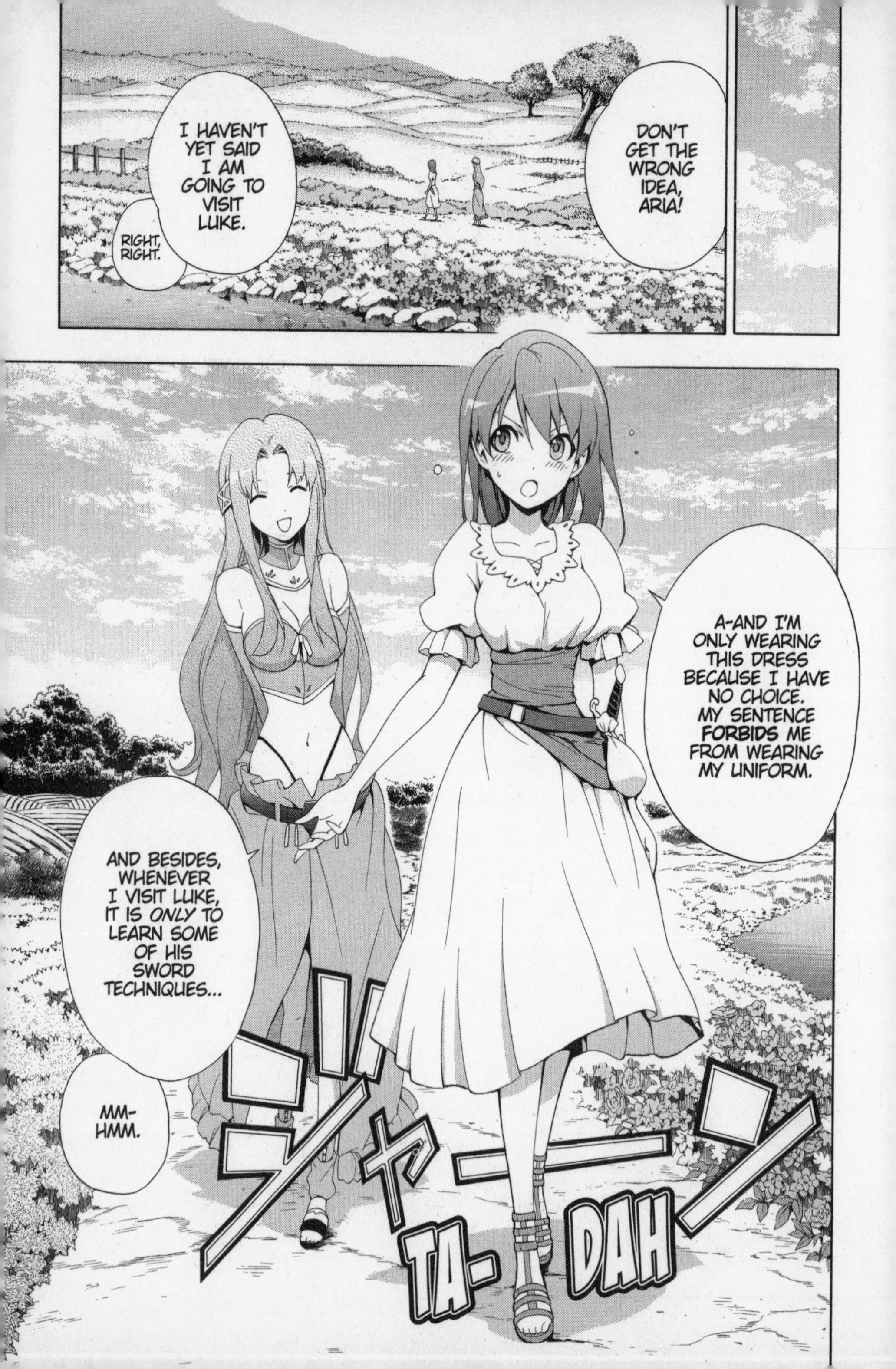
DON'T GET THE WRONG IDEA, ARIA!
I HAVEN'T YET SAID I AM GOING TO VISIT LUKE.
RIGHT, RIGHT.
A-AND I'M ONLY WEARING THIS DRESS BECAUSE I HAVE NO CHOICE. MY SENTENCE **FORBIDS** ME FROM WEARING MY UNIFORM.
AND BESIDES, WHENEVER I VISIT LUKE, IT IS *ONLY* TO LEARN SOME OF HIS SWORD TECHNIQUES...
MM-HMM.
TA- DAH

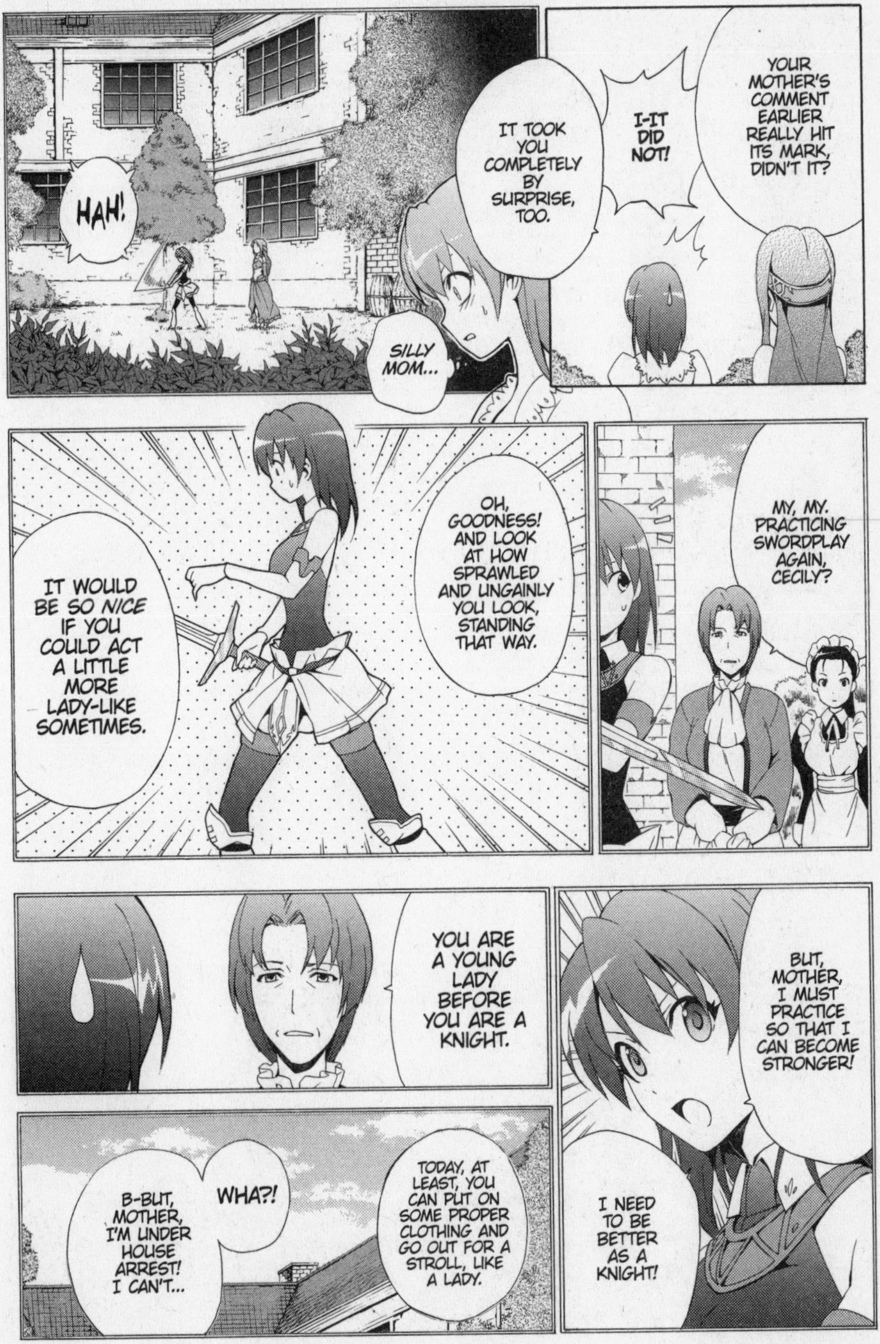
YOUR MOTHER'S COMMENT EARLIER REALLY HIT ITS MARK, DIDN'T IT?
I-IT DID NOT!
IT TOOK YOU COMPLETELY BY SURPRISE, TOO.
HAH!
SILLY MOM...
MY, MY. PRACTICING SWORDPLAY AGAIN, CECILY?
OH, GOODNESS! AND LOOK AT HOW SPRAWLED AND UNGAINLY YOU LOOK, STANDING THAT WAY.
IT WOULD BE SO *NICE* IF YOU COULD ACT A LITTLE MORE LADY-LIKE SOMETIMES.
BUT, MOTHER, I MUST PRACTICE SO THAT I CAN BECOME STRONGER!
I NEED TO BE BETTER AS A KNIGHT!
YOU ARE A YOUNG LADY BEFORE YOU ARE A KNIGHT.
TODAY, AT LEAST, YOU CAN PUT ON SOME PROPER CLOTHING AND GO OUT FOR A STROLL, LIKE A LADY.
WHA?!
B-BUT, MOTHER, I'M UNDER HOUSE ARREST! I CAN'T...

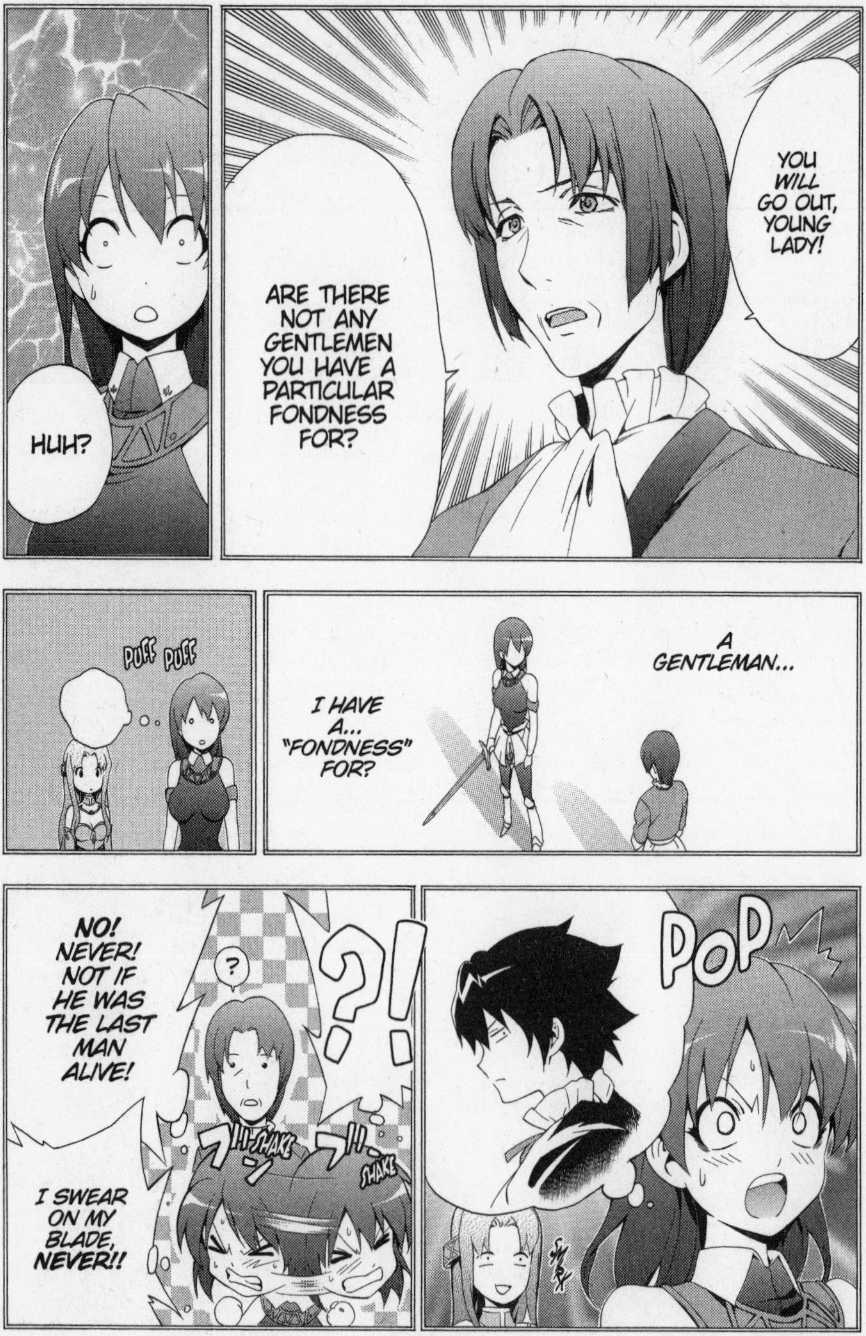
YOU WILL GO OUT, YOUNG LADY!
ARE THERE NOT ANY GENTLEMEN YOU HAVE A PARTICULAR FONDNESS FOR?
HUH?
A GENTLEMAN...
I HAVE A... "FONDNESS" FOR?
PUFF PUFF
POP
?!
?
NO! NEVER! NOT IF HE WAS THE LAST MAN ALIVE!
SHAKE
SHAKE
I SWEAR ON MY BLADE, NEVER!!

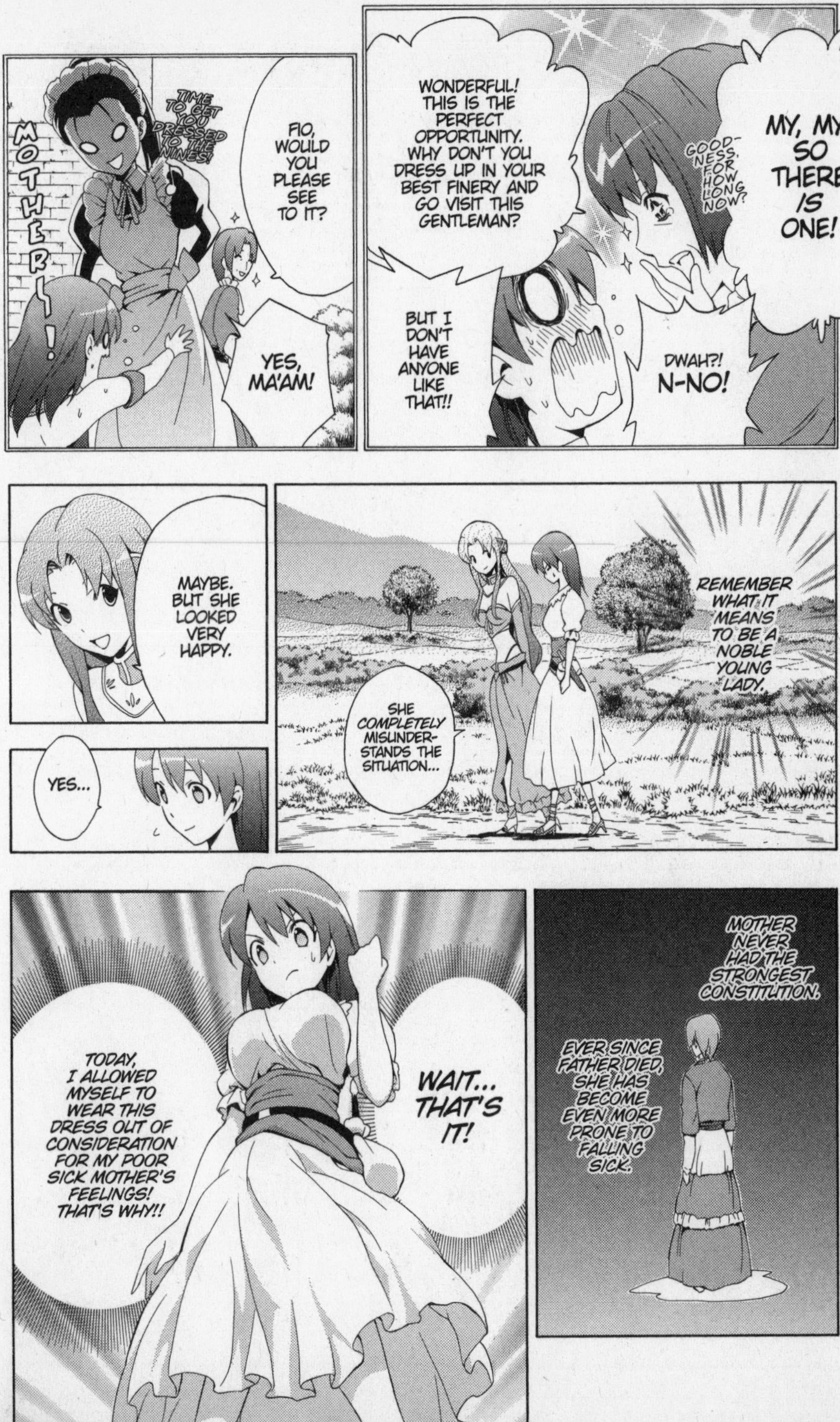
MY, MY! SO THERE IS ONE!
GOODNESS, FOR HOW LONG NOW?
WONDERFUL! THIS IS THE PERFECT OPPORTUNITY. WHY DON'T YOU DRESS UP IN YOUR BEST FINERY AND GO VISIT THIS GENTLEMAN?
DWAH?! N-NO!
BUT I DON'T HAVE ANYONE LIKE THAT!!
FIO, WOULD YOU PLEASE SEE TO IT?
YES, MA'AM!
TIME TO GET YOU DRESSED TO THE NINES!
MOTHER!
REMEMBER WHAT IT MEANS TO BE A NOBLE YOUNG LADY.
SHE COMPLETELY MISUNDERSTANDS THE SITUATION...
MAYBE. BUT SHE LOOKED VERY HAPPY.
YES...
MOTHER NEVER HAD THE STRONGEST CONSTITUTION.
EVER SINCE FATHER DIED, SHE HAS BECOME EVEN MORE PRONE TO FALLING SICK.
WAIT... THAT'S IT!
TODAY, I ALLOWED MYSELF TO WEAR THIS DRESS OUT OF CONSIDERATION FOR MY POOR SICK MOTHER'S FEELINGS! THAT'S WHY!!

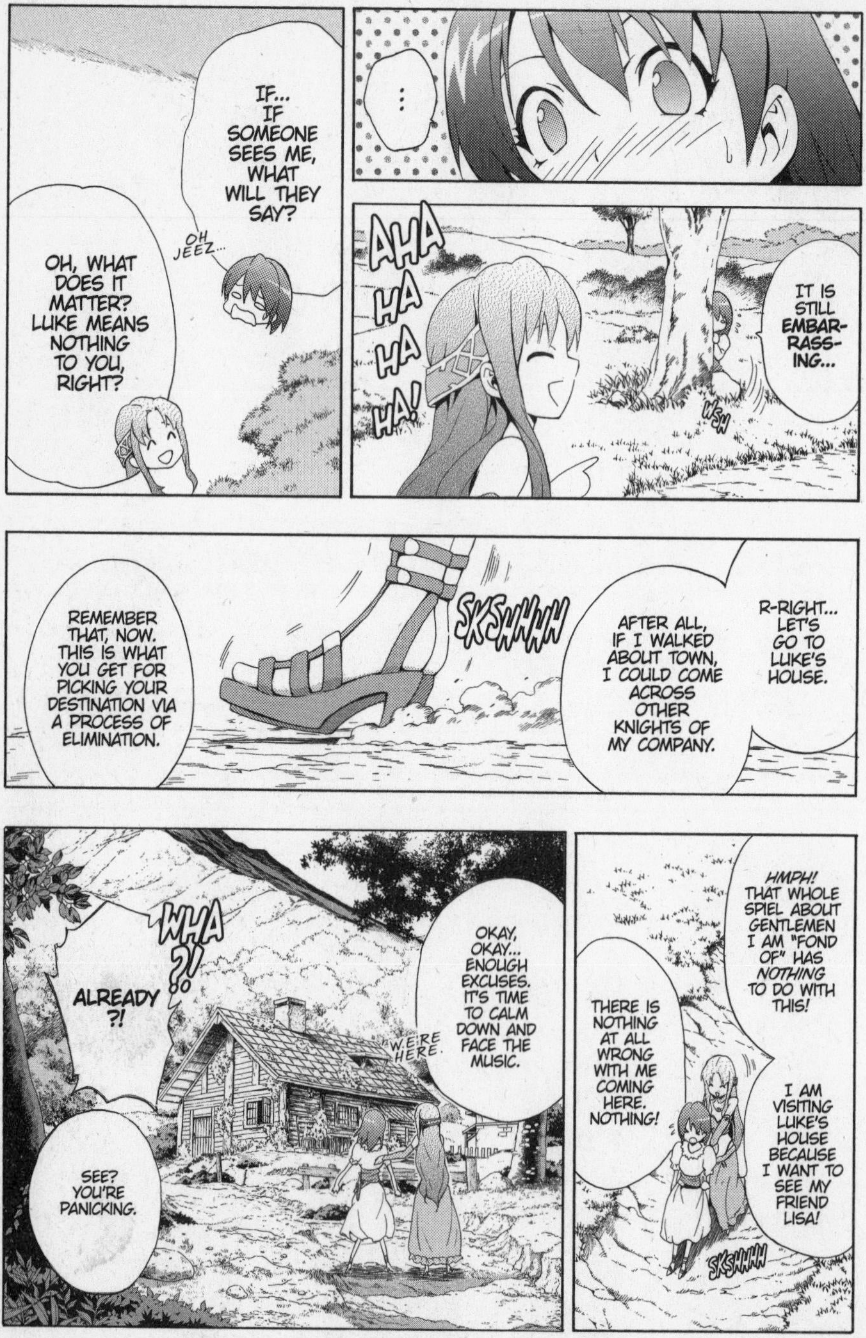
…
AHA HA HA HA!
IT IS STILL EMBARRASSING...
WSH
IF... IF SOMEONE SEES ME, WHAT WILL THEY SAY?
OH JEEZ...
OH, WHAT DOES IT MATTER? LUKE MEANS NOTHING TO YOU, RIGHT?
R-RIGHT... LET'S GO TO LUKE'S HOUSE.
AFTER ALL, IF I WALKED ABOUT TOWN, I COULD COME ACROSS OTHER KNIGHTS OF MY COMPANY.
SKSHHHH
REMEMBER THAT, NOW. THIS IS WHAT YOU GET FOR PICKING YOUR DESTINATION VIA A PROCESS OF ELIMINATION.
HMPH! THAT WHOLE SPIEL ABOUT GENTLEMEN I AM "FOND OF" HAS NOTHING TO DO WITH THIS!
I AM VISITING LUKE'S HOUSE BECAUSE I WANT TO SEE MY FRIEND LISA!
THERE IS NOTHING AT ALL WRONG WITH ME COMING HERE. NOTHING!
SKSHHH
OKAY, OKAY... ENOUGH EXCUSES. IT'S TIME TO CALM DOWN AND FACE THE MUSIC.
WE'RE HERE.
WHA?!
ALREADY?!
SEE? YOU'RE PANICKING.

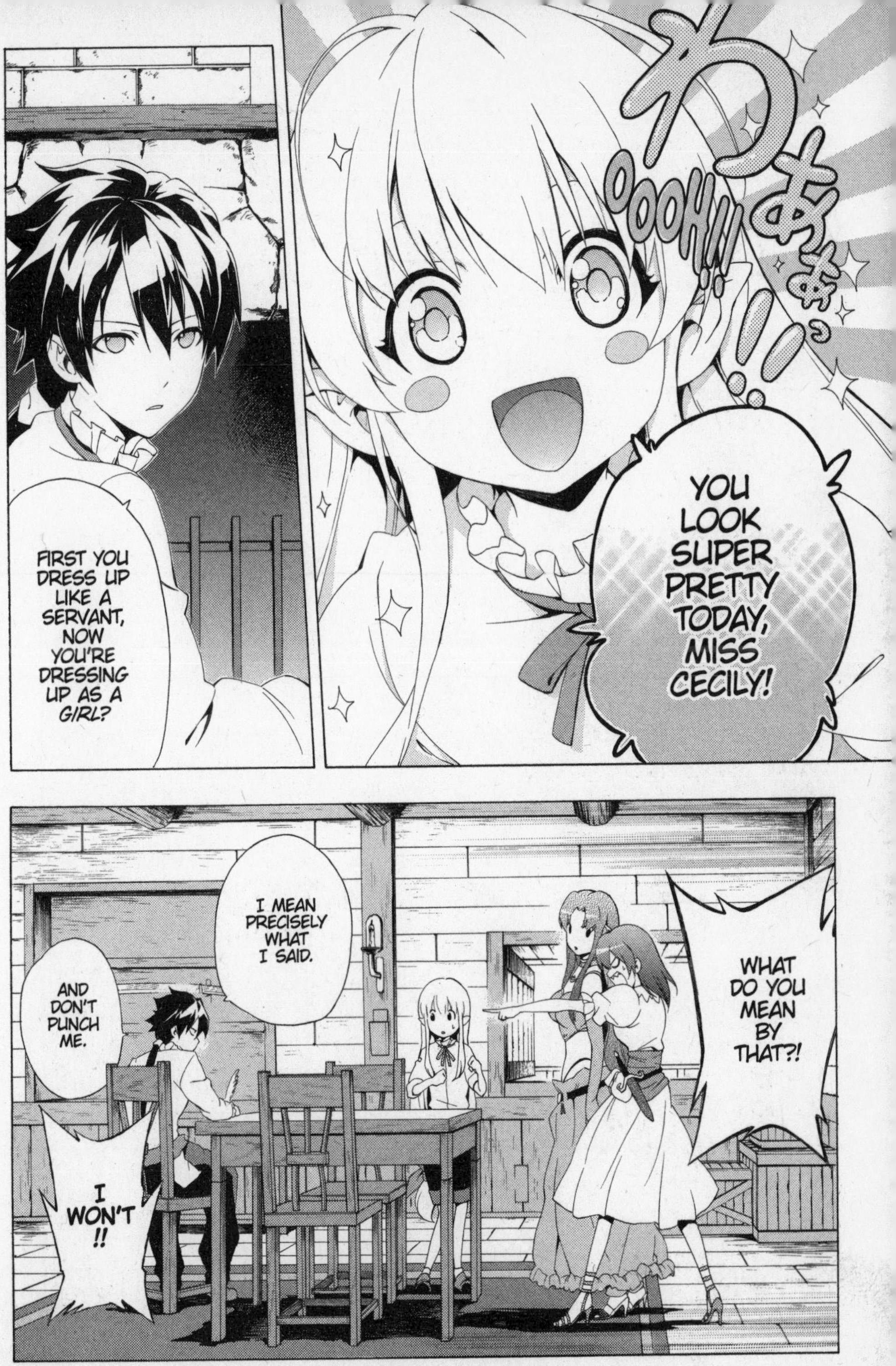
わあぁっ
OOOH!!!
YOU LOOK SUPER PRETTY TODAY, MISS CECILY!
FIRST YOU DRESS UP LIKE A SERVANT, NOW YOU'RE DRESSING UP AS A GIRL?
WHAT DO YOU MEAN BY THAT?!
I MEAN PRECISELY WHAT I SAID.
AND DON'T PUNCH ME.
I WON'T!!

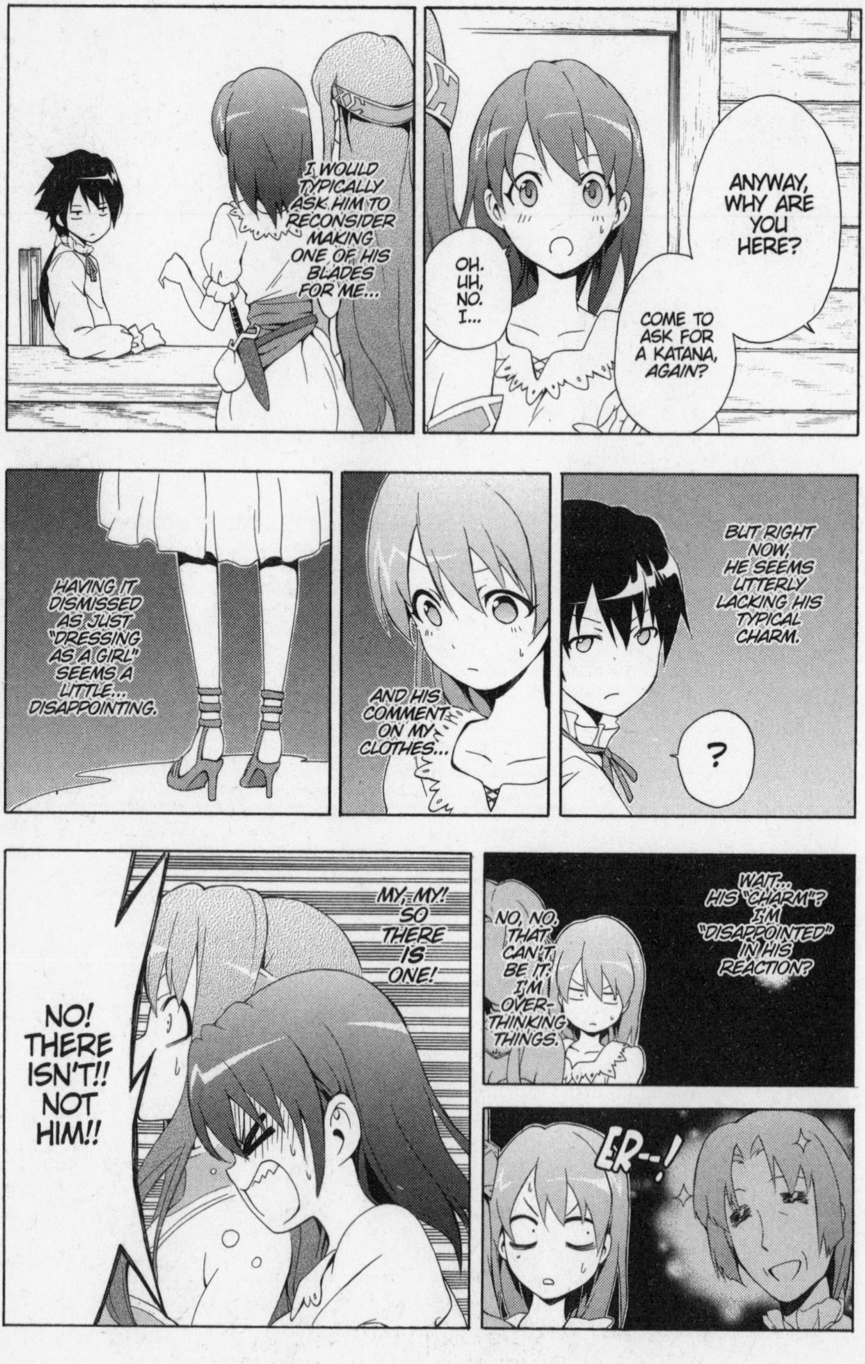
ANYWAY, WHY ARE YOU HERE?
COME TO ASK FOR A KATANA, AGAIN?
OH. UH, NO. I...
I WOULD TYPICALLY ASK HIM TO RECONSIDER MAKING ONE OF HIS BLADES FOR ME...
BUT RIGHT NOW, HE SEEMS UTTERLY LACKING HIS TYPICAL CHARM.
?
AND HIS COMMENT ON MY CLOTHES...
HAVING IT DISMISSED AS JUST "DRESSING AS A GIRL" SEEMS A LITTLE... DISAPPOINTING.
WAIT... HIS "CHARM"? I'M "DISAPPOINTED" IN HIS REACTION?
NO, NO. THAT CAN'T BE IT. I'M OVER-THINKING THINGS.
ER--!
MY, MY! SO THERE IS ONE!
NO! THERE ISN'T!! NOT HIM!!

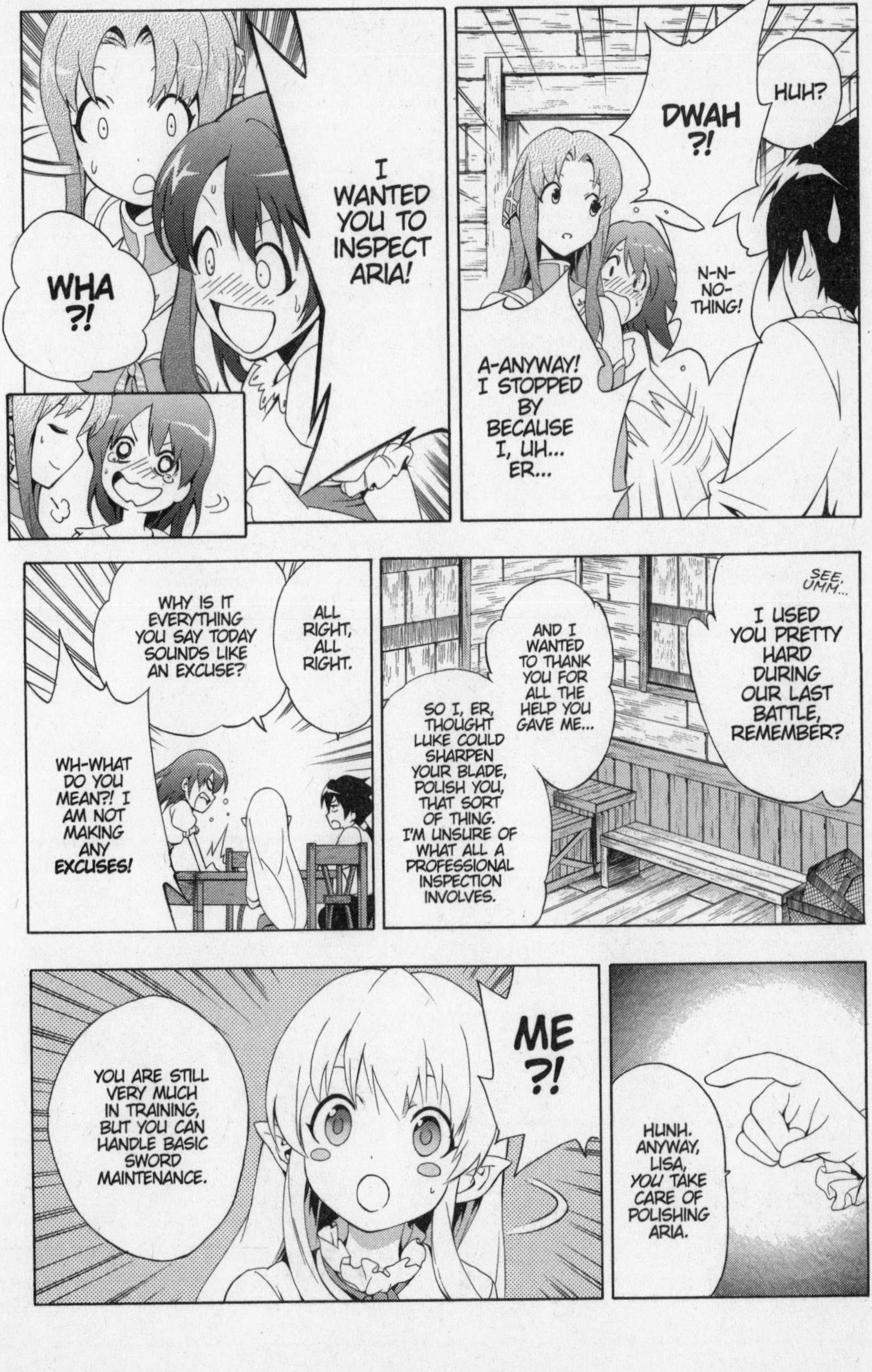
HUH?
DWAH ?!
N-N-NO-THING!
A-ANYWAY! I STOPPED BY BECAUSE I, UH... ER...
I WANTED YOU TO INSPECT ARIA!
WHA ?!
SEE, UMM...
I USED YOU PRETTY HARD DURING OUR LAST BATTLE, REMEMBER?
AND I WANTED TO THANK YOU FOR ALL THE HELP YOU GAVE ME...
SO I, ER, THOUGHT LUKE COULD SHARPEN YOUR BLADE, POLISH YOU, THAT SORT OF THING. I'M UNSURE OF WHAT ALL A PROFESSIONAL INSPECTION INVOLVES.
ALL RIGHT, ALL RIGHT.
WHY IS IT EVERYTHING YOU SAY TODAY SOUNDS LIKE AN EXCUSE?
WH-WHAT DO YOU MEAN?! I AM NOT MAKING ANY EXCUSES!
HUNH. ANYWAY, LISA, *YOU* TAKE CARE OF POLISHING ARIA.
ME ?!
YOU ARE STILL VERY MUCH IN TRAINING, BUT YOU CAN HANDLE BASIC SWORD MAINTENANCE.

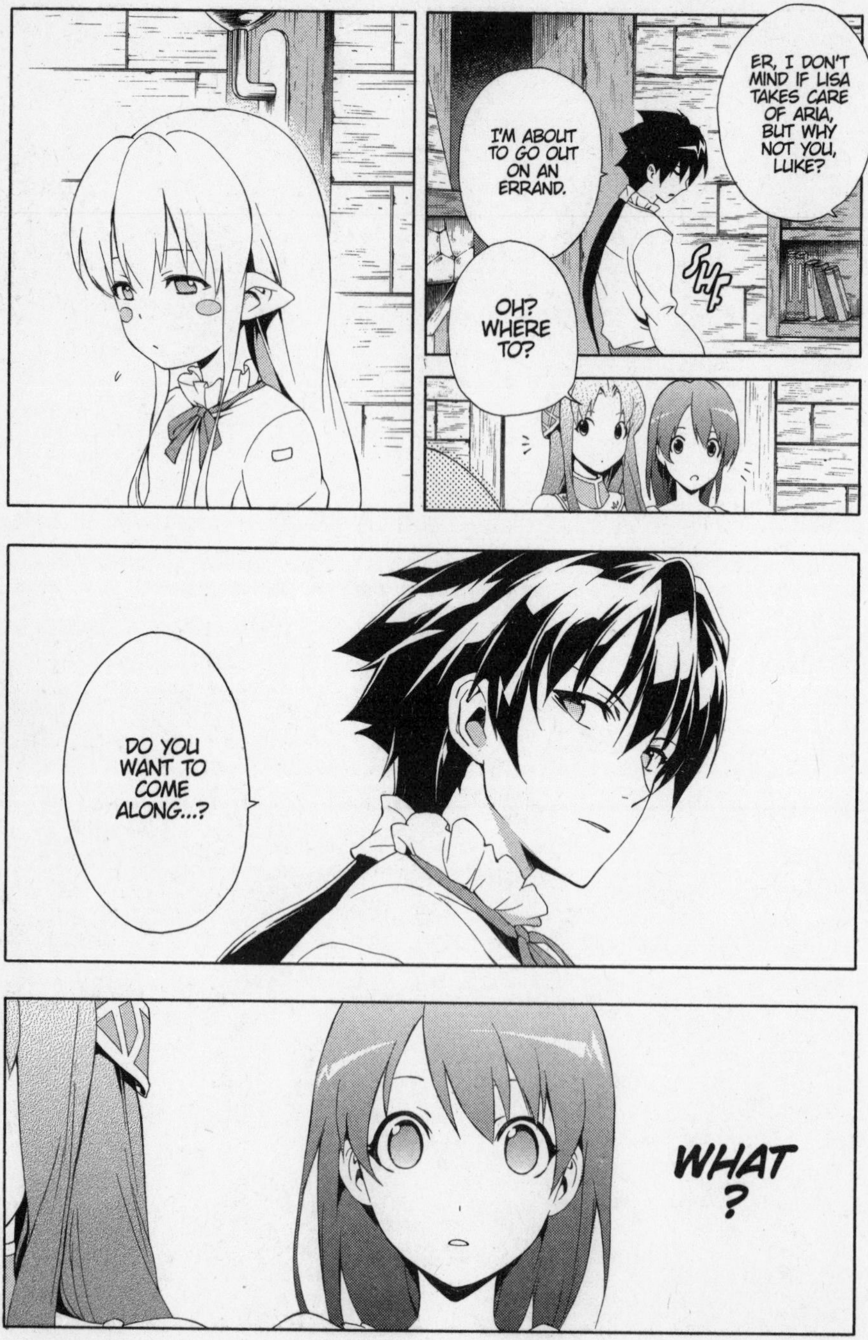
ER, I DON'T MIND IF LISA TAKES CARE OF ARIA, BUT WHY NOT YOU, LUKE?
I'M ABOUT TO GO OUT ON AN ERRAND.
SHF
OH? WHERE TO?
DO YOU WANT TO COME ALONG...?
WHAT?

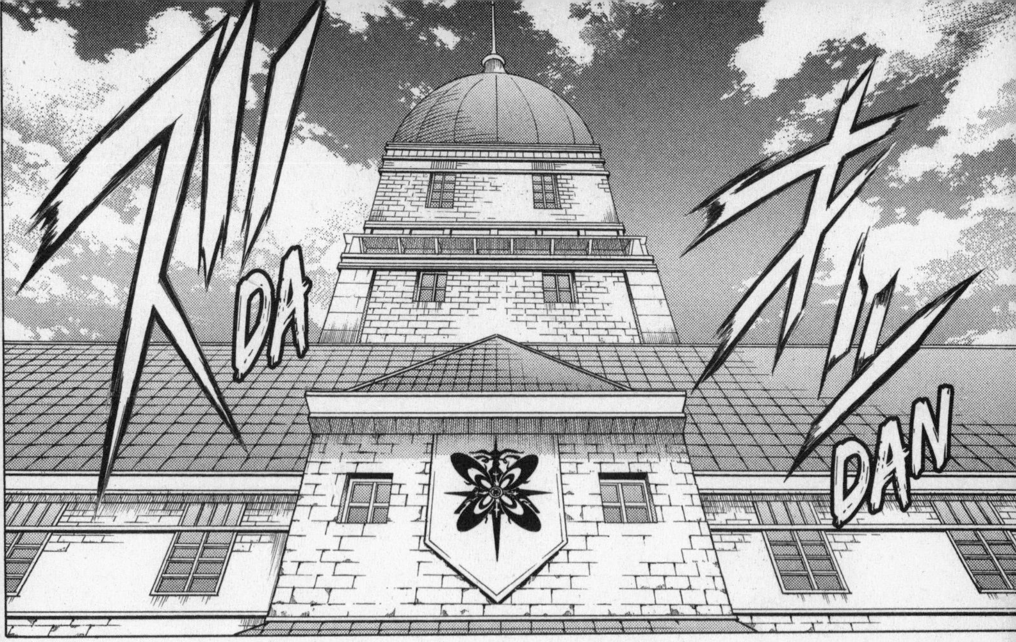
DA
DAN

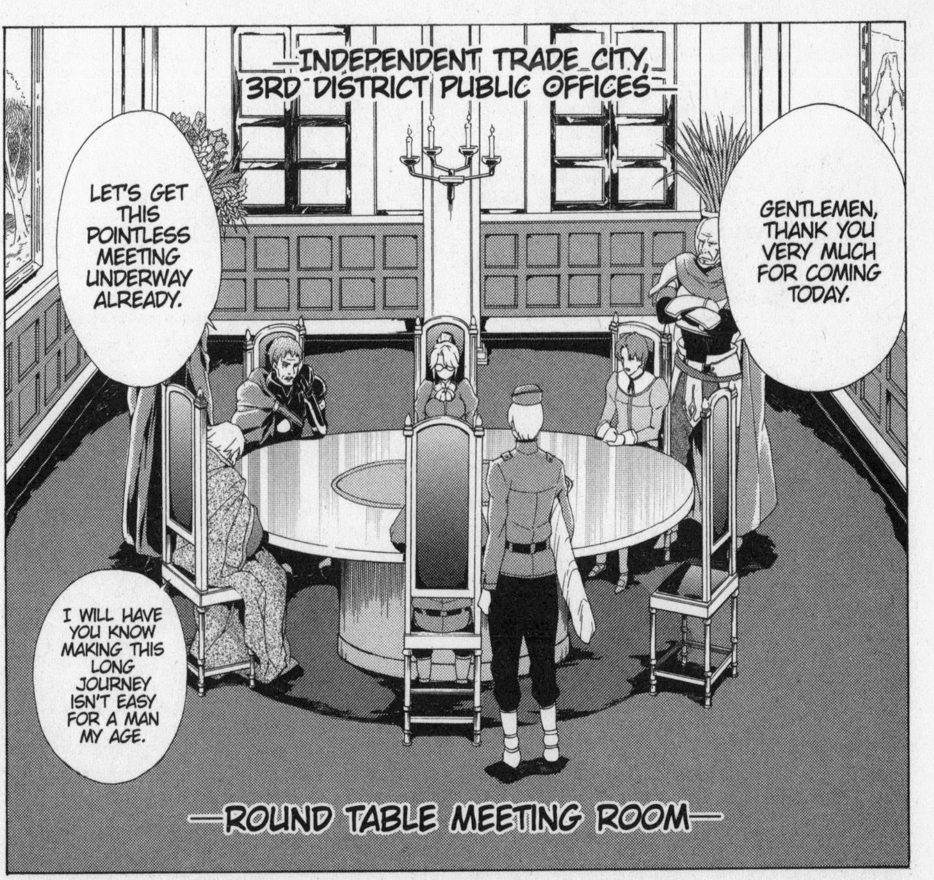
—INDEPENDENT TRADE CITY, 3RD DISTRICT PUBLIC OFFICES—
GENTLEMEN, THANK YOU VERY MUCH FOR COMING TODAY.
LET'S GET THIS POINTLESS MEETING UNDERWAY ALREADY.
I WILL HAVE YOU KNOW MAKING THIS LONG JOURNEY ISN'T EASY FOR A MAN MY AGE.
—ROUND TABLE MEETING ROOM—

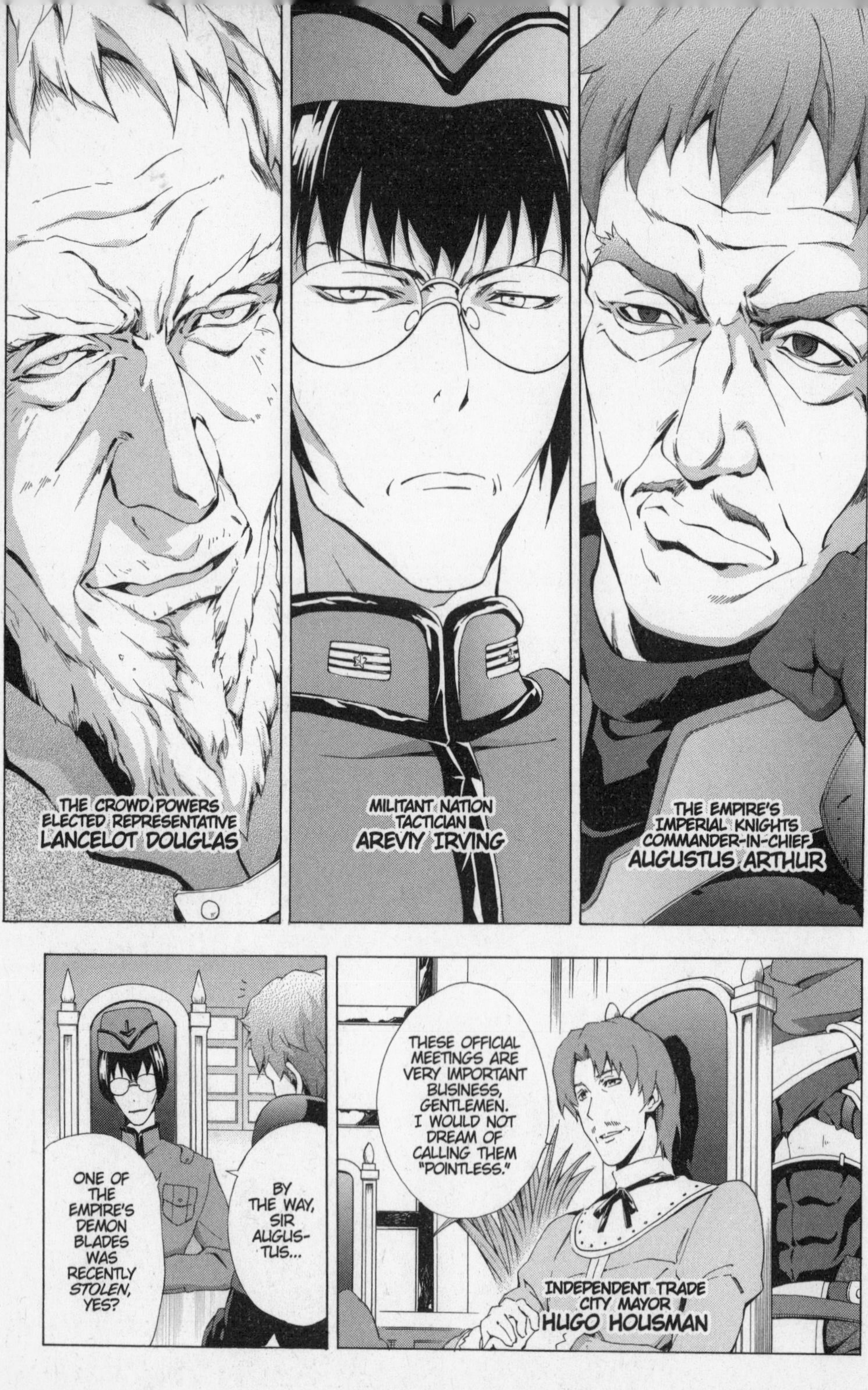
THE EMPIRE'S IMPERIAL KNIGHTS COMMANDER-IN-CHIEF AUGUSTUS ARTHUR
MILITANT NATION TACTICIAN AREVIY IRVING
THE CROWD POWERS ELECTED REPRESENTATIVE LANCELOT DOUGLAS
THESE OFFICIAL MEETINGS ARE VERY IMPORTANT BUSINESS, GENTLEMEN. I WOULD NOT DREAM OF CALLING THEM "POINTLESS."
INDEPENDENT TRADE CITY MAYOR HUGO HOUSMAN
BY THE WAY, SIR AUGUSTUS...
ONE OF THE EMPIRE'S DEMON BLADES WAS RECENTLY STOLEN, YES?

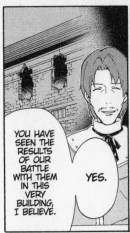

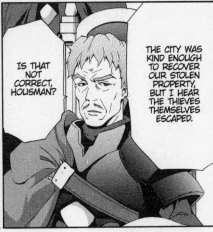

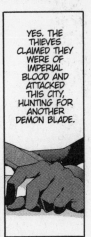

YES. THE THIEVES CLAIMED THEY WERE OF IMPERIAL BLOOD AND ATTACKED THIS CITY, HUNTING FOR ANOTHER DEMON BLADE.
THE CITY WAS KIND ENOUGH TO RECOVER OUR STOLEN PROPERTY, BUT I HEAR THE THIEVES THEMSELVES ESCAPED.
IS THAT NOT CORRECT, HOUSMAN?
YES.
YOU HAVE SEEN THE RESULTS OF OUR BATTLE WITH THEM IN THIS VERY BUILDING, I BELIEVE.
THEY NEARLY DESTROYED THE ENTIRE EAST WING.
HEH HEH...
THEY WERE QUITE VICIOUS FIGHTERS.
THIEVES *CLAIMING* TO BE OF IMPERIAL BLOOD, YES?
WHAT ARE YOU TRYING TO SAY, IRVING? SPIT IT OUT.
IT IS NOTHING. I SIMPLY WONDERED IF THE EMPIRE MIGHT HAVE SOME REASON TO *COLLECT* DEMON BLADES...
WE ARE *NOT* COLLECTING THEM.
WE SIMPLY RETRIEVED PROPERTY WE ALREADY OWNED.
WHERE DID YOU HEAR SUCH A RUMOR?
I COULD NOT SAY.
RUMORS ARE RUMORS. WHO REMEMBERS **WHERE** THEY HEAR THEM?

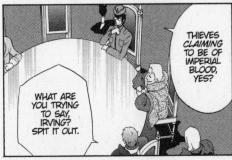

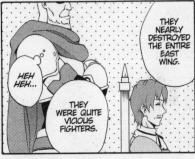

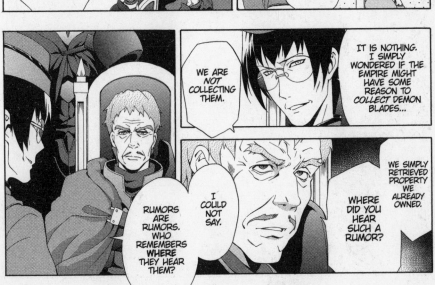

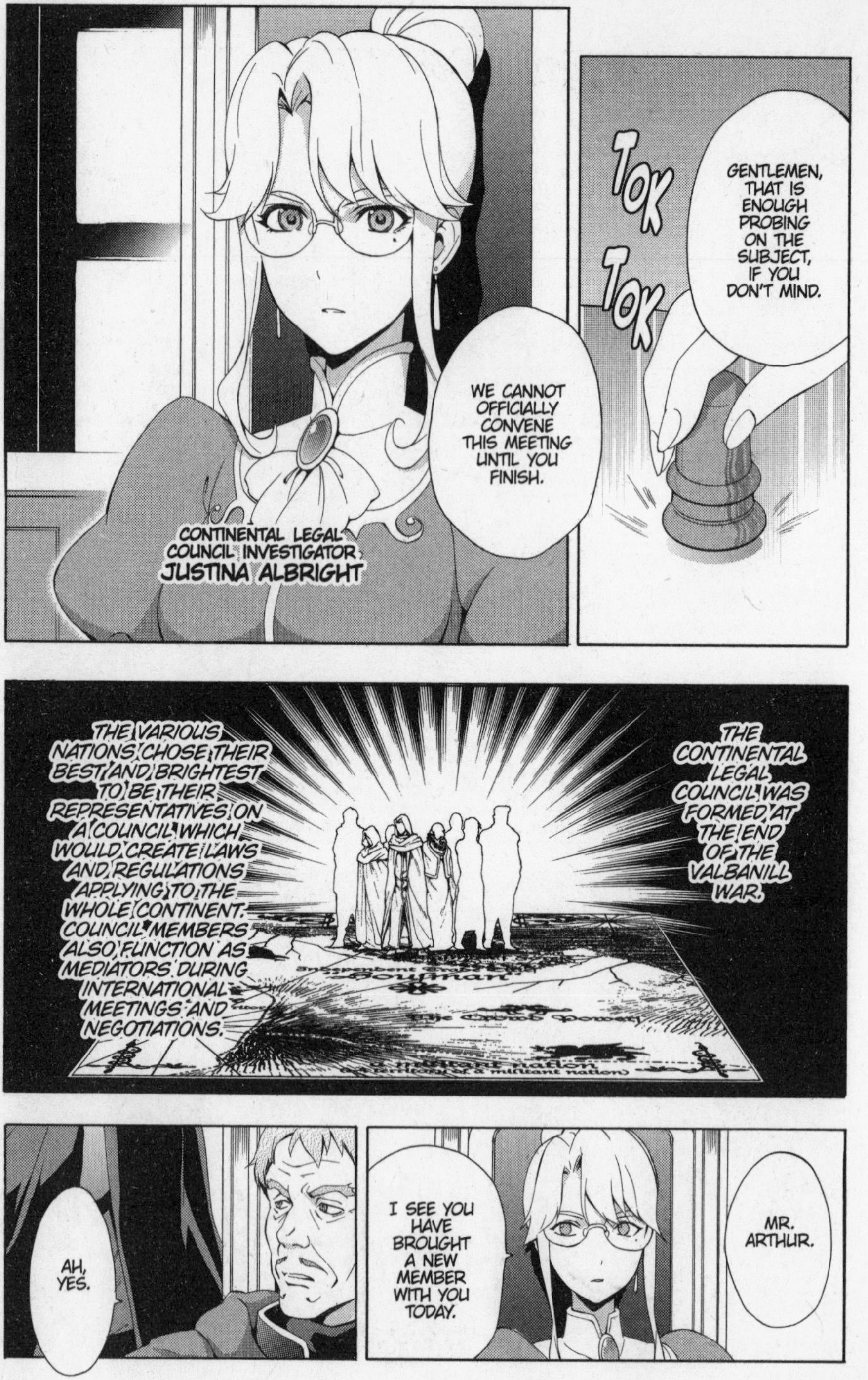
TOK TOK
GENTLEMEN, THAT IS ENOUGH PROBING ON THE SUBJECT, IF YOU DON'T MIND.
WE CANNOT OFFICIALLY CONVENE THIS MEETING UNTIL YOU FINISH.
CONTINENTAL LEGAL COUNCIL INVESTIGATOR JUSTINA ALBRIGHT
THE CONTINENTAL LEGAL COUNCIL WAS FORMED AT THE END OF THE VALBANILL WAR.
THE VARIOUS NATIONS CHOSE THEIR BEST AND BRIGHTEST TO BE THEIR REPRESENTATIVES ON A COUNCIL WHICH WOULD CREATE LAWS AND REGULATIONS APPLYING TO THE WHOLE CONTINENT. COUNCIL MEMBERS ALSO FUNCTION AS MEDIATORS DURING INTERNATIONAL MEETINGS AND NEGOTIATIONS.
MR. ARTHUR.
I SEE YOU HAVE BROUGHT A NEW MEMBER WITH YOU TODAY.
AH, YES.

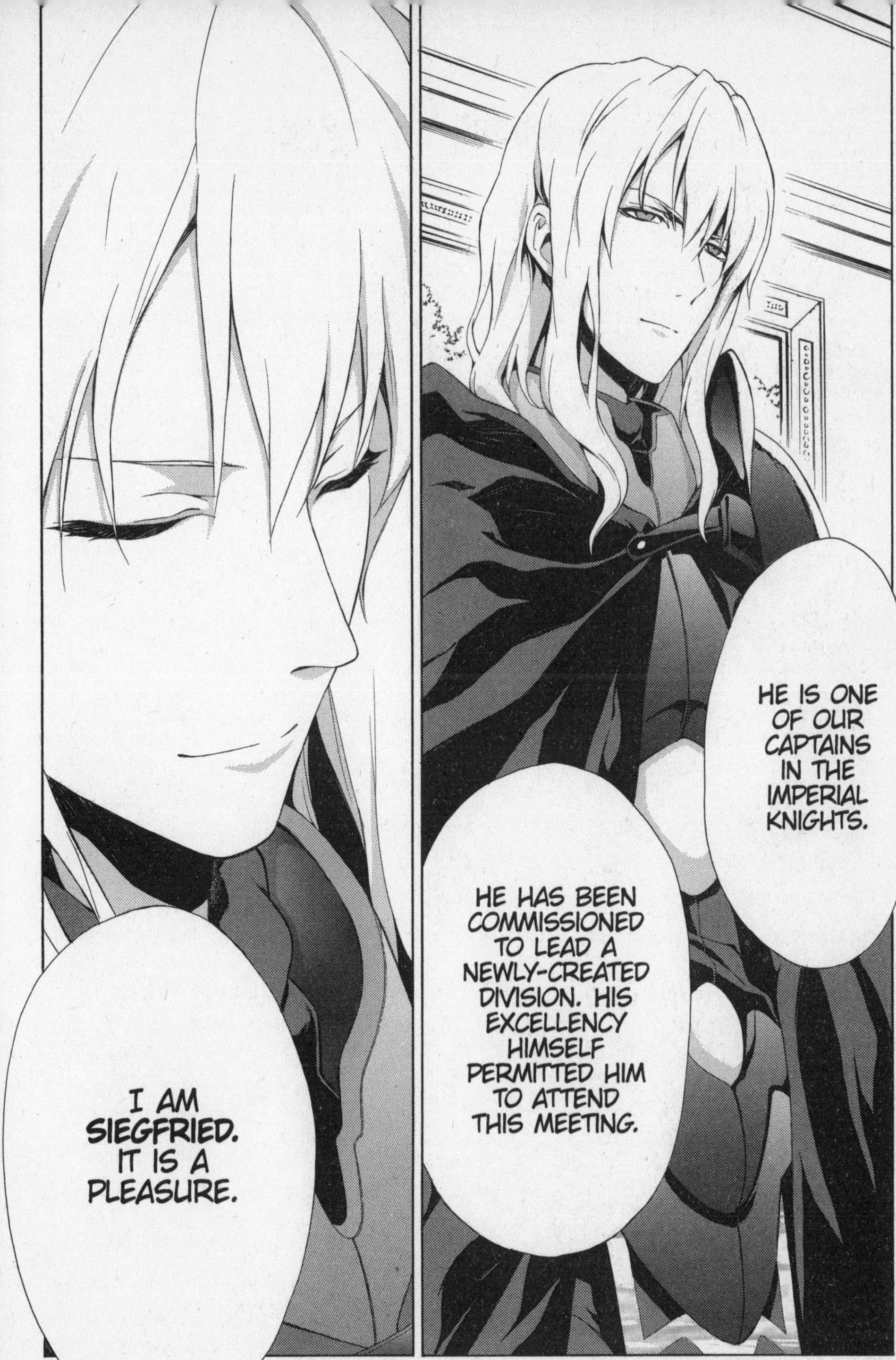
HE IS ONE OF OUR CAPTAINS IN THE IMPERIAL KNIGHTS.
HE HAS BEEN COMMISSIONED TO LEAD A NEWLY-CREATED DIVISION. HIS EXCELLENCY HIMSELF PERMITTED HIM TO ATTEND THIS MEETING.
I AM SIEGFRIED. IT IS A PLEASURE.

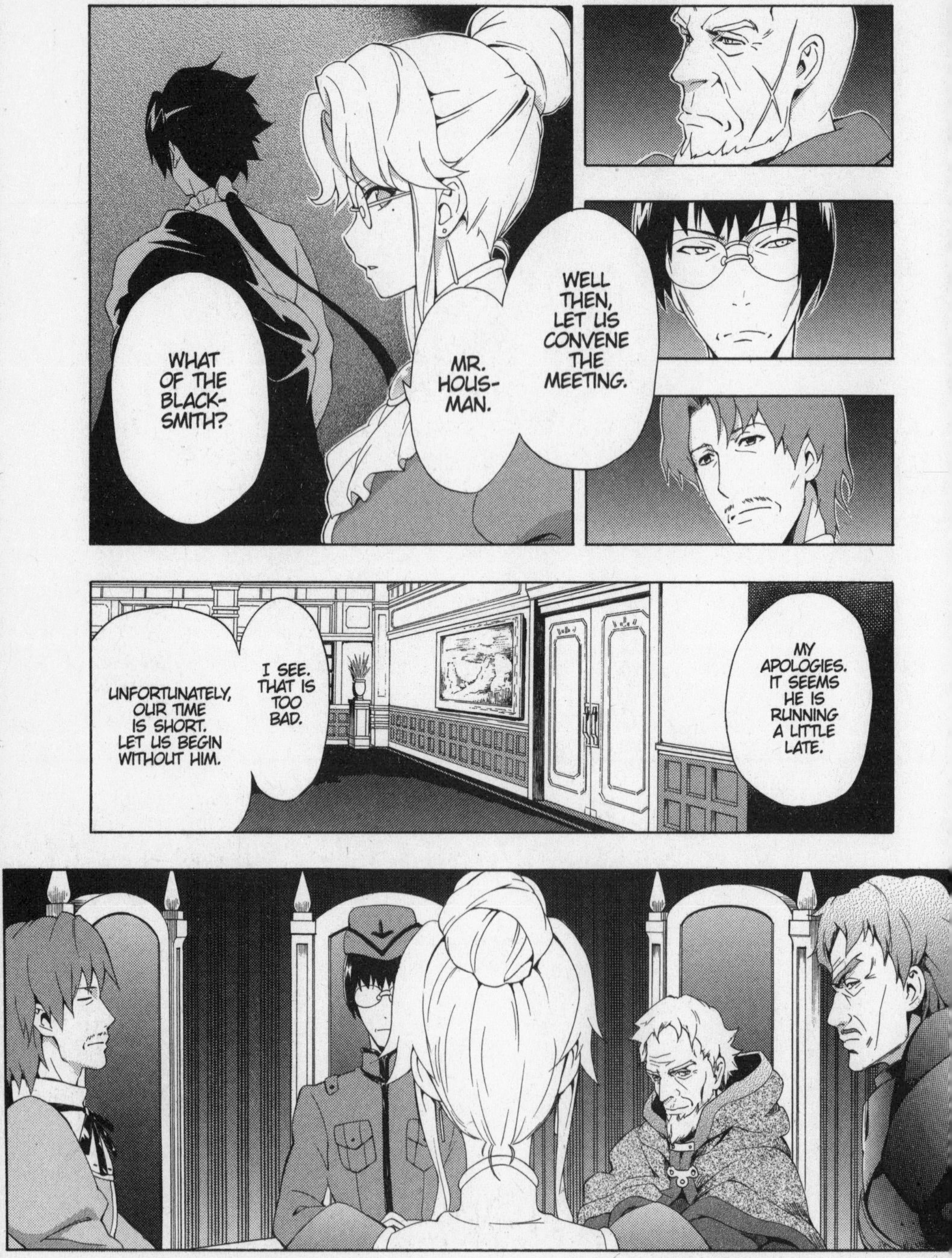
WELL THEN, LET US CONVENE THE MEETING.
MR. HOUSMAN.
WHAT OF THE BLACKSMITH?
MY APOLOGIES. IT SEEMS HE IS RUNNING A LITTLE LATE.
I SEE. THAT IS TOO BAD.
UNFORTUNATELY, OUR TIME IS SHORT. LET US BEGIN WITHOUT HIM.

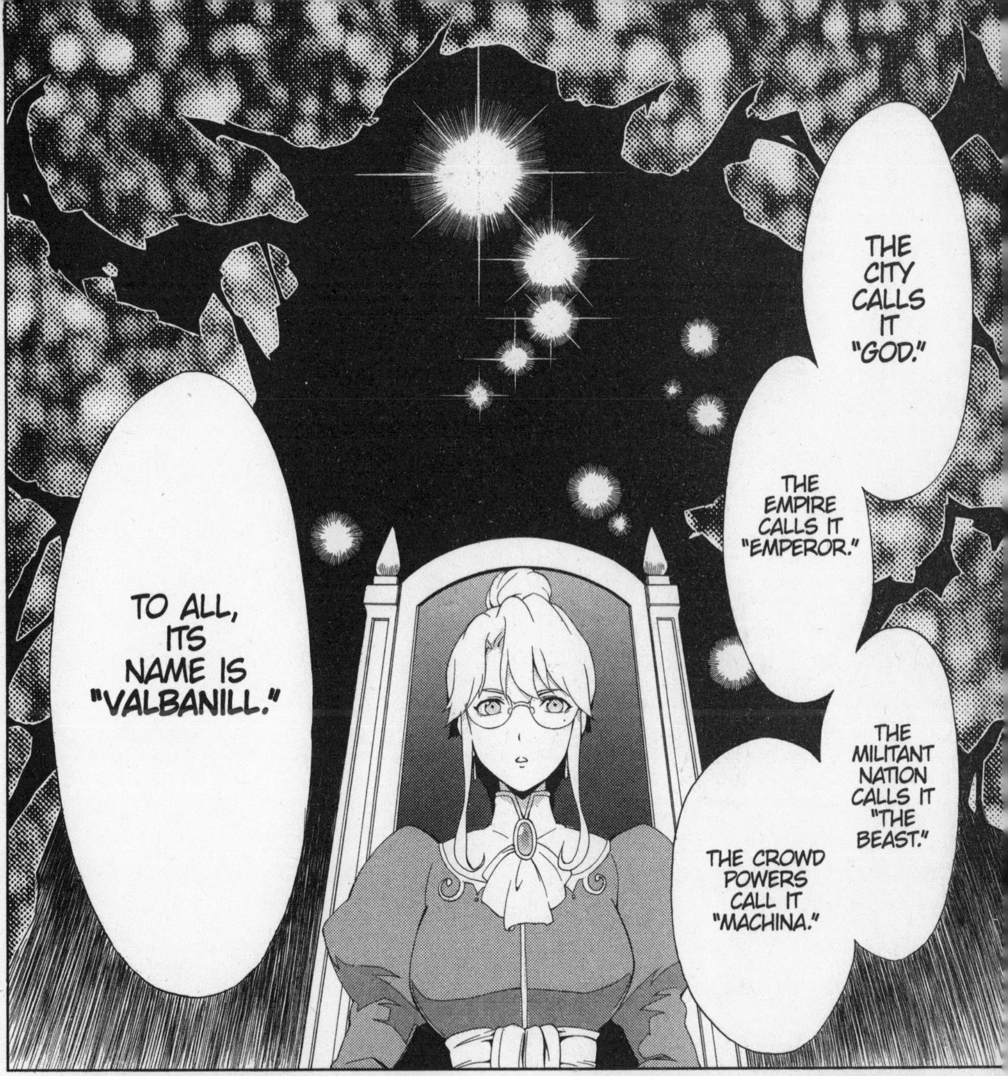
THE CITY CALLS IT "GOD."
THE EMPIRE CALLS IT "EMPEROR."
THE MILITANT NATION CALLS IT "THE BEAST."
THE CROWD POWERS CALL IT "MACHINA."
TO ALL, ITS NAME IS "VALBANILL."
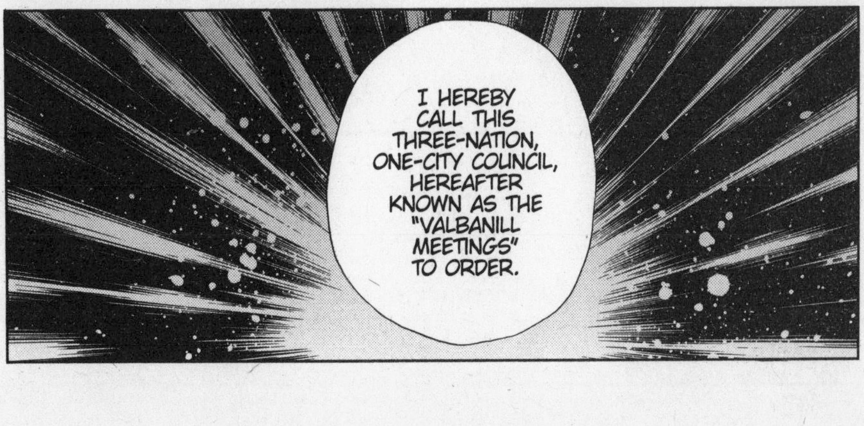
I HEREBY CALL THIS THREE-NATION, ONE-CITY COUNCIL, HEREAFTER KNOWN AS THE "VALBANILL MEETINGS" TO ORDER.

✳Cecily Campbell✳

アトリエ 工房リーザ
atelier Liza BRANCH OFFICE I

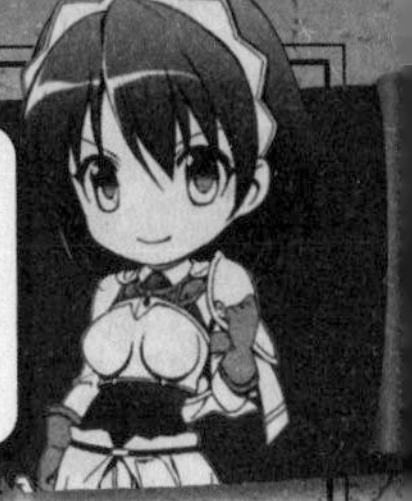
Let's begin this volume's Atelier Liza Branch Office! Has yours been chosen?

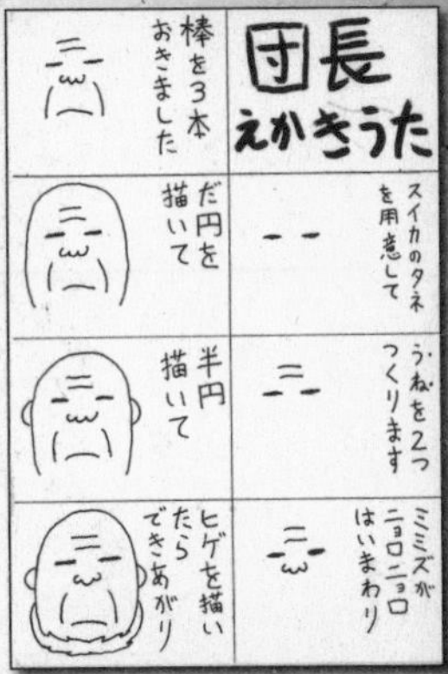
団長
えかきうた
棒を3本おきました
スイカのタネを用意して
だ円を描いて
うねを2つつくります
半円描いて
ミミズがニョロニョロはいまわり
ヒゲを描いたらできあがり

↑ Tochigi, Tsutomu Ochiai

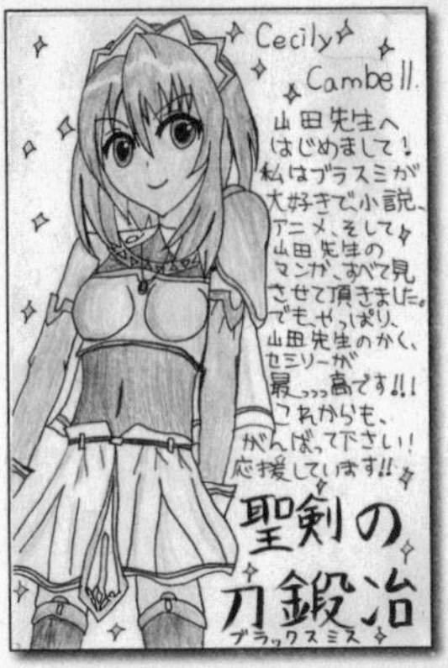
Cecily Cambell.
山田先生へ はじめまして! 私はブラスミが大好きで小説、アニメ、そして山田先生のマンガ、すべて見させて頂きました。でも、やっぱり、山田先生のかく、セシリーが最っっっ高です!!! これからも、がんばって下さい! 応援しています!!
聖剣の刀鍛冶
ブラックスミス

↑ Aichi, Micchan

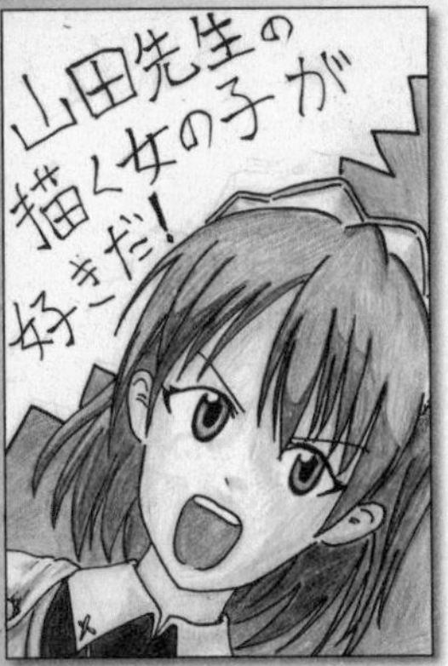
山田先生の描く女の子が好きだ!

↑ Aichi, Takeno

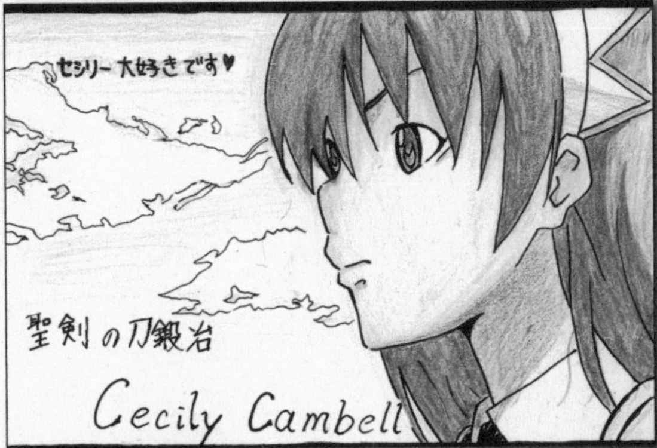
セシリー大好きです♥
聖剣の刀鍛冶
Cecily Cambell

↑ Aichi, Oren

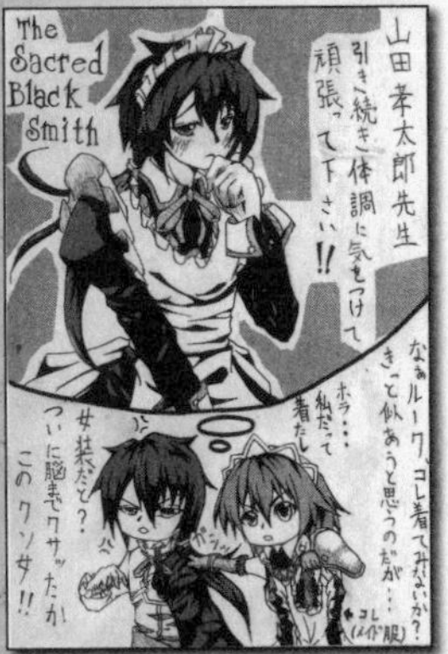
The Sacred Black Smith
山田孝太郎先生 引き続き体調に気をつけて頑張って下さい!!
なぁルーク、コレ着てみないか? きっと似あうと思うのだが…
ホラ、私だって着たし
女装だと? ついに脳までクサッたかこのクソ女!!
←コレ(メイド服)

↑ Saitama, Kengo Tokuda

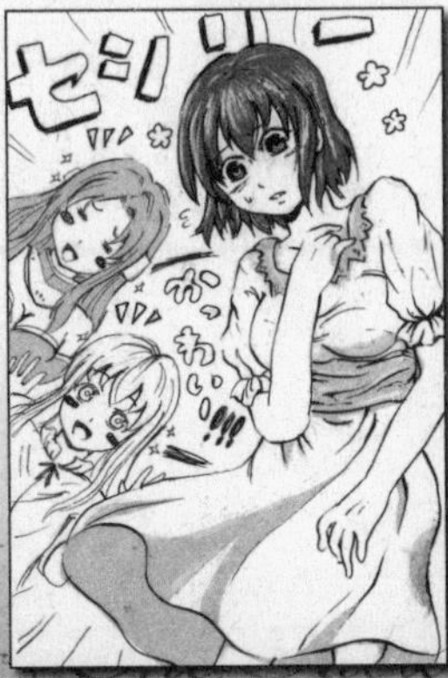
セシリー

↑ Kanagawa, Sakura

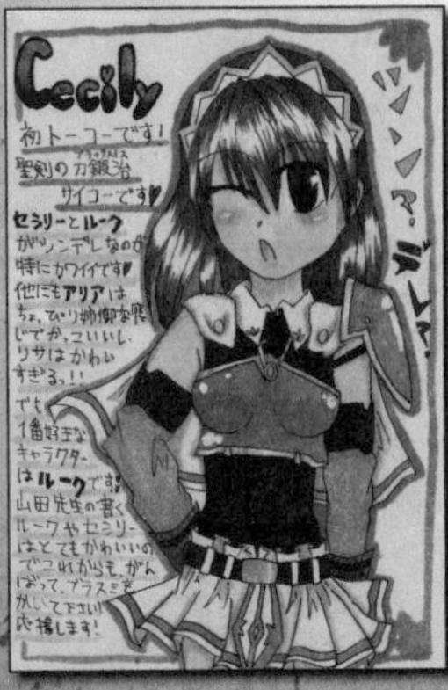
Cecily
初トーコーです! 聖剣の刀鍛冶サイコーです♥
セシリーとルークがツンデレなのが特にカワイイです♥ 他にもアリアはちょっぴり小悪魔系じでかっこいいし、リサはかわいすぎる…!!
でも1番好きなキャラクターはルークです! 山田先生の書くルークやセシリーはとてもかわいいのでこれからも、がんばって、ブラスミ完結して下さい! 応援します!

↑ Miyazaki, Ahri

Thank you for your gracious interest. Luke could learn a thing or two from all of you.

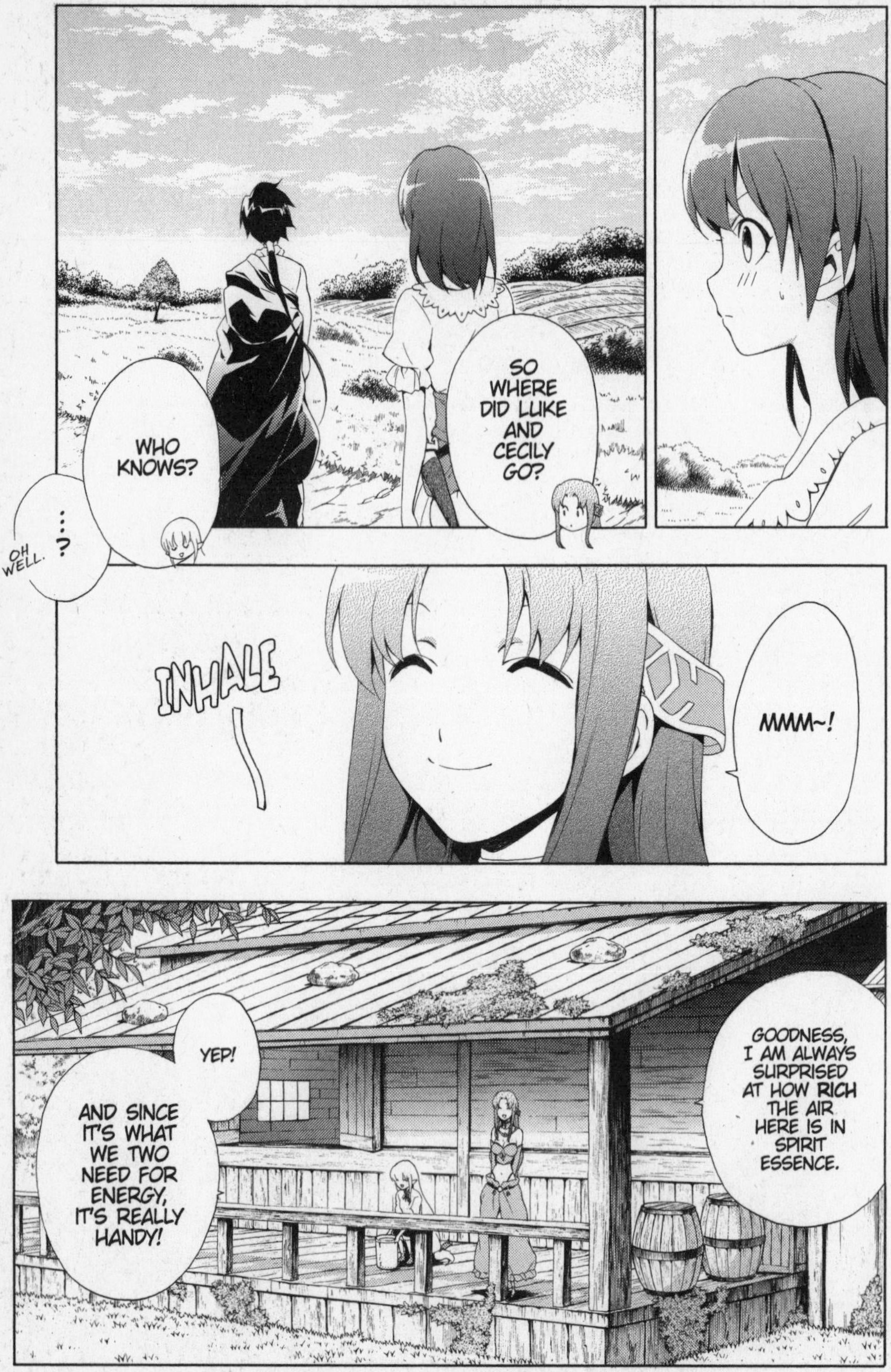
SO WHERE DID LUKE AND CECILY GO?
WHO KNOWS?
...?
OH WELL.
MMMM~!
INHALE
GOODNESS, I AM ALWAYS SURPRISED AT HOW RICH THE AIR HERE IS IN SPIRIT ESSENCE.
YEP!
AND SINCE IT'S WHAT WE TWO NEED FOR ENERGY, IT'S REALLY HANDY!

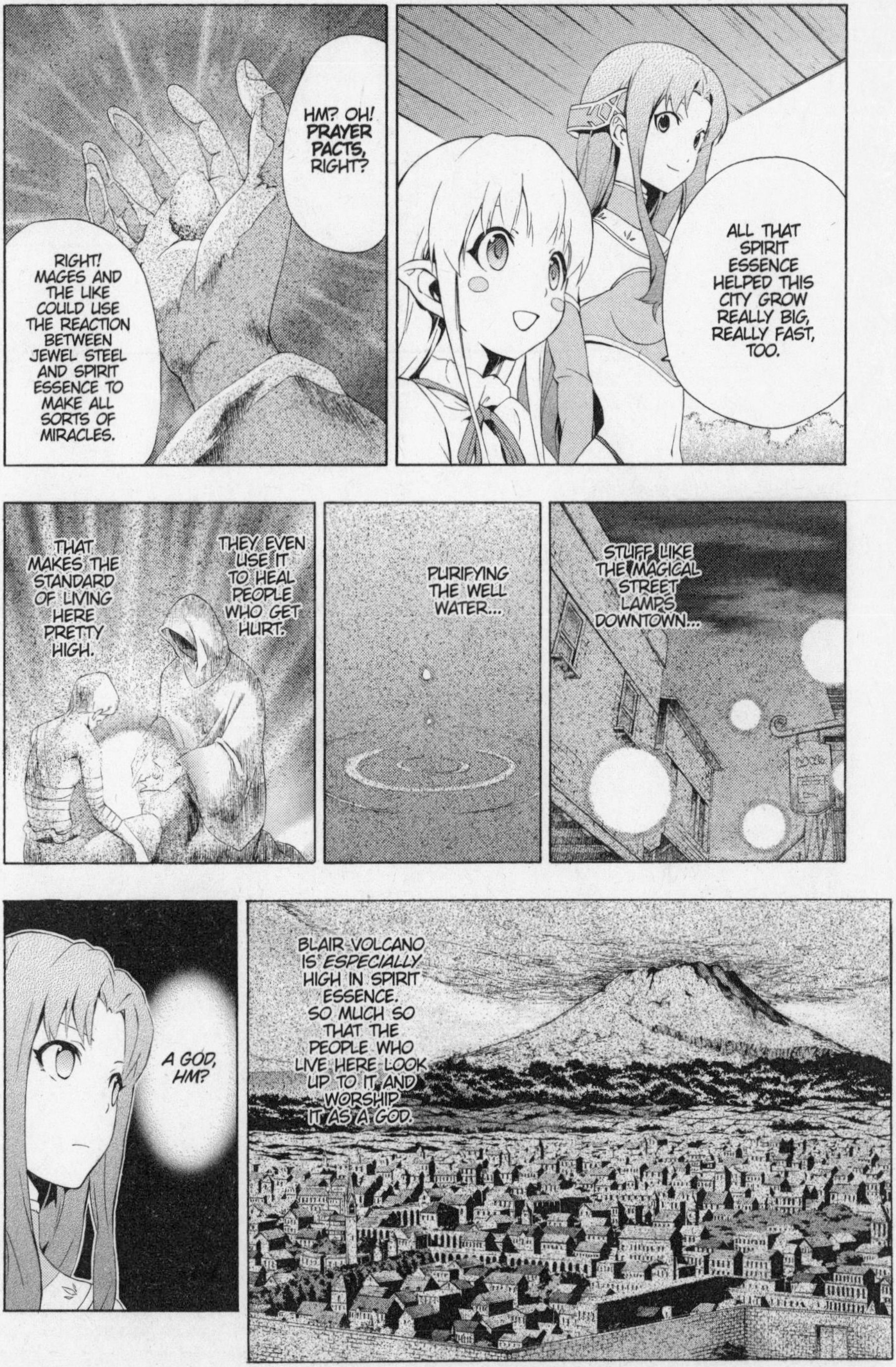
ALL THAT SPIRIT ESSENCE HELPED THIS CITY GROW REALLY BIG, REALLY FAST, TOO.
HM? OH! **PRAYER PACTS**, RIGHT?
RIGHT! MAGES AND THE LIKE COULD USE THE REACTION BETWEEN JEWEL STEEL AND SPIRIT ESSENCE TO MAKE ALL SORTS OF MIRACLES.
STUFF LIKE THE MAGICAL STREET LAMPS DOWNTOWN...
PURIFYING THE WELL WATER...
THEY EVEN USE IT TO HEAL PEOPLE WHO GET HURT.
THAT MAKES THE STANDARD OF LIVING HERE PRETTY HIGH.
BLAIR VOLCANO IS *ESPECIALLY* HIGH IN SPIRIT ESSENCE. SO MUCH SO THAT THE PEOPLE WHO LIVE HERE LOOK UP TO IT AND WORSHIP IT AS A GOD.
A GOD, HM?

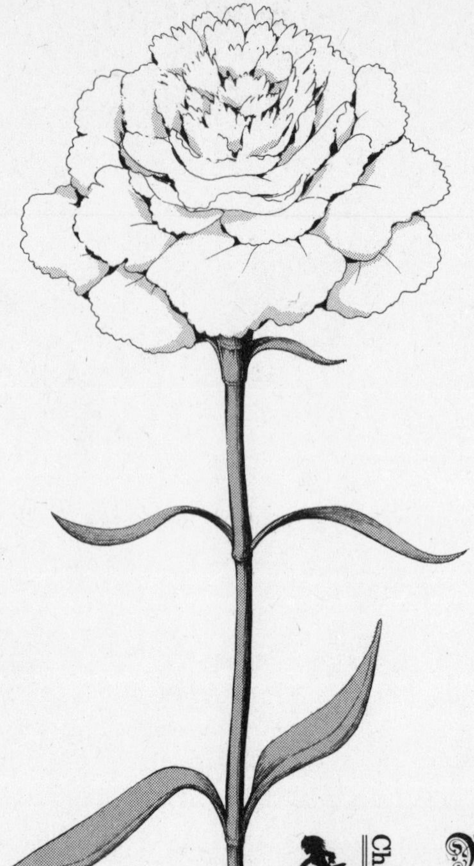

Chapter 14 Blacksmith (Part 2)

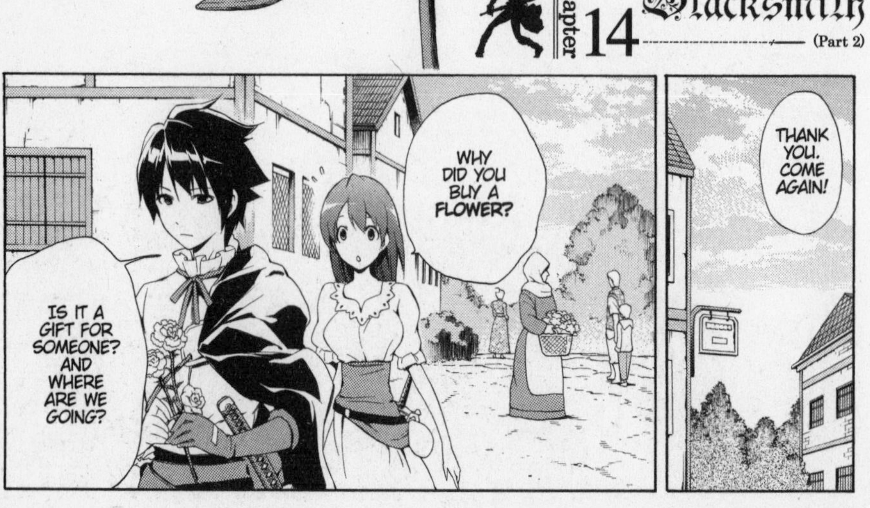
THANK YOU. COME AGAIN!
WHY DID YOU BUY A FLOWER?
IS IT A GIFT FOR SOMEONE? AND WHERE ARE WE GOING?

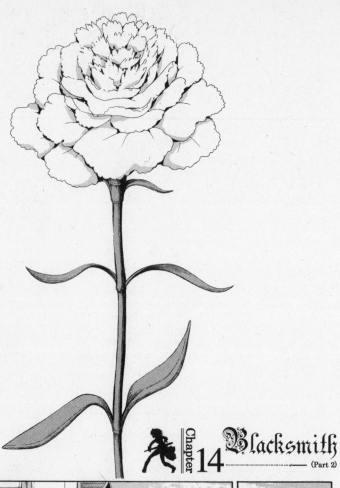

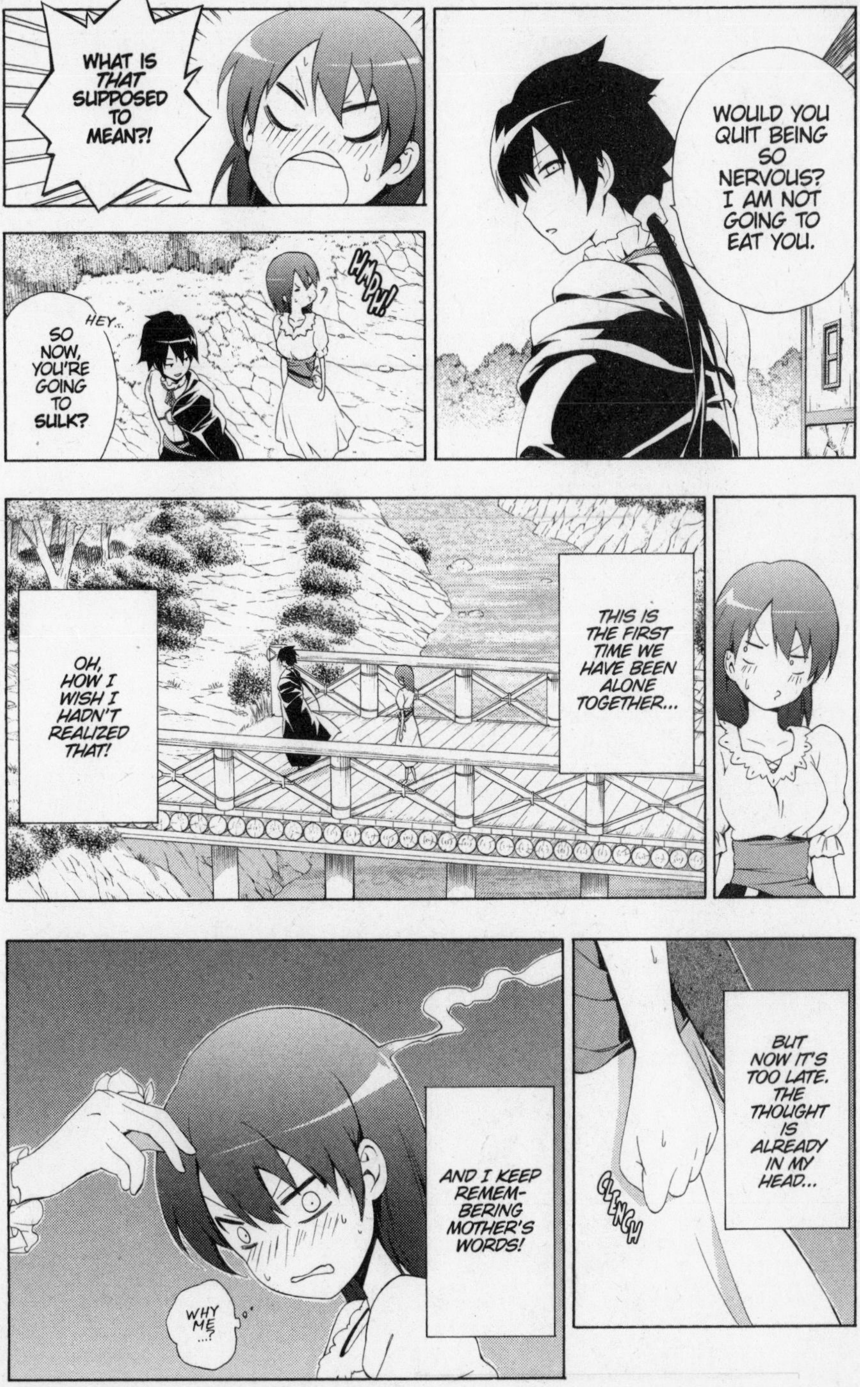
WOULD YOU QUIT BEING SO NERVOUS? I AM NOT GOING TO EAT YOU.
WHAT IS *THAT* SUPPOSED TO MEAN?!
HMPH!
HEY...
SO NOW, YOU'RE GOING TO SULK?
THIS IS THE FIRST TIME WE HAVE BEEN ALONE TOGETHER...
OH, HOW I WISH I HADN'T REALIZED THAT!
BUT NOW IT'S TOO LATE. THE THOUGHT IS ALREADY IN MY HEAD...
CLENCH
AND I KEEP REMEMBERING MOTHER'S WORDS!
WHY ME ...?

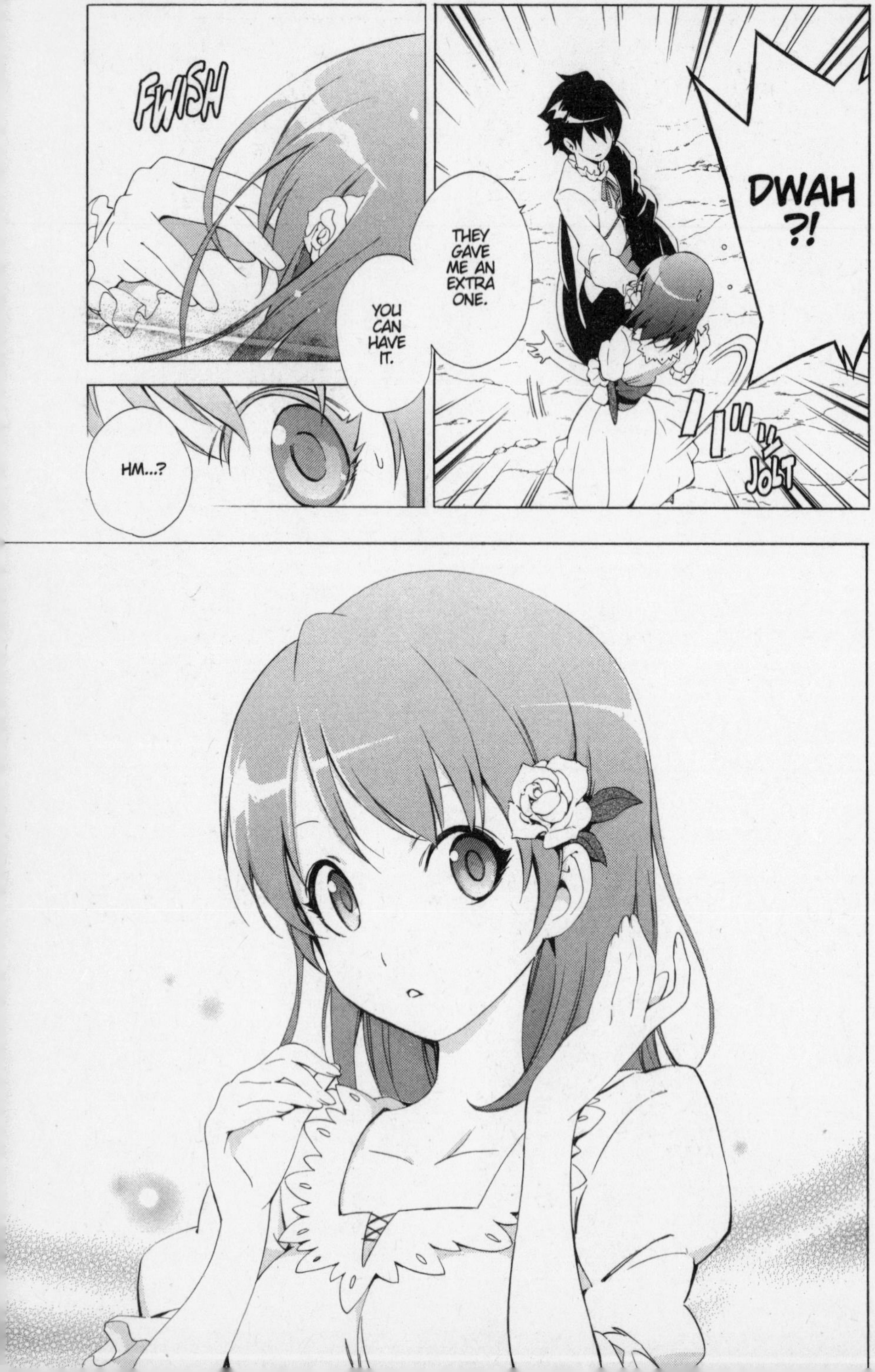
DWAH ?!
JOLT
FWISH
THEY GAVE ME AN EXTRA ONE.
YOU CAN HAVE IT.
HM...?

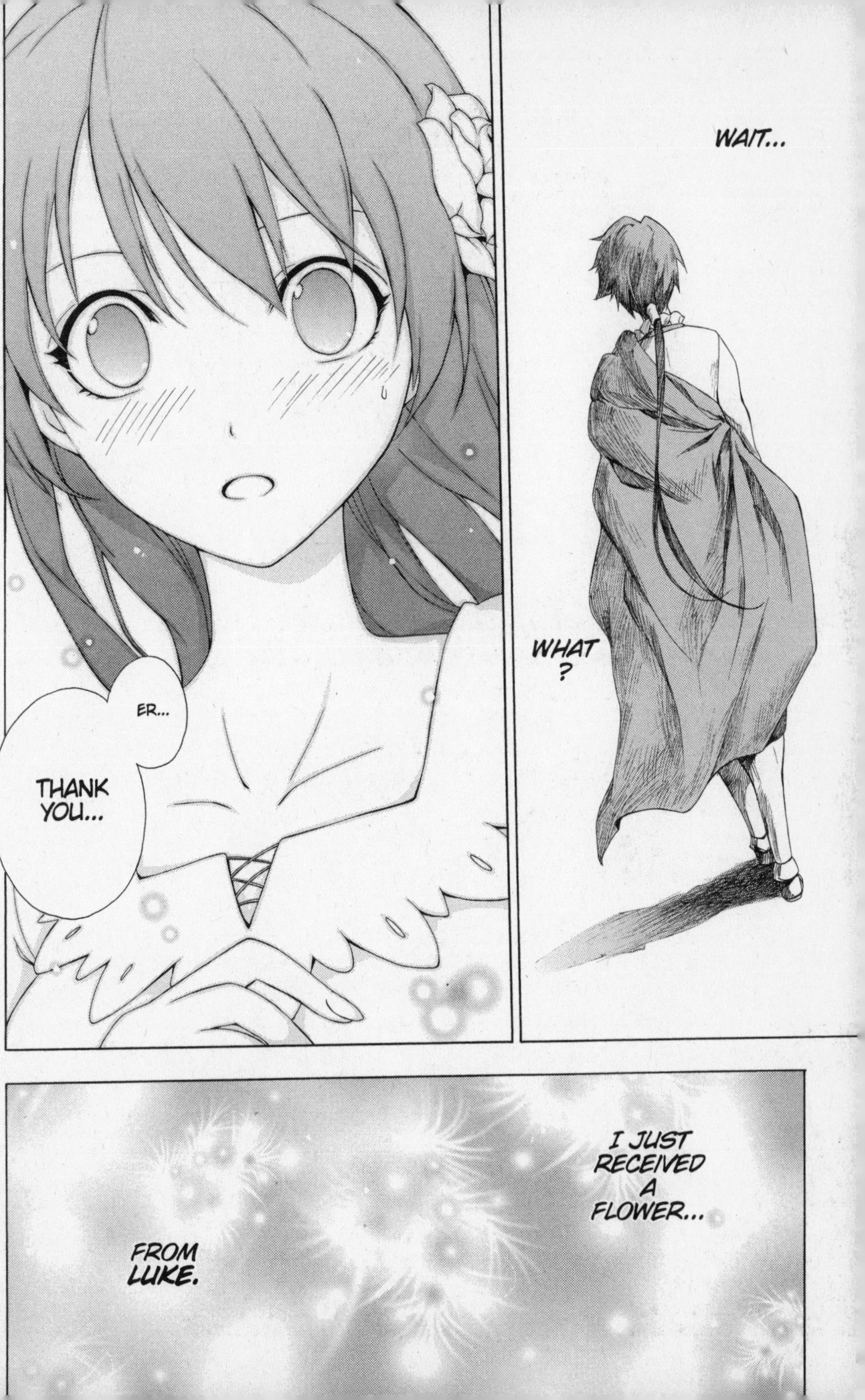
WAIT...
WHAT?
ER...
THANK YOU...
I JUST RECEIVED A FLOWER...
FROM LUKE.

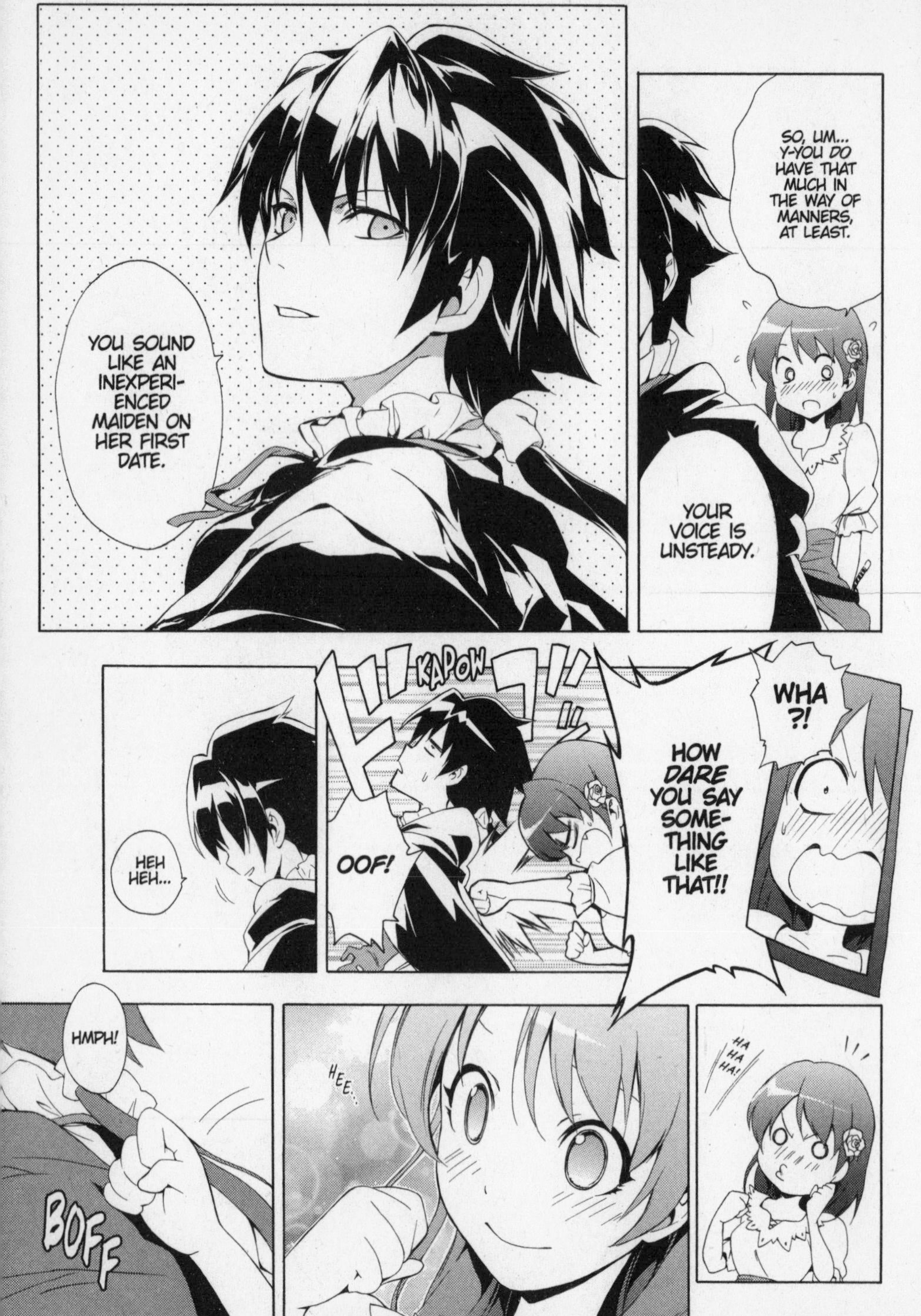
SO, UM... Y-YOU DO HAVE THAT MUCH IN THE WAY OF MANNERS, AT LEAST.
YOUR VOICE IS UNSTEADY.
YOU SOUND LIKE AN INEXPERI-ENCED MAIDEN ON HER FIRST DATE.
WHA ?!
KAPOW
HOW DARE YOU SAY SOME-THING LIKE THAT!!
OOF!
HEH HEH...
HA HA HA!
HEE...
HMPH!
BOFF

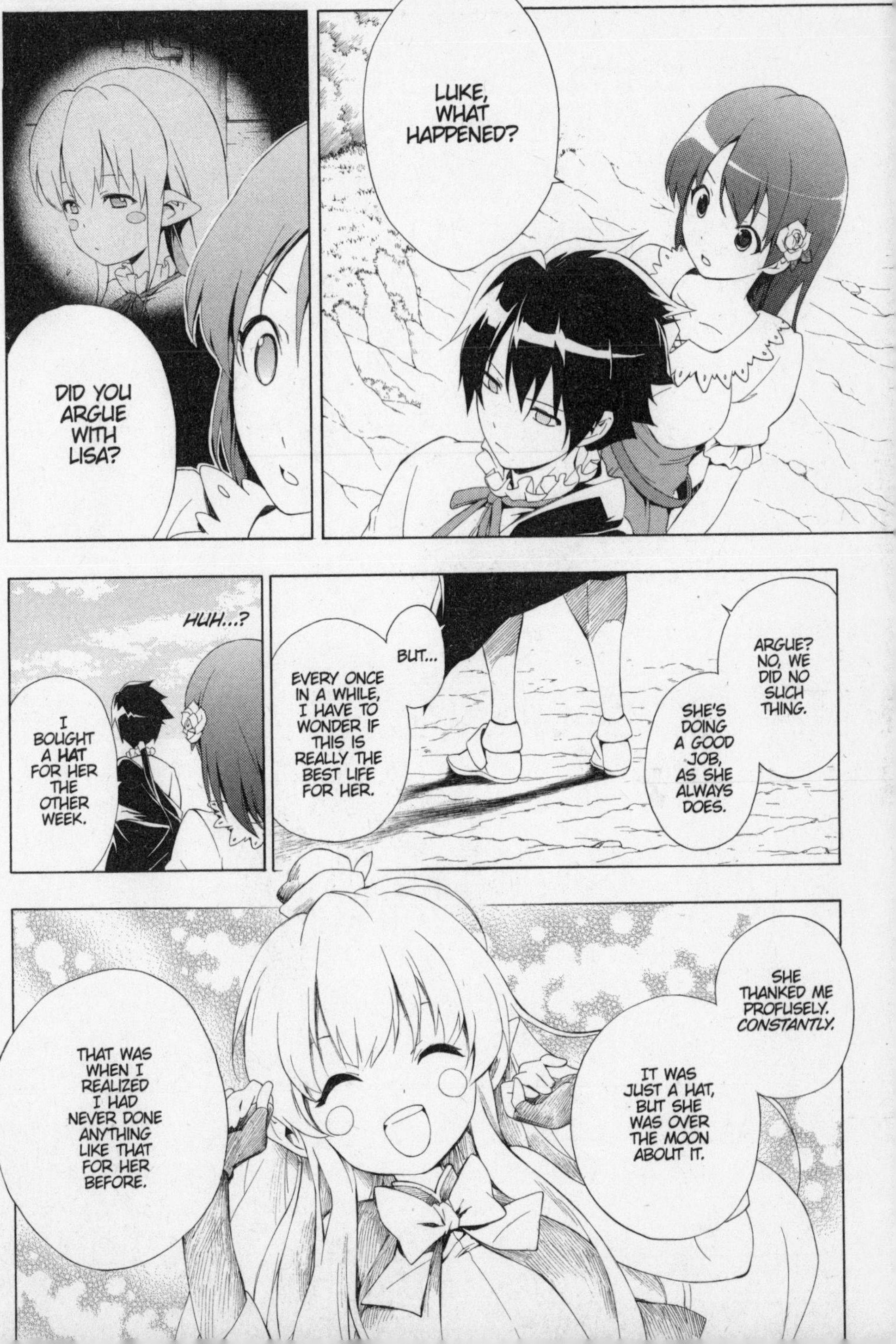
LUKE, WHAT HAPPENED?
DID YOU ARGUE WITH LISA?
ARGUE? NO, WE DID NO SUCH THING.
SHE'S DOING A GOOD JOB, AS SHE ALWAYS DOES.
BUT...
EVERY ONCE IN A WHILE, I HAVE TO WONDER IF THIS IS REALLY THE BEST LIFE FOR HER.
HUH...?
I BOUGHT A HAT FOR HER THE OTHER WEEK.
SHE THANKED ME PROFUSELY. CONSTANTLY.
IT WAS JUST A HAT, BUT SHE WAS OVER THE MOON ABOUT IT.
THAT WAS WHEN I REALIZED I HAD NEVER DONE ANYTHING LIKE THAT FOR HER BEFORE.

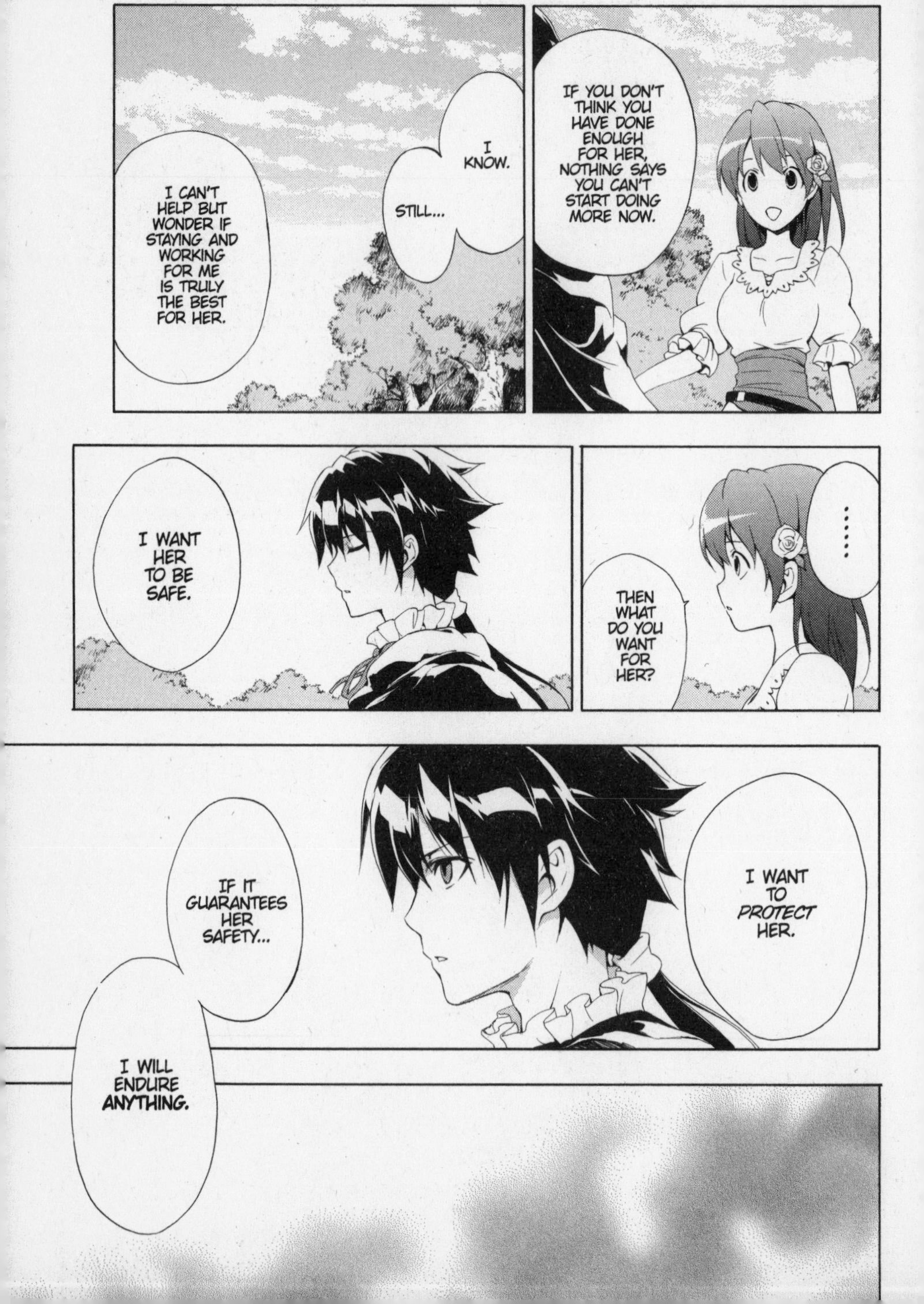
IF YOU DON'T THINK YOU HAVE DONE ENOUGH FOR HER, NOTHING SAYS YOU CAN'T START DOING MORE NOW.
I KNOW.
STILL...
I CAN'T HELP BUT WONDER IF STAYING AND WORKING FOR ME IS TRULY THE BEST FOR HER.
......
THEN WHAT DO YOU WANT FOR HER?
I WANT HER TO BE SAFE.
I WANT TO *PROTECT* HER.
IF IT GUARANTEES HER SAFETY...
I WILL ENDURE **ANYTHING.**

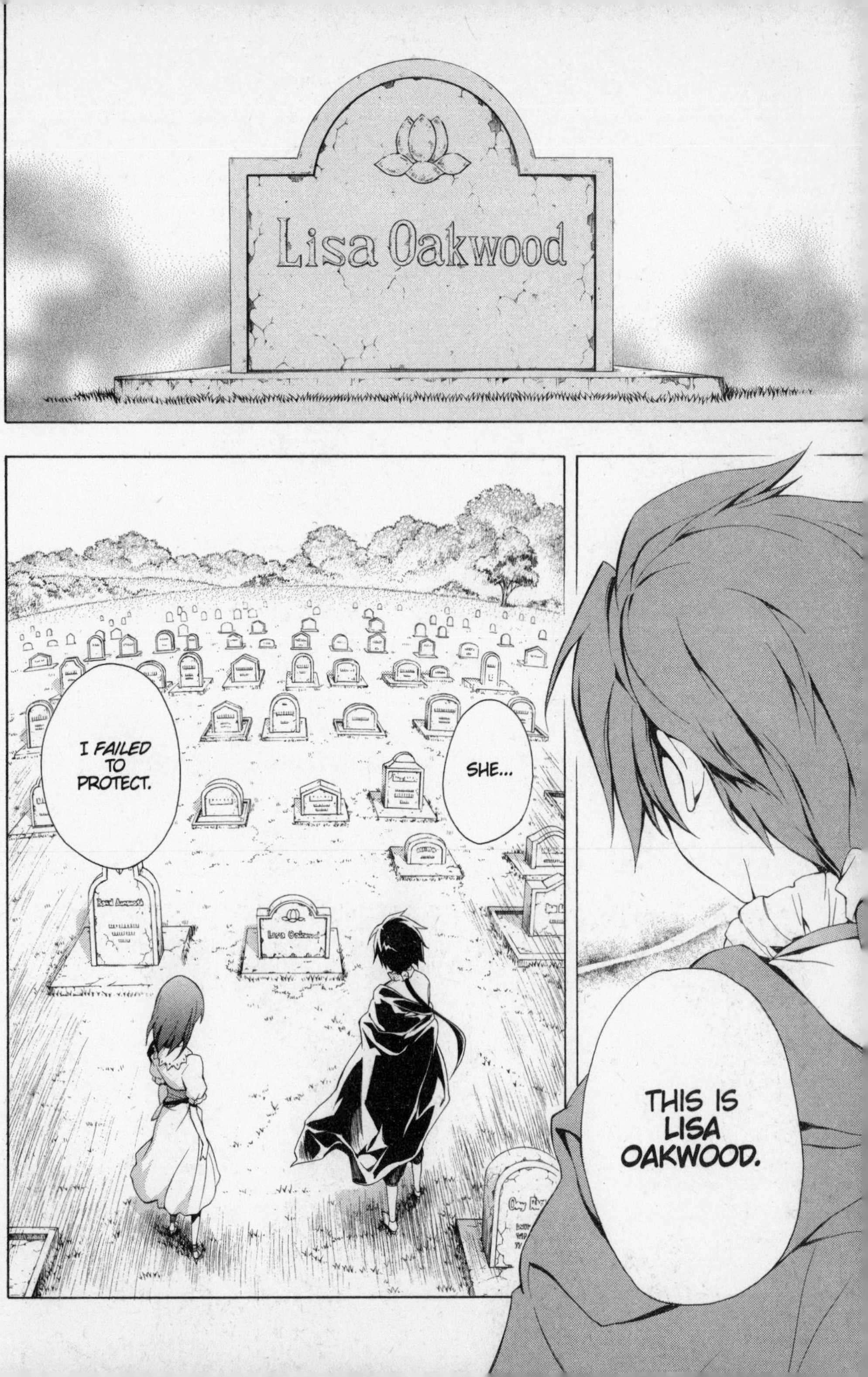
Lisa Oakwood
THIS IS LISA OAKWOOD.
SHE...
I FAILED TO PROTECT.

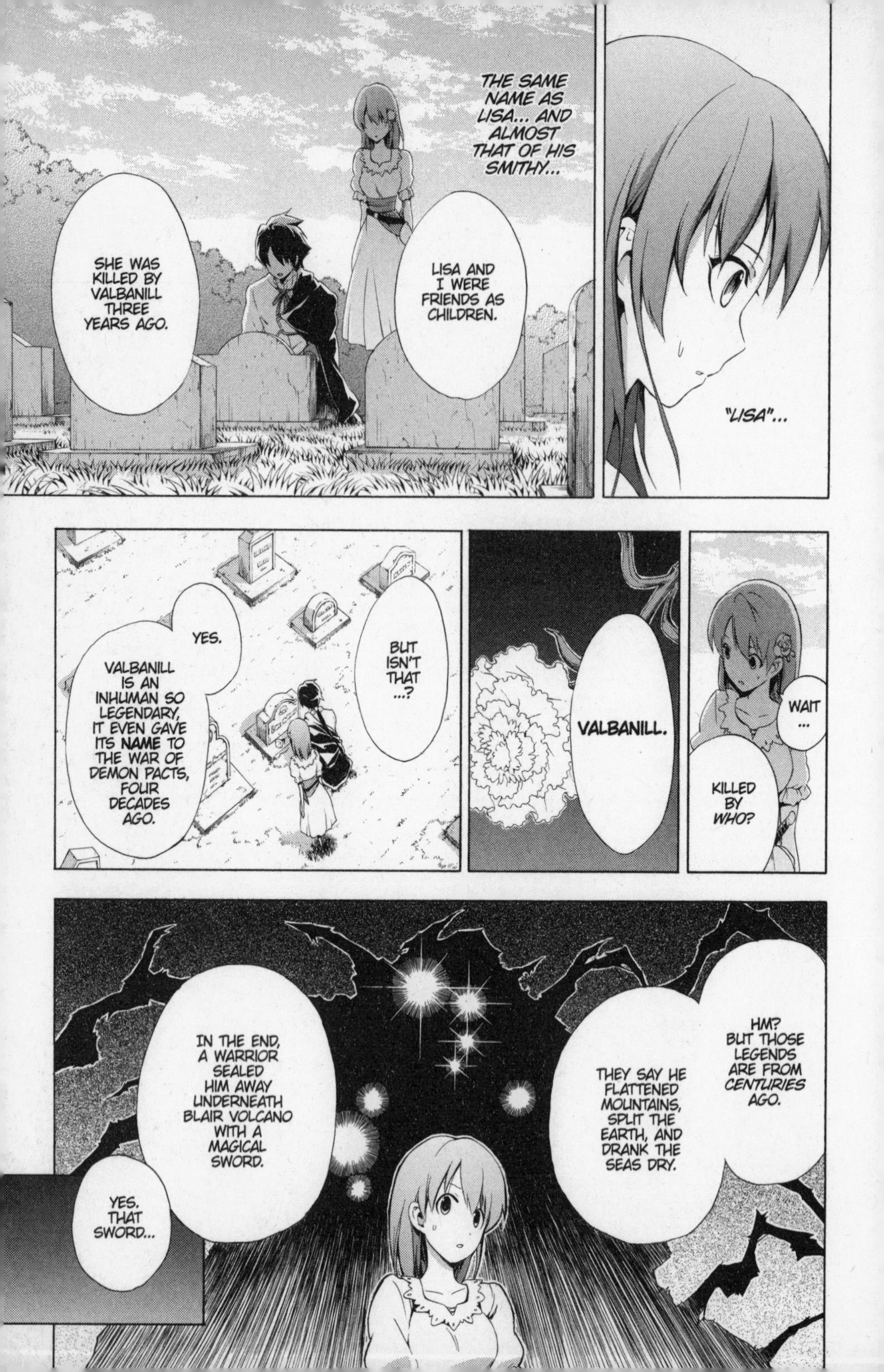
"LISA"...
THE SAME NAME AS LISA... AND ALMOST THAT OF HIS SMITHY...
LISA AND I WERE FRIENDS AS CHILDREN.
SHE WAS KILLED BY VALBANILL THREE YEARS AGO.
WAIT ...
KILLED BY WHO?
VALBANILL.
BUT ISN'T THAT ...?
YES.
VALBANILL IS AN INHUMAN SO LEGENDARY, IT EVEN GAVE ITS NAME TO THE WAR OF DEMON PACTS, FOUR DECADES AGO.
HM? BUT THOSE LEGENDS ARE FROM CENTURIES AGO.
THEY SAY HE FLATTENED MOUNTAINS, SPLIT THE EARTH, AND DRANK THE SEAS DRY.
IN THE END, A WARRIOR SEALED HIM AWAY UNDERNEATH BLAIR VOLCANO WITH A MAGICAL SWORD.
YES. THAT SWORD...

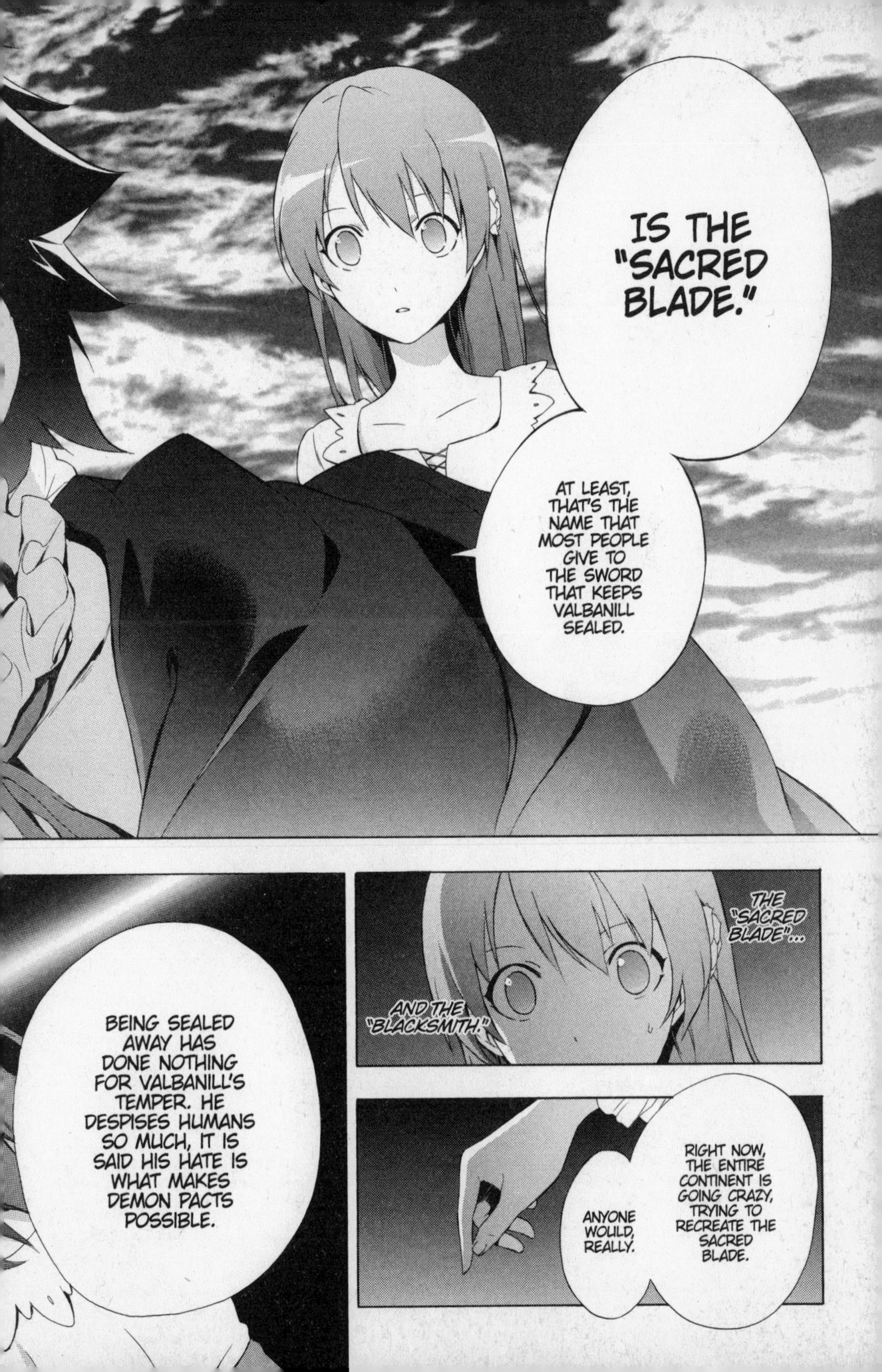
IS THE "SACRED BLADE."
AT LEAST, THAT'S THE NAME THAT MOST PEOPLE GIVE TO THE SWORD THAT KEEPS VALBANILL SEALED.
THE "SACRED BLADE"...
AND THE "BLACKSMITH."
RIGHT NOW, THE ENTIRE CONTINENT IS GOING CRAZY, TRYING TO RECREATE THE SACRED BLADE.
ANYONE WOULD, REALLY.
BEING SEALED AWAY HAS DONE NOTHING FOR VALBANILL'S TEMPER. HE DESPISES HUMANS SO MUCH, IT IS SAID HIS HATE IS WHAT MAKES DEMON PACTS POSSIBLE.

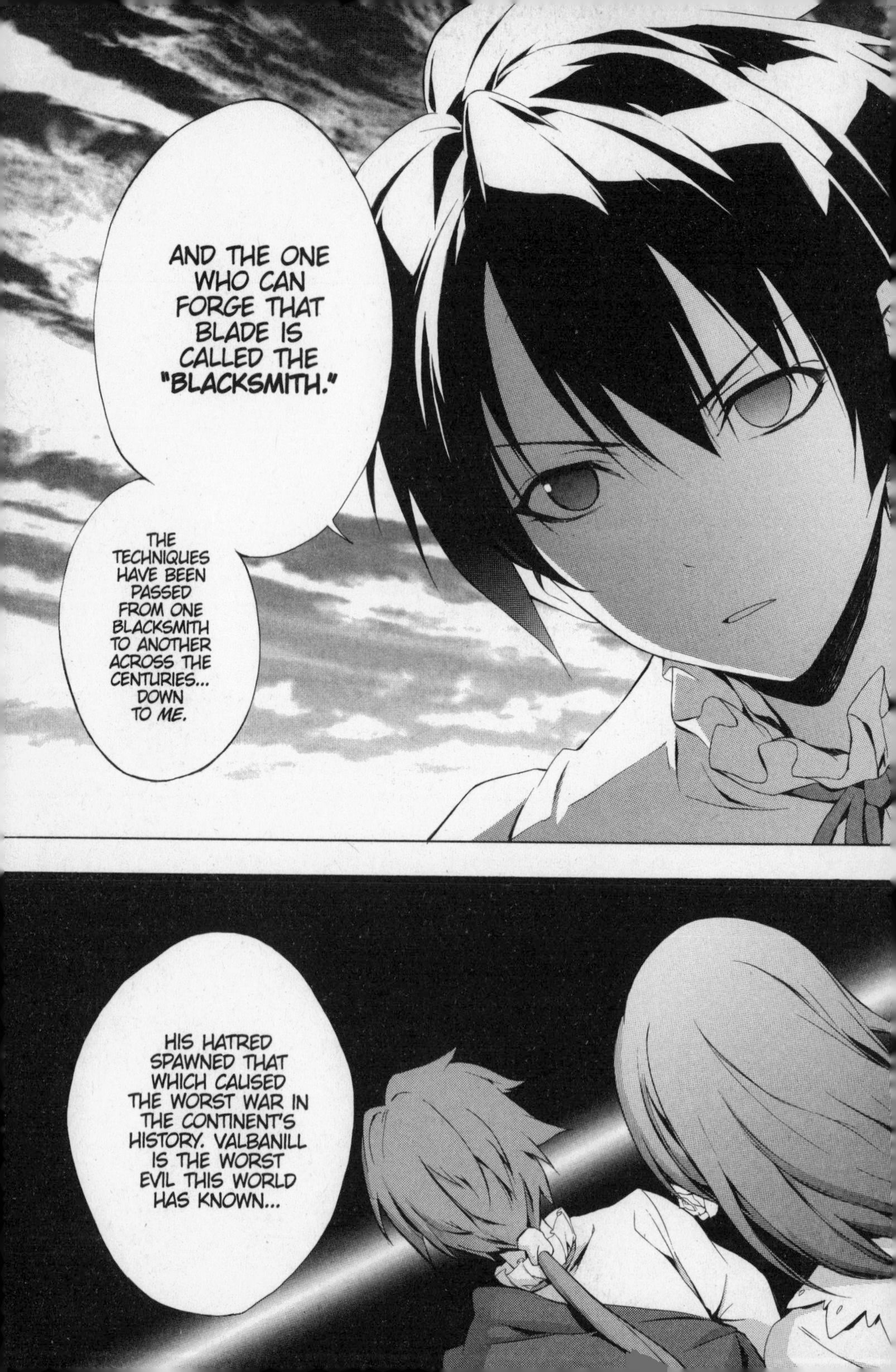
AND THE ONE WHO CAN FORGE THAT BLADE IS CALLED THE "BLACKSMITH."
THE TECHNIQUES HAVE BEEN PASSED FROM ONE BLACKSMITH TO ANOTHER ACROSS THE CENTURIES... DOWN TO *ME*.
HIS HATRED SPAWNED THAT WHICH CAUSED THE WORST WAR IN THE CONTINENT'S HISTORY. VALBANILL IS THE WORST EVIL THIS WORLD HAS KNOWN...

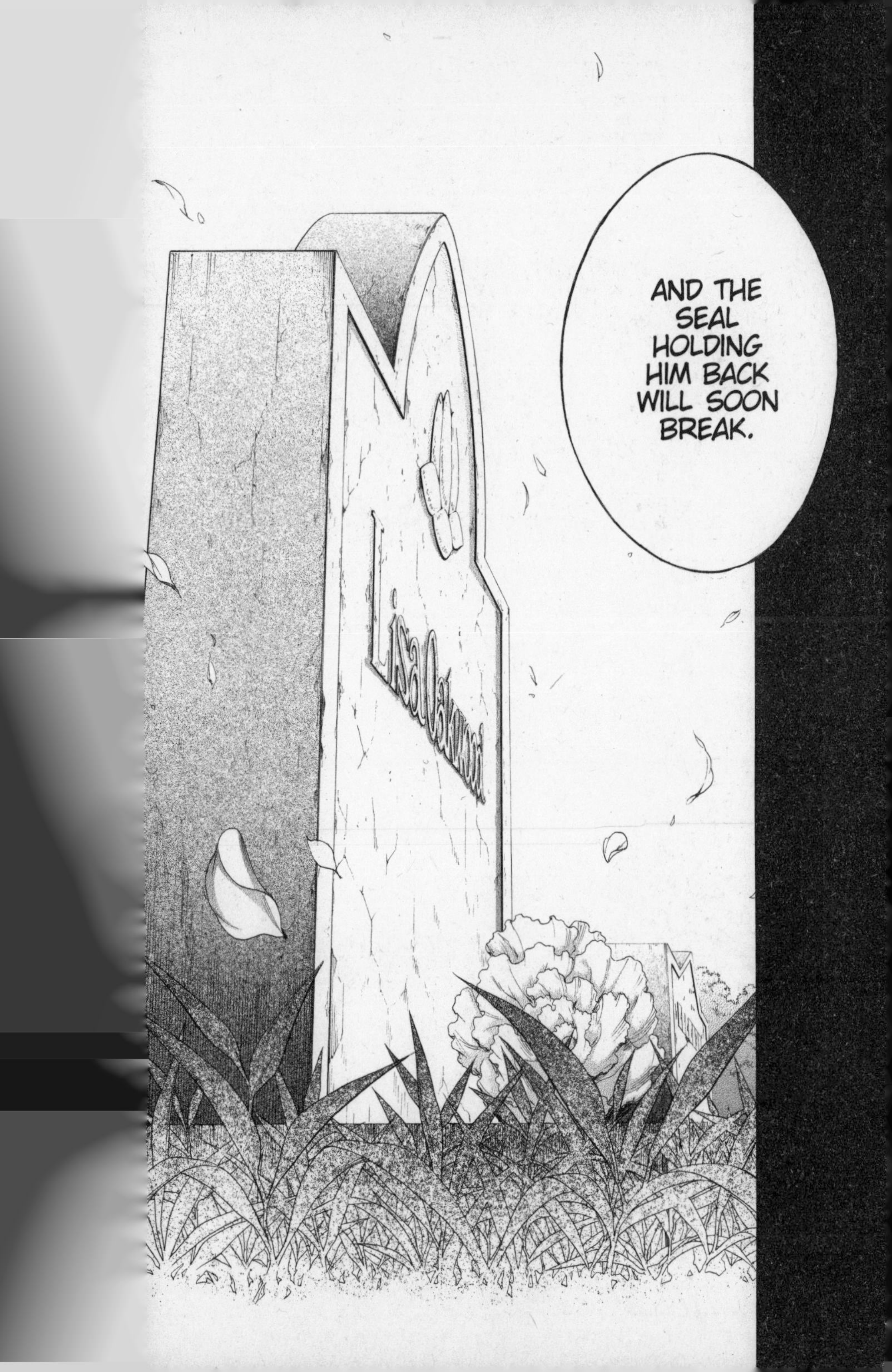
AND THE SEAL HOLDING HIM BACK WILL SOON BREAK.
Lisa Oakwood

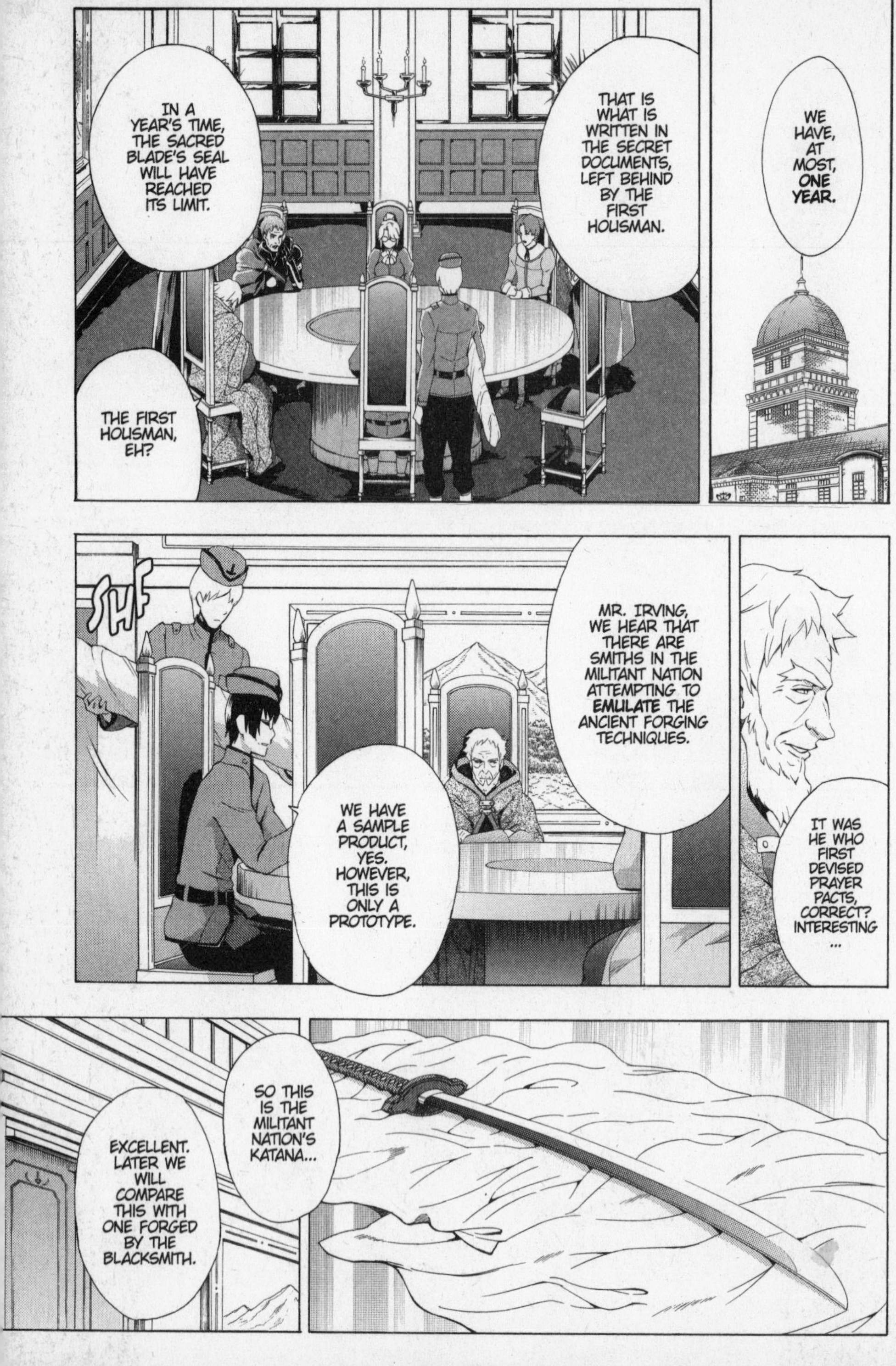
WE HAVE, AT MOST, ONE YEAR.
THAT IS WHAT IS WRITTEN IN THE SECRET DOCUMENTS, LEFT BEHIND BY THE FIRST HOUSMAN.
IN A YEAR'S TIME, THE SACRED BLADE'S SEAL WILL HAVE REACHED ITS LIMIT.
THE FIRST HOUSMAN, EH?
IT WAS HE WHO FIRST DEVISED PRAYER PACTS, CORRECT? INTERESTING ...
MR. IRVING, WE HEAR THAT THERE ARE SMITHS IN THE MILITANT NATION ATTEMPTING TO EMULATE THE ANCIENT FORGING TECHNIQUES.
SHF
WE HAVE A SAMPLE PRODUCT, YES. HOWEVER, THIS IS ONLY A PROTOTYPE.
SO THIS IS THE MILITANT NATION'S KATANA...
EXCELLENT. LATER WE WILL COMPARE THIS WITH ONE FORGED BY THE BLACKSMITH.

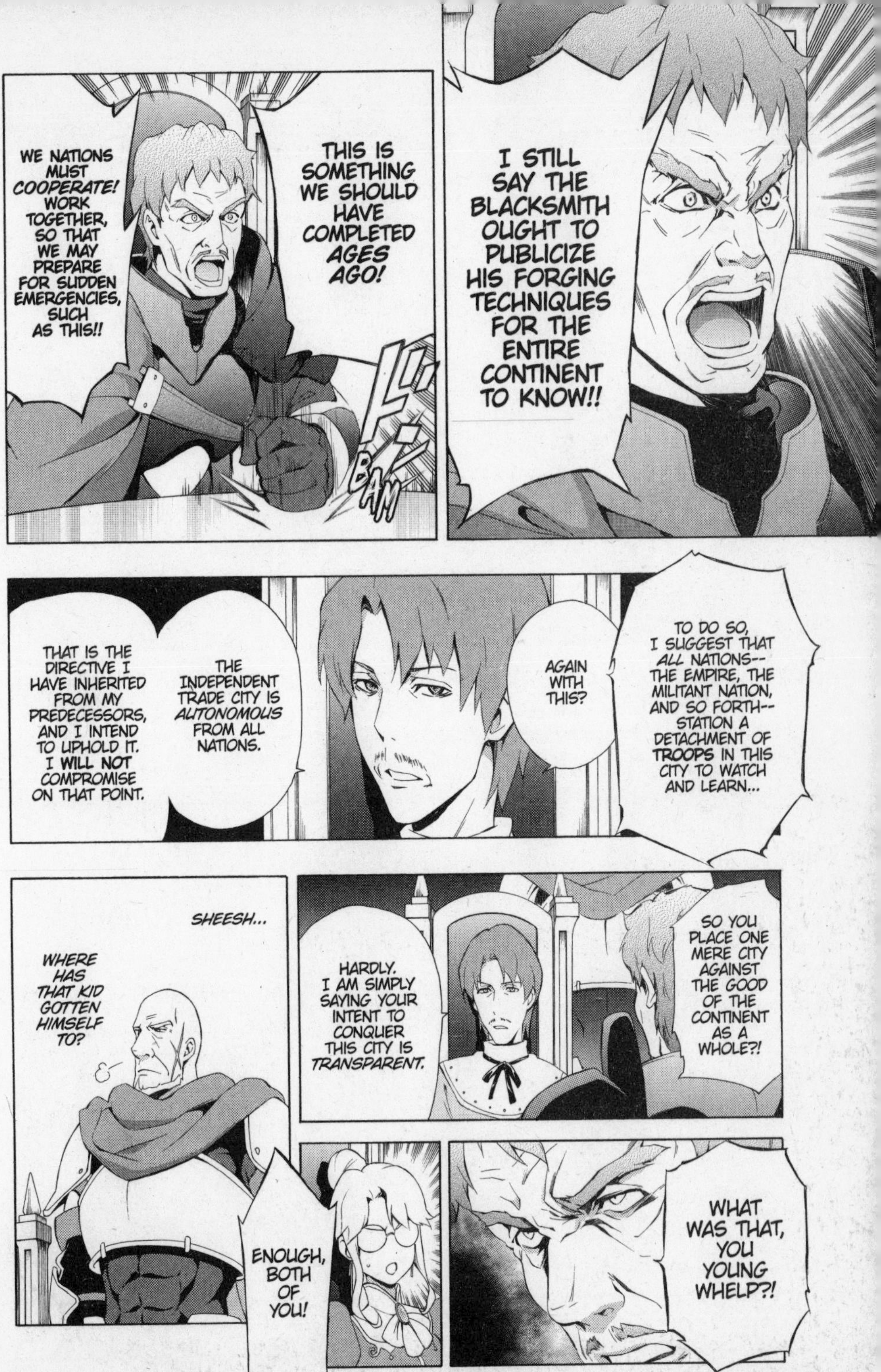
I STILL SAY THE BLACKSMITH OUGHT TO PUBLICIZE HIS FORGING TECHNIQUES FOR THE ENTIRE CONTINENT TO KNOW!!
THIS IS SOMETHING WE SHOULD HAVE COMPLETED AGES AGO!
WE NATIONS MUST COOPERATE! WORK TOGETHER, SO THAT WE MAY PREPARE FOR SUDDEN EMERGENCIES, SUCH AS THIS!!
BAM
TO DO SO, I SUGGEST THAT ALL NATIONS-- THE EMPIRE, THE MILITANT NATION, AND SO FORTH-- STATION A DETACHMENT OF TROOPS IN THIS CITY TO WATCH AND LEARN...
AGAIN WITH THIS?
THE INDEPENDENT TRADE CITY IS AUTONOMOUS FROM ALL NATIONS.
THAT IS THE DIRECTIVE I HAVE INHERITED FROM MY PREDECESSORS, AND I INTEND TO UPHOLD IT. I WILL NOT COMPROMISE ON THAT POINT.
SO YOU PLACE ONE MERE CITY AGAINST THE GOOD OF THE CONTINENT AS A WHOLE?!
HARDLY. I AM SIMPLY SAYING YOUR INTENT TO CONQUER THIS CITY IS TRANSPARENT.
WHAT WAS THAT, YOU YOUNG WHELP?!
ENOUGH, BOTH OF YOU!
SHEESH...
WHERE HAS THAT KID GOTTEN HIMSELF TO?

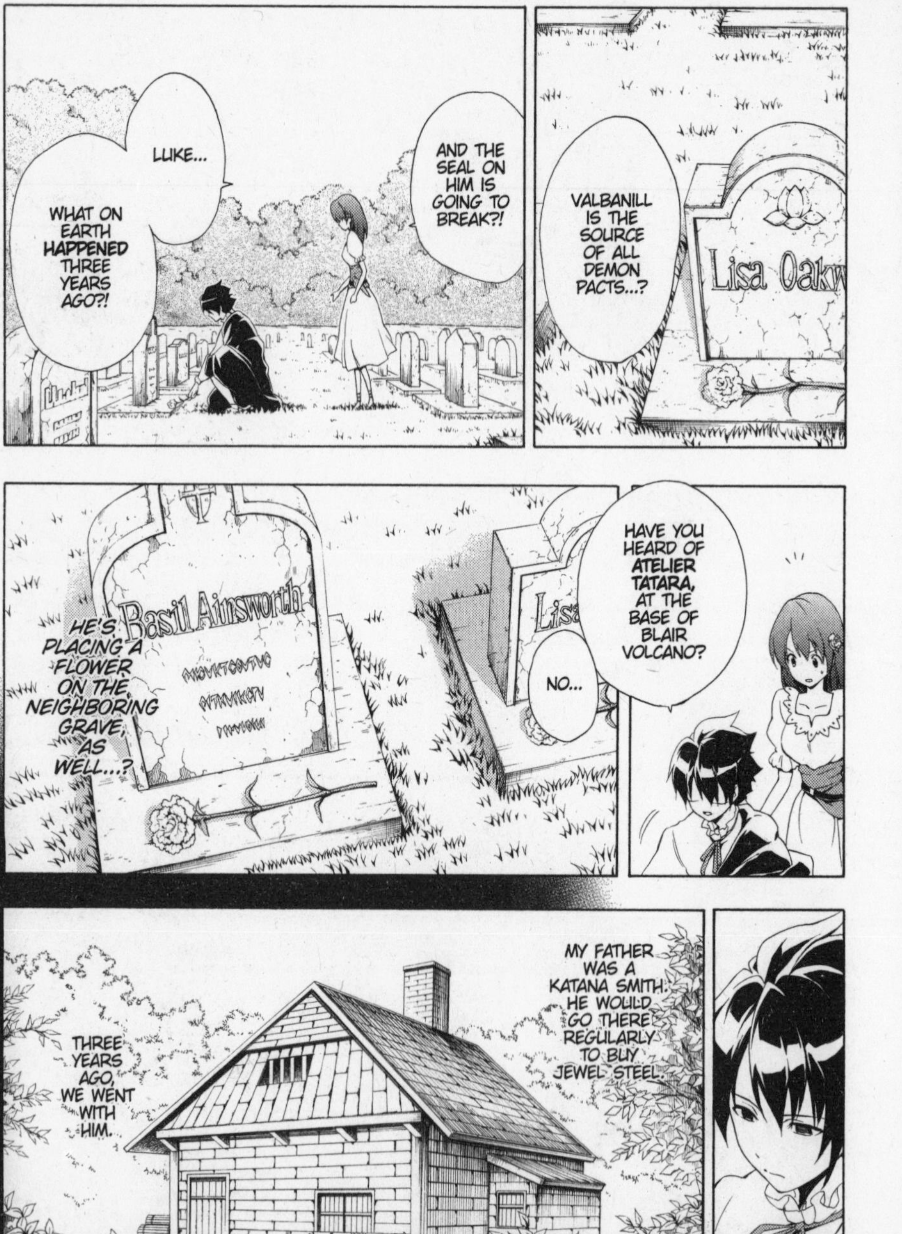
VALBANILL IS THE SOURCE OF ALL DEMON PACTS...?
Lisa Oakw
AND THE SEAL ON HIM IS GOING TO BREAK?!
LUKE...
WHAT ON EARTH HAPPENED THREE YEARS AGO?!
HAVE YOU HEARD OF ATELIER TATARA, AT THE BASE OF BLAIR VOLCANO?
NO...
Lisa
Basil Ainsworth
HE'S PLACING A FLOWER ON THE NEIGHBORING GRAVE, AS WELL...?
MY FATHER WAS A KATANA SMITH. HE WOULD GO THERE REGULARLY TO BUY JEWEL STEEL.
THREE YEARS AGO, WE WENT WITH HIM.

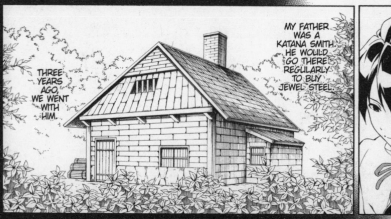

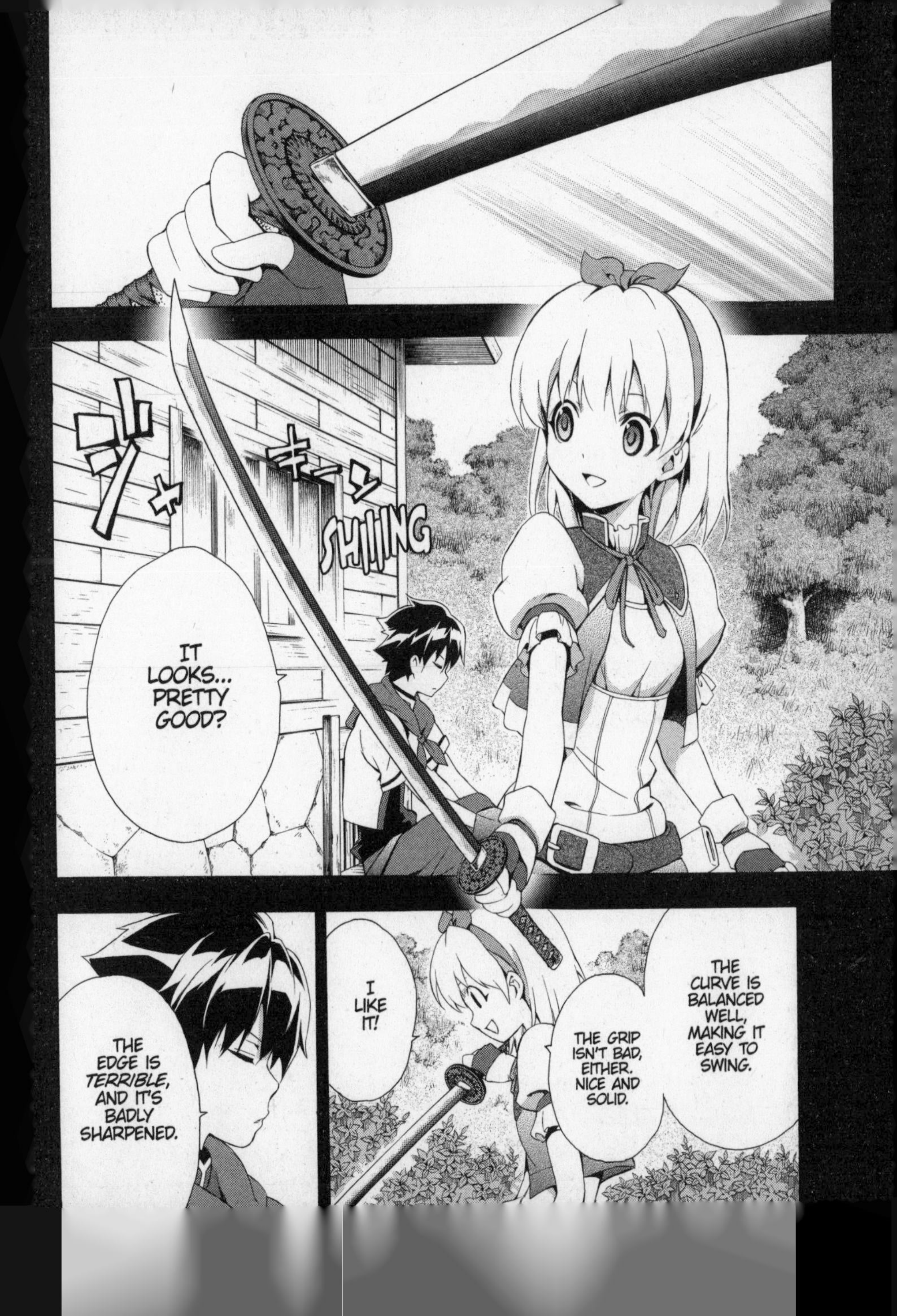
SHIIIING
IT LOOKS... PRETTY GOOD?
THE CURVE IS BALANCED WELL, MAKING IT EASY TO SWING.
THE GRIP ISN'T BAD, EITHER. NICE AND SOLID.
I LIKE IT!
THE EDGE IS *TERRIBLE*, AND IT'S BADLY SHARPENED.

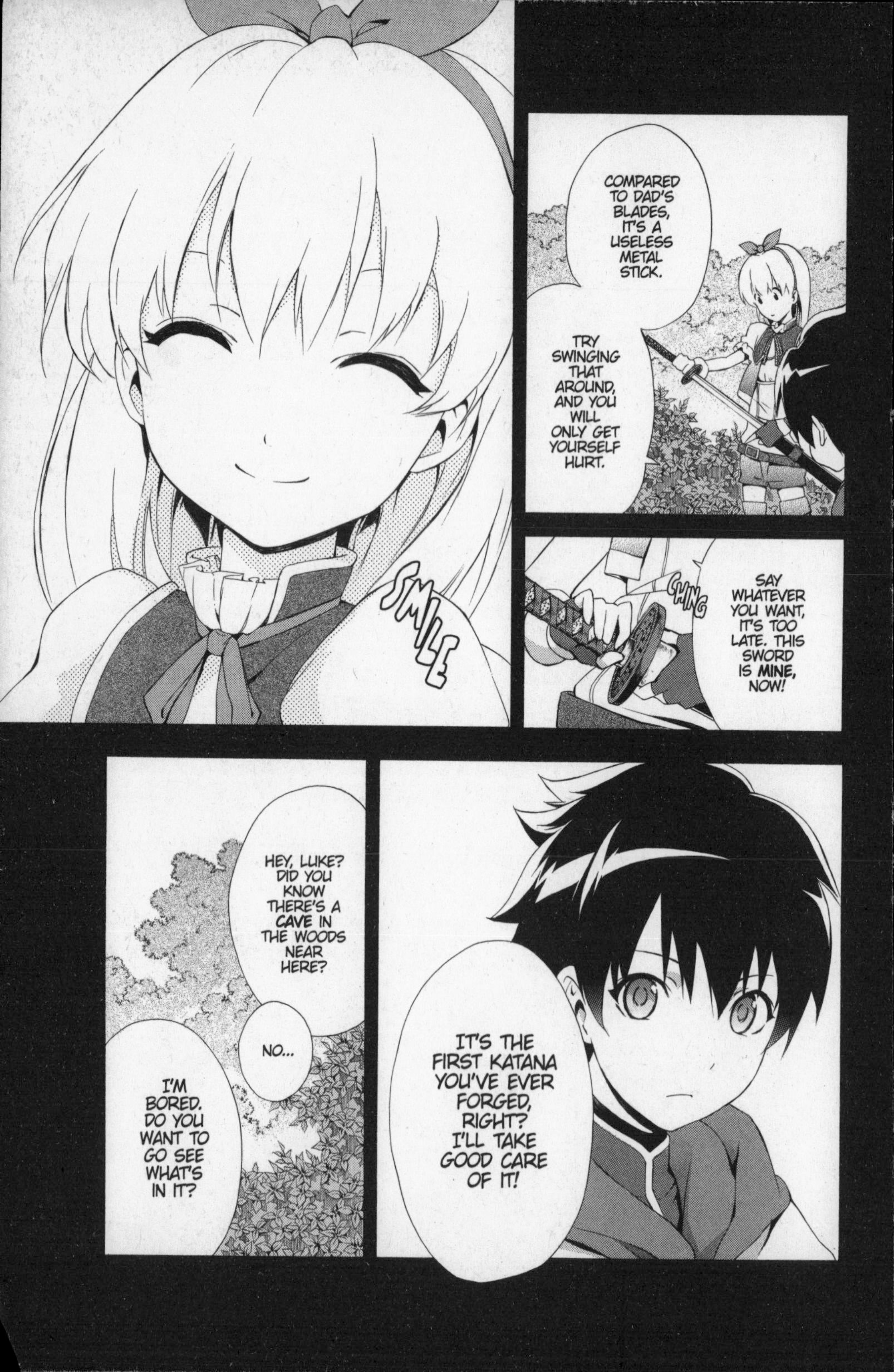
COMPARED TO DAD'S BLADES, IT'S A USELESS METAL STICK.
TRY SWINGING THAT AROUND, AND YOU WILL ONLY GET YOURSELF HURT.
SAY WHATEVER YOU WANT, IT'S TOO LATE. THIS SWORD IS **MINE**, NOW!
CHING
SMILE
IT'S THE FIRST KATANA YOU'VE EVER FORGED, RIGHT? I'LL TAKE GOOD CARE OF IT!
HEY, LUKE? DID YOU KNOW THERE'S A **CAVE** IN THE WOODS NEAR HERE?
NO...
I'M BORED. DO YOU WANT TO GO SEE WHAT'S IN IT?

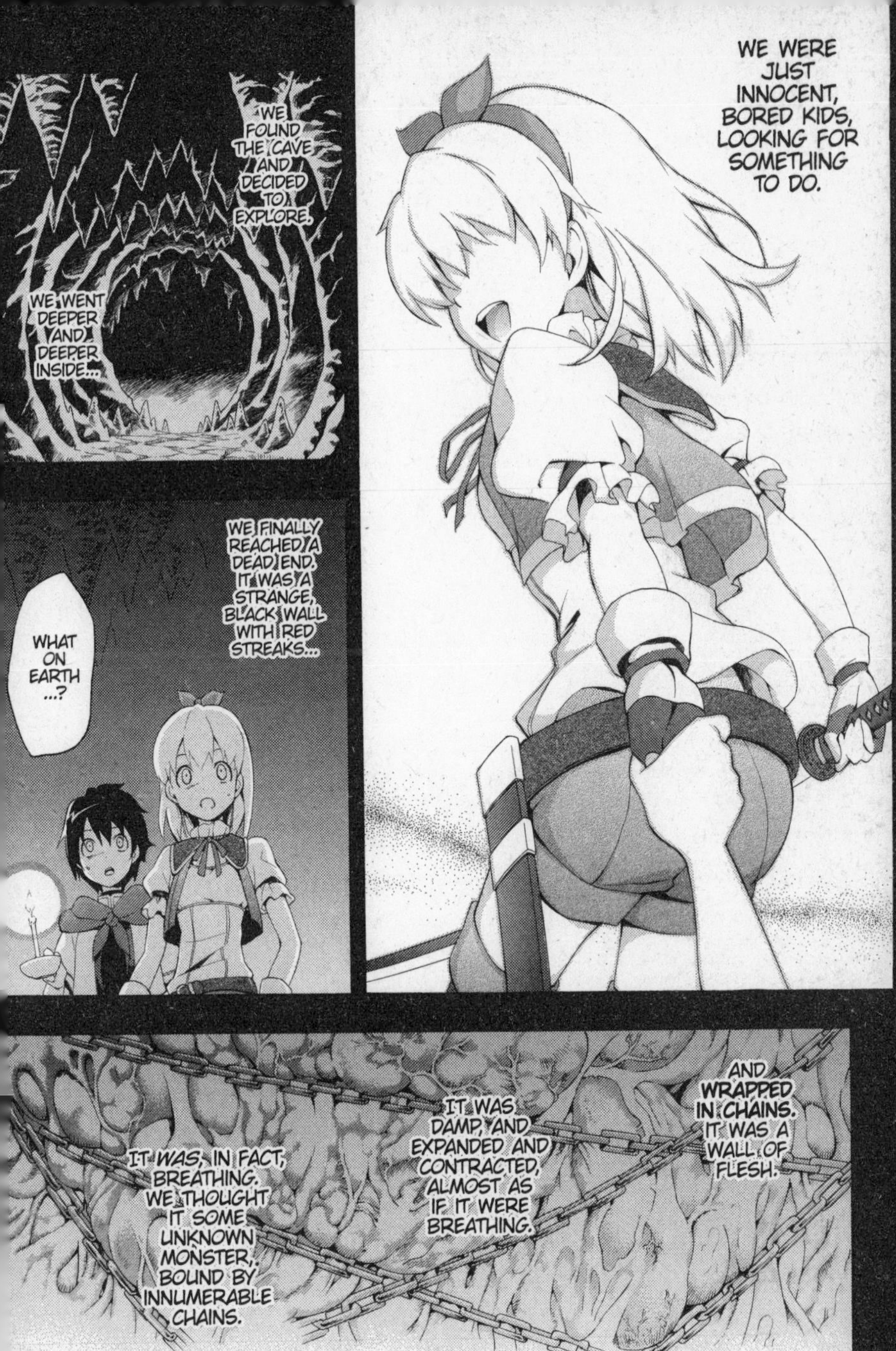
WE WERE JUST INNOCENT, BORED KIDS, LOOKING FOR SOMETHING TO DO.
WE FOUND THE CAVE AND DECIDED TO EXPLORE.
WE WENT DEEPER AND DEEPER INSIDE...
WE FINALLY REACHED A DEAD END. IT WAS A STRANGE, BLACK WALL WITH RED STREAKS...
WHAT ON EARTH ...?
AND WRAPPED IN CHAINS. IT WAS A WALL OF FLESH.
IT WAS DAMP, AND EXPANDED AND CONTRACTED, ALMOST AS IF IT WERE BREATHING.
IT WAS, IN FACT, BREATHING. WE THOUGHT IT SOME UNKNOWN MONSTER, BOUND BY INNUMERABLE CHAINS.

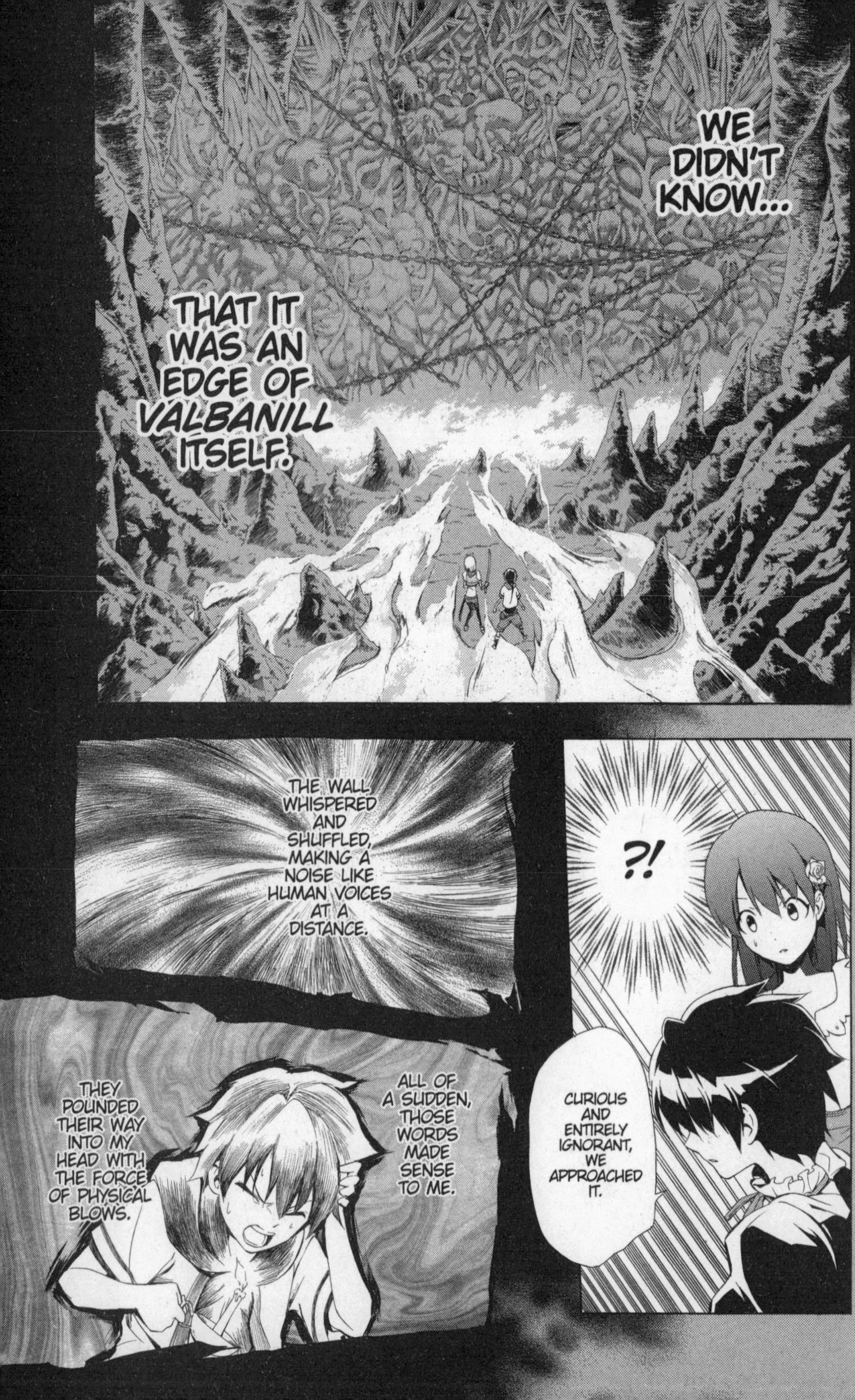
WE DIDN'T KNOW...
THAT IT WAS AN EDGE OF VALBANILL ITSELF.
?!
CURIOUS AND ENTIRELY IGNORANT, WE APPROACHED IT.
THE WALL WHISPERED AND SHUFFLED, MAKING A NOISE LIKE HUMAN VOICES AT A DISTANCE.
ALL OF A SUDDEN, THOSE WORDS MADE SENSE TO ME.
THEY POUNDED THEIR WAY INTO MY HEAD WITH THE FORCE OF PHYSICAL BLOWS.

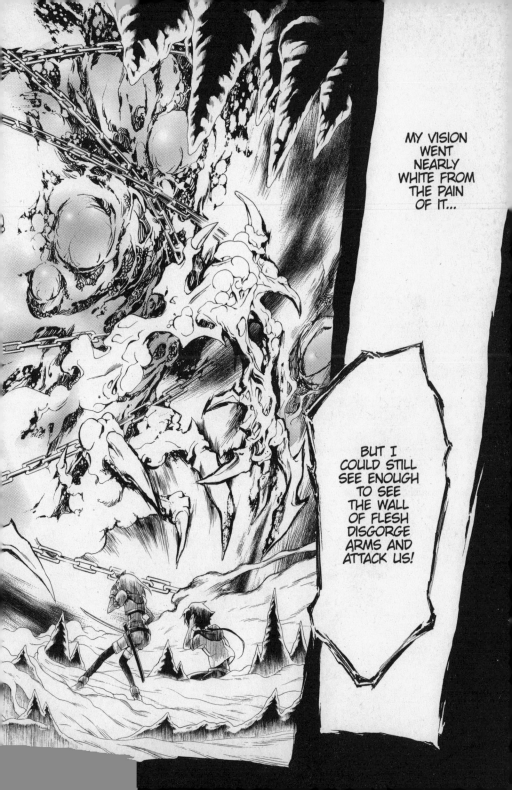

MY VISION WENT NEARLY WHITE FROM THE PAIN OF IT...

BUT I COULD STILL SEE ENOUGH TO SEE THE WALL OF FLESH DISGORGE ARMS AND ATTACK US!

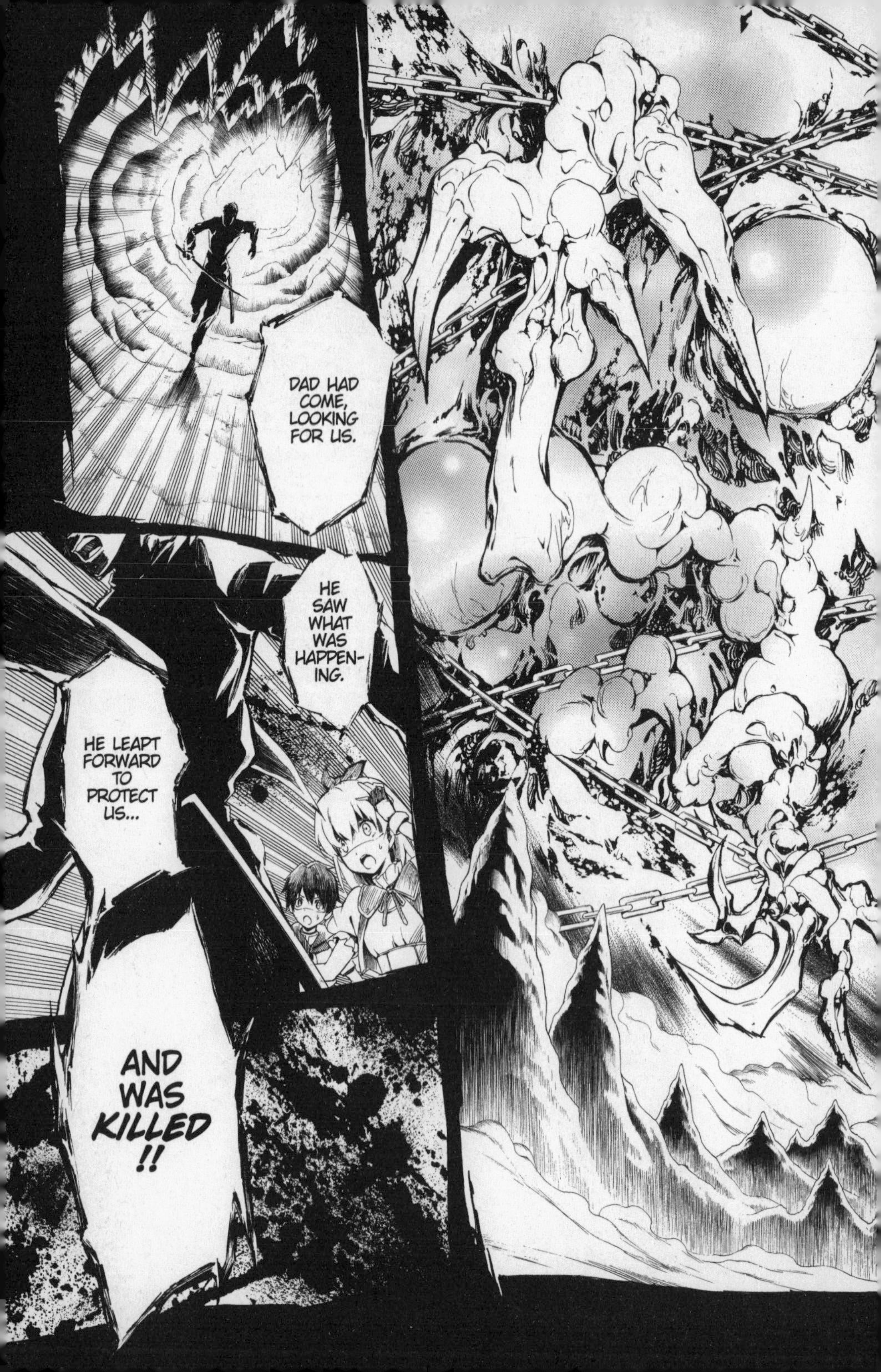
DAD HAD COME, LOOKING FOR US.
HE SAW WHAT WAS HAPPEN-ING.
HE LEAPT FORWARD TO PROTECT US...
AND WAS KILLED!!

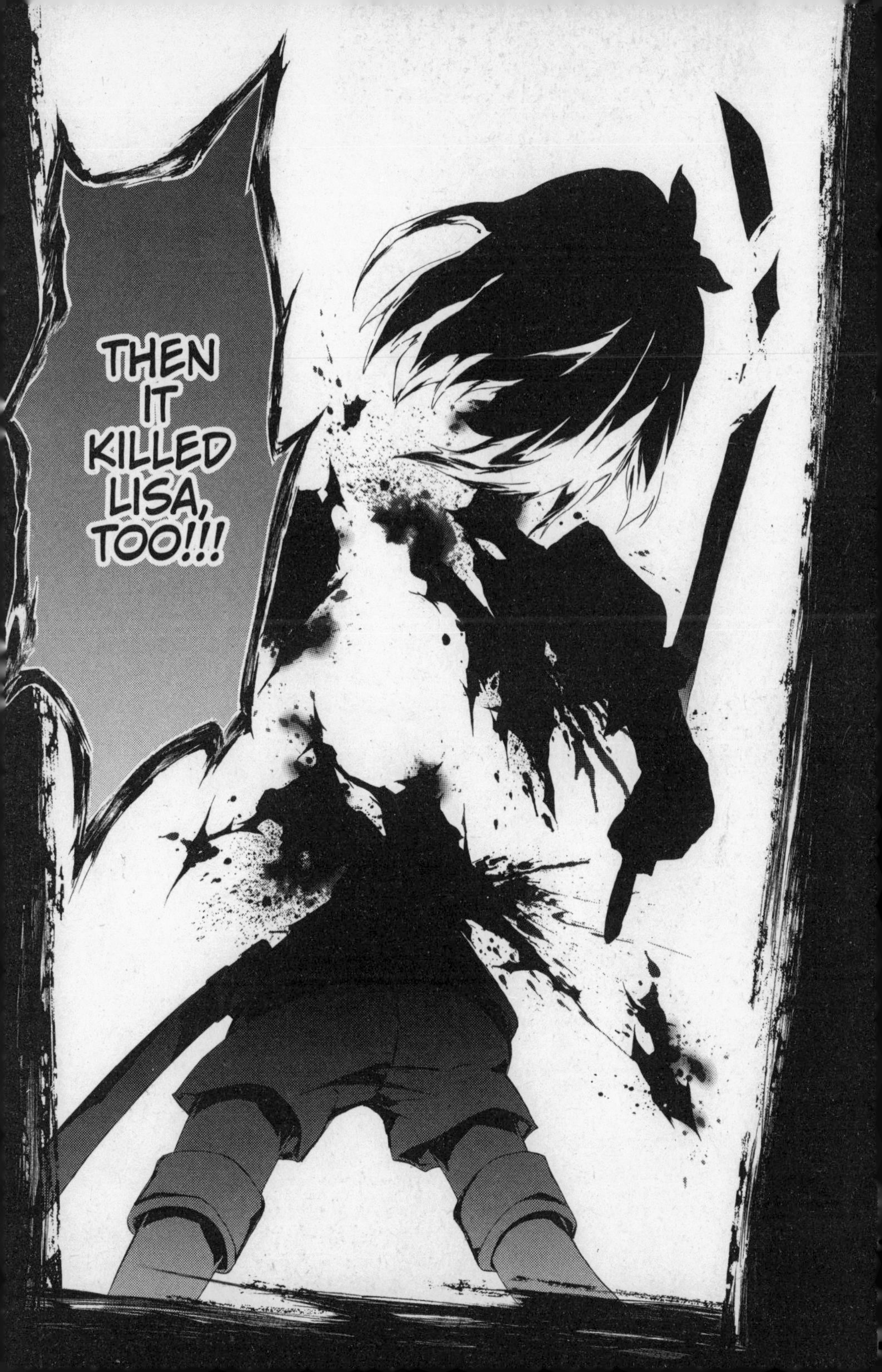
THEN IT KILLED LISA, TOO!!!

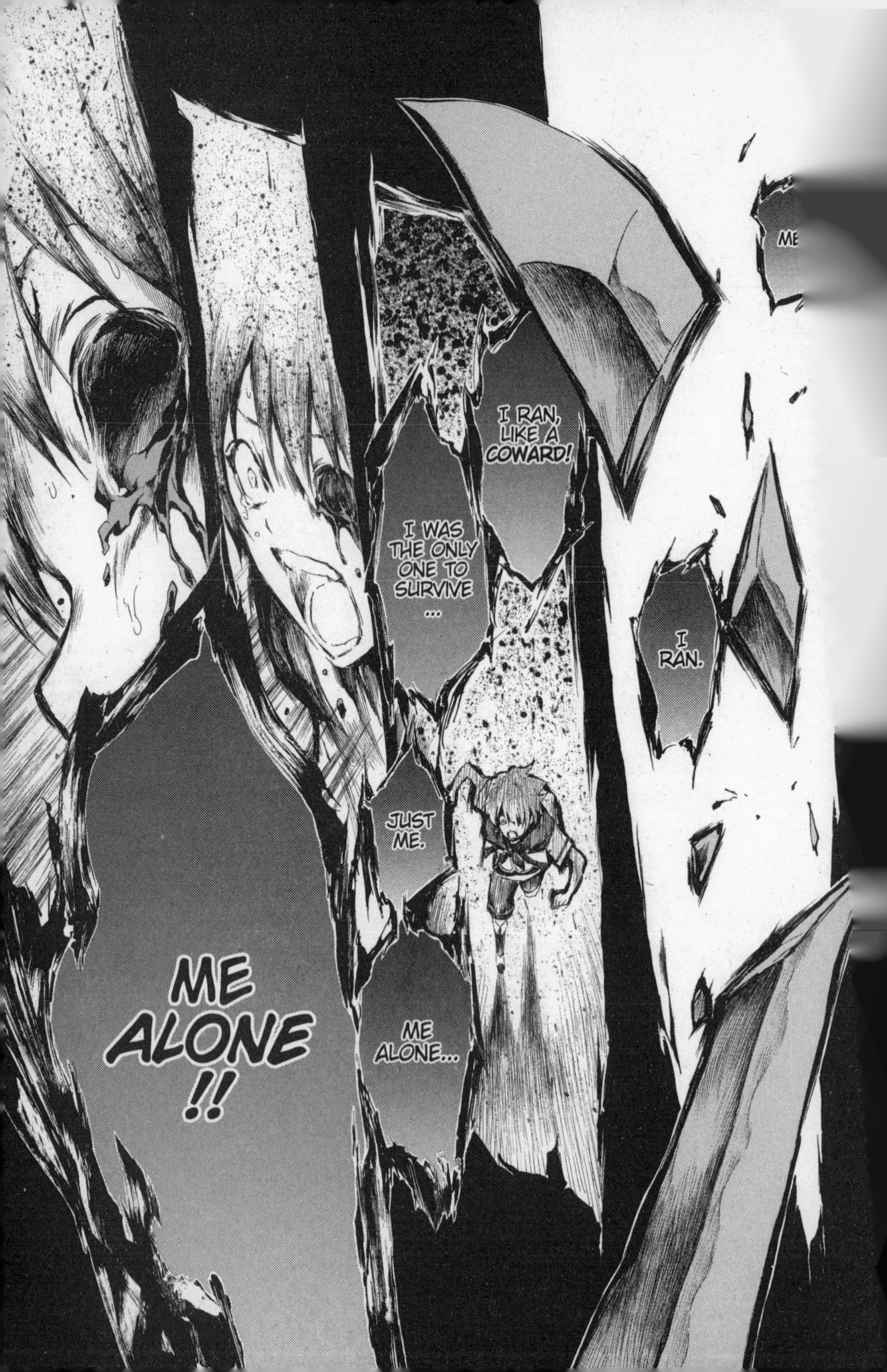
ME
I RAN.
I RAN, LIKE A COWARD!
I WAS THE ONLY ONE TO SURVIVE ...
JUST ME.
ME ALONE...
ME ALONE !!

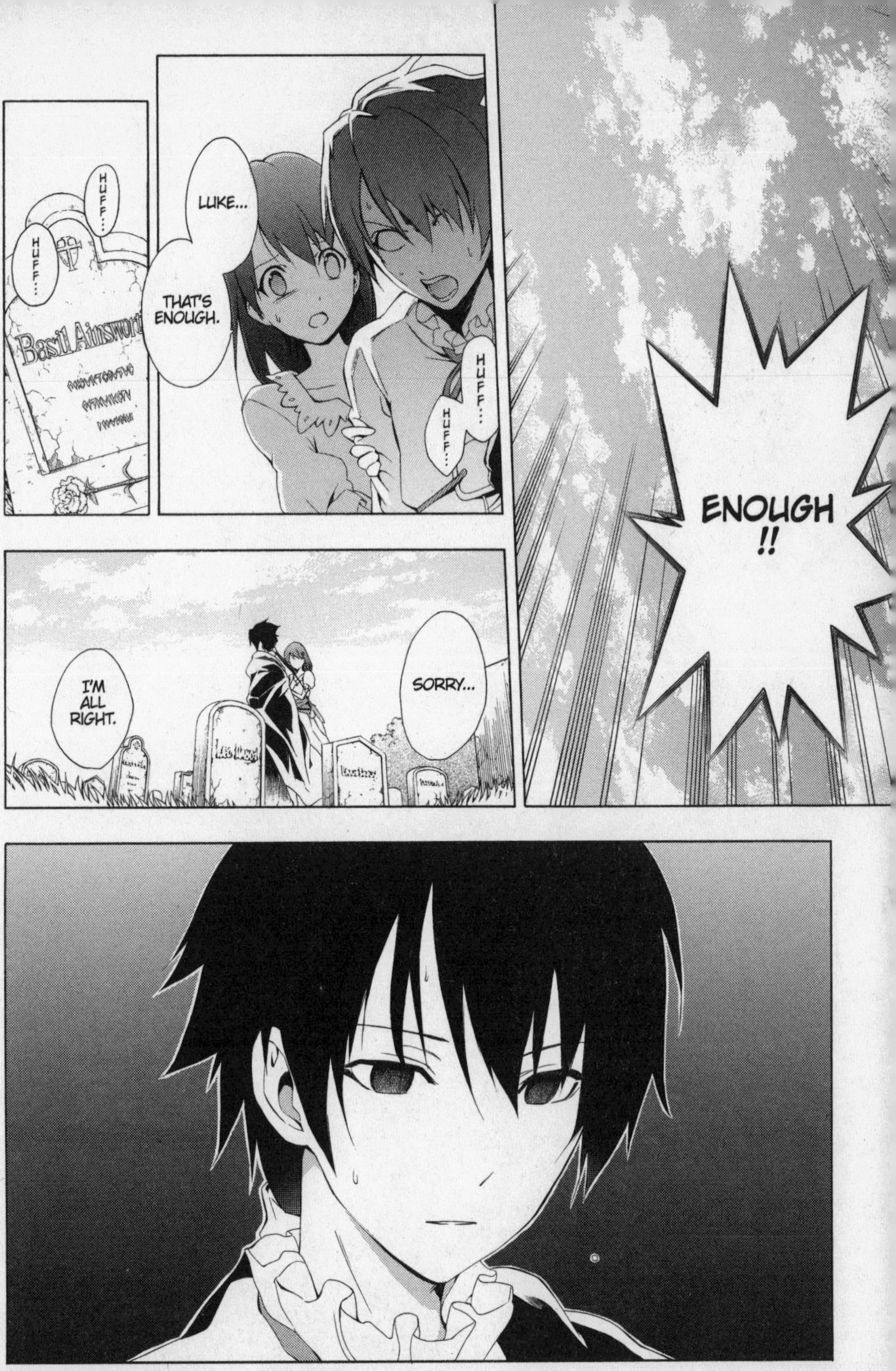
ENOUGH!!
LUKE...
THAT'S ENOUGH.
HUFF... HUFF...
HUFF... HUFF...
Basil Ainswort
SORRY...
I'M ALL RIGHT.

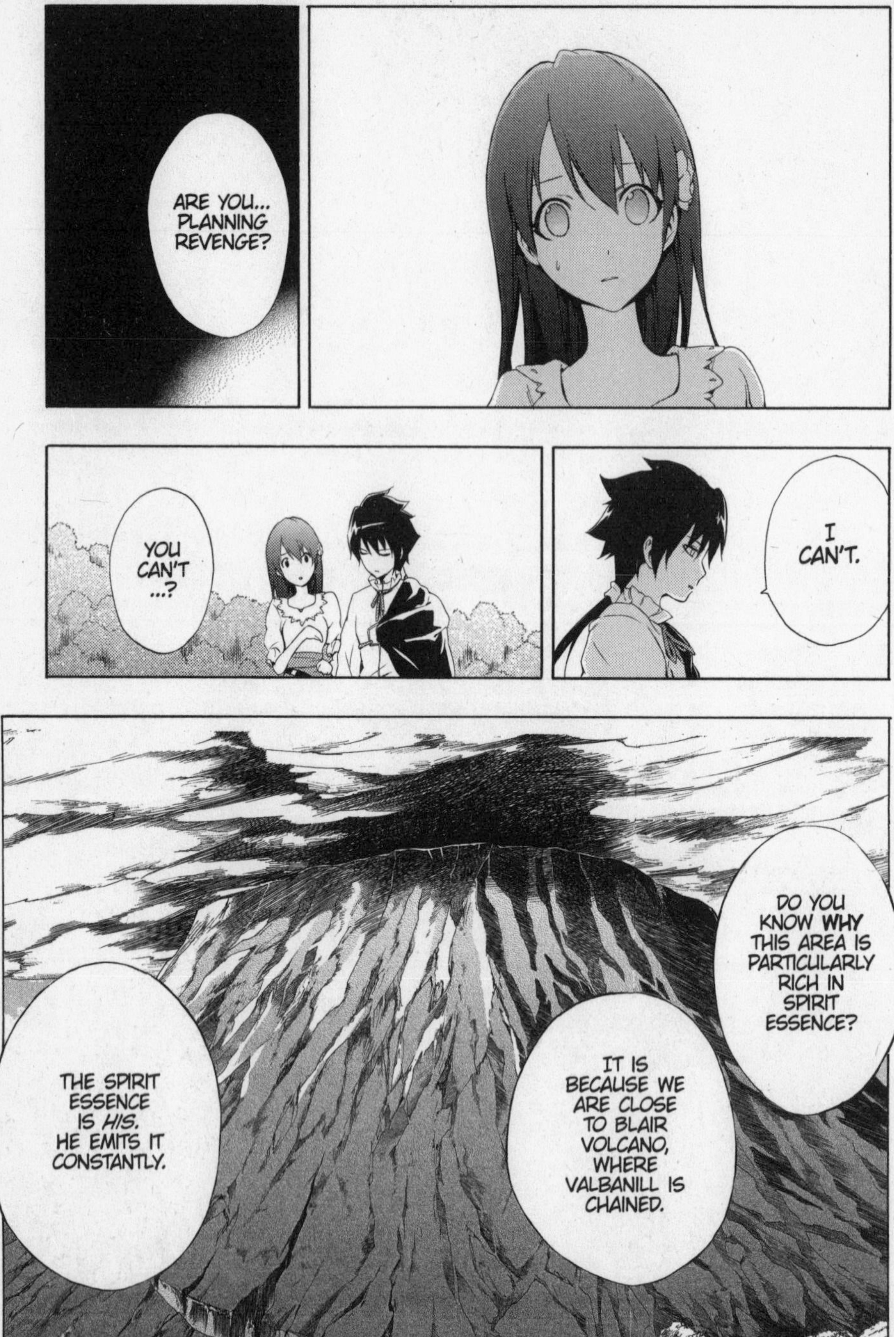
ARE YOU... PLANNING REVENGE?
I CAN'T.
YOU CAN'T ...?
DO YOU KNOW WHY THIS AREA IS PARTICULARLY RICH IN SPIRIT ESSENCE?
IT IS BECAUSE WE ARE CLOSE TO BLAIR VOLCANO, WHERE VALBANILL IS CHAINED.
THE SPIRIT ESSENCE IS *HIS*. HE EMITS IT CONSTANTLY.

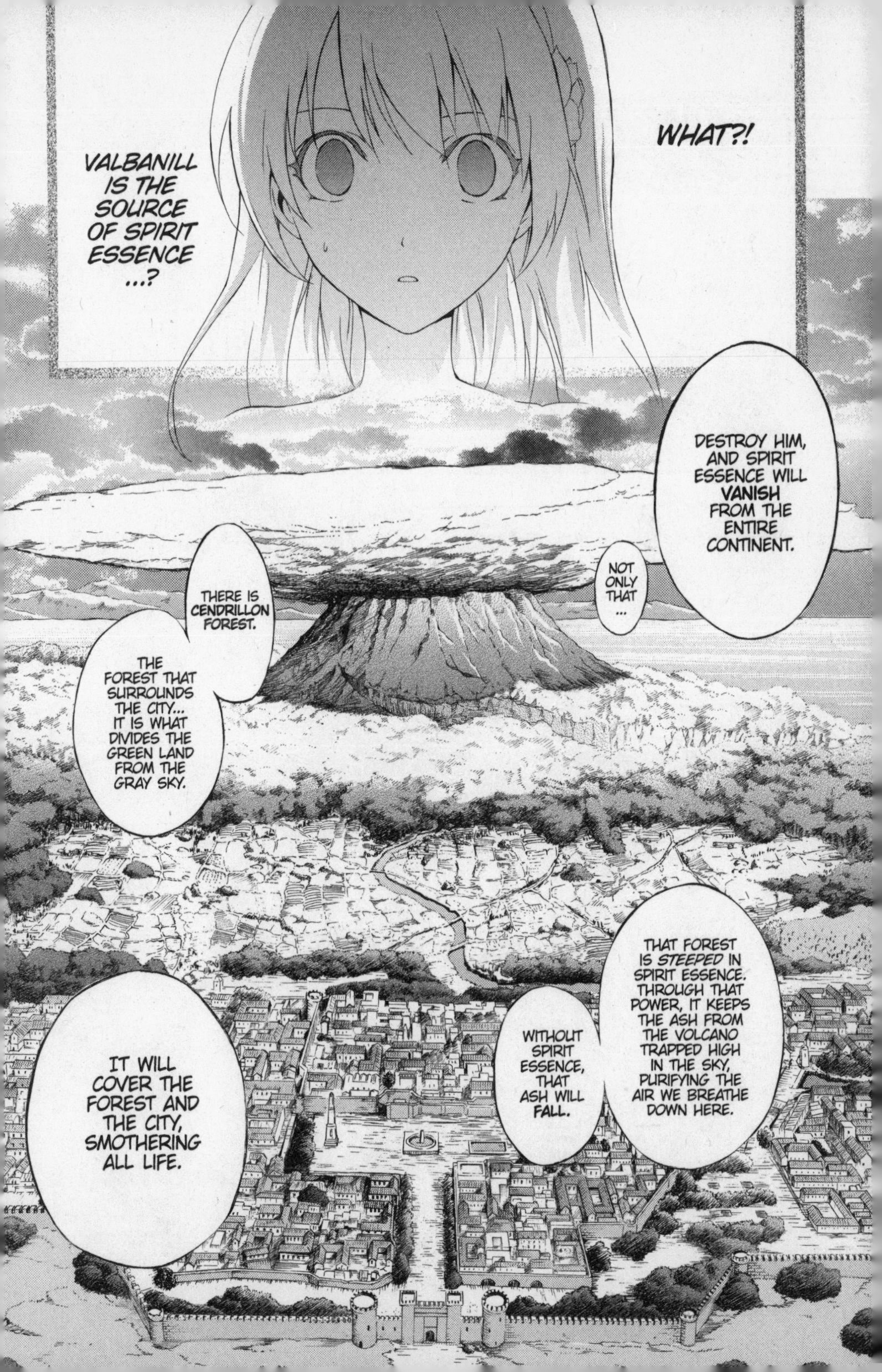
WHAT?!
VALBANILL IS THE SOURCE OF SPIRIT ESSENCE ...?
DESTROY HIM, AND SPIRIT ESSENCE WILL **VANISH** FROM THE ENTIRE CONTINENT.
NOT ONLY THAT ...
THERE IS CENDRILLON FOREST.
THE FOREST THAT SURROUNDS THE CITY... IT IS WHAT DIVIDES THE GREEN LAND FROM THE GRAY SKY.
THAT FOREST IS *STEEPED* IN SPIRIT ESSENCE. THROUGH THAT POWER, IT KEEPS THE ASH FROM THE VOLCANO TRAPPED HIGH IN THE SKY, PURIFYING THE AIR WE BREATHE DOWN HERE.
WITHOUT SPIRIT ESSENCE, THAT ASH WILL **FALL.**
IT WILL COVER THE FOREST AND THE CITY, SMOTHERING ALL LIFE.

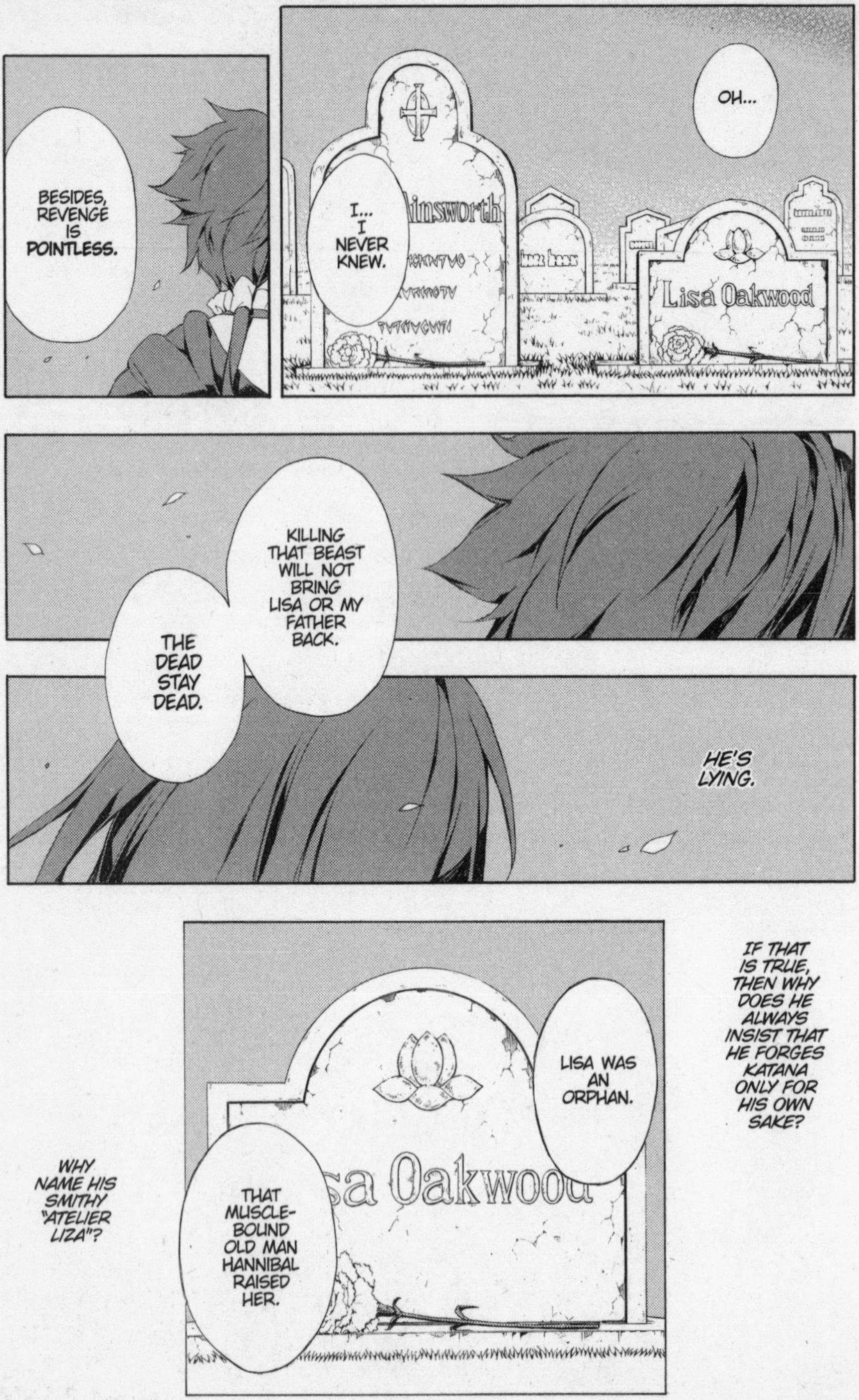
OH...
I... I NEVER KNEW.
Lisa Oakwood
BESIDES, REVENGE IS POINTLESS.
KILLING THAT BEAST WILL NOT BRING LISA OR MY FATHER BACK.
THE DEAD STAY DEAD.
HE'S LYING.
IF THAT IS TRUE, THEN WHY DOES HE ALWAYS INSIST THAT HE FORGES KATANA ONLY FOR HIS OWN SAKE?
LISA WAS AN ORPHAN.
sa Oakwood
THAT MUSCLE-BOUND OLD MAN HANNIBAL RAISED HER.
WHY NAME HIS SMITHY "ATELIER LIZA"?

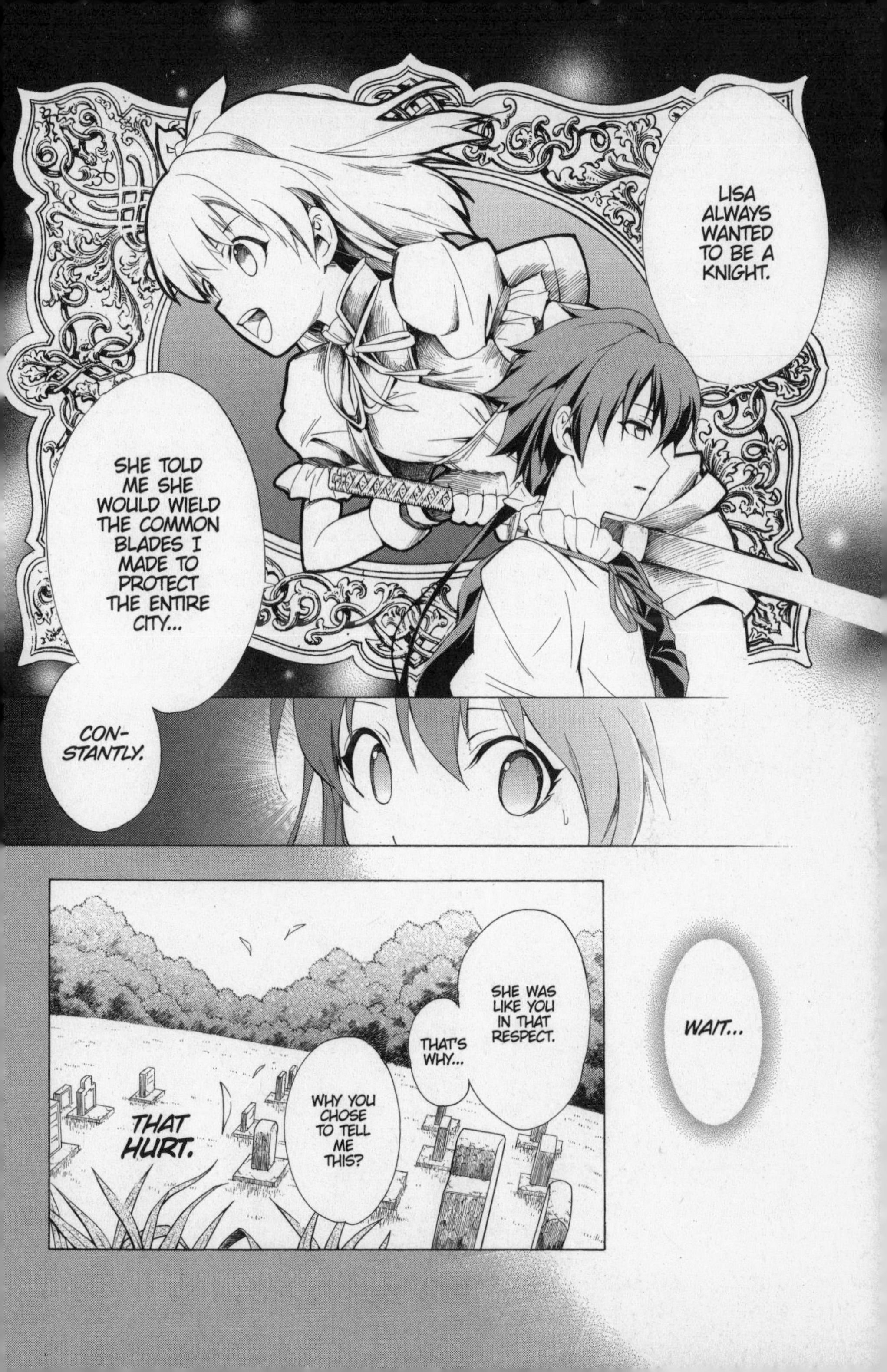
LISA ALWAYS WANTED TO BE A KNIGHT.
SHE TOLD ME SHE WOULD WIELD THE COMMON BLADES I MADE TO PROTECT THE ENTIRE CITY...
CON-STANTLY.
WAIT...
SHE WAS LIKE YOU IN THAT RESPECT.
THAT'S WHY...
WHY YOU CHOSE TO TELL ME THIS?
THAT HURT.

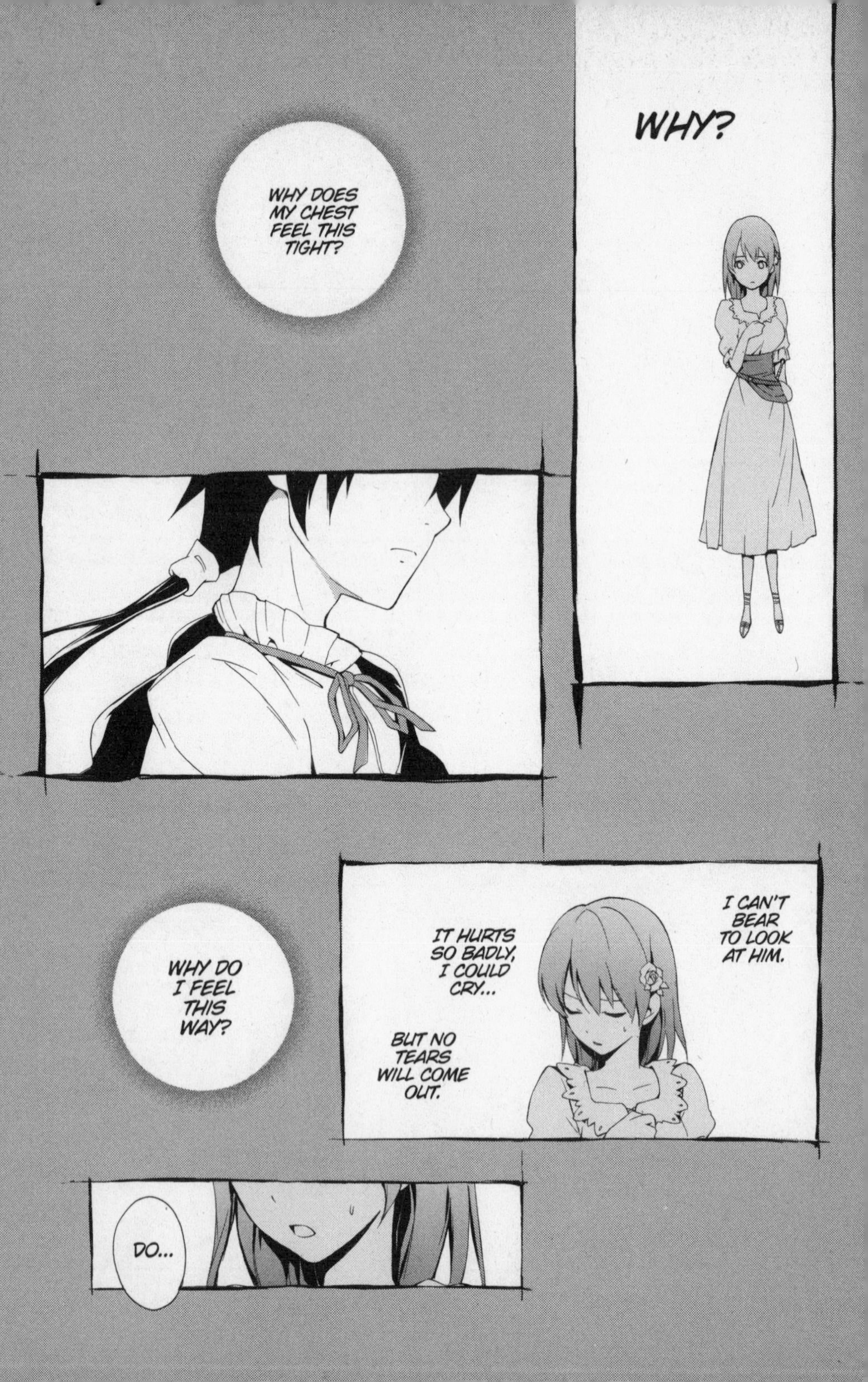
WHY?
WHY DOES MY CHEST FEEL THIS TIGHT?
I CAN'T BEAR TO LOOK AT HIM.
IT HURTS SO BADLY, I COULD CRY...
BUT NO TEARS WILL COME OUT.
WHY DO I FEEL THIS WAY?
DO...

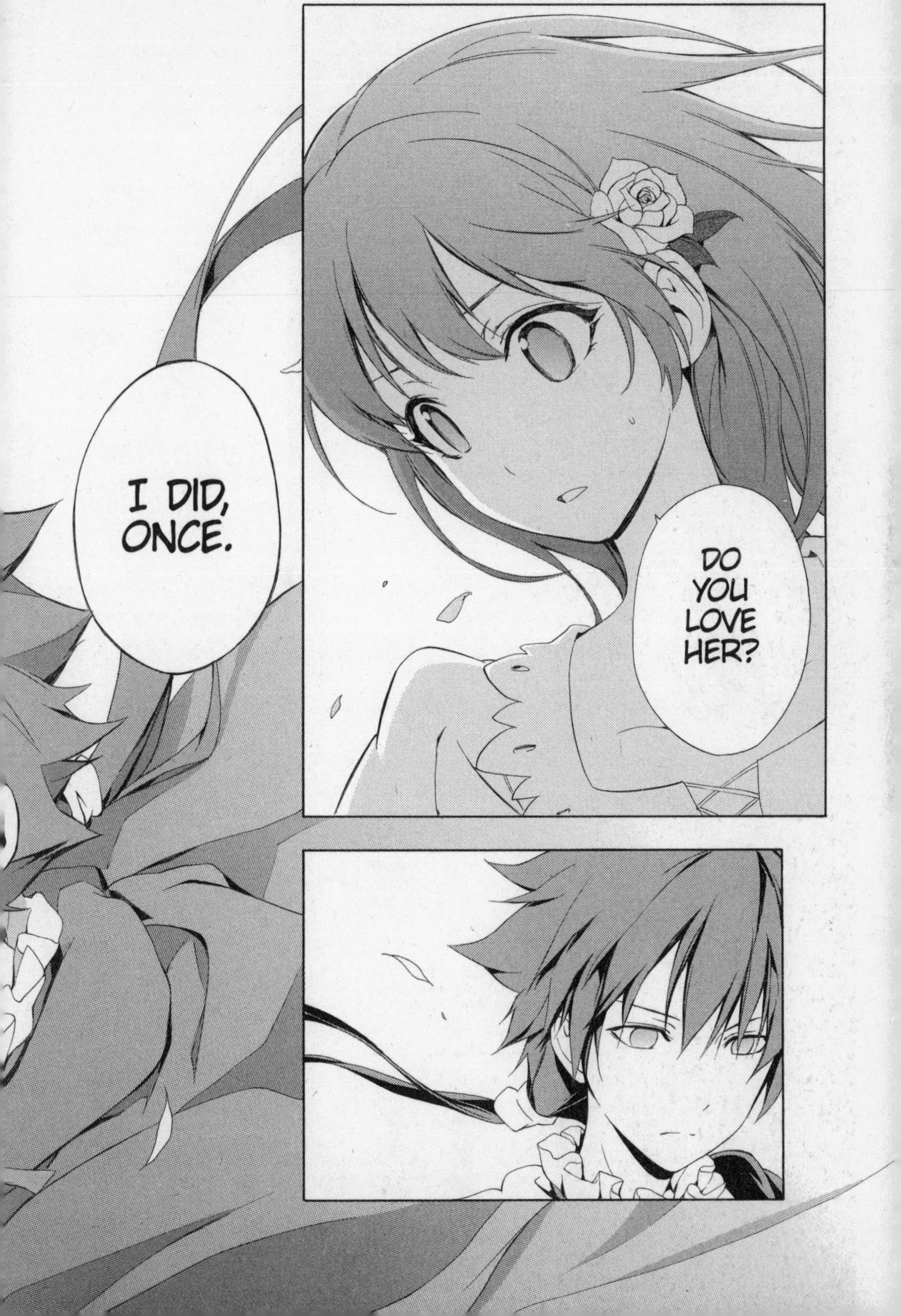
DO YOU LOVE HER?
I DID, ONCE.

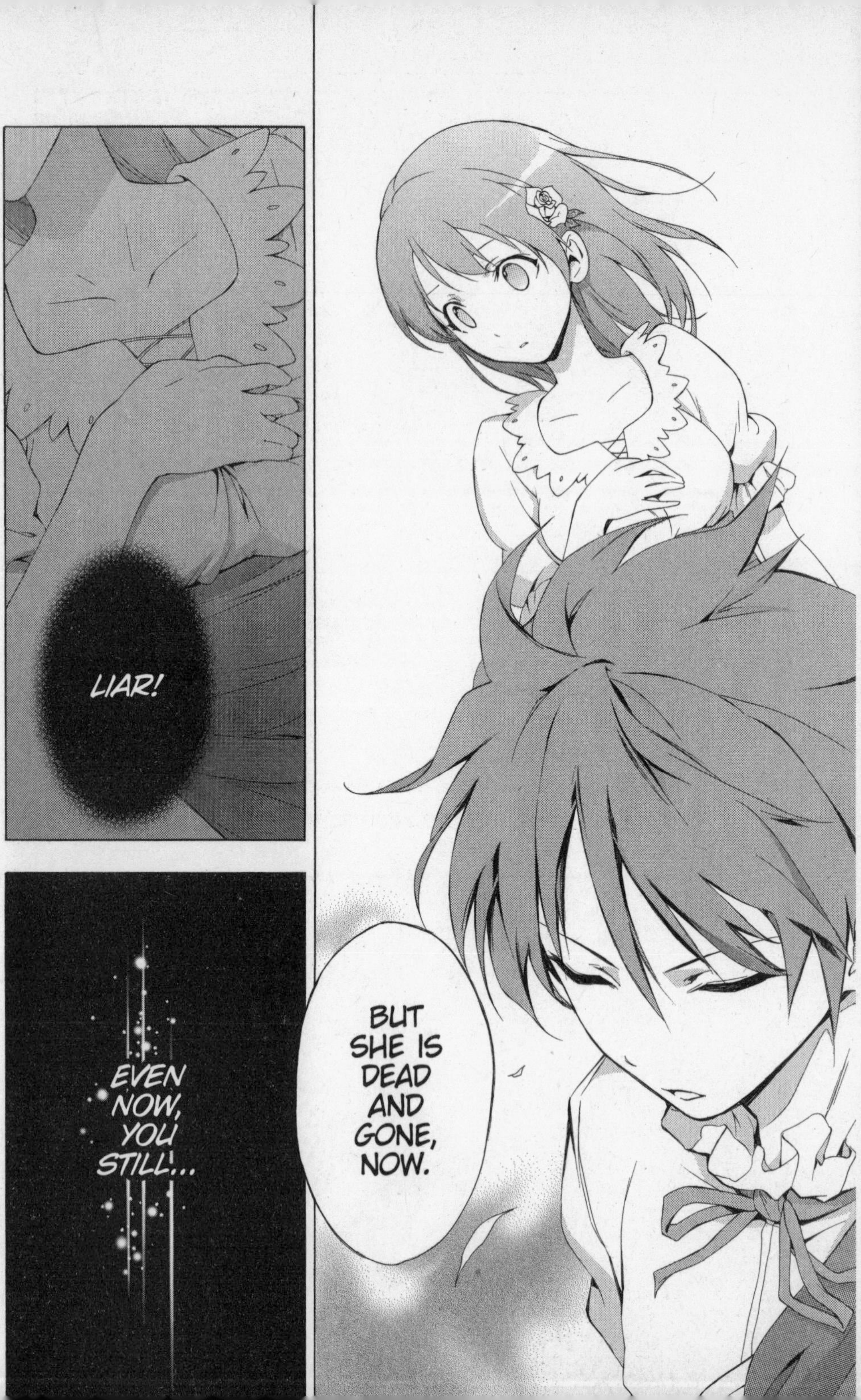
BUT SHE IS DEAD AND GONE, NOW.
LIAR!
EVEN NOW, YOU STILL...

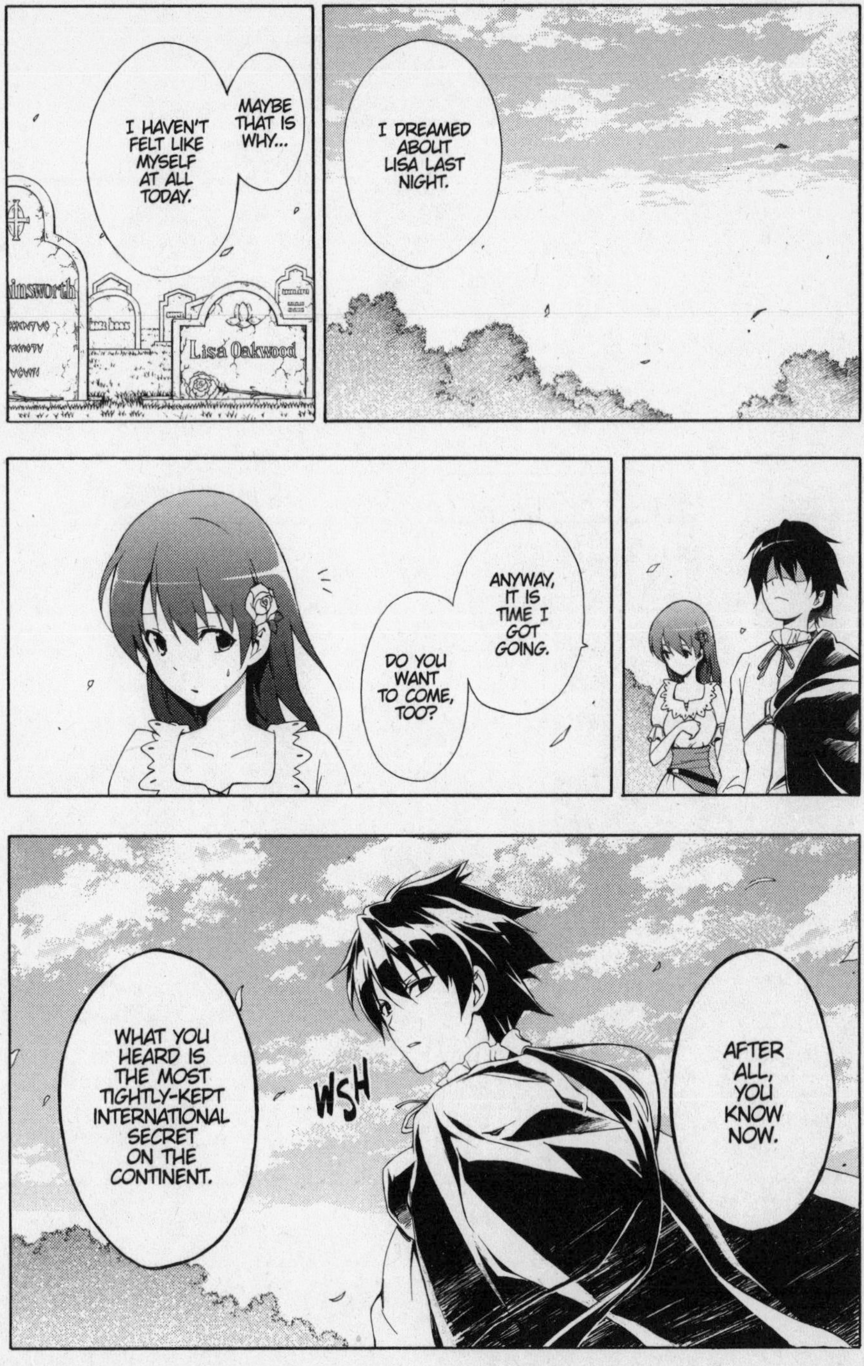
I DREAMED ABOUT LISA LAST NIGHT.
MAYBE THAT IS WHY...
I HAVEN'T FELT LIKE MYSELF AT ALL TODAY.
Lisa Oakwood
ANYWAY, IT IS TIME I GOT GOING.
DO YOU WANT TO COME, TOO?
AFTER ALL, YOU KNOW NOW.
WSH
WHAT YOU HEARD IS THE MOST TIGHTLY-KEPT INTERNATIONAL SECRET ON THE CONTINENT.

✳ Luke Ainsworth ✳

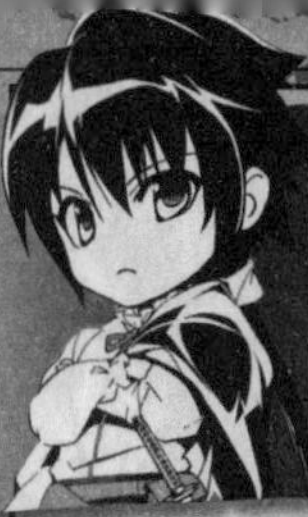

Hunh. These works of art are nearly as good as the blades I forge. Not bad.

アトリエ 工房リーザ

atelier Liza BRANCH OFFICE II

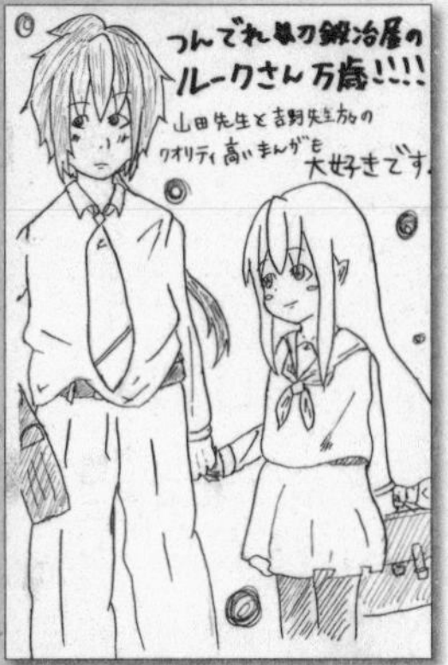
つんでれ系刀鍛冶屋のルークさん万歳!!!!
山田先生と吉野先生方のクオリティ高いまんがも大好きです。

Tokyo, Yosuke

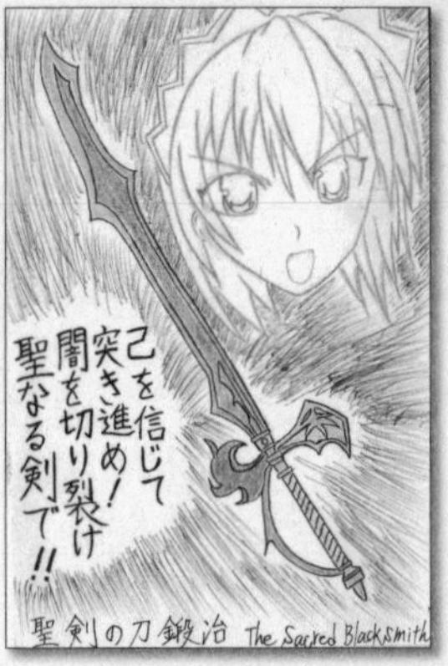
己を信じて突き進め! 闇を切り裂け 聖なる剣で!!
聖剣の刀鍛冶 The Sacred Blacksmith

Saitama, Yuuki Yamazaki

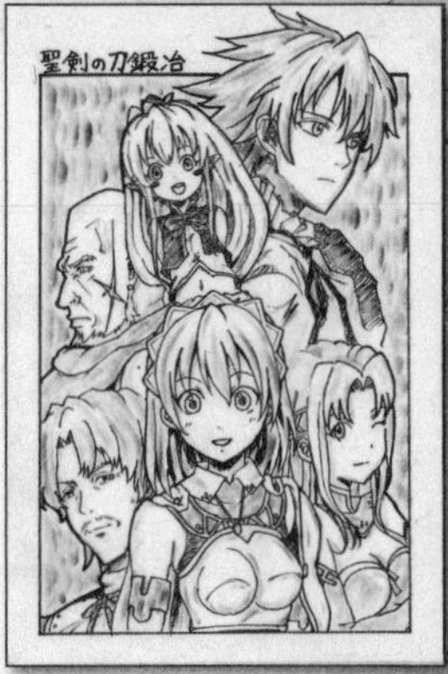
聖剣の刀鍛冶

Kagoshima, Akane Hiragawa

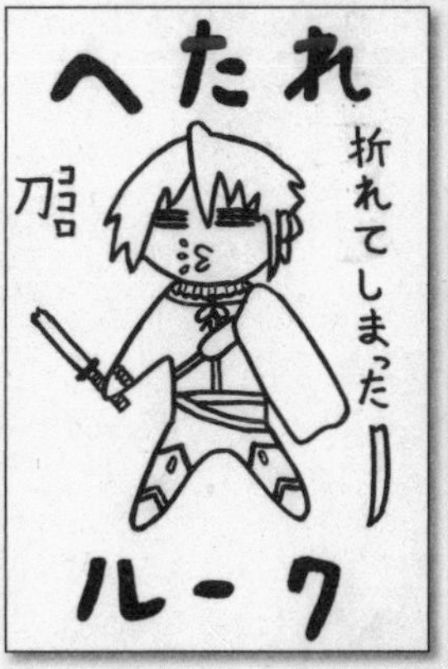
へたれ
刀
ココロ
折れてしまった
ルーク

Aichi, Excalibur

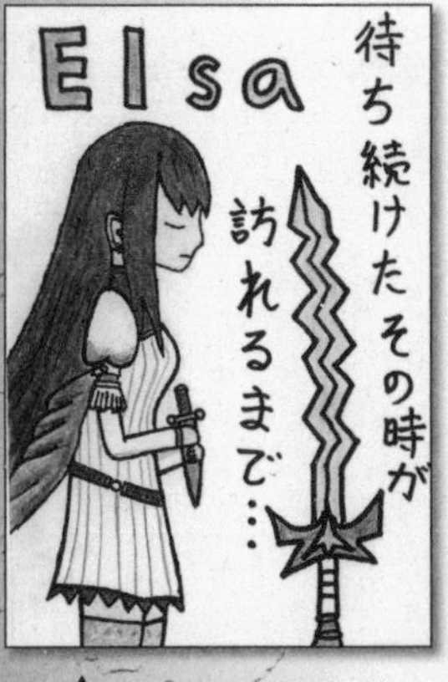
Elsa
待ち続けたその時が訪れるまで…

Aichi, the Demon Blade Smith

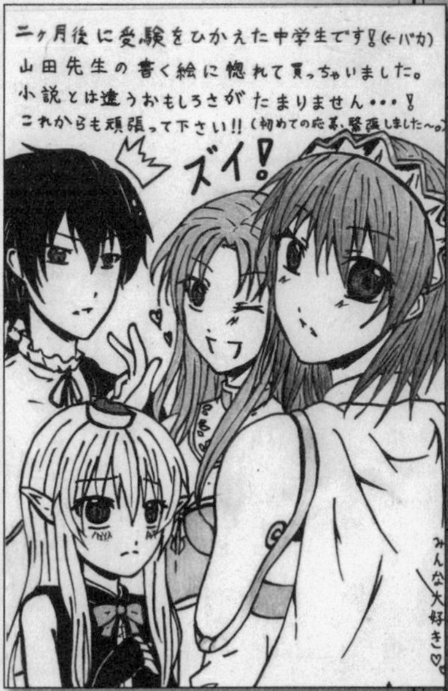
二ヶ月後に受験をひかえた中学生です!(←バカ)
山田先生の書く絵に惚れて買っちゃいました。
小説とは違うおもしろさがたまりません…!
これからも頑張って下さい!!(初めての応募、緊張しました〜。)
ズイ!
みんな大好き♡

Ibaraki, Matsuri Tachibana

Taking exams is like forging a blade. You use all of the knowledge and techniques you have gained to display your greatest level of skill.

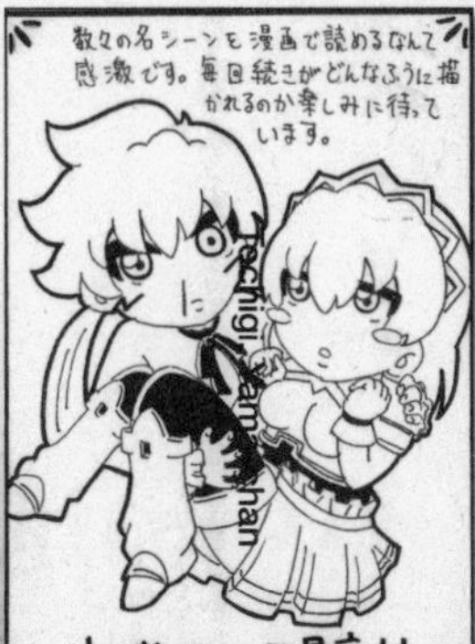
数々の名シーンを漫画で読めるなんて感激です。毎回続きがどんなふうに描かれるのか楽しみに待っています。
ウブなルーク最高!!

Tochigi, Kam[illegible]han

Gifu, Daiki Maruyama

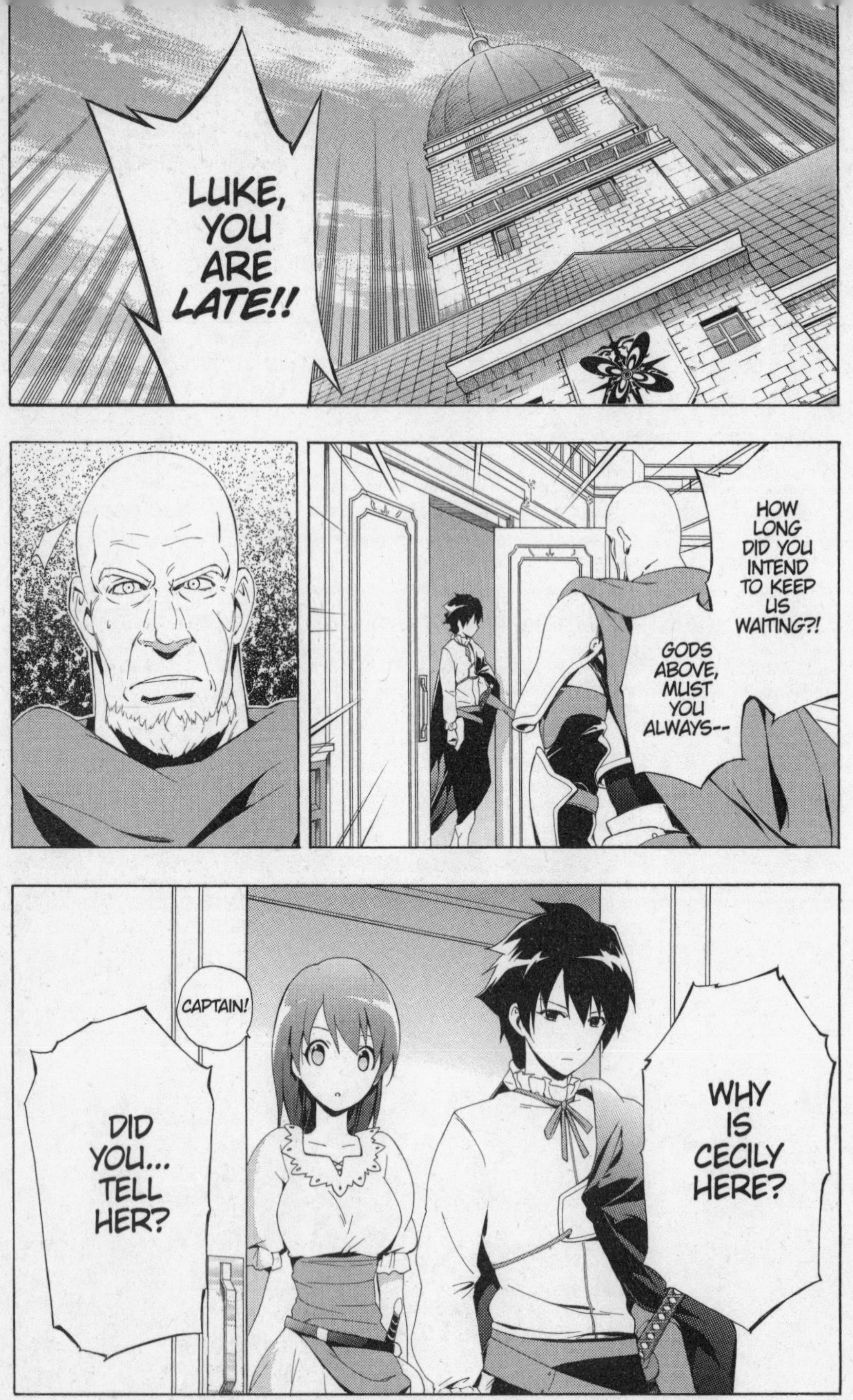
LUKE, YOU ARE LATE!!
HOW LONG DID YOU INTEND TO KEEP US WAITING?!
GODS ABOVE, MUST YOU ALWAYS--
WHY IS CECILY HERE?
CAPTAIN!
DID YOU... TELL HER?

Chapter 15 Blacksmith ------------------ (Part 3)

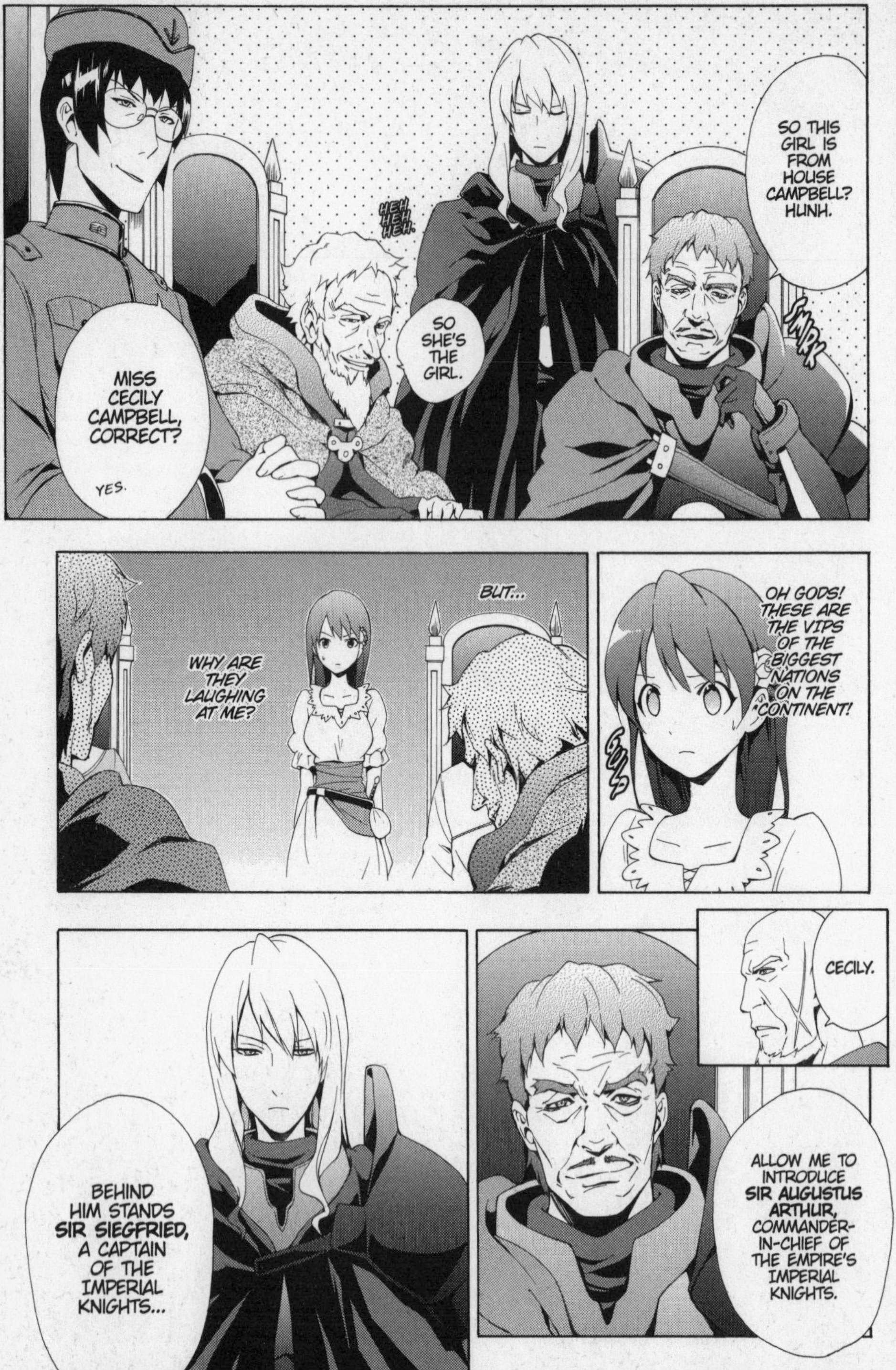
SO THIS GIRL IS FROM HOUSE CAMPBELL? HUNH.
SMIRK
HEH HEH HEH.
SO SHE'S THE GIRL.
MISS CECILY CAMPBELL, CORRECT?
YES.
OH GODS! THESE ARE THE VIPS OF THE BIGGEST NATIONS ON THE CONTINENT!
BUT...
WHY ARE THEY LAUGHING AT ME?
CECILY.
ALLOW ME TO INTRODUCE SIR AUGUSTUS ARTHUR, COMMANDER-IN-CHIEF OF THE EMPIRE'S IMPERIAL KNIGHTS.
BEHIND HIM STANDS SIR SIEGFRIED, A CAPTAIN OF THE IMPERIAL KNIGHTS...

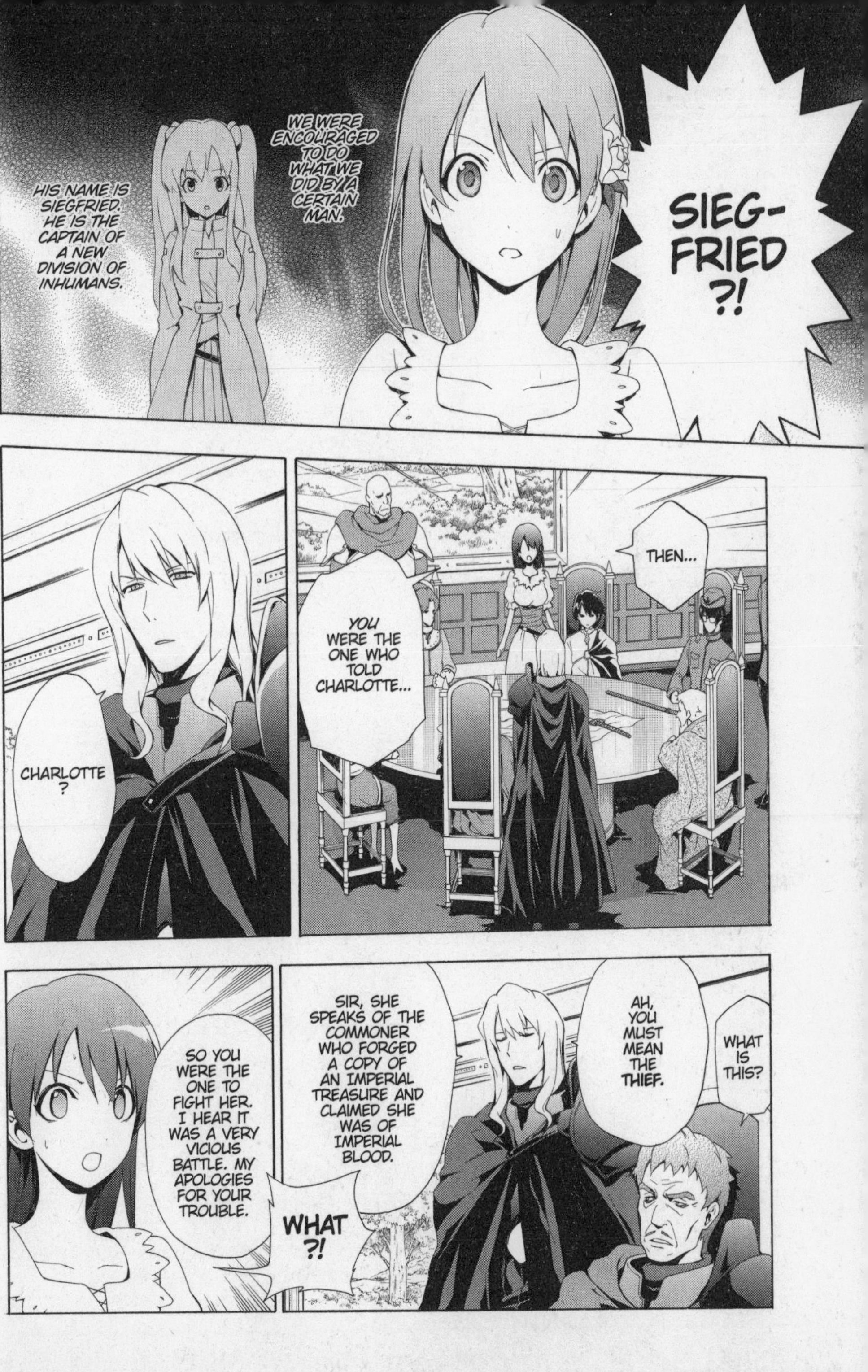
WE WERE ENCOURAGED TO DO WHAT WE DID BY A CERTAIN MAN.
HIS NAME IS SIEGFRIED. HE IS THE CAPTAIN OF A NEW DIVISION OF INHUMANS.
SIEG-FRIED ?!
THEN...
YOU WERE THE ONE WHO TOLD CHARLOTTE...
CHARLOTTE ?
WHAT IS THIS?
AH, YOU MUST MEAN THE THIEF.
SIR, SHE SPEAKS OF THE COMMONER WHO FORGED A COPY OF AN IMPERIAL TREASURE AND CLAIMED SHE WAS OF IMPERIAL BLOOD.
SO YOU WERE THE ONE TO FIGHT HER. I HEAR IT WAS A VERY VICIOUS BATTLE. MY APOLOGIES FOR YOUR TROUBLE.
WHAT ?!

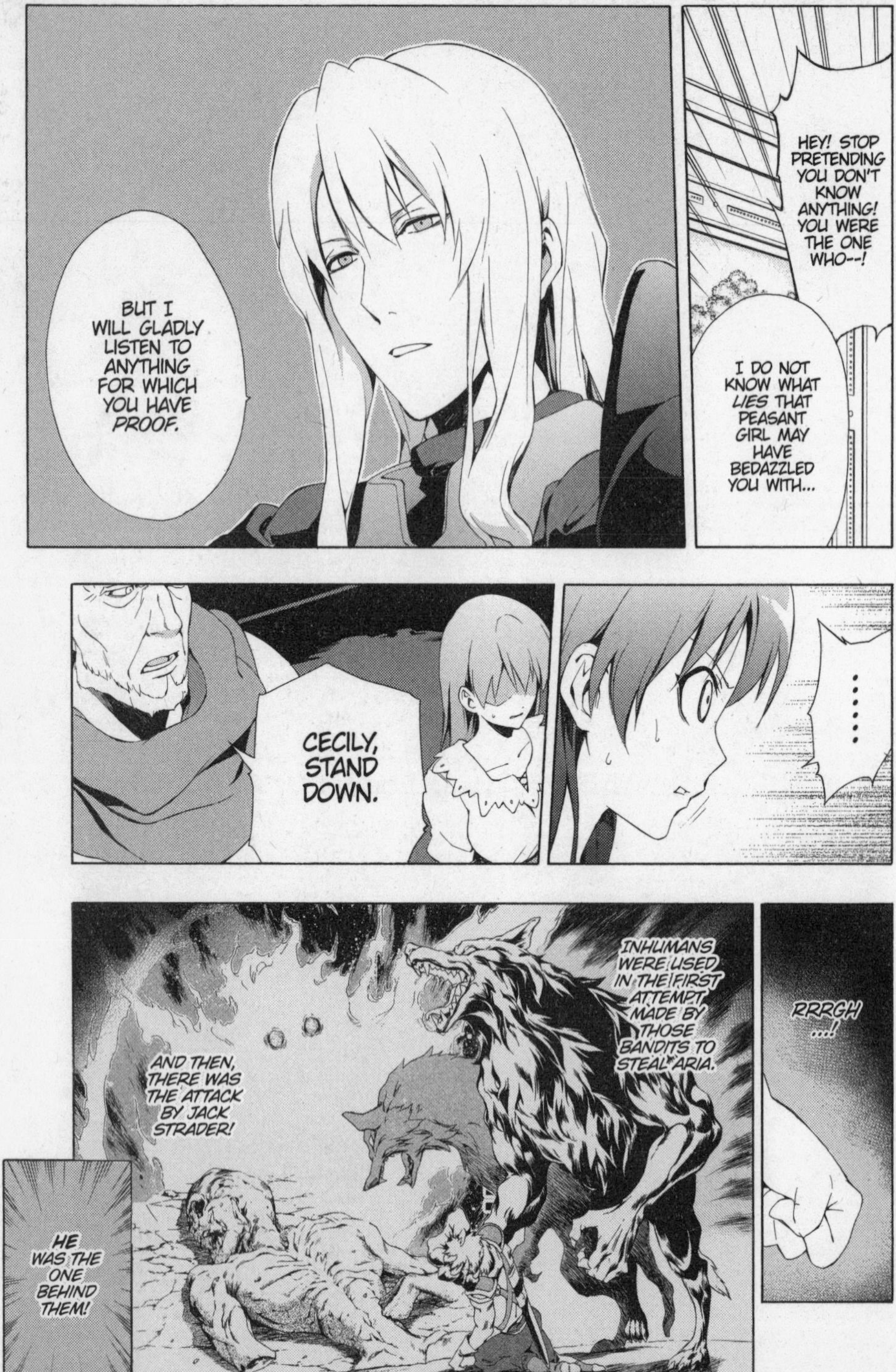
HEY! STOP PRETENDING YOU DON'T KNOW ANYTHING! YOU WERE THE ONE WHO--!
I DO NOT KNOW WHAT *LIES* THAT PEASANT GIRL MAY HAVE BEDAZZLED YOU WITH...
BUT I WILL GLADLY LISTEN TO ANYTHING FOR WHICH YOU HAVE *PROOF*.
......
CECILY, STAND DOWN.
RRRGH ...!
INHUMANS WERE USED IN THE FIRST ATTEMPT MADE BY THOSE BANDITS TO STEAL ARIA.
AND THEN, THERE WAS THE ATTACK BY JACK STRADER!
HE WAS THE ONE BEHIND THEM!

I STAND, RIGHT BEFORE THE MAN WHO COULD BE **RESPONSIBLE** FOR EVERYTHING THAT HAS HAPPENED.

IS THERE NOTHING I CAN DO?!

GENTLEMEN, LET US RETURN TO THE SUBJECT AT HAND.

LUKE AINSWORTH, YOU HAVE BROUGHT WITH YOU YOUR LATEST CREATION, CORRECT?

TONK

SIIIGH...

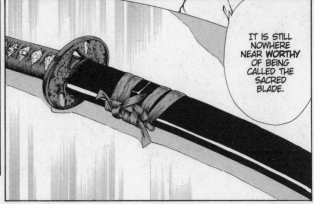

IT IS STILL NOWHERE NEAR **WORTHY** OF BEING CALLED THE SACRED BLADE.

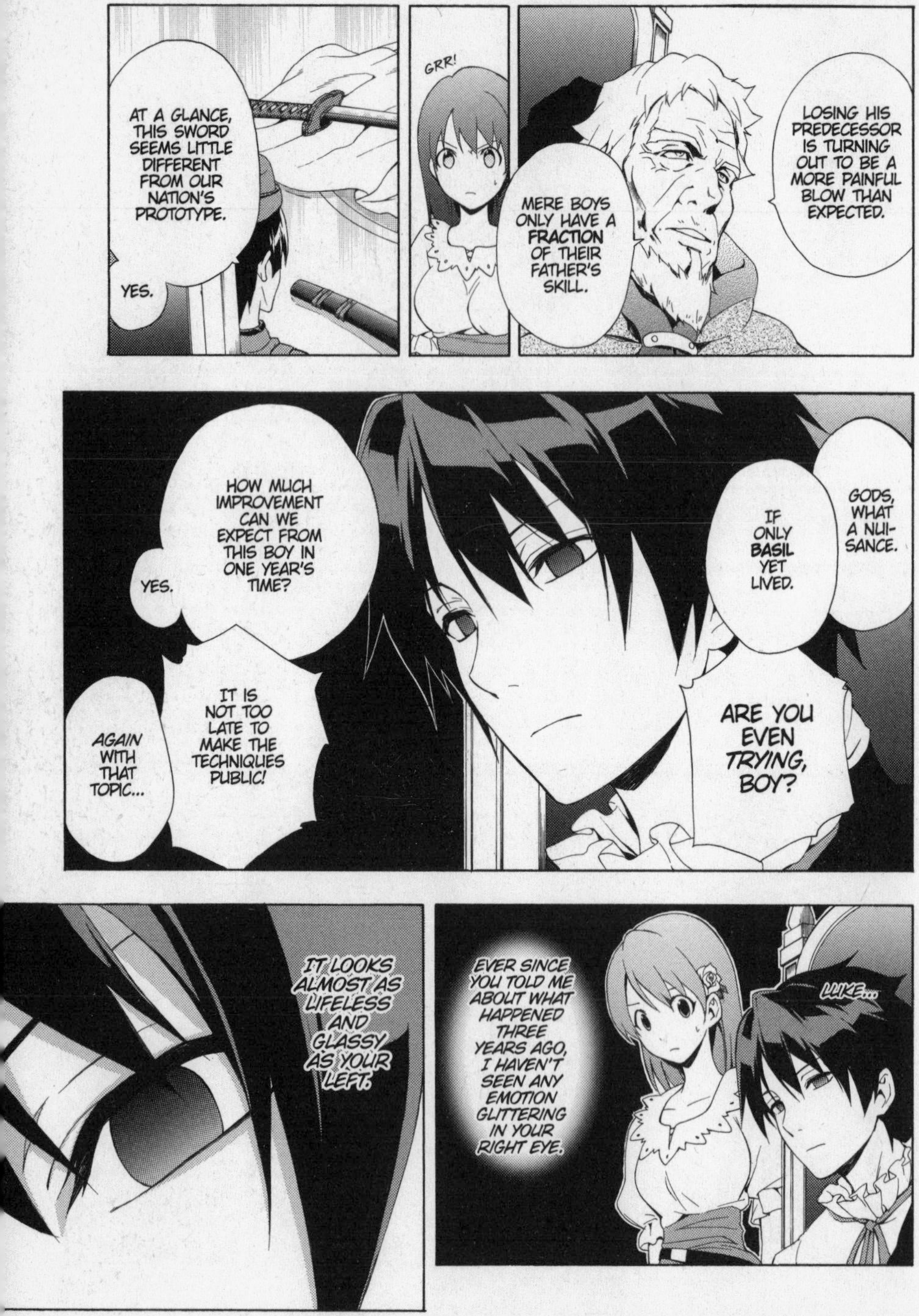
LOSING HIS PREDECESSOR IS TURNING OUT TO BE A MORE PAINFUL BLOW THAN EXPECTED.
MERE BOYS ONLY HAVE A FRACTION OF THEIR FATHER'S SKILL.
GRR!
AT A GLANCE, THIS SWORD SEEMS LITTLE DIFFERENT FROM OUR NATION'S PROTOTYPE.
YES.
GODS, WHAT A NUI-SANCE.
IF ONLY BASIL YET LIVED.
ARE YOU EVEN TRYING, BOY?
HOW MUCH IMPROVEMENT CAN WE EXPECT FROM THIS BOY IN ONE YEAR'S TIME?
YES.
IT IS NOT TOO LATE TO MAKE THE TECHNIQUES PUBLIC!
AGAIN WITH THAT TOPIC...
LUKE...
EVER SINCE YOU TOLD ME ABOUT WHAT HAPPENED THREE YEARS AGO, I HAVEN'T SEEN ANY EMOTION GLITTERING IN YOUR RIGHT EYE.
IT LOOKS ALMOST AS LIFELESS AND GLASSY AS YOUR LEFT.

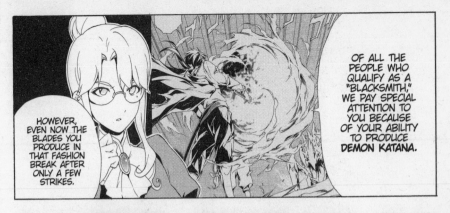

OF ALL THE PEOPLE WHO QUALIFY AS A "BLACKSMITH," WE PAY SPECIAL ATTENTION TO YOU BECAUSE OF YOUR ABILITY TO PRODUCE DEMON KATANA.
HOWEVER, EVEN NOW THE BLADES YOU PRODUCE IN THAT FASHION BREAK AFTER ONLY A FEW STRIKES.
EXACTLY! THAT TALENT OF YOURS IS THE ONLY REASON WE LET YOU KEEP THAT PET DEMON OF YOURS.
WE ARE DOING YOU A FAVOR, BOY.
YOU COULD AT LEAST DO SOMETHING TO REPAY US.
REALLY?
WHY DON'T YOU TELL IT LIKE IT IS? YOU ARE USING ME, NOTHING MORE.
BOY...!
LISA...
IS SHE A DEMON THAT LUKE MADE BY GIVING UP HIS LEFT EYE, DURING THAT TRAGEDY THREE YEARS AGO?
IS THAT KATANA-FORGING POWER SHE GIVES HIM THE REASON HE WAS THE ONLY ONE WHO SURVIVED?
YOU THERE, CAMPBELL GIRL. HAS HE TOLD YOU?

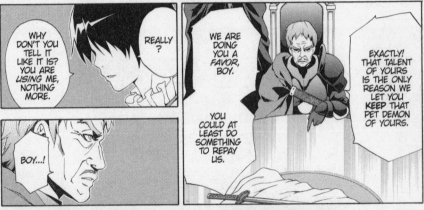

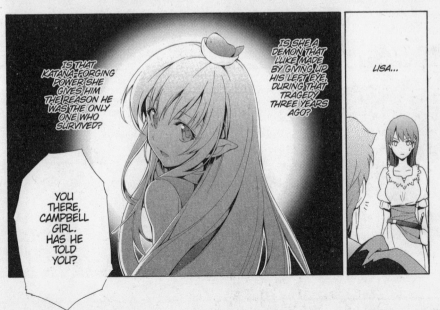

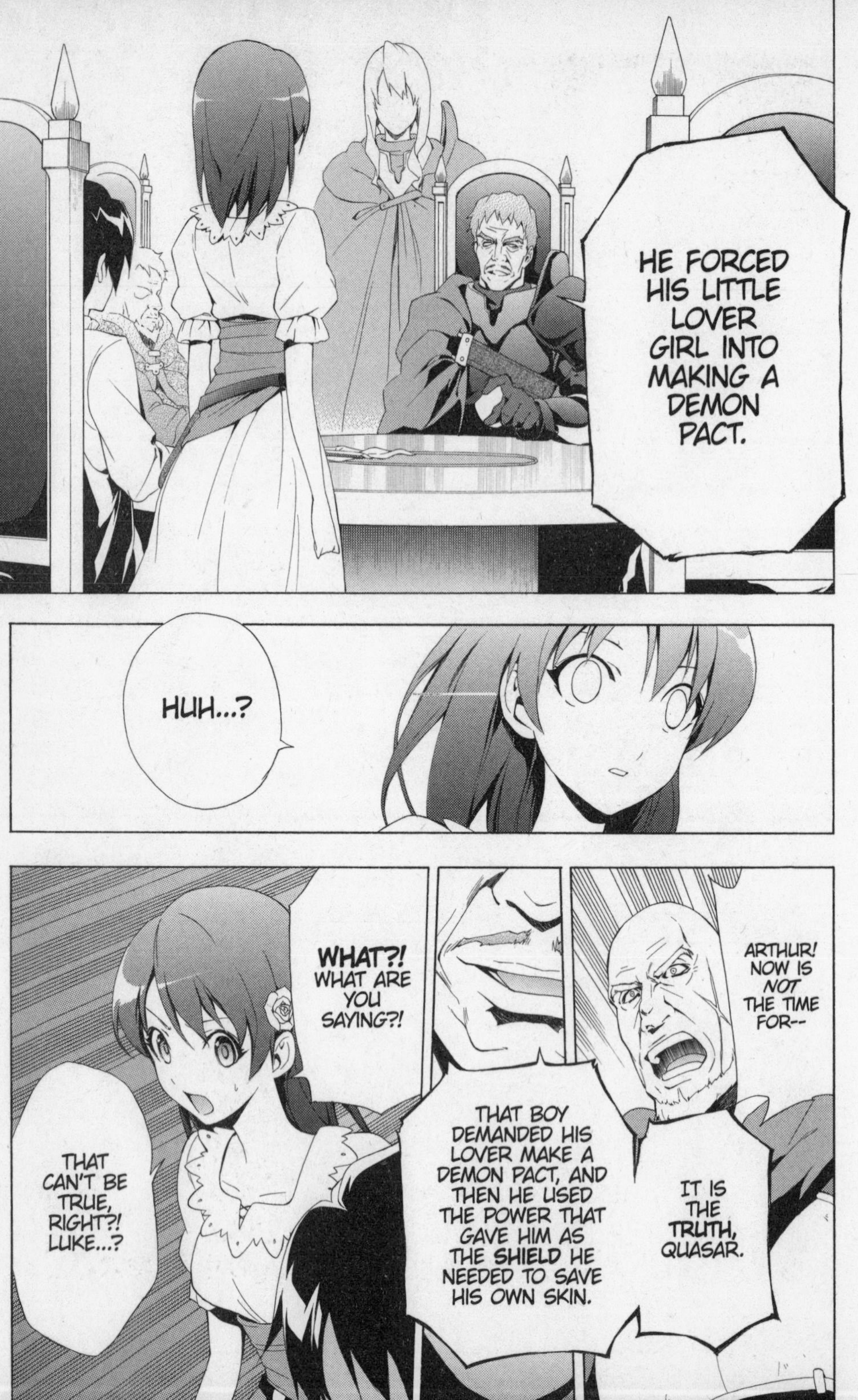

HE FORCED HIS LITTLE LOVER GIRL INTO MAKING A DEMON PACT.
HUH...?
ARTHUR! NOW IS *NOT* THE TIME FOR--
IT IS THE **TRUTH**, QUASAR.
THAT BOY DEMANDED HIS LOVER MAKE A DEMON PACT, AND THEN HE USED THE POWER THAT GAVE HIM AS THE **SHIELD** HE NEEDED TO SAVE HIS OWN SKIN.
WHAT?! WHAT ARE YOU SAYING?!
THAT CAN'T BE TRUE, RIGHT?! LUKE...?

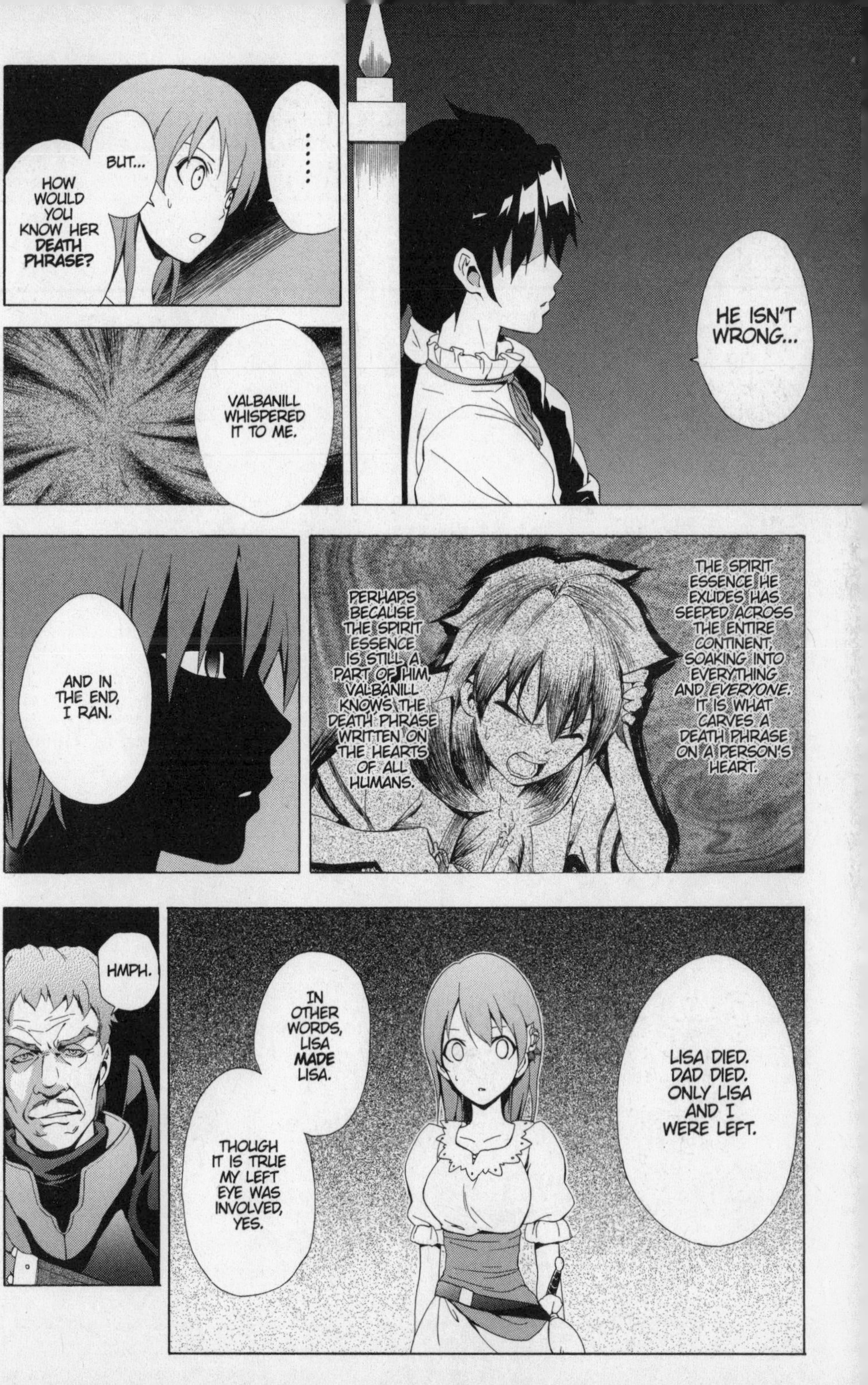
HE ISN'T WRONG...
......
BUT... HOW WOULD YOU KNOW HER DEATH PHRASE?
VALBANILL WHISPERED IT TO ME.
THE SPIRIT ESSENCE HE EXUDES HAS SEEPED ACROSS THE ENTIRE CONTINENT, SOAKING INTO EVERYTHING AND EVERYONE. IT IS WHAT CARVES A DEATH PHRASE ON A PERSON'S HEART.
PERHAPS BECAUSE THE SPIRIT ESSENCE IS STILL A PART OF HIM, VALBANILL KNOWS THE DEATH PHRASE WRITTEN ON THE HEARTS OF ALL HUMANS.
AND IN THE END, I RAN.
LISA DIED. DAD DIED. ONLY LISA AND I WERE LEFT.
IN OTHER WORDS, LISA MADE LISA.
THOUGH IT IS TRUE MY LEFT EYE WAS INVOLVED, YES.
HMPH.

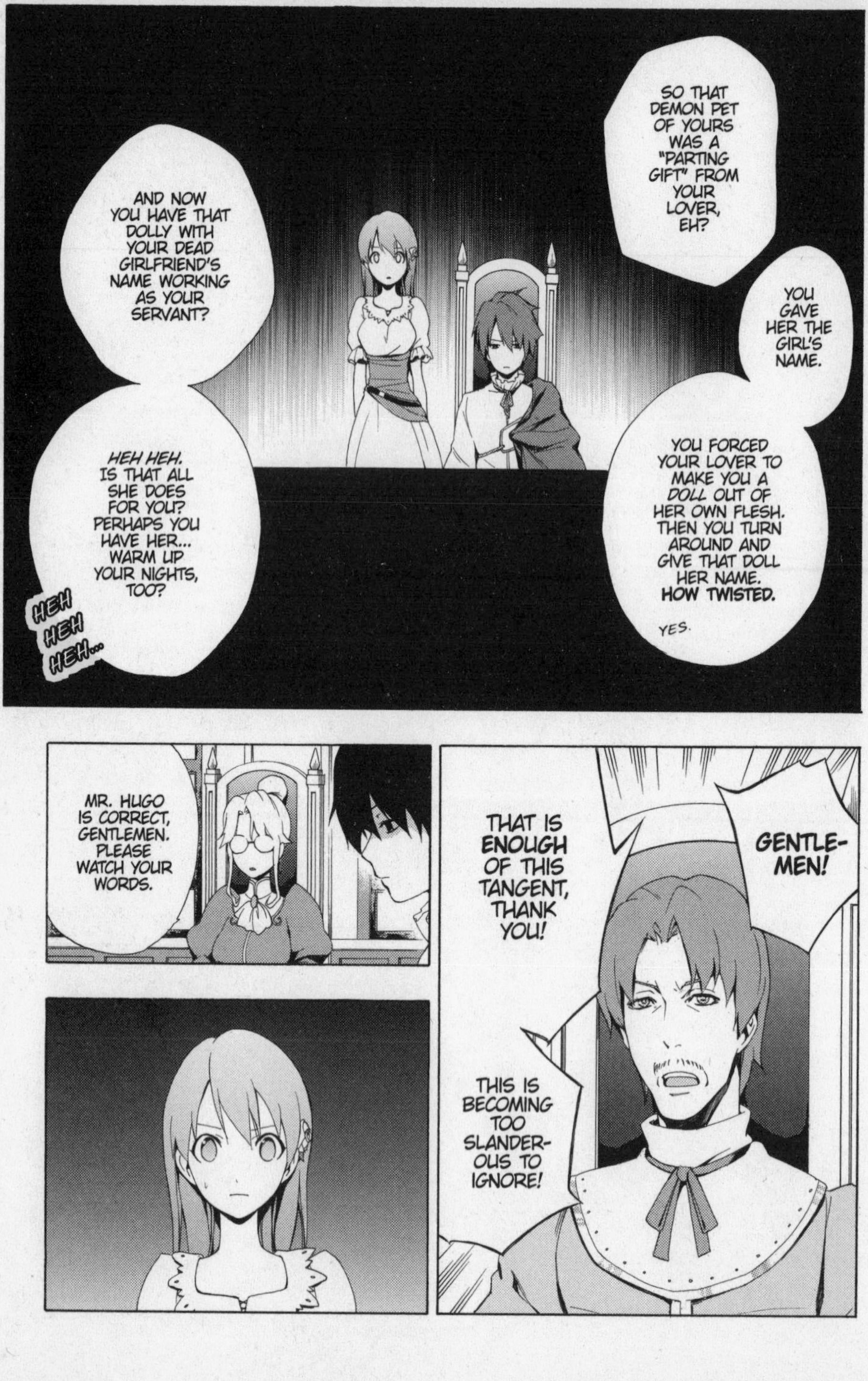
SO THAT DEMON PET OF YOURS WAS A "PARTING GIFT" FROM YOUR LOVER, EH?
AND NOW YOU HAVE THAT DOLLY WITH YOUR DEAD GIRLFRIEND'S NAME WORKING AS YOUR SERVANT?
YOU GAVE HER THE GIRL'S NAME.
YOU FORCED YOUR LOVER TO MAKE YOU A *DOLL* OUT OF HER OWN FLESH. THEN YOU TURN AROUND AND GIVE THAT DOLL HER NAME. **HOW TWISTED.**
YES.
HEH HEH. IS THAT ALL SHE DOES FOR YOU? PERHAPS YOU HAVE HER... WARM UP YOUR NIGHTS, TOO?
HEH HEH HEH...
GENTLE-MEN!
THAT IS **ENOUGH** OF THIS TANGENT, THANK YOU!
THIS IS BECOMING TOO SLANDER-OUS TO IGNORE!
MR. HUGO IS CORRECT, GENTLEMEN. PLEASE WATCH YOUR WORDS.

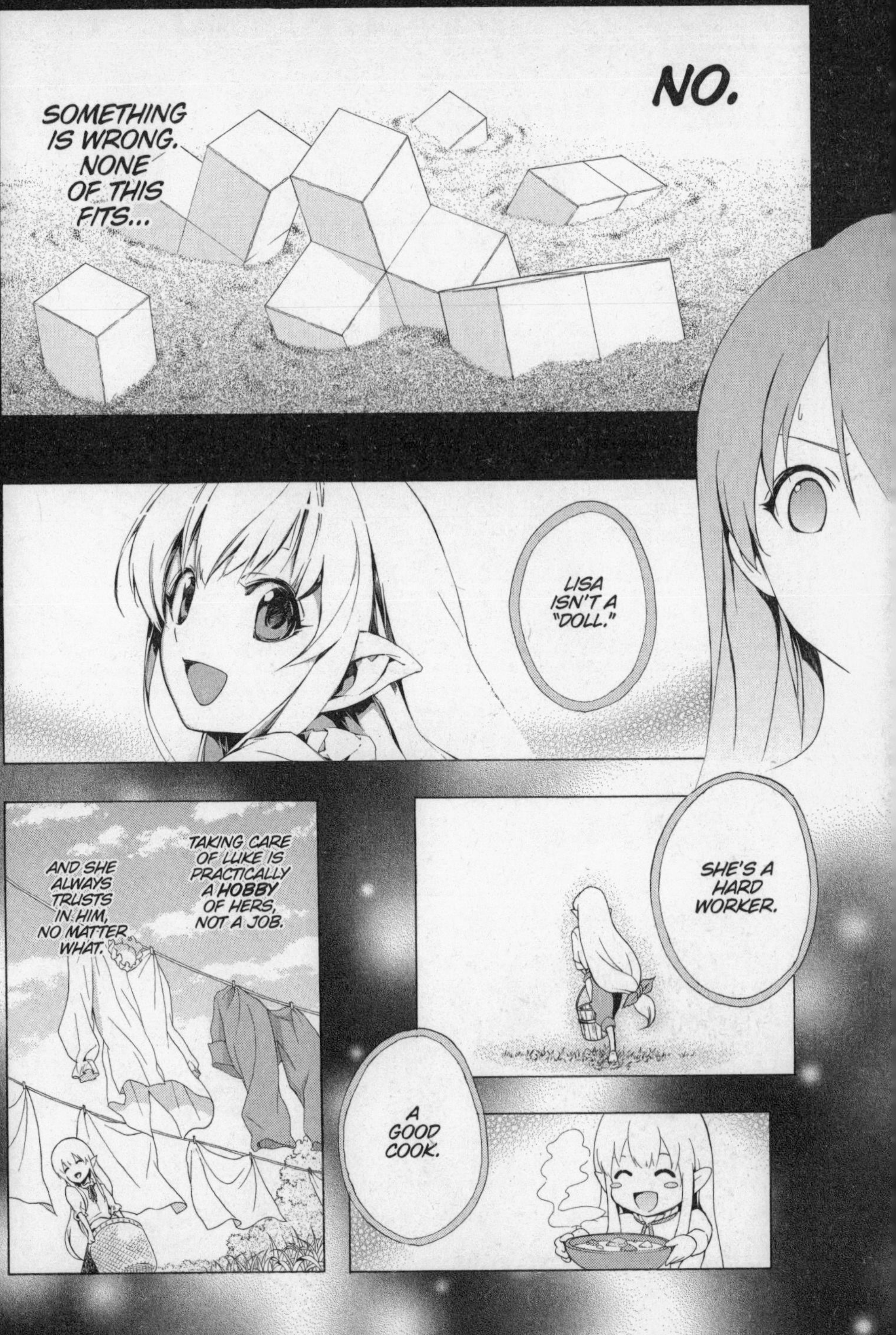
NO.
SOMETHING IS WRONG. NONE OF THIS FITS...
LISA ISN'T A "DOLL."
SHE'S A HARD WORKER.
A GOOD COOK.
TAKING CARE OF LUKE IS PRACTICALLY A HOBBY OF HERS, NOT A JOB.
AND SHE ALWAYS TRUSTS IN HIM, NO MATTER WHAT.

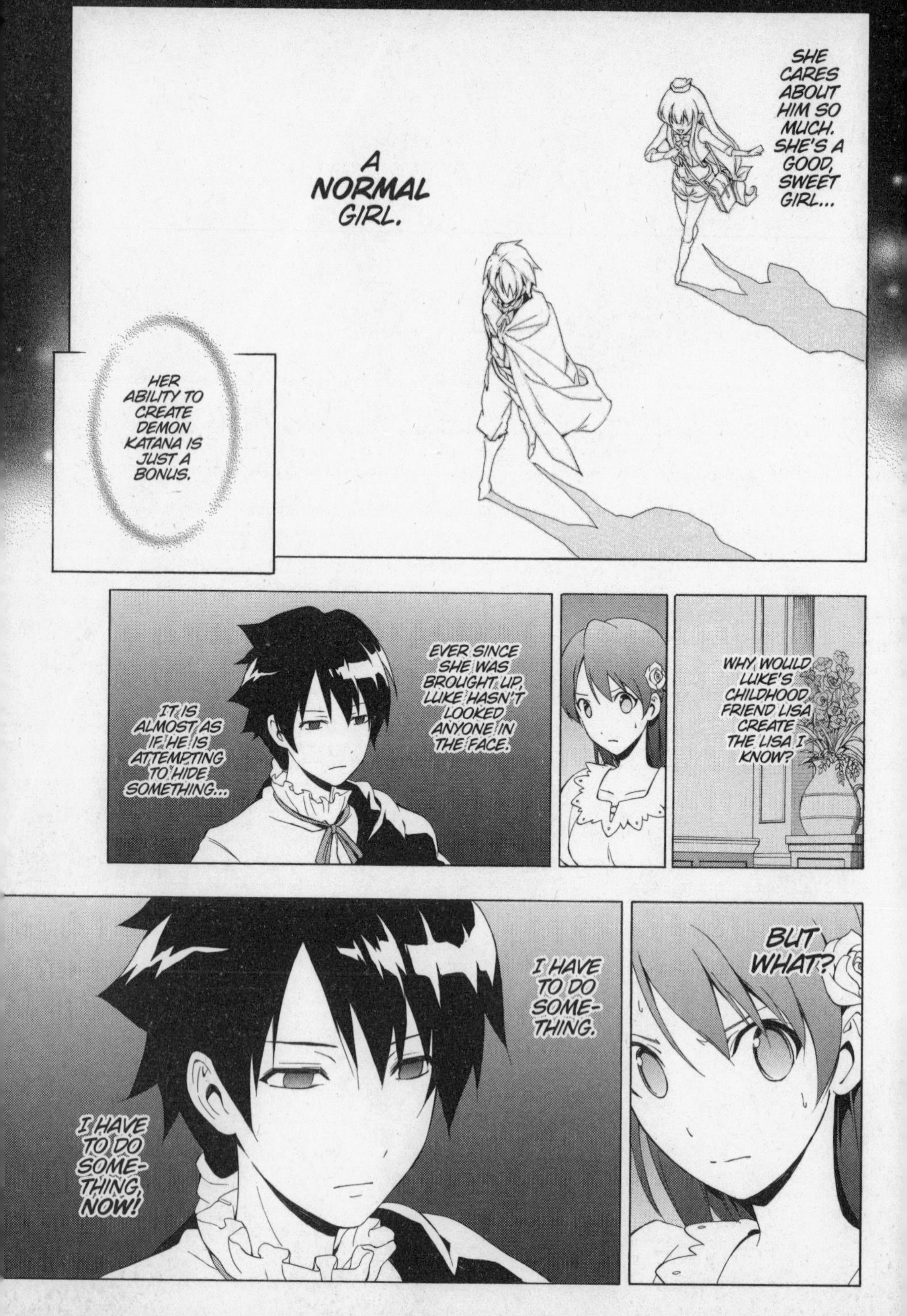
SHE CARES ABOUT HIM SO MUCH. SHE'S A GOOD, SWEET GIRL...
A NORMAL GIRL.
HER ABILITY TO CREATE DEMON KATANA IS JUST A BONUS.
WHY WOULD LUKE'S CHILDHOOD FRIEND LISA CREATE THE LISA I KNOW?
EVER SINCE SHE WAS BROUGHT UP, LUKE HASN'T LOOKED ANYONE IN THE FACE.
IT IS ALMOST AS IF HE IS ATTEMPTING TO HIDE SOMETHING...
BUT WHAT?
I HAVE TO DO SOME-THING.
I HAVE TO DO SOME-THING, NOW!

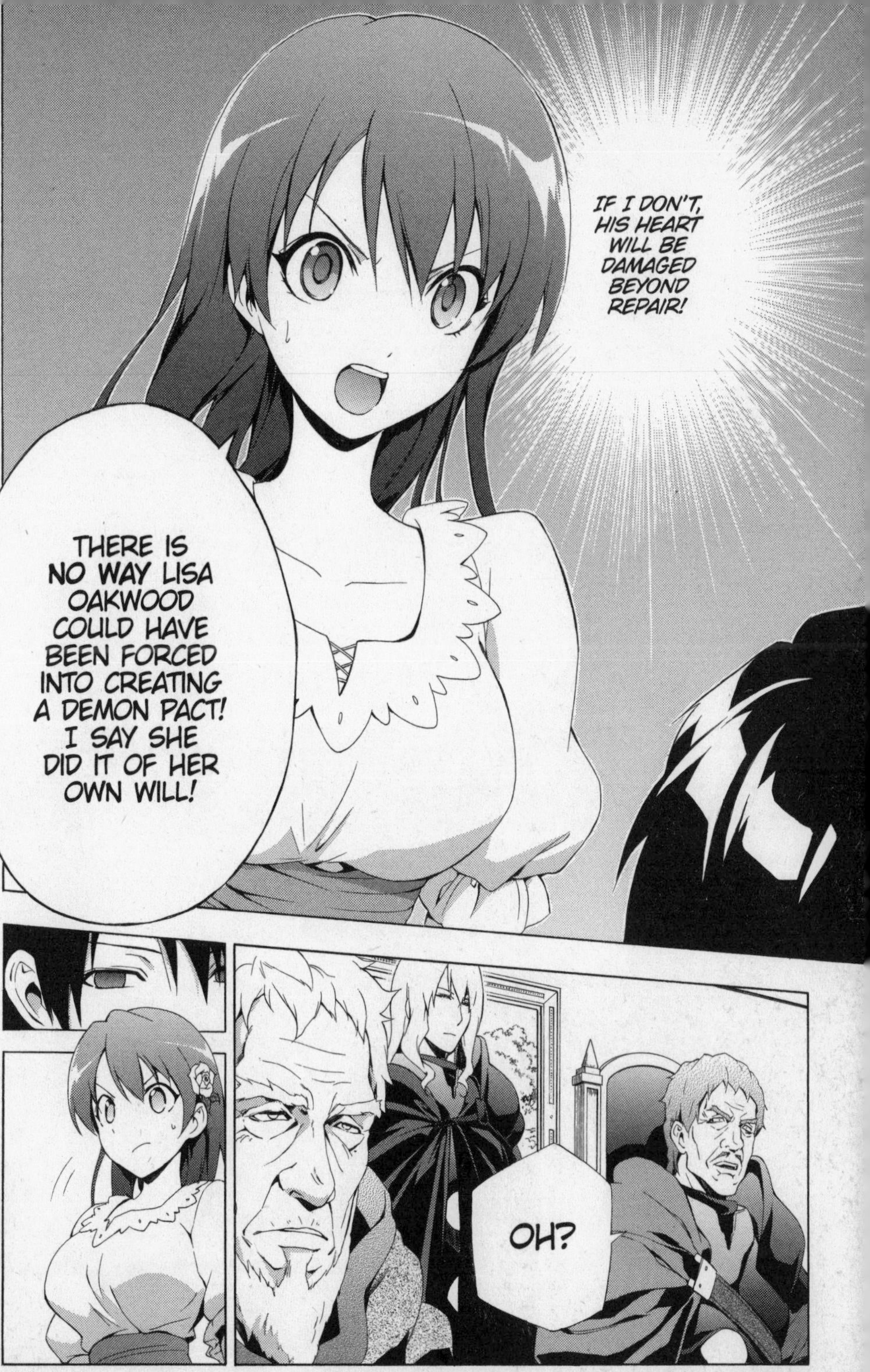
IF I DON'T, HIS HEART WILL BE DAMAGED BEYOND REPAIR!
THERE IS NO WAY LISA OAKWOOD COULD HAVE BEEN FORCED INTO CREATING A DEMON PACT! I SAY SHE DID IT OF HER OWN WILL!
OH?

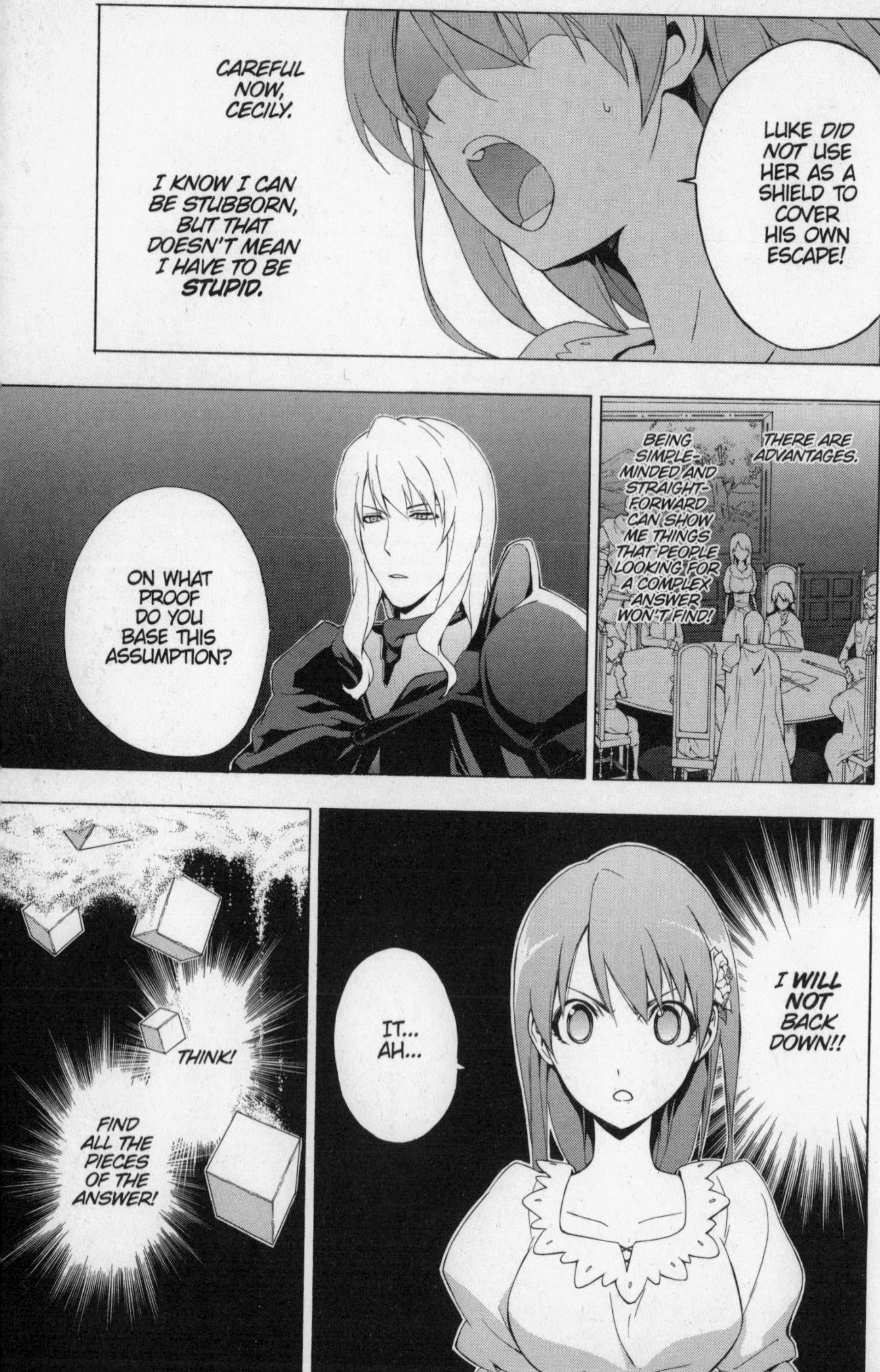
LUKE DID NOT USE HER AS A SHIELD TO COVER HIS OWN ESCAPE!
CAREFUL NOW, CECILY.
I KNOW I CAN BE STUBBORN, BUT THAT DOESN'T MEAN I HAVE TO BE STUPID.
THERE ARE ADVANTAGES.
BEING SIMPLE-MINDED AND STRAIGHT-FORWARD CAN SHOW ME THINGS THAT PEOPLE LOOKING FOR A COMPLEX ANSWER WON'T FIND!
ON WHAT PROOF DO YOU BASE THIS ASSUMPTION?
I WILL NOT BACK DOWN!!
IT... AH...
THINK!
FIND ALL THE PIECES OF THE ANSWER!

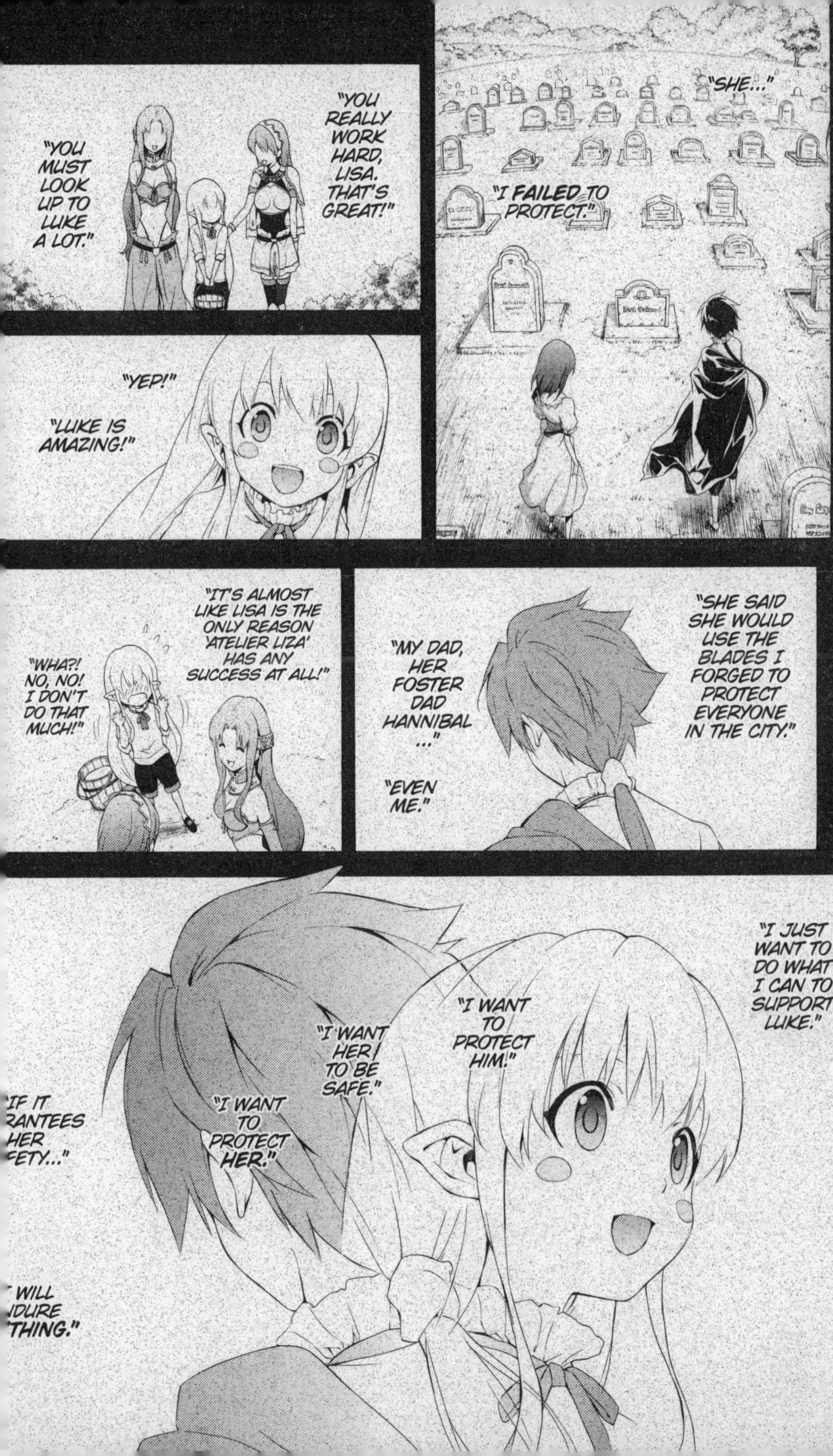
"SHE..."
"I FAILED TO PROTECT."
"YOU REALLY WORK HARD, LISA. THAT'S GREAT!"
"YOU MUST LOOK UP TO LUKE A LOT."
"YEP!"
"LUKE IS AMAZING!"
"SHE SAID SHE WOULD USE THE BLADES I FORGED TO PROTECT EVERYONE IN THE CITY."
"MY DAD, HER FOSTER DAD HANNIBAL ..."
"EVEN ME."
"IT'S ALMOST LIKE LISA IS THE ONLY REASON 'ATELIER LIZA' HAS ANY SUCCESS AT ALL!"
"WHA?! NO, NO! I DON'T DO THAT MUCH!"
"I JUST WANT TO DO WHAT I CAN TO SUPPORT LUKE."
"I WANT TO PROTECT HIM."
"I WANT HER TO BE SAFE."
"I WANT TO PROTECT HER."
"IF IT RANTEES HER FETY..."
T WILL NDURE THING."

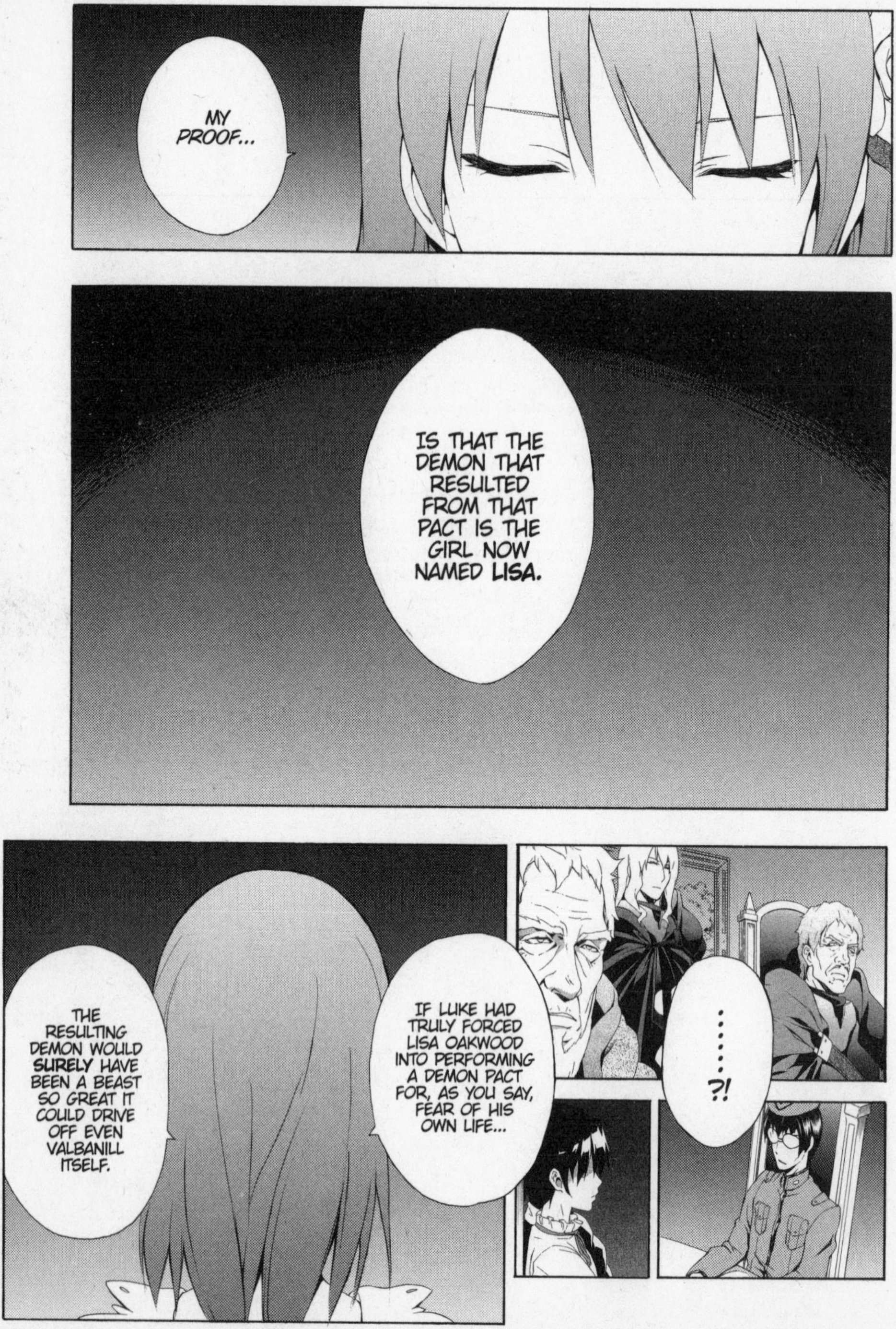
MY PROOF...
IS THAT THE DEMON THAT RESULTED FROM THAT PACT IS THE GIRL NOW NAMED **LISA.**
......
?!
IF LUKE HAD TRULY FORCED LISA OAKWOOD INTO PERFORMING A DEMON PACT FOR, AS YOU SAY, FEAR OF HIS OWN LIFE...
THE RESULTING DEMON WOULD **SURELY** HAVE BEEN A BEAST SO GREAT IT COULD DRIVE OFF EVEN VALBANILL ITSELF.

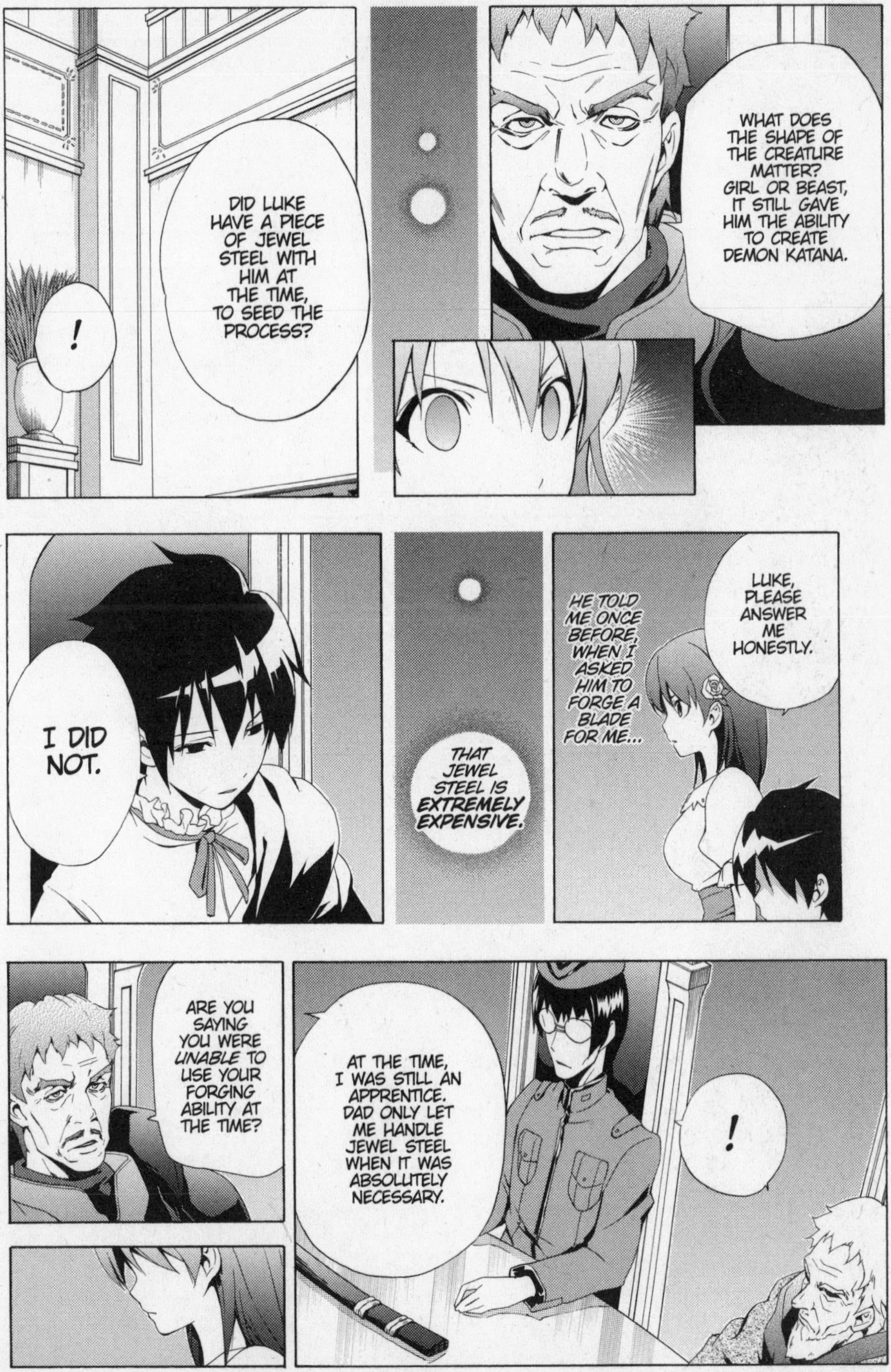
WHAT DOES THE SHAPE OF THE CREATURE MATTER? GIRL OR BEAST, IT STILL GAVE HIM THE ABILITY TO CREATE DEMON KATANA.
DID LUKE HAVE A PIECE OF JEWEL STEEL WITH HIM AT THE TIME, TO SEED THE PROCESS?
!
LUKE, PLEASE ANSWER ME HONESTLY.
HE TOLD ME ONCE BEFORE, WHEN I ASKED HIM TO FORGE A BLADE FOR ME...
THAT JEWEL STEEL IS EXTREMELY EXPENSIVE.
I DID NOT.
!
AT THE TIME, I WAS STILL AN APPRENTICE. DAD ONLY LET ME HANDLE JEWEL STEEL WHEN IT WAS ABSOLUTELY NECESSARY.
ARE YOU SAYING YOU WERE UNABLE TO USE YOUR FORGING ABILITY AT THE TIME?

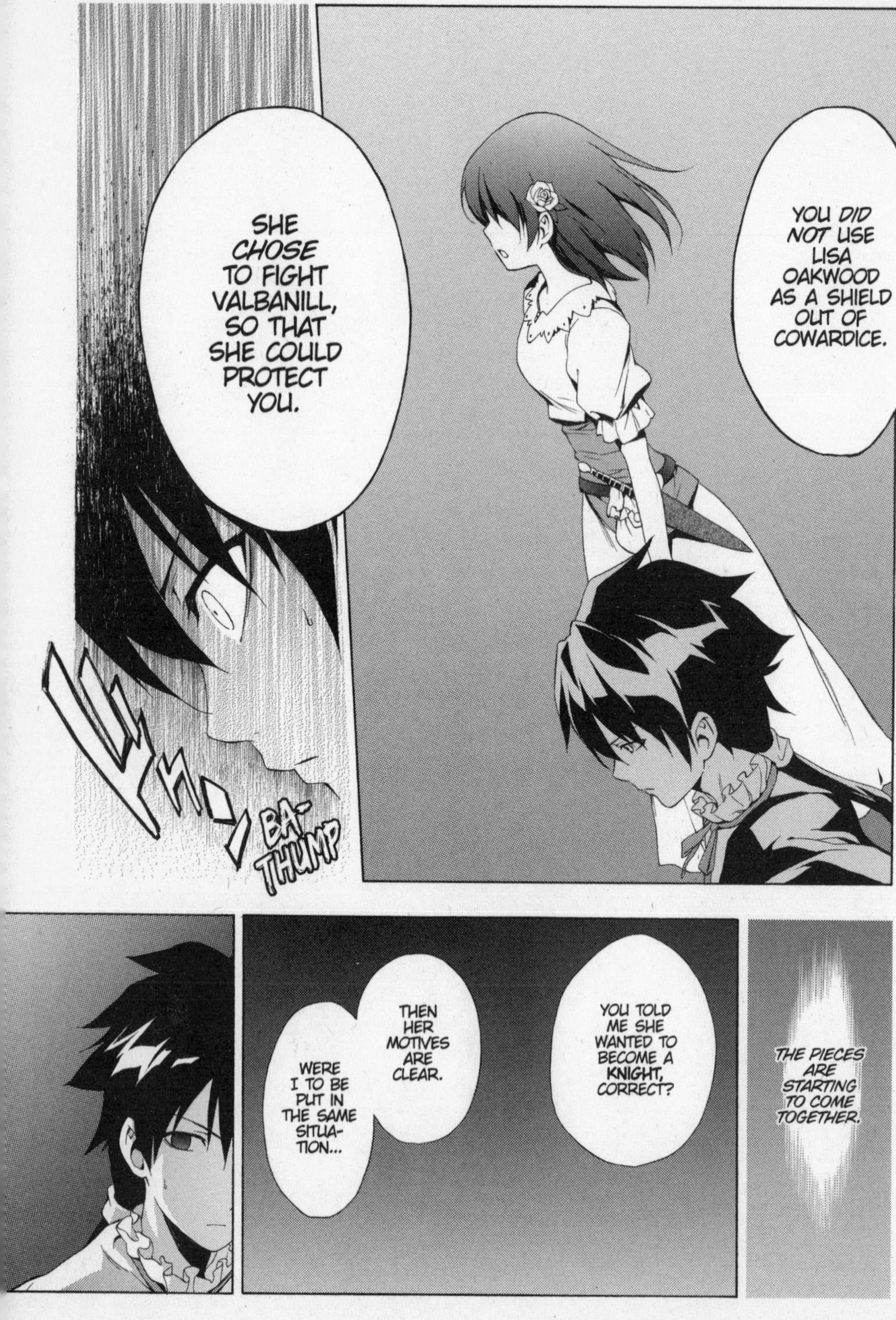
YOU DID NOT USE LISA OAKWOOD AS A SHIELD OUT OF COWARDICE.
SHE CHOSE TO FIGHT VALBANILL, SO THAT SHE COULD PROTECT YOU.
BA-THUMP
THE PIECES ARE STARTING TO COME TOGETHER.
YOU TOLD ME SHE WANTED TO BECOME A KNIGHT, CORRECT?
THEN HER MOTIVES ARE CLEAR.
WERE I TO BE PUT IN THE SAME SITUA-TION...

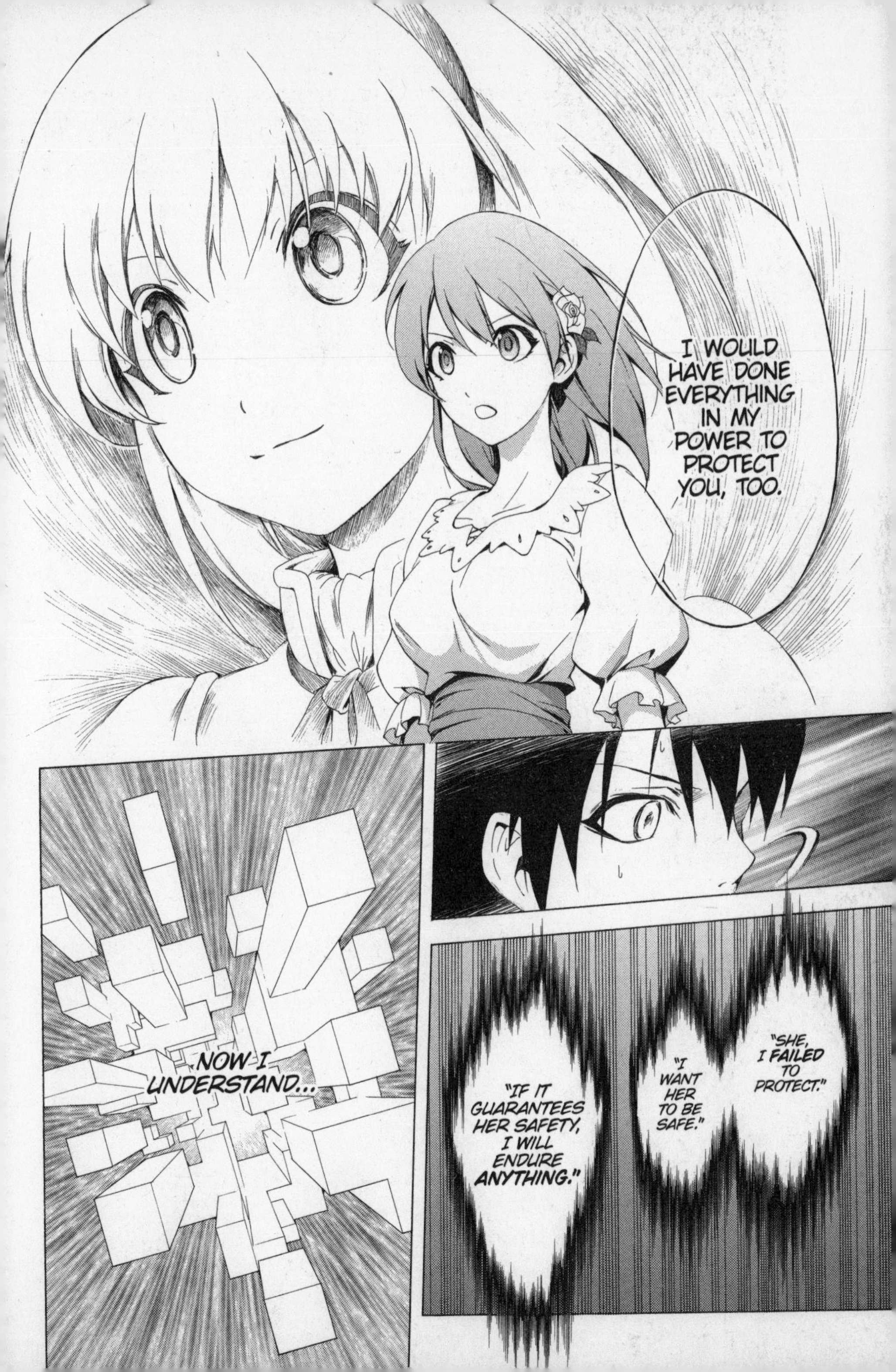
I WOULD HAVE DONE EVERYTHING IN MY POWER TO PROTECT YOU, TOO.
"SHE, I FAILED TO PROTECT."
"I WANT HER TO BE SAFE."
"IF IT GUARANTEES HER SAFETY, I WILL ENDURE ANYTHING."
NOW I UNDERSTAND...

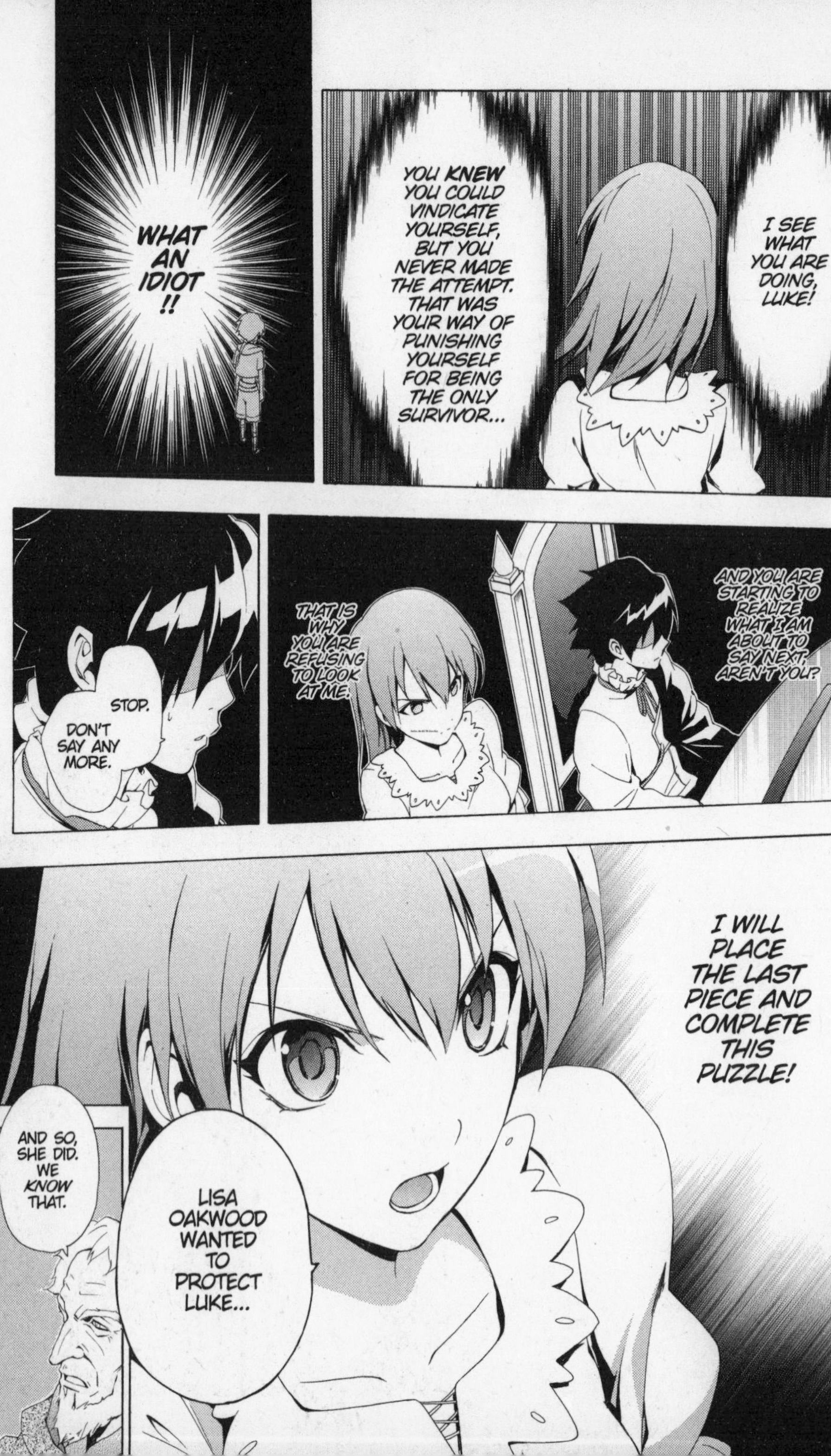
I SEE WHAT YOU ARE DOING, LUKE!
YOU KNEW YOU COULD VINDICATE YOURSELF, BUT YOU NEVER MADE THE ATTEMPT. THAT WAS YOUR WAY OF PUNISHING YOURSELF FOR BEING THE ONLY SURVIVOR...
WHAT AN IDIOT !!
AND YOU ARE STARTING TO REALIZE WHAT I AM ABOUT TO SAY NEXT, AREN'T YOU?
THAT IS WHY YOU ARE REFUSING TO LOOK AT ME.
STOP.
DON'T SAY ANY MORE.
I WILL PLACE THE LAST PIECE AND COMPLETE THIS PUZZLE!
LISA OAKWOOD WANTED TO PROTECT LUKE...
AND SO, SHE DID. WE KNOW THAT.

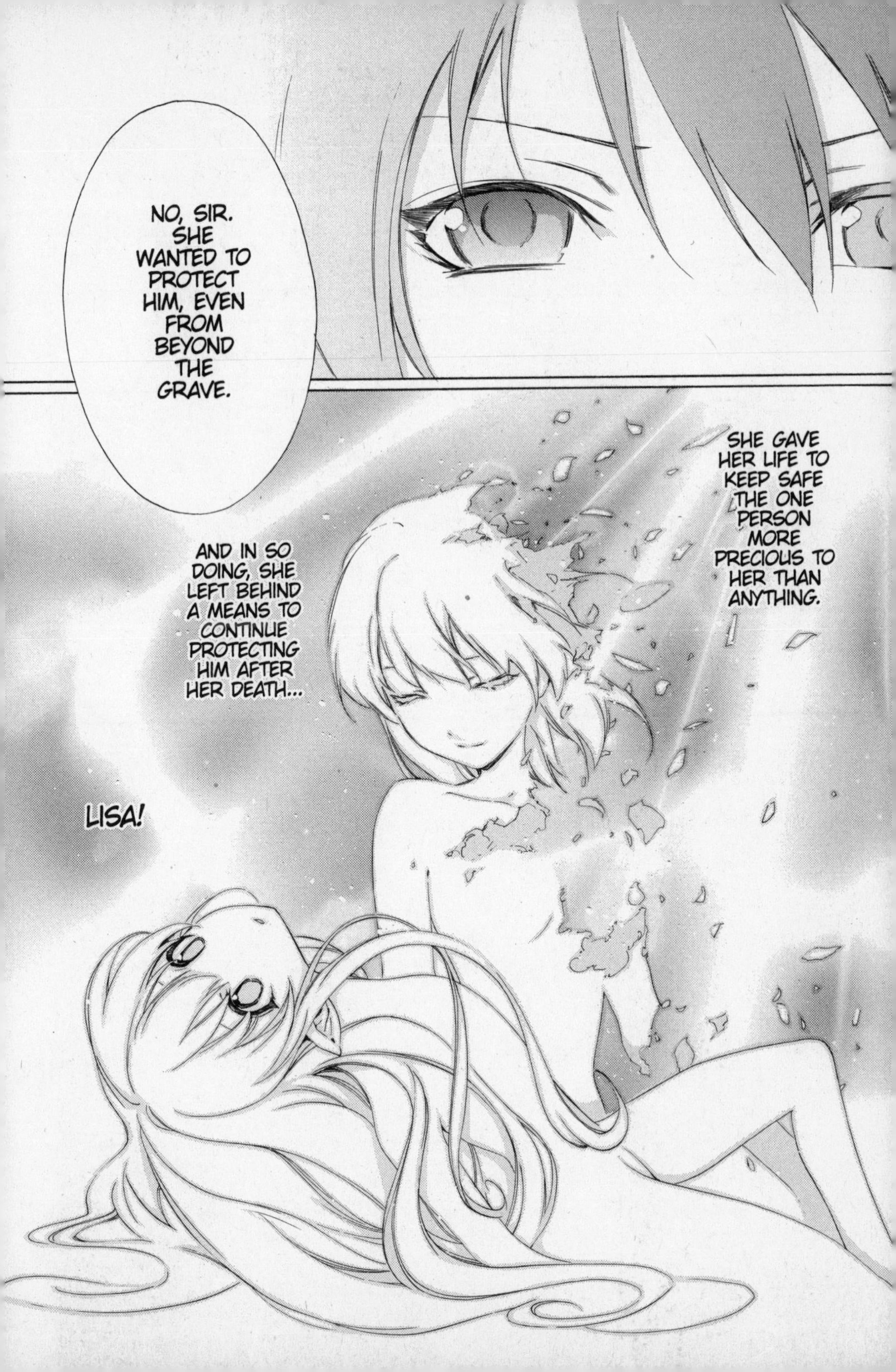
NO, SIR. SHE WANTED TO PROTECT HIM, EVEN FROM BEYOND THE GRAVE.
SHE GAVE HER LIFE TO KEEP SAFE THE ONE PERSON MORE PRECIOUS TO HER THAN ANYTHING.
AND IN SO DOING, SHE LEFT BEHIND A MEANS TO CONTINUE PROTECTING HIM AFTER HER DEATH...
LISA!

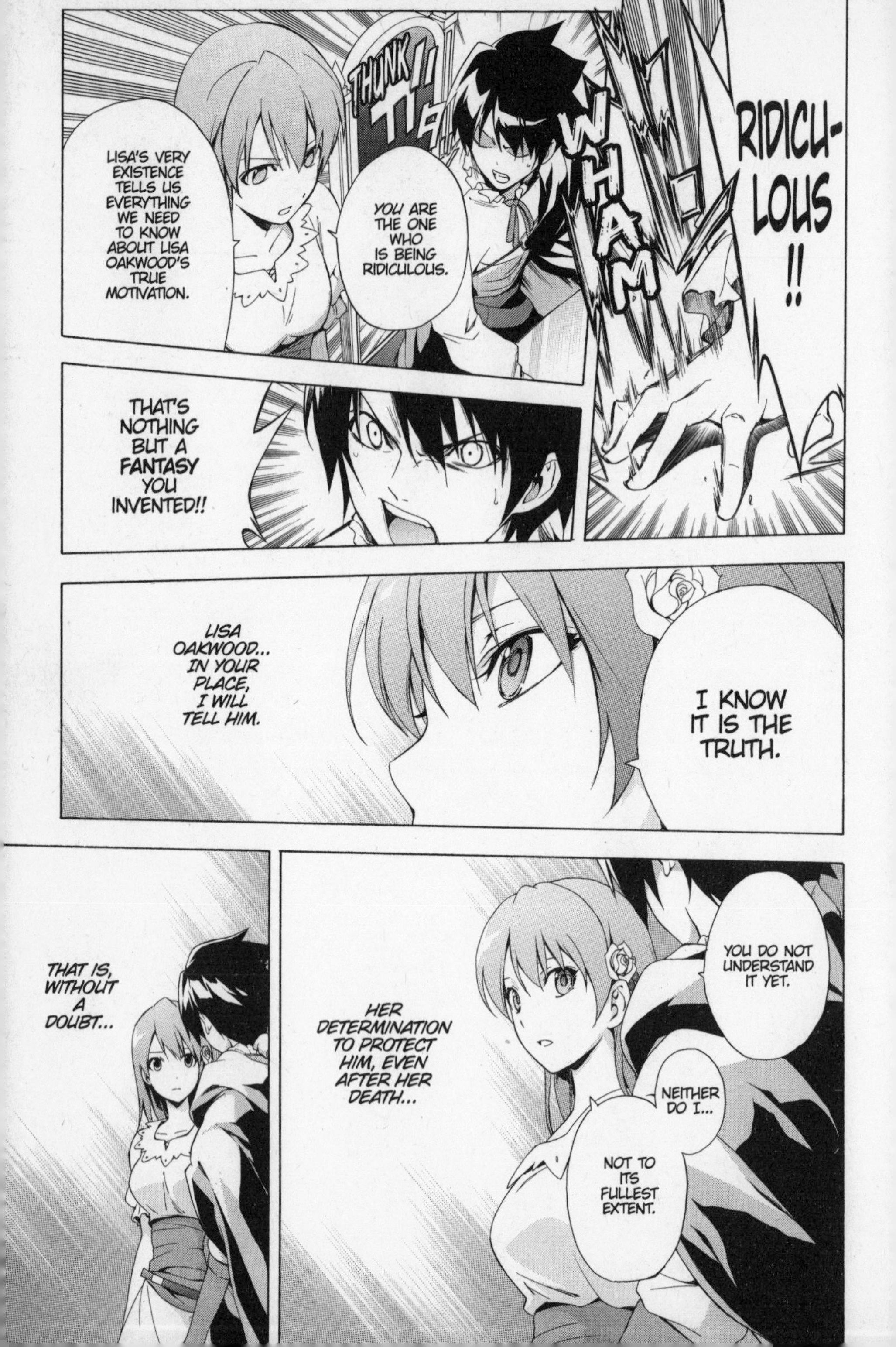
RIDICU-LOUS!!
WHAM
THUNK!!
YOU ARE THE ONE WHO IS BEING RIDICULOUS.
LISA'S VERY EXISTENCE TELLS US EVERYTHING WE NEED TO KNOW ABOUT LISA OAKWOOD'S TRUE MOTIVATION.
THAT'S NOTHING BUT A FANTASY YOU INVENTED!!
I KNOW IT IS THE TRUTH.
LISA OAKWOOD... IN YOUR PLACE, I WILL TELL HIM.
YOU DO NOT UNDERSTAND IT YET.
NEITHER DO I...
NOT TO ITS FULLEST EXTENT.
HER DETERMINATION TO PROTECT HIM, EVEN AFTER HER DEATH...
THAT IS, WITHOUT A DOUBT...

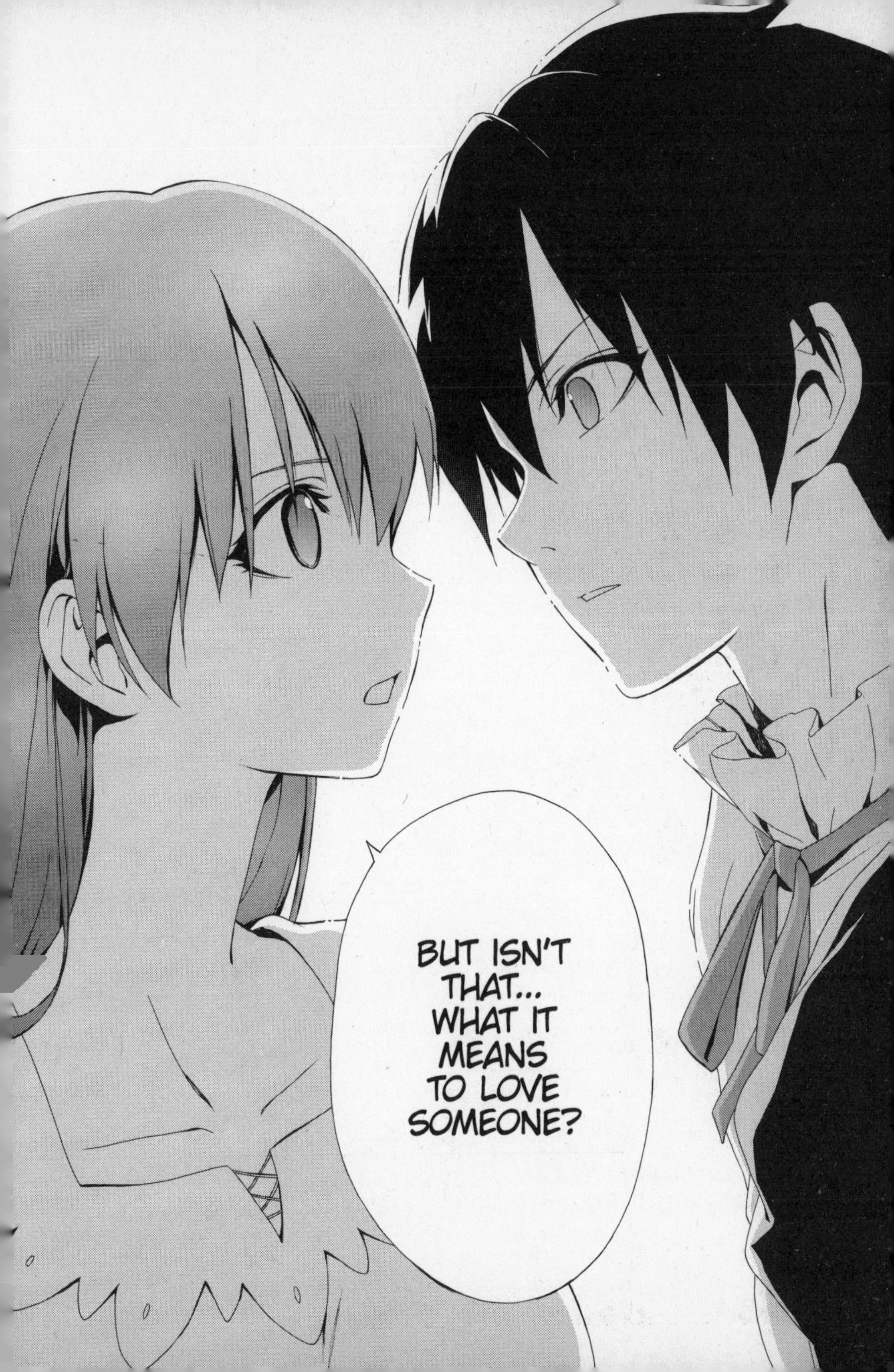
BUT ISN'T THAT... WHAT IT MEANS TO LOVE SOMEONE?

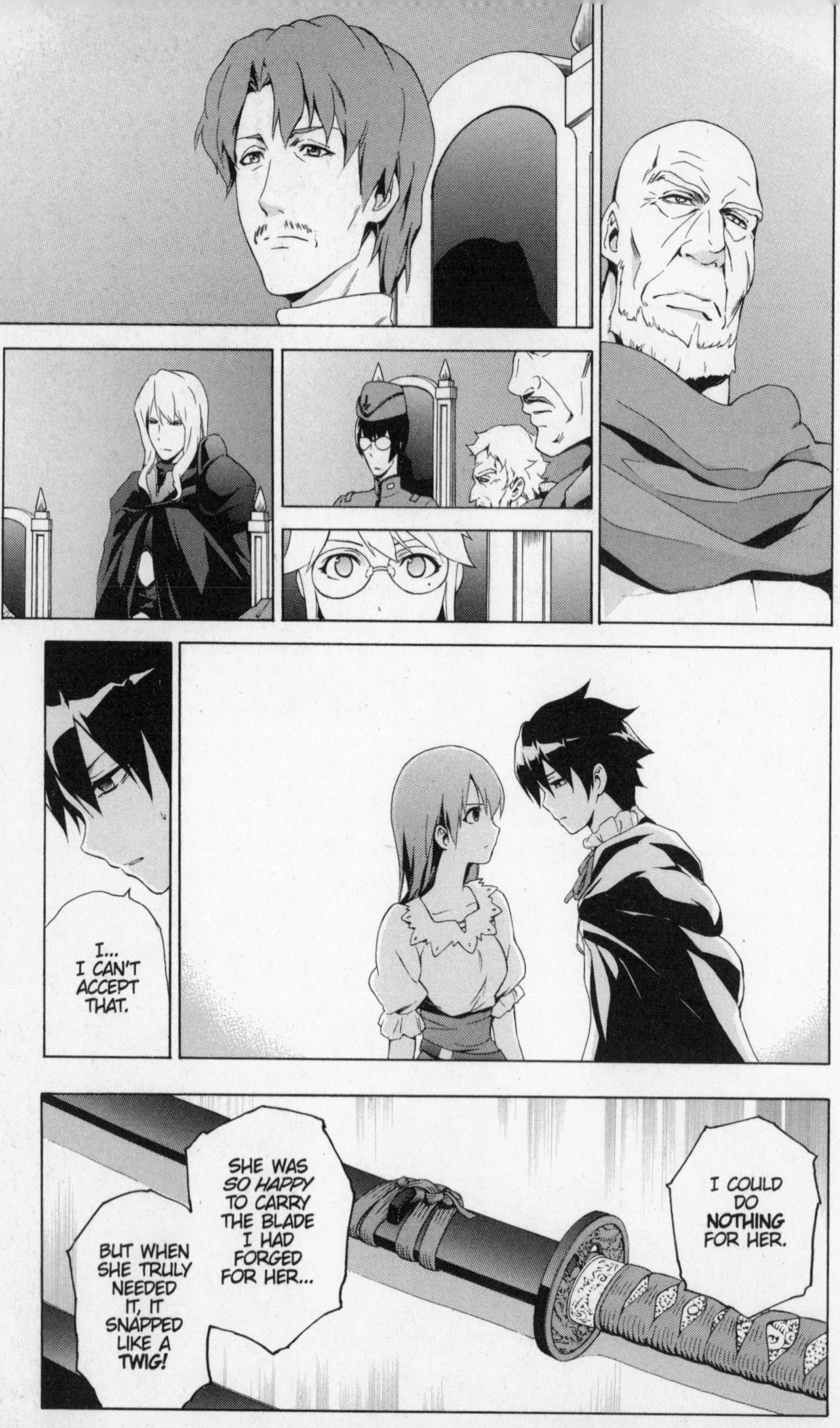
I... I CAN'T ACCEPT THAT.
I COULD DO NOTHING FOR HER.
SHE WAS SO HAPPY TO CARRY THE BLADE I HAD FORGED FOR HER...
BUT WHEN SHE TRULY NEEDED IT, IT SNAPPED LIKE A TWIG!

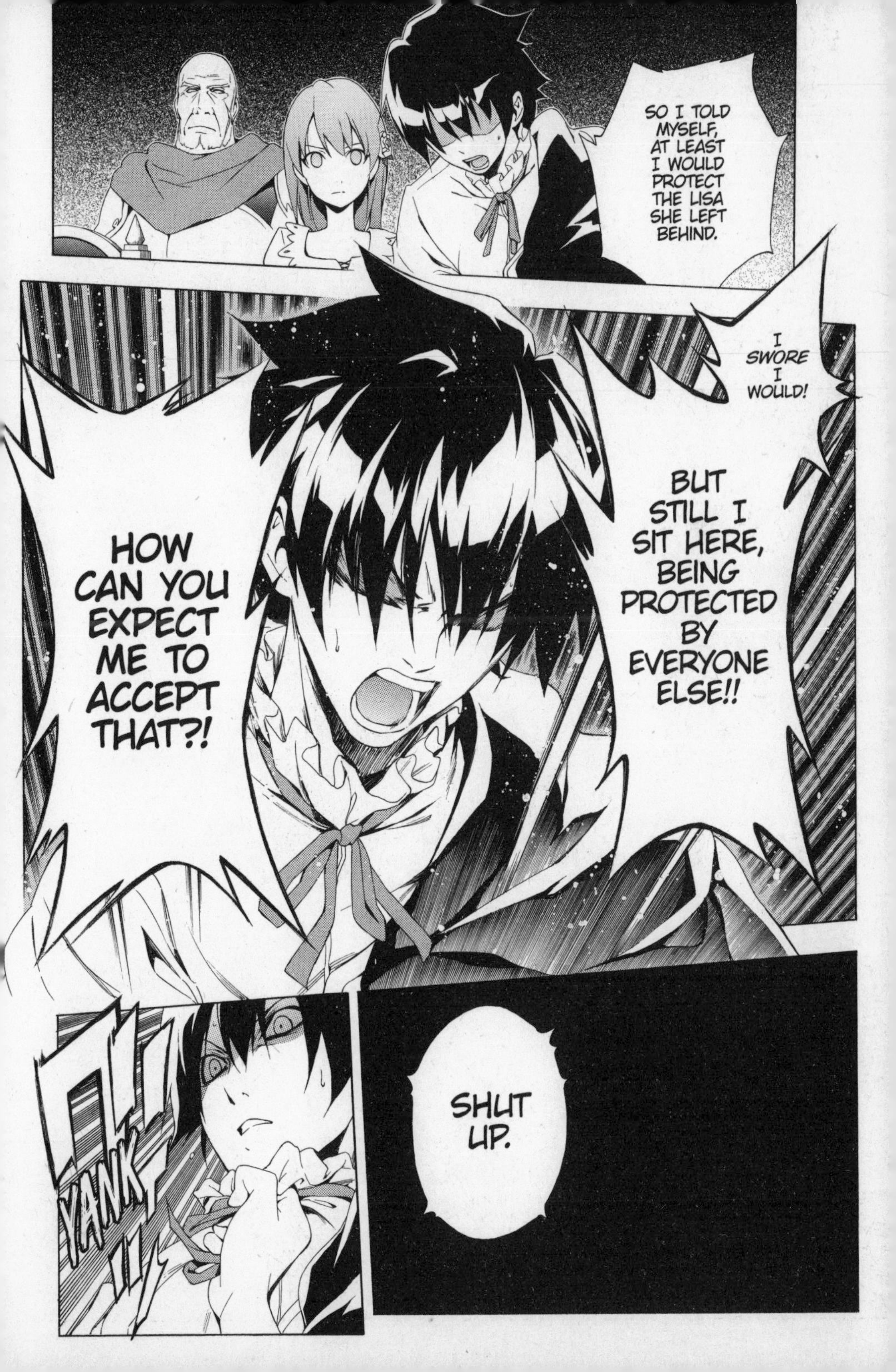
SO I TOLD MYSELF, AT LEAST I WOULD PROTECT THE LISA SHE LEFT BEHIND.
I SWORE I WOULD!
BUT STILL I SIT HERE, BEING PROTECTED BY EVERYONE ELSE!!
HOW CAN YOU EXPECT ME TO ACCEPT THAT?!
SHUT UP.
YANK

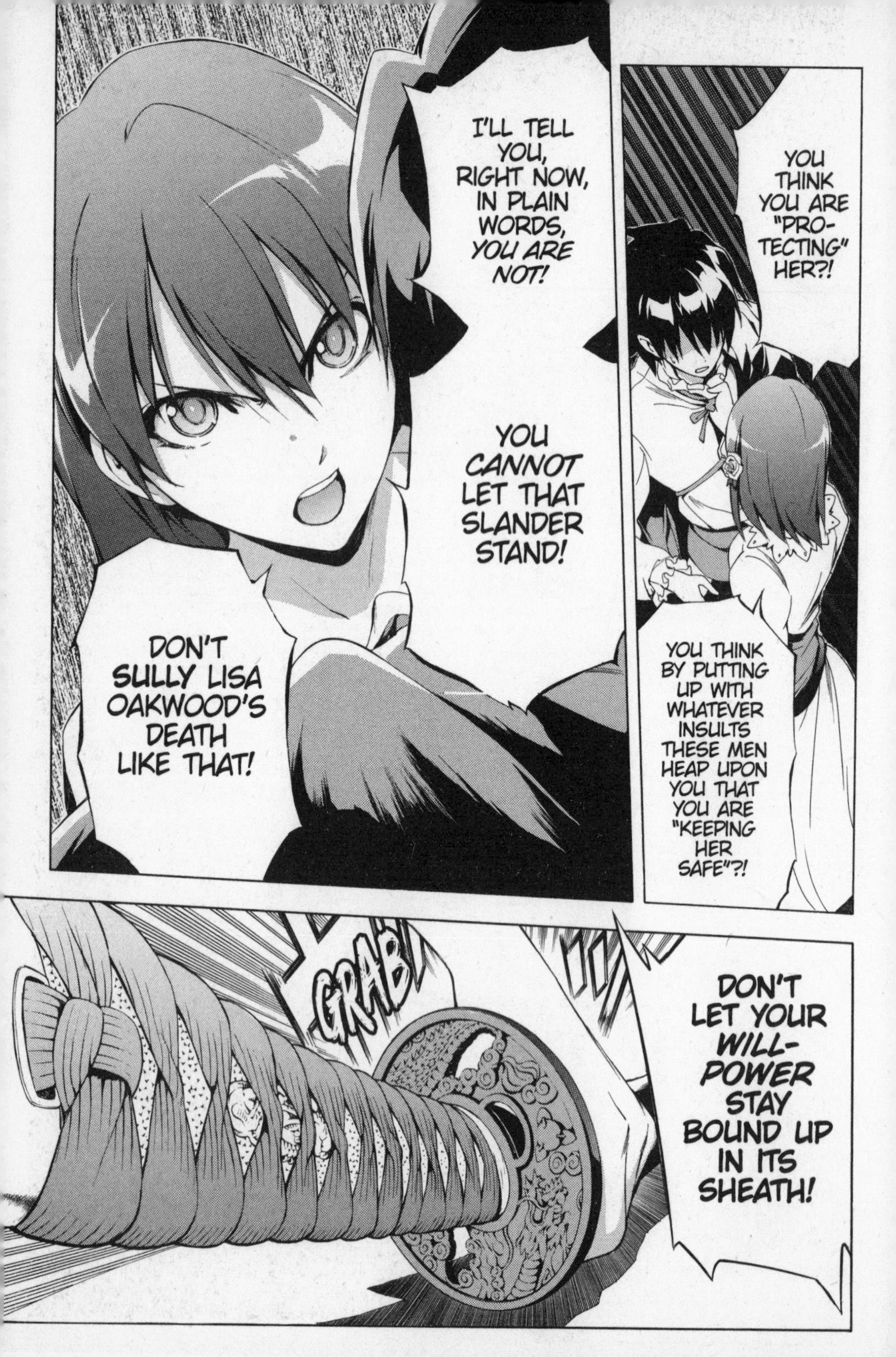
YOU THINK YOU ARE "PRO-TECTING" HER?!
YOU THINK BY PUTTING UP WITH WHATEVER INSULTS THESE MEN HEAP UPON YOU THAT YOU ARE "KEEPING HER SAFE"?!
I'LL TELL YOU, RIGHT NOW, IN PLAIN WORDS, *YOU ARE NOT!*
YOU *CANNOT* LET THAT SLANDER STAND!
DON'T SULLY LISA OAKWOOD'S DEATH LIKE THAT!
DON'T LET YOUR *WILL-POWER* STAY BOUND UP IN ITS SHEATH!
GRAB

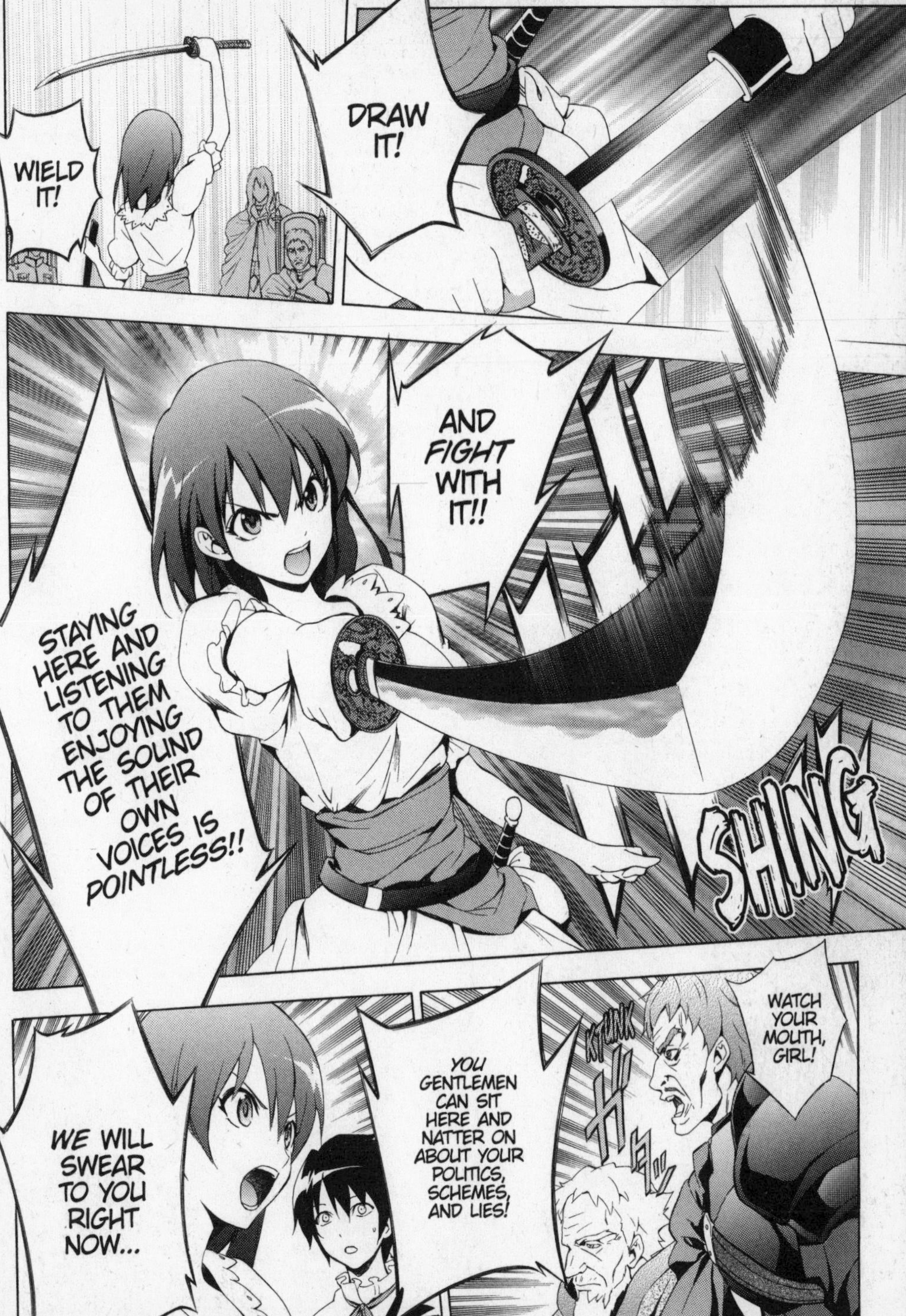
DRAW IT!
WIELD IT!
AND FIGHT WITH IT!!
SHING
STAYING HERE AND LISTENING TO THEM ENJOYING THE SOUND OF THEIR OWN VOICES IS POINTLESS!!
WATCH YOUR MOUTH, GIRL!
YOU GENTLEMEN CAN SIT HERE AND NATTER ON ABOUT YOUR POLITICS, SCHEMES, AND LIES!
WE WILL SWEAR TO YOU RIGHT NOW...

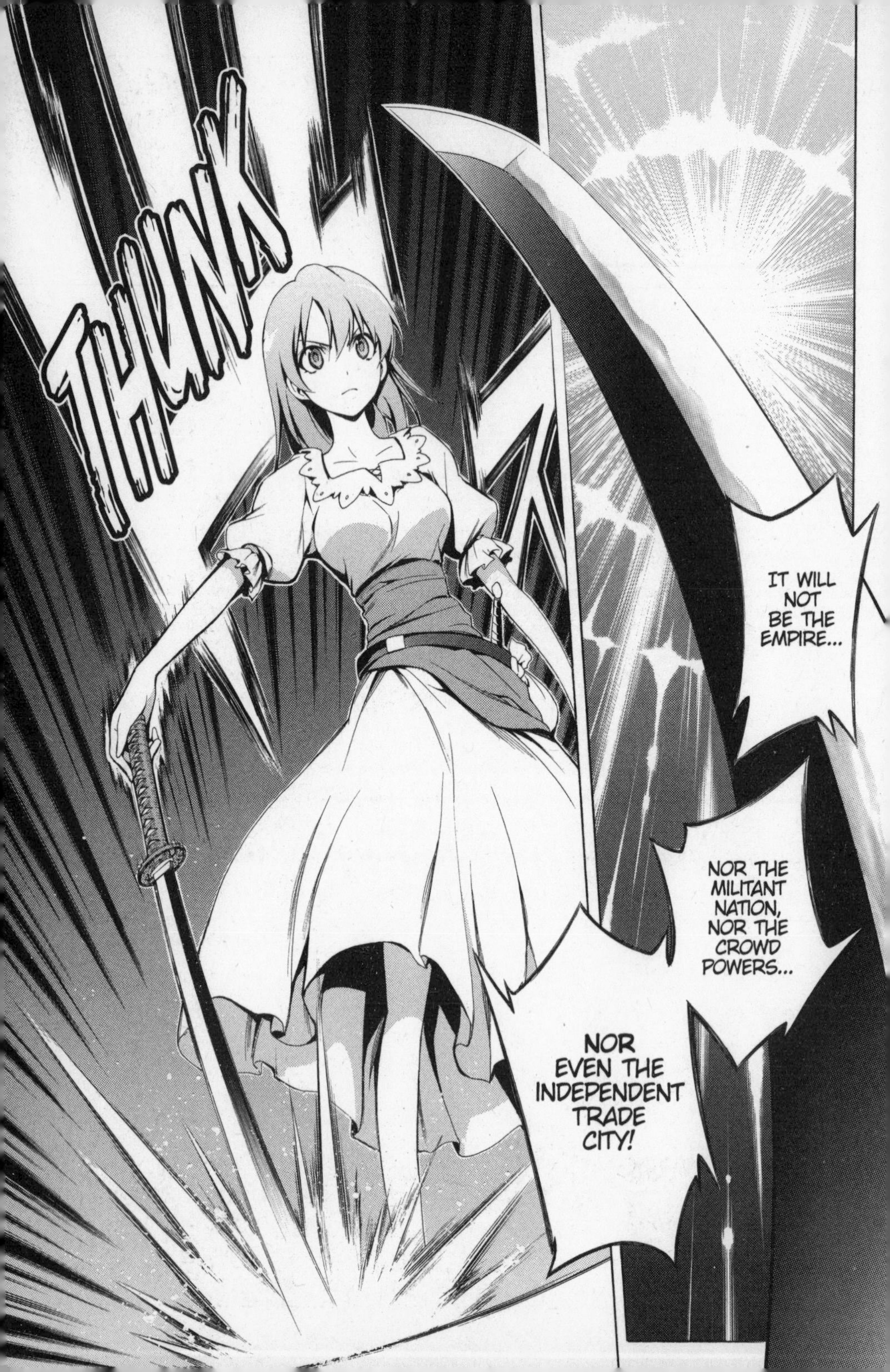
THUNK
IT WILL NOT BE THE EMPIRE...
NOR THE MILITANT NATION, NOR THE CROWD POWERS...
NOR EVEN THE INDEPENDENT TRADE CITY!

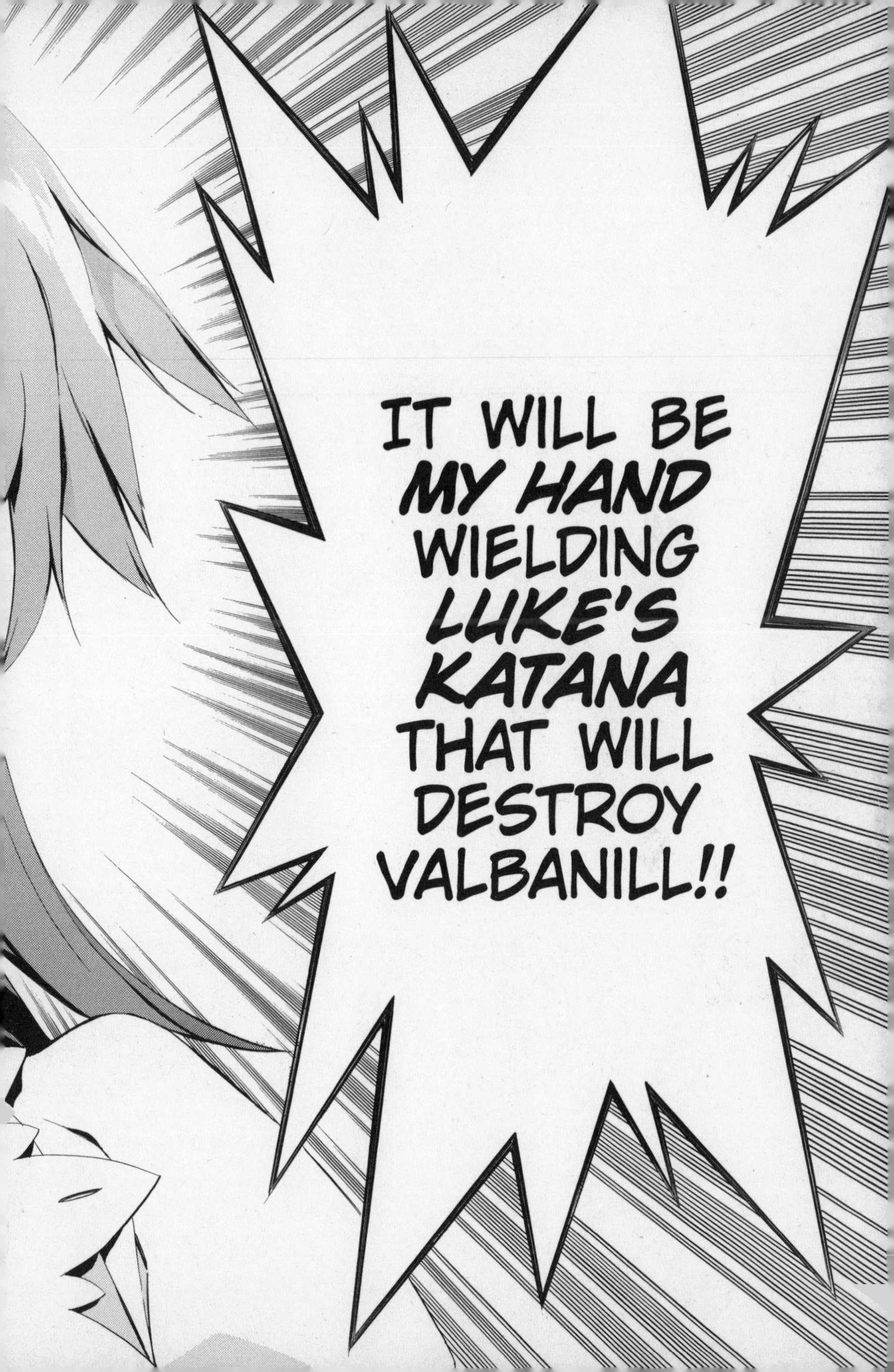
IT WILL BE MY HAND WIELDING LUKE'S KATANA THAT WILL DESTROY VALBANILL!!

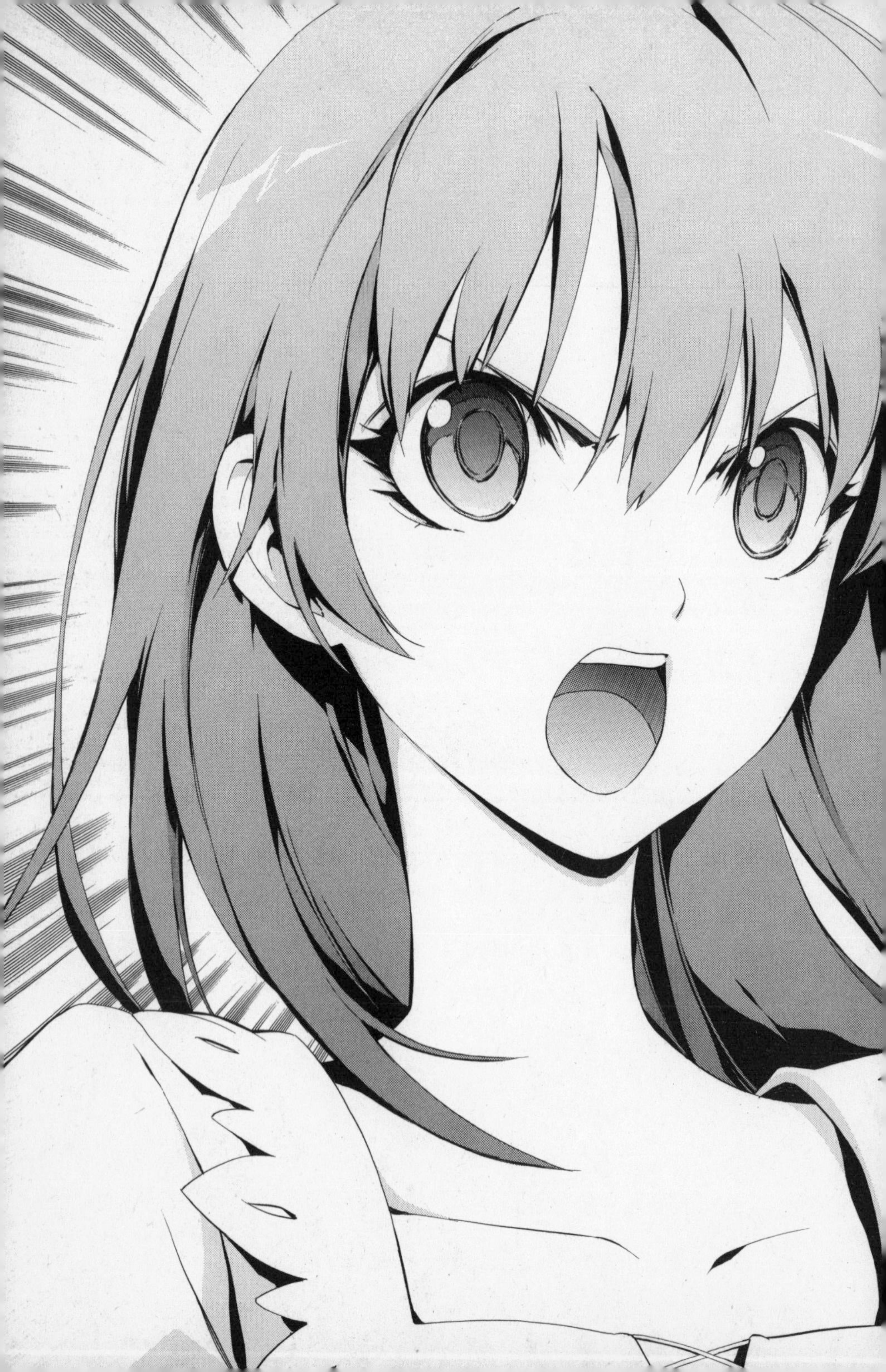

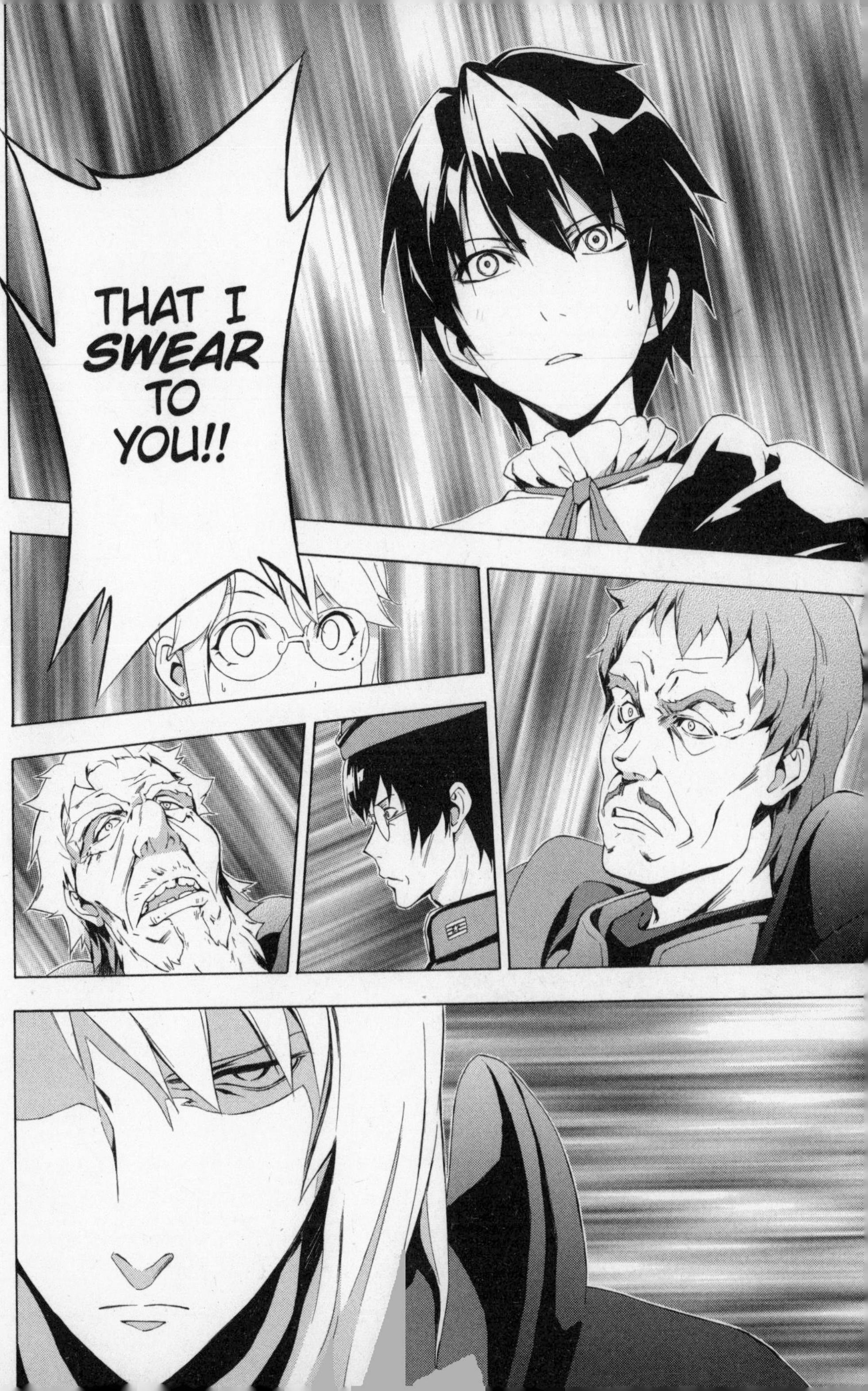
THAT I SWEAR TO YOU!!

✳ Lisa Oakwood ✳

アトリエ
工房リーザ
atelier Liza BRANCH OFFICE III

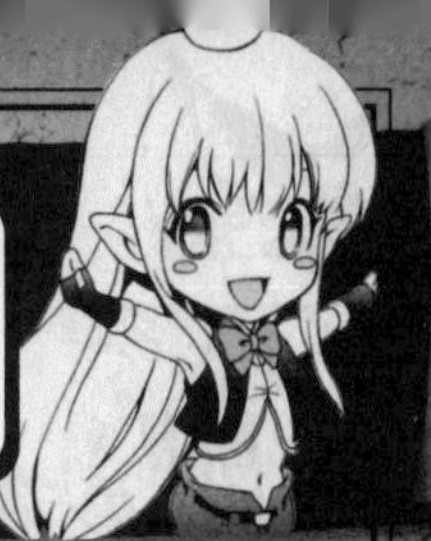
Oooh!♥
Can't you just feel the love in each of these pieces?

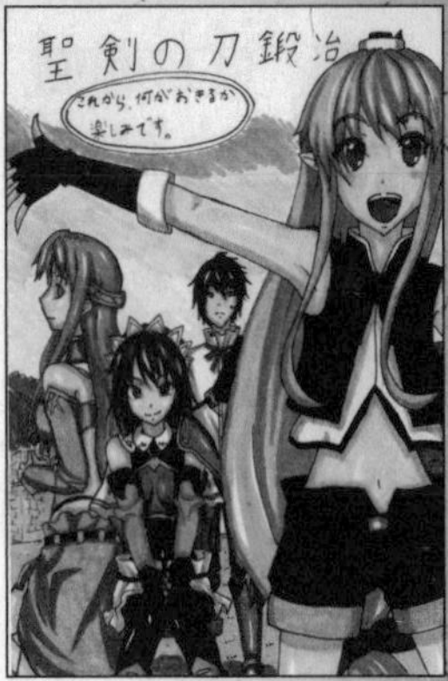
聖剣の刀鍛冶
これから、何がおきるか楽しみです。

↑ Yamaguchi, Shonen Tensai

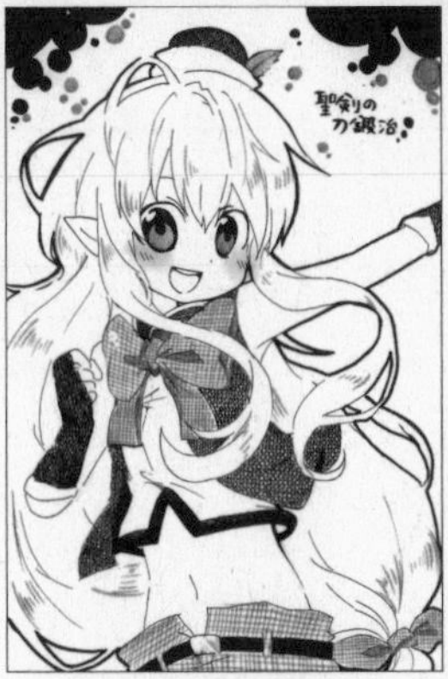
聖剣の刀鍛冶

↑ Osaka, Yu Shuta

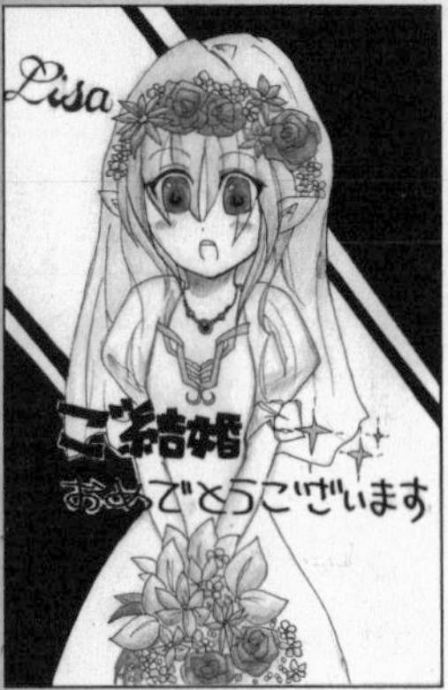
Lisa
ご結婚
おめでとうございます

↑ Aichi, Ito Kanji

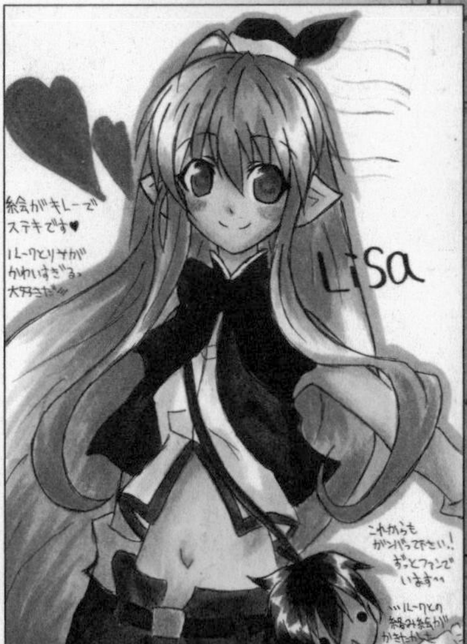
絵がキレーでステキです♥
ルークとリサがかわいすぎる。
Lisa
これからもガンバって下さい!
ずっとファンでいます。

↑ Chiba, Shuya Himesora

Aichi, K.K.→

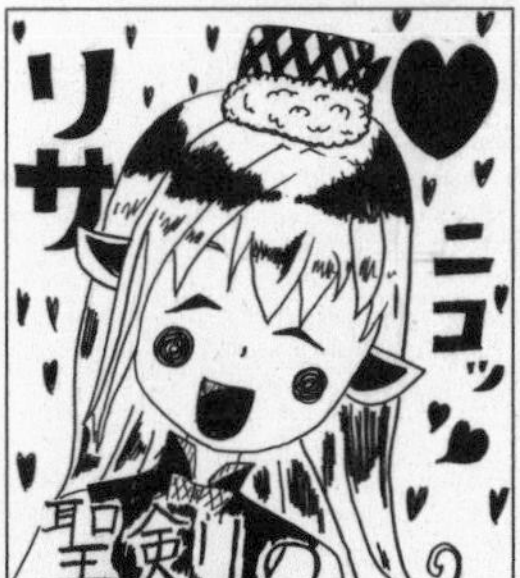
リサ
ニコッ
聖剣の
刀鍛冶
ブラックスミス

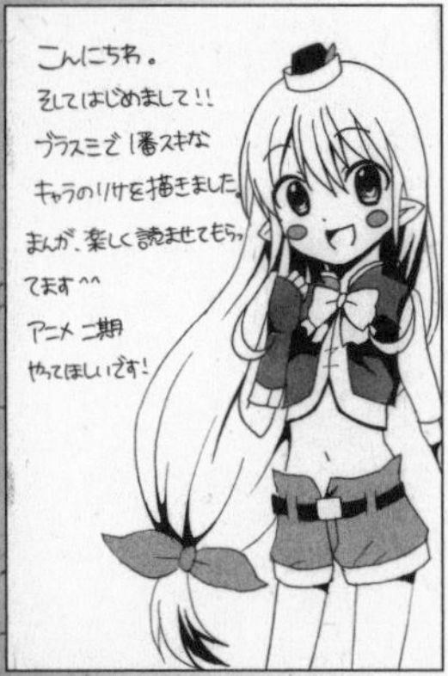
こんにちわ。
そしてはじめまして!!
ブラスミで1番スキな
キャラのリサを描きました。
まんが、楽しく読ませてもらってます^^
アニメ二期
やってほしいです!

↑ Miyagi, Kotoko Tanimura

Aichi, Yakitori→

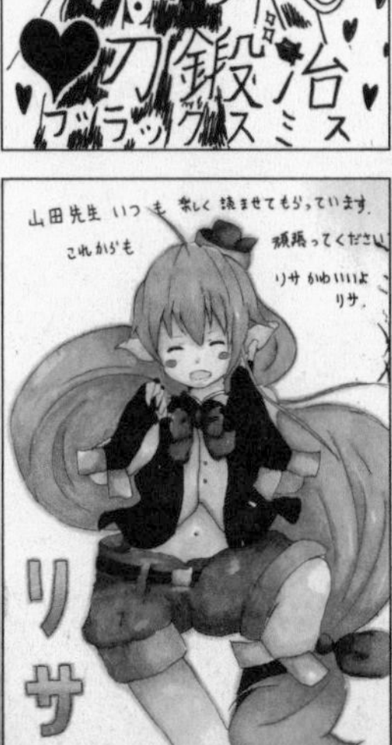
山田先生 いつも 楽しく 読ませてもらっています。
これからも 頑張ってください
リサかわいいよ リサ。
リサ

Wow, everybody's so good! I hope I can be as good as you all when I grow up!

cred Blacksmith

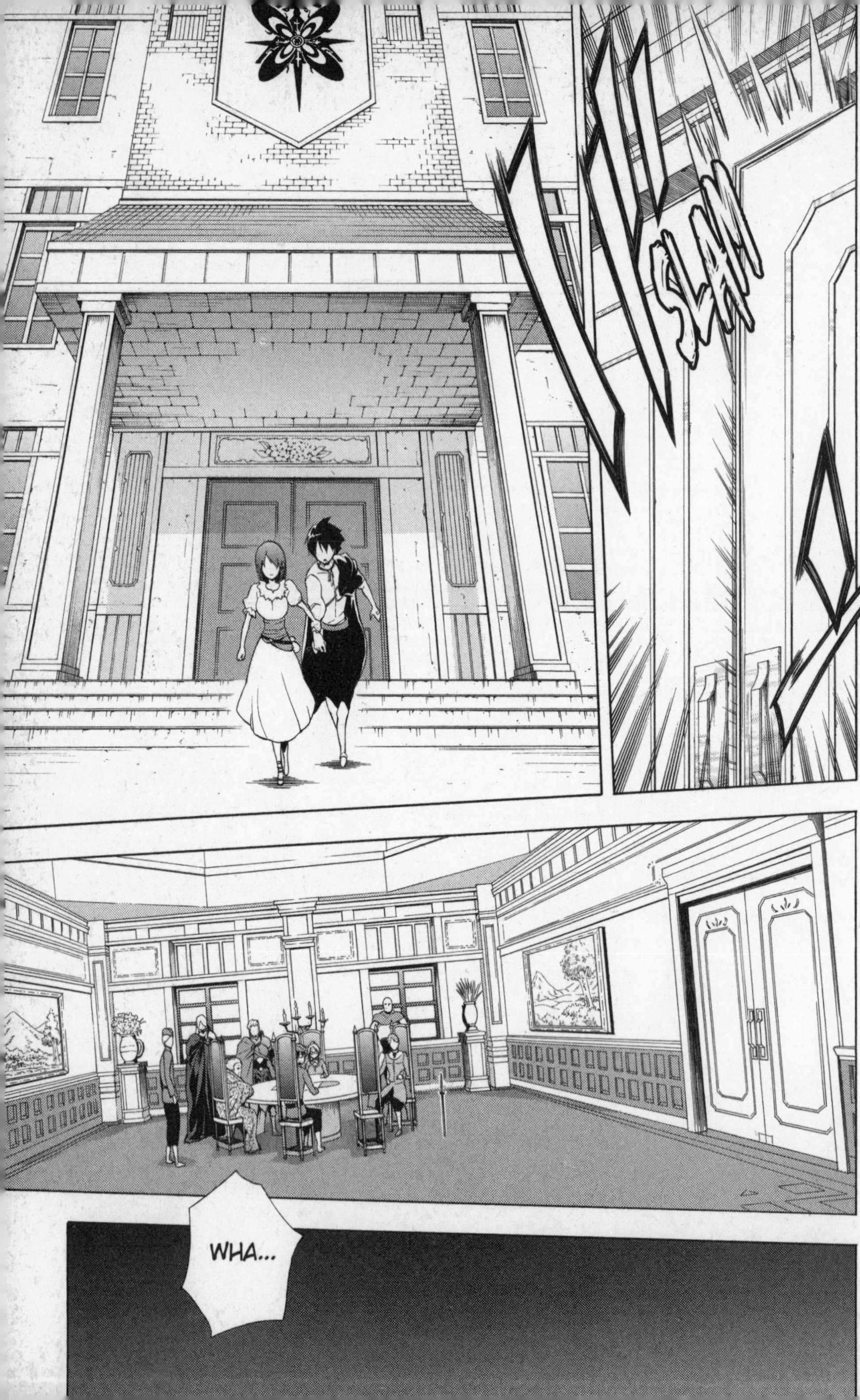
SLAM
WHA...

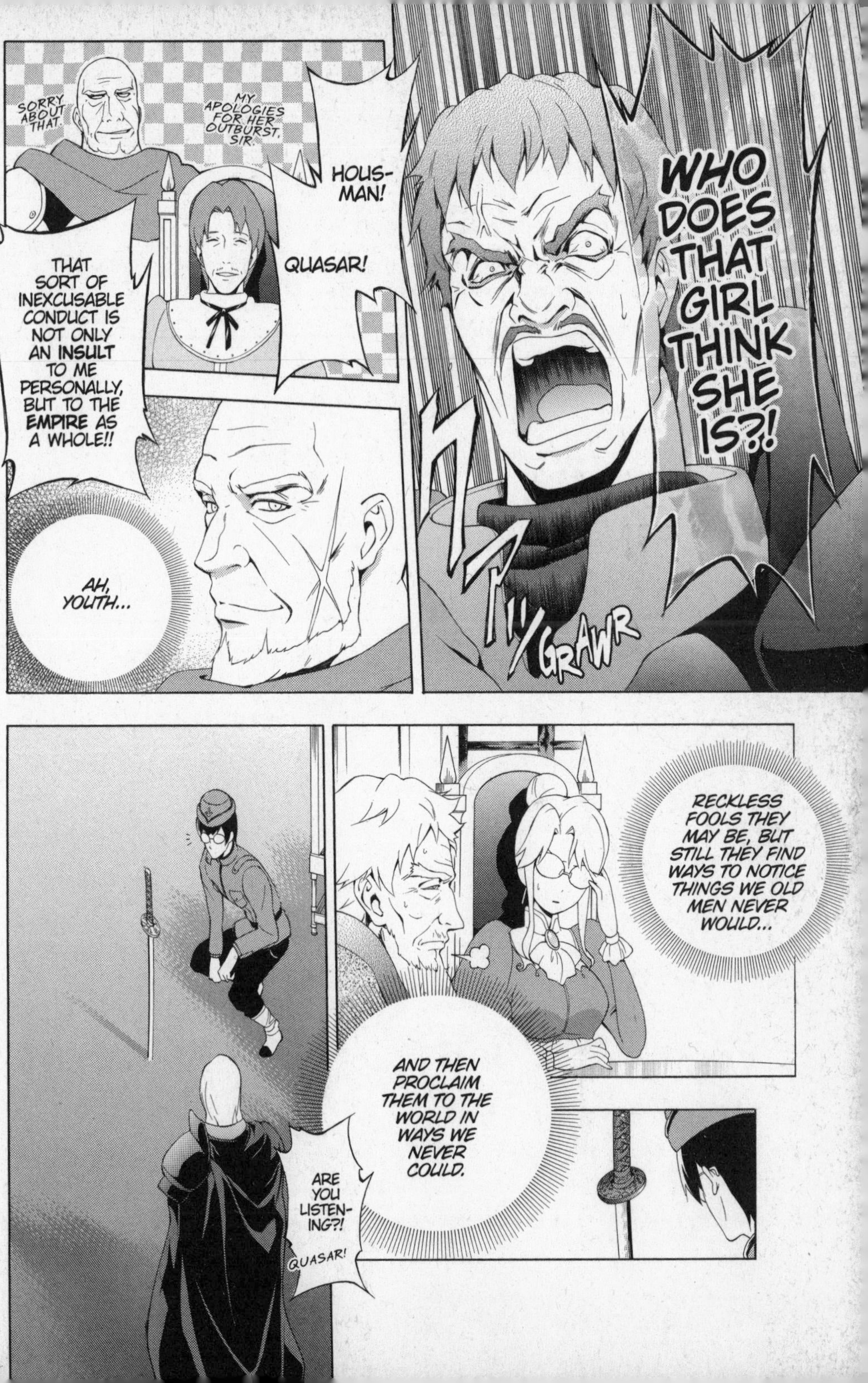
WHO DOES THAT GIRL THINK SHE IS?!
GRAWR
HOUS-MAN!
QUASAR!
MY APOLOGIES FOR HER OUTBURST, SIR.
SORRY ABOUT THAT.
THAT SORT OF INEXCUSABLE CONDUCT IS NOT ONLY AN INSULT TO ME PERSONALLY, BUT TO THE EMPIRE AS A WHOLE!!
AH, YOUTH...
RECKLESS FOOLS THEY MAY BE, BUT STILL THEY FIND WAYS TO NOTICE THINGS WE OLD MEN NEVER WOULD...
AND THEN PROCLAIM THEM TO THE WORLD IN WAYS WE NEVER COULD.
ARE YOU LISTEN-ING?!
QUASAR!

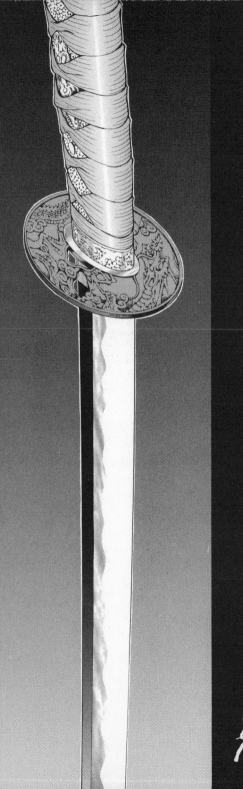

Chapter 16 **Blacksmith** (Part 4)

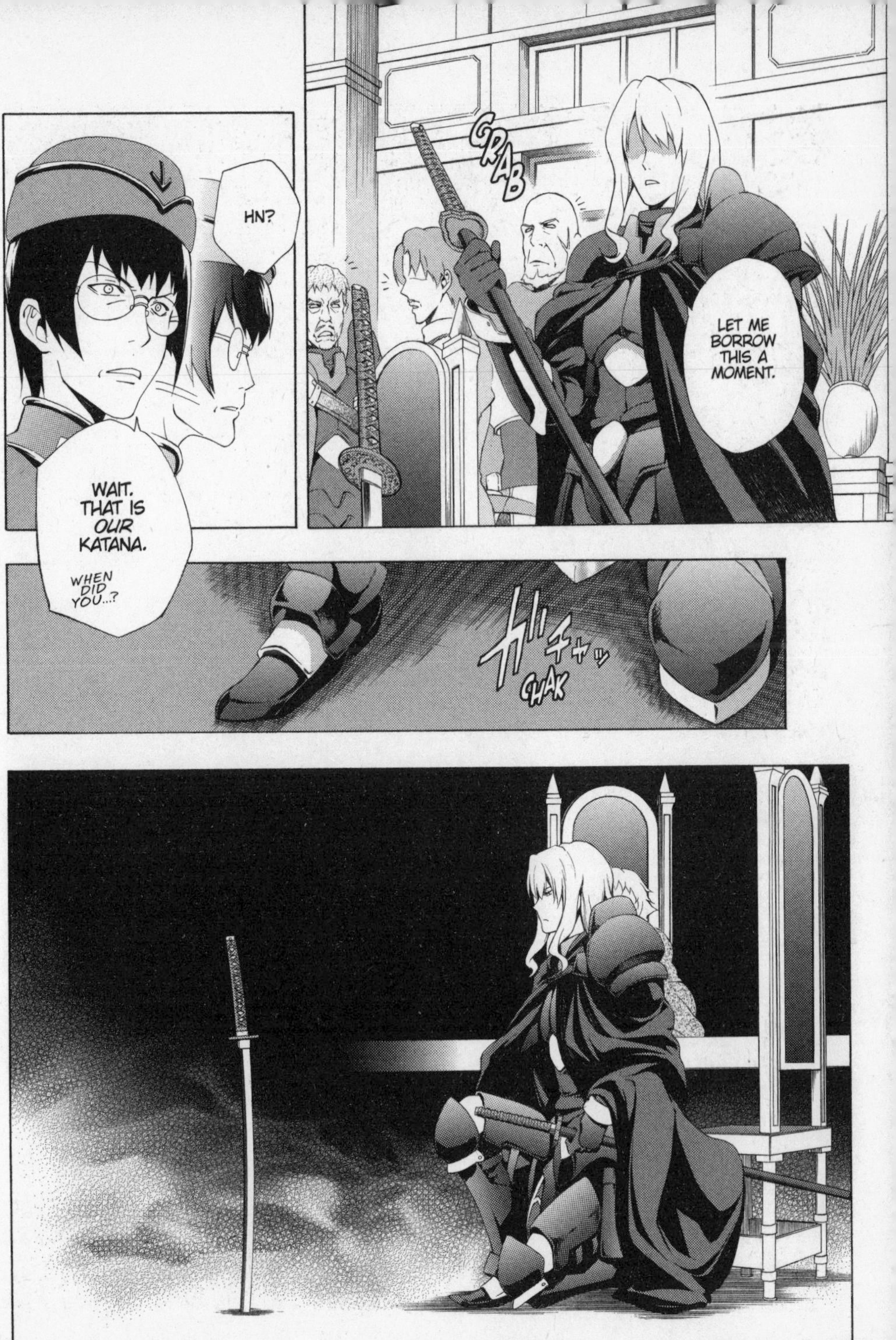
GRAB
LET ME BORROW THIS A MOMENT.
HN?
WAIT. THAT IS *OUR* KATANA.
WHEN DID YOU...?
カチャッ
CHAK

AN IAI* STANCE...?!

*Iai-do is a Japanese martial art concerned with perfecting the movements of drawing a sword, striking, then returning the blade to the sheath.

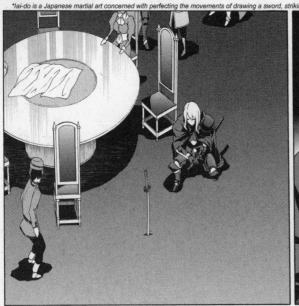

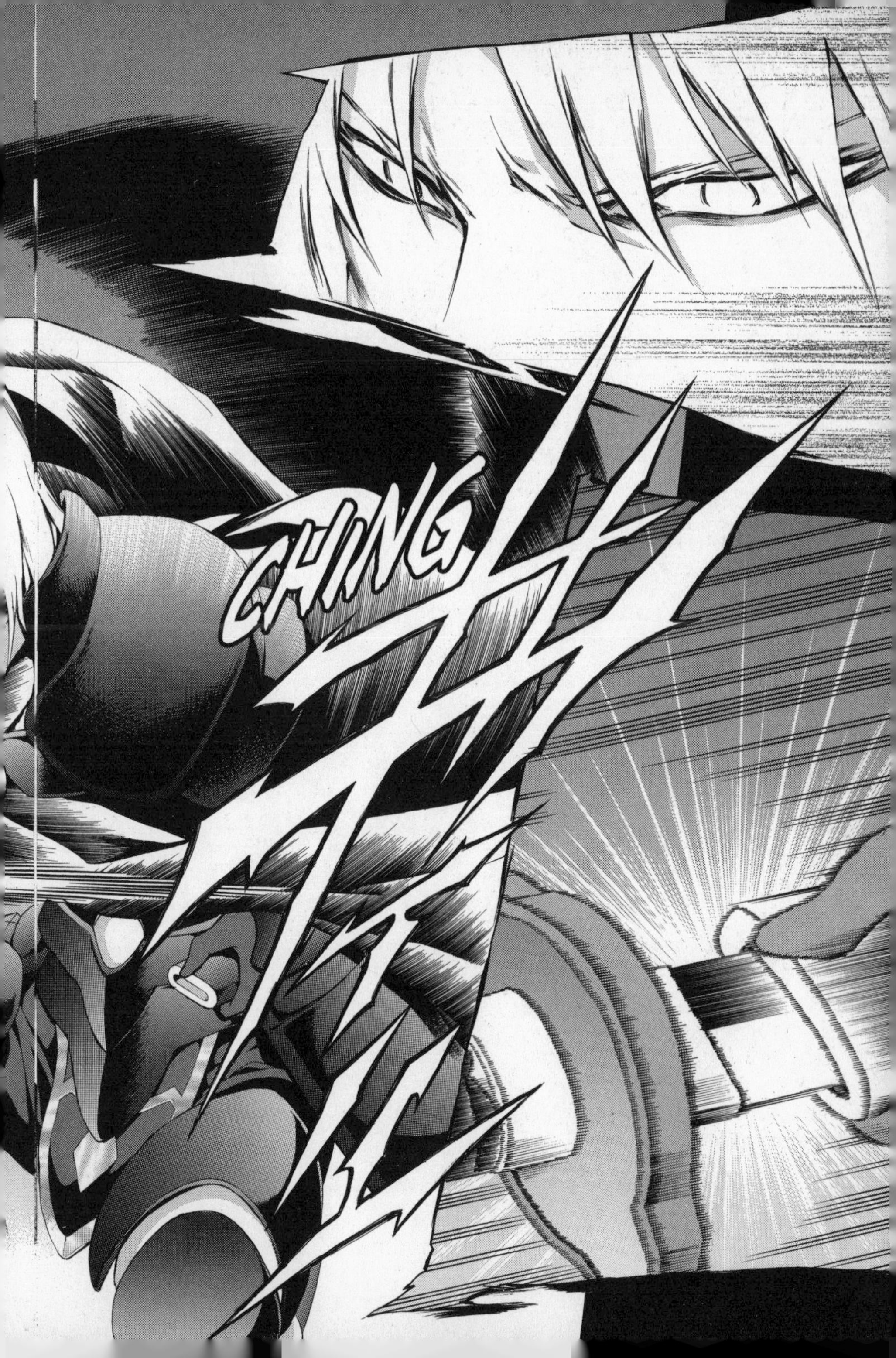
CHING

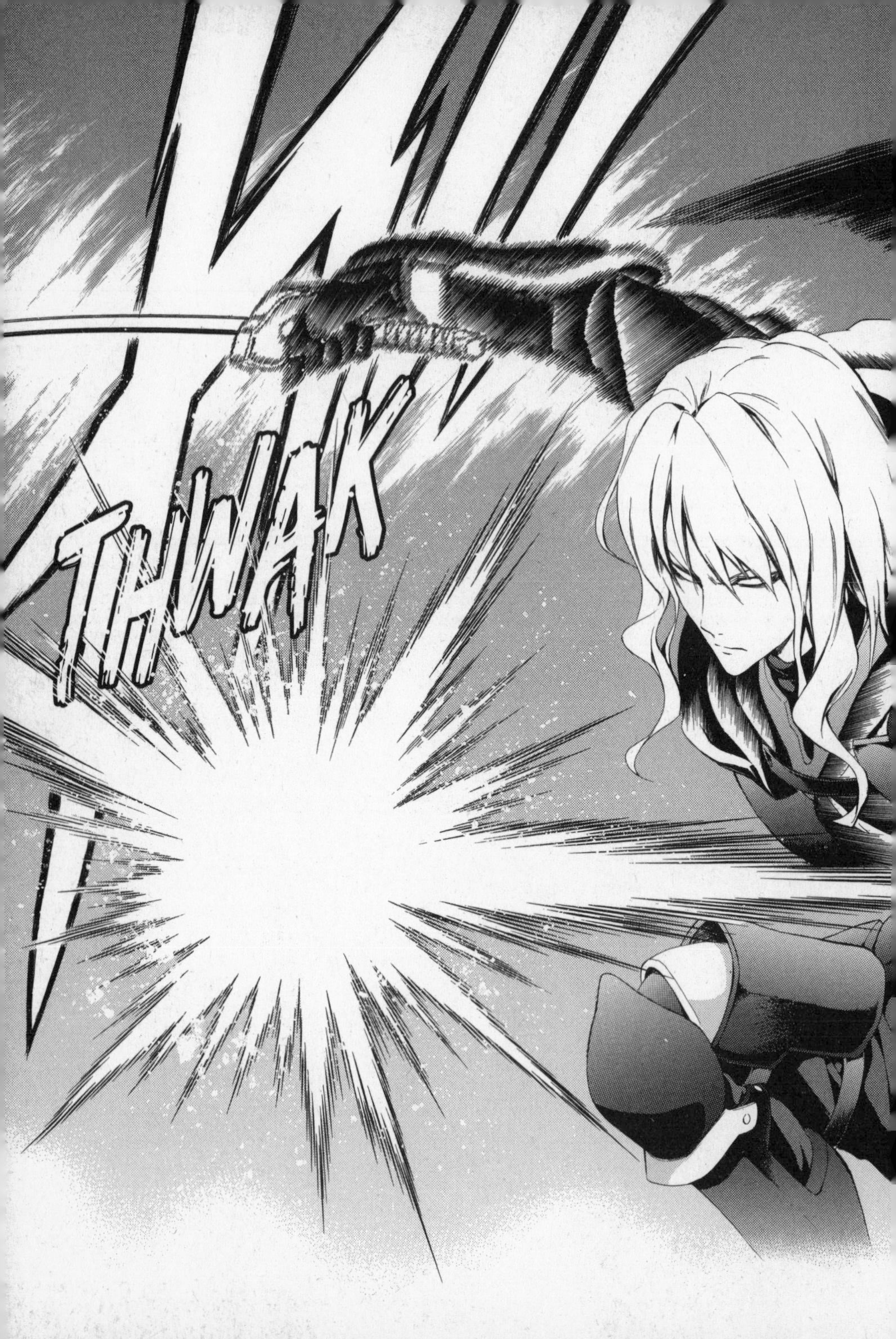
THWAK

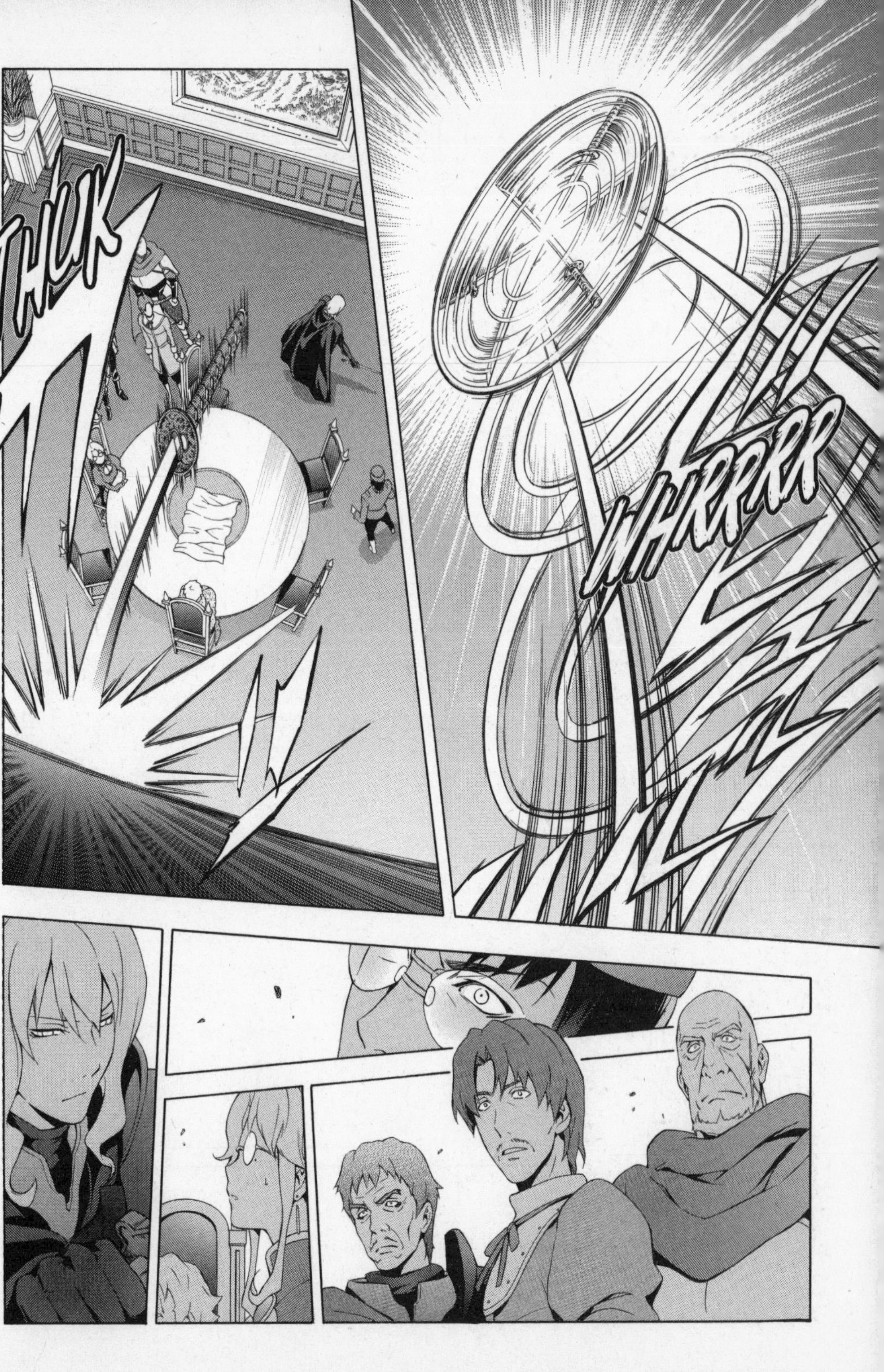
WHIRRRR
THUK

YOU THERE! HOW DARE YOU TREAT OUR SACRED BLADE AS--

HEY!

THUMP

HMPH.

TOSS

WHAT?!

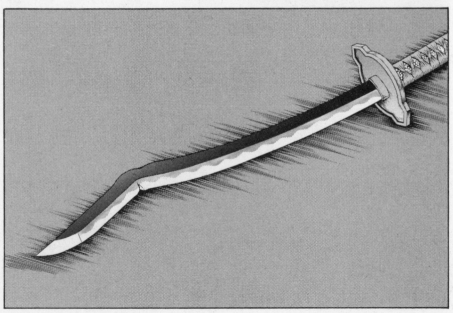

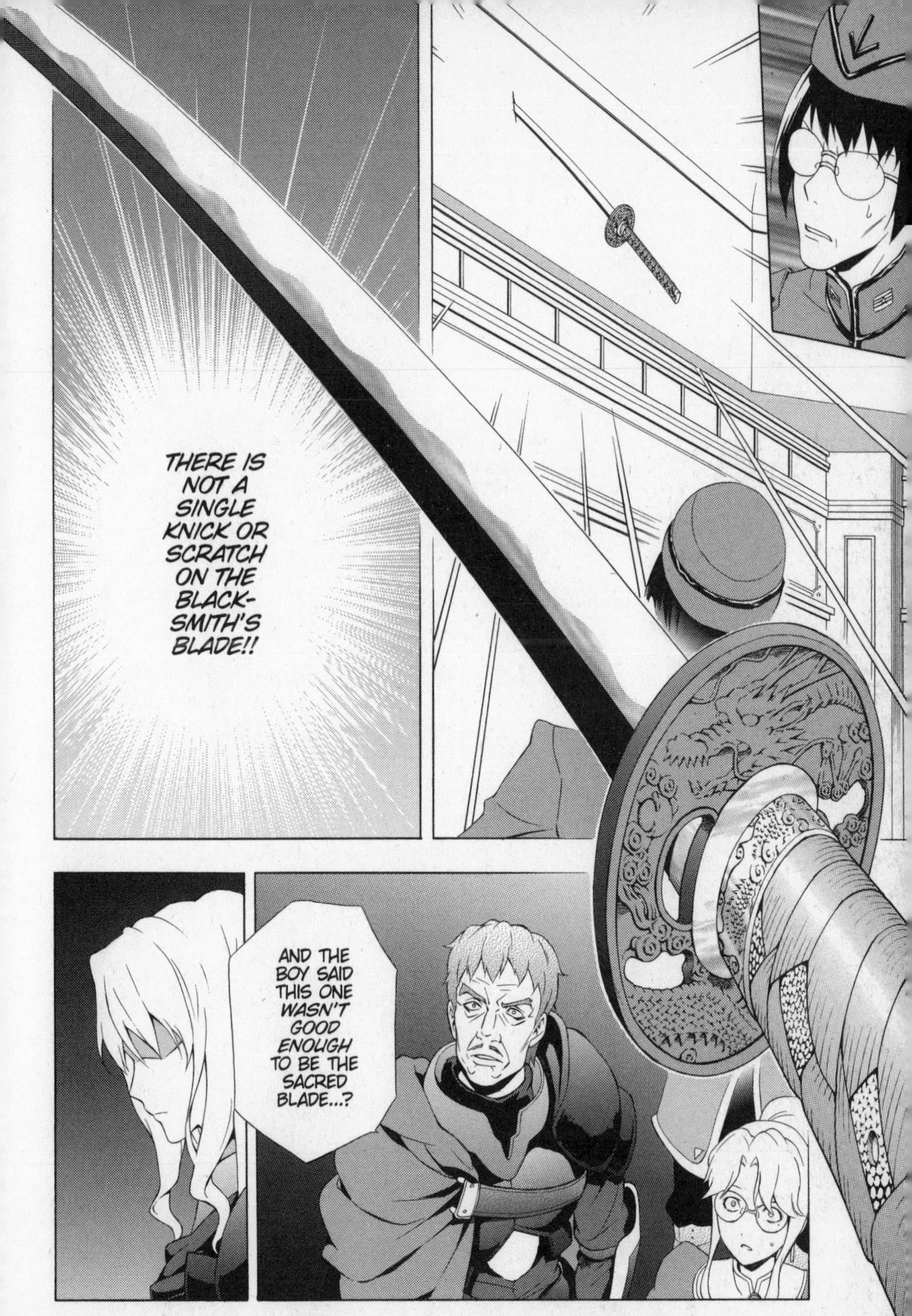
THERE IS NOT A SINGLE KNICK OR SCRATCH ON THE BLACK-SMITH'S BLADE!!
AND THE BOY SAID THIS ONE WASN'T GOOD ENOUGH TO BE THE SACRED BLADE...?

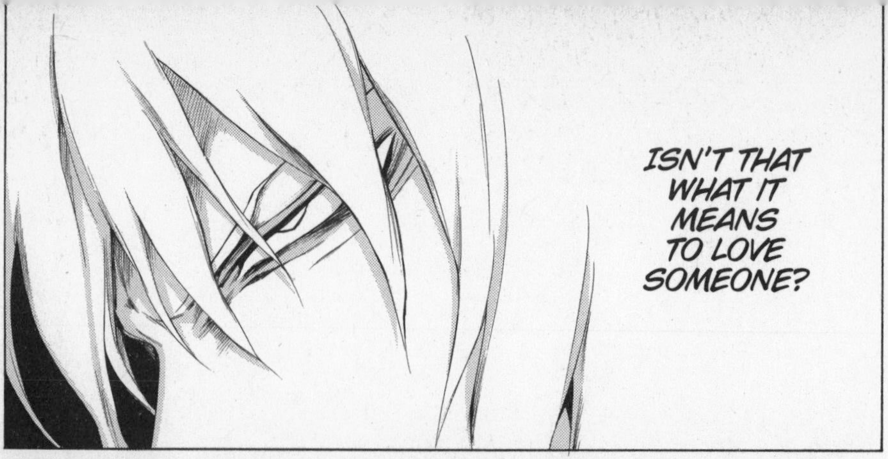
ISN'T THAT WHAT IT MEANS TO LOVE SOMEONE?

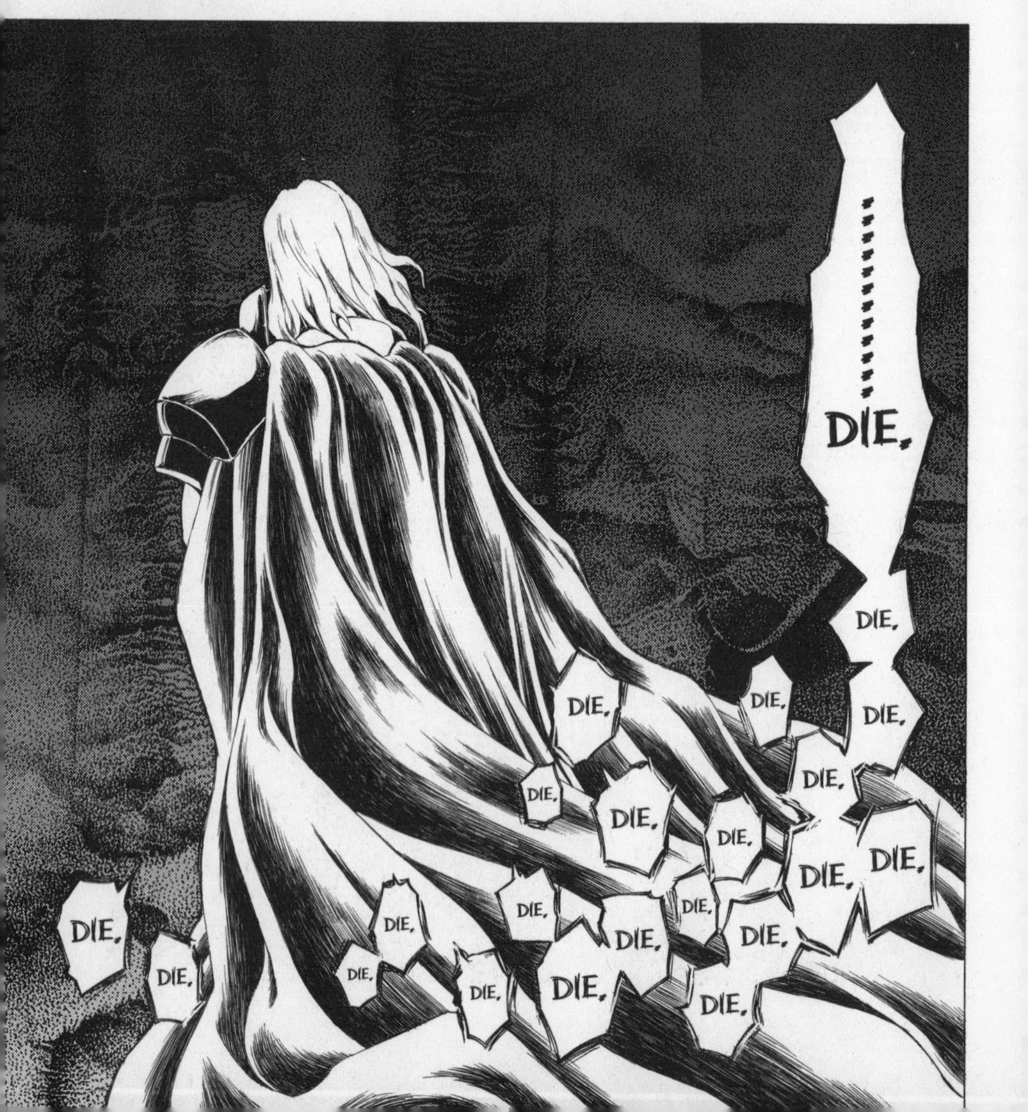
....
DIE.
DIE.
DIE.
DIE.
DIE.
DIE.
DIE.
DIE.
DIE.
DIE.
DIE.
DIE.
DIE.
DIE.
DIE.
DIE.
DIE.
DIE.
DIE.
DIE.
DIE.
DIE.

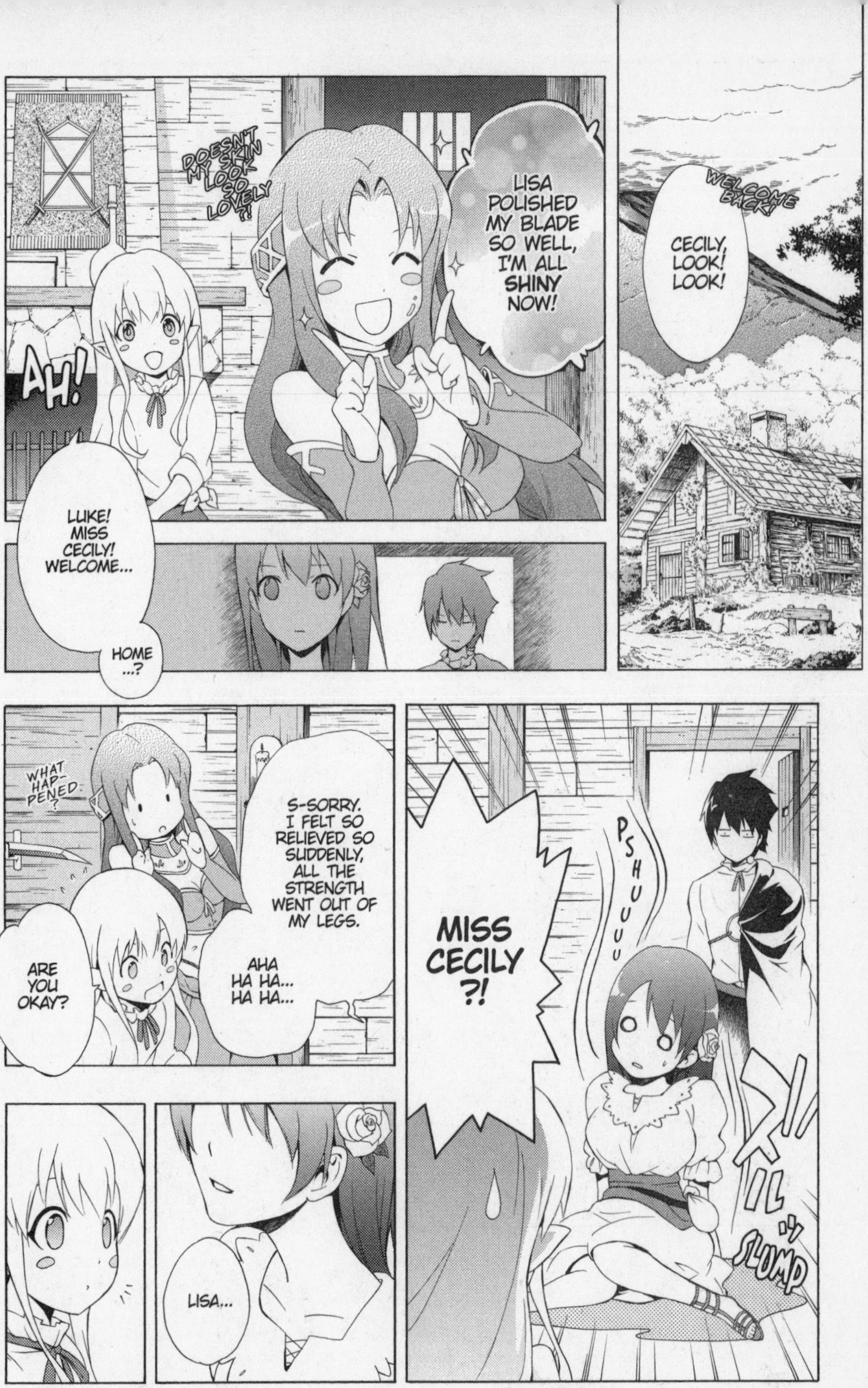
WELCOME BACK!
CECILY, LOOK! LOOK!
LISA POLISHED MY BLADE SO WELL, I'M ALL SHINY NOW!
DOESN'T MY SKIN LOOK SO LOVELY?!
AH!
LUKE! MISS CECILY! WELCOME...
HOME ...?
MISS CECILY ?!
PSHUUUUU
SLUMP
WHAT HAPPENED?
S-SORRY. I FELT SO RELIEVED SO SUDDENLY, ALL THE STRENGTH WENT OUT OF MY LEGS.
AHA HA HA... HA HA...
ARE YOU OKAY?
LISA...

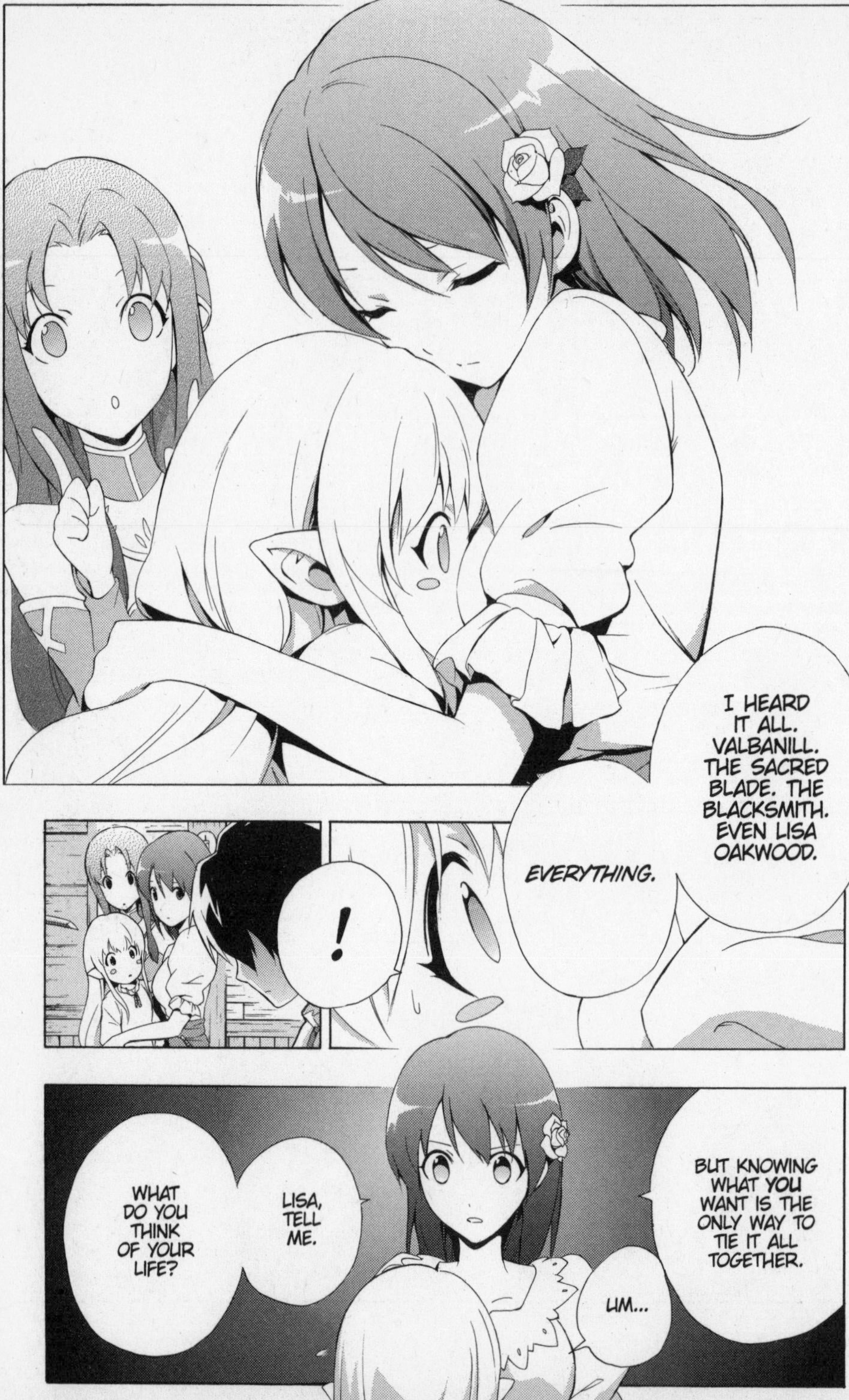
I HEARD IT ALL. VALBANILL. THE SACRED BLADE. THE BLACKSMITH. EVEN LISA OAKWOOD.
EVERYTHING.
!
BUT KNOWING WHAT YOU WANT IS THE ONLY WAY TO TIE IT ALL TOGETHER.
UM...
LISA, TELL ME.
WHAT DO YOU THINK OF YOUR LIFE?

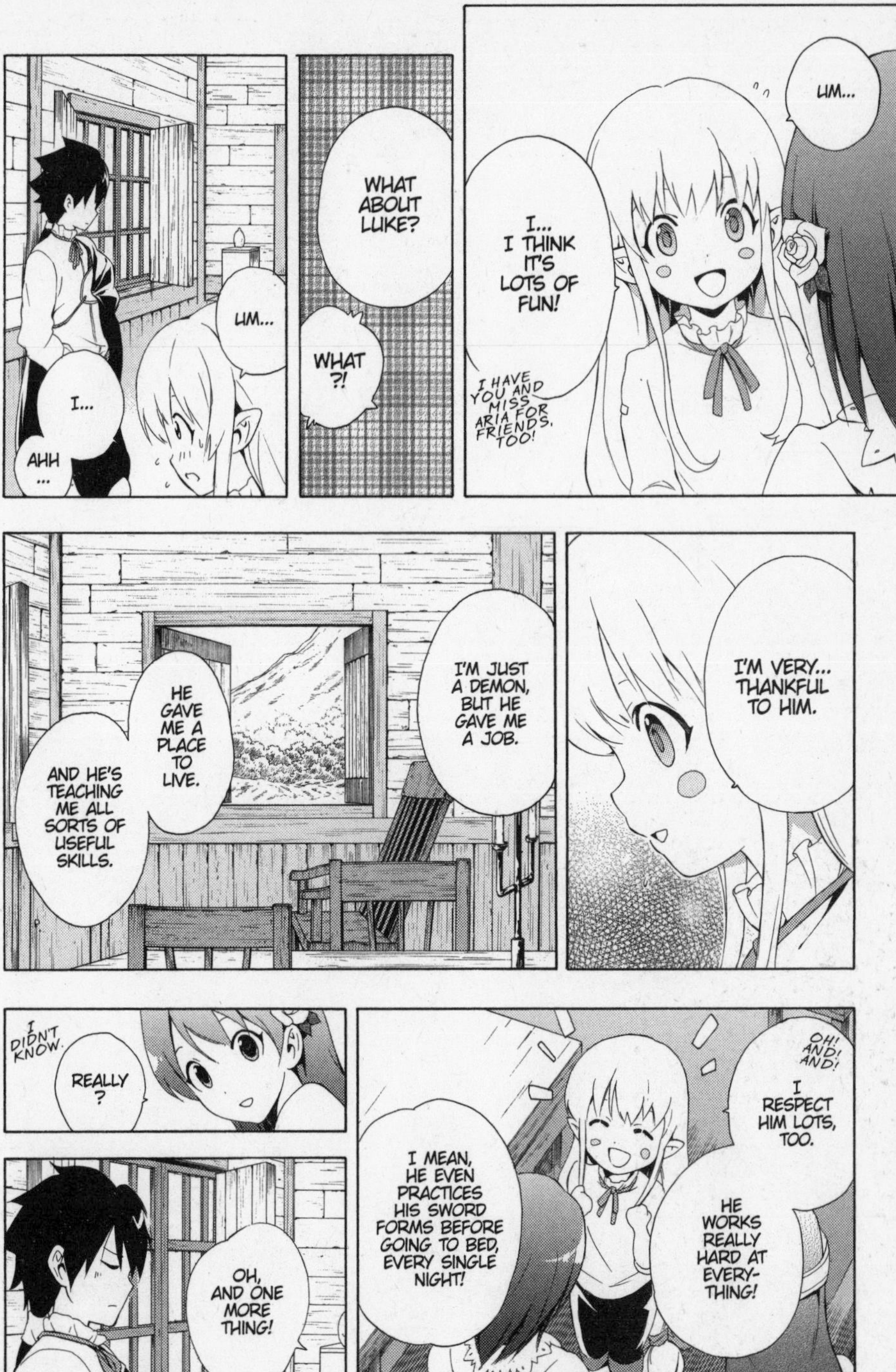
UM...
I... I THINK IT'S LOTS OF FUN!
I HAVE YOU AND MISS ARIA FOR FRIENDS, TOO!
WHAT ABOUT LUKE?
WHAT ?!
UM...
I...
AHH ...
I'M VERY... THANKFUL TO HIM.
I'M JUST A DEMON, BUT HE GAVE ME A JOB.
HE GAVE ME A PLACE TO LIVE.
AND HE'S TEACHING ME ALL SORTS OF USEFUL SKILLS.
OH! AND! AND!
I RESPECT HIM LOTS, TOO.
HE WORKS REALLY HARD AT EVERY-THING!
I MEAN, HE EVEN PRACTICES HIS SWORD FORMS BEFORE GOING TO BED, EVERY SINGLE NIGHT!
REALLY ?
I DIDN'T KNOW.
OH, AND ONE MORE THING!

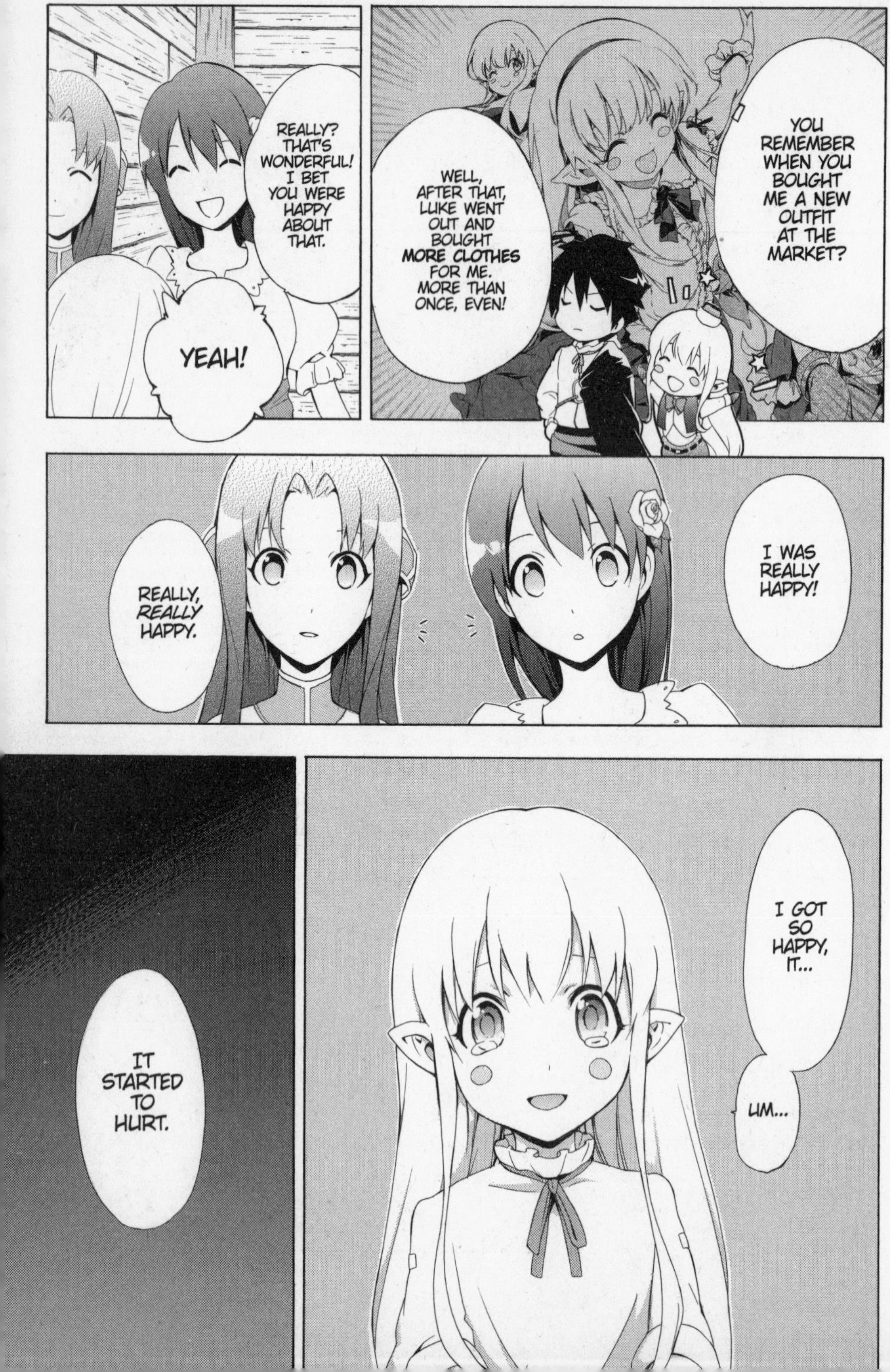
YOU REMEMBER WHEN YOU BOUGHT ME A NEW OUTFIT AT THE MARKET?
WELL, AFTER THAT, LUKE WENT OUT AND BOUGHT **MORE CLOTHES** FOR ME. MORE THAN ONCE, EVEN!
REALLY? THAT'S WONDERFUL! I BET YOU WERE HAPPY ABOUT THAT.
YEAH!
I WAS REALLY HAPPY!
REALLY, *REALLY* HAPPY.
I GOT SO HAPPY, IT...
UM...
IT STARTED TO HURT.

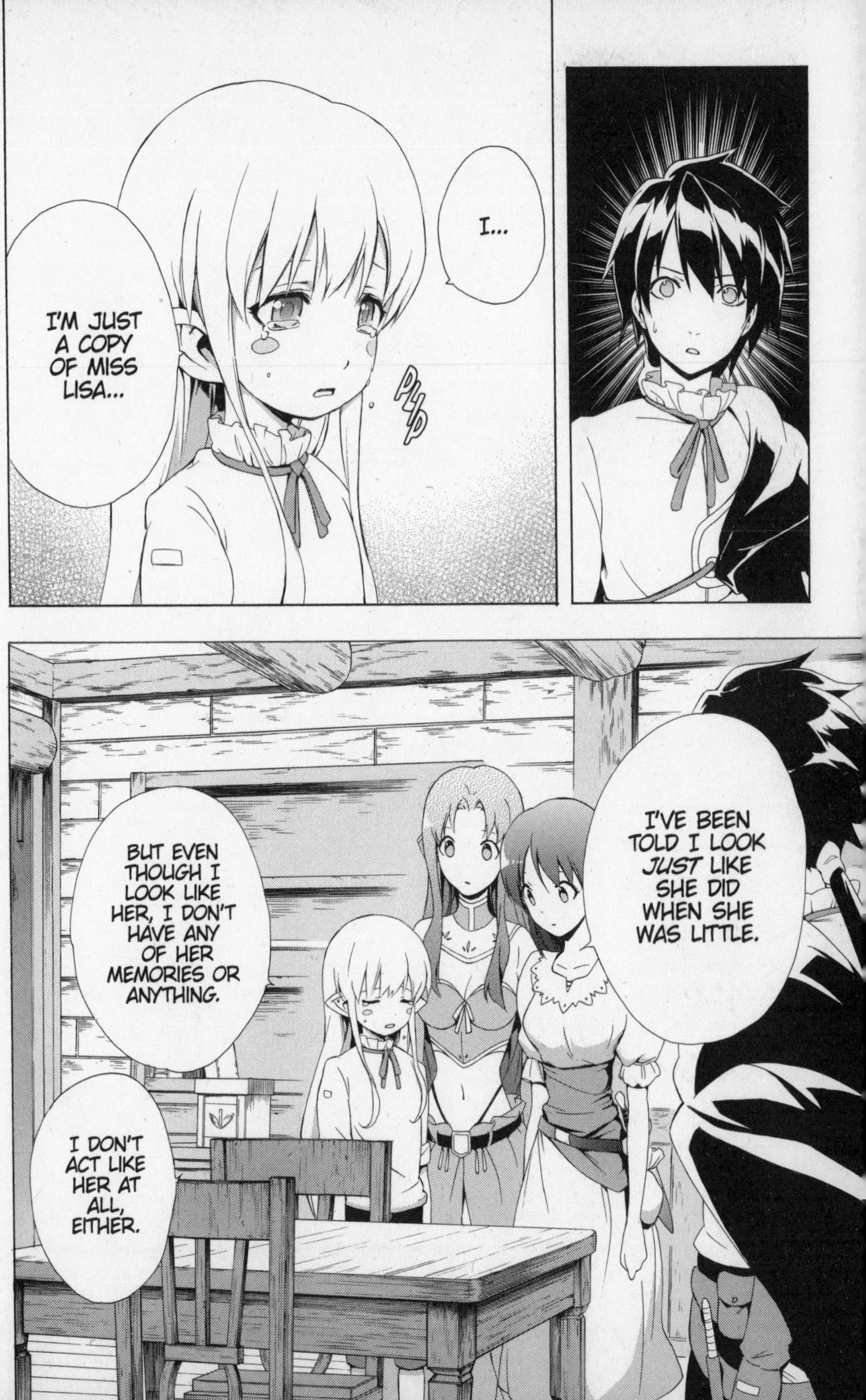
I...
I'M JUST A COPY OF MISS LISA...
PLIP
I'VE BEEN TOLD I LOOK *JUST* LIKE SHE DID WHEN SHE WAS LITTLE.
BUT EVEN THOUGH I LOOK LIKE HER, I DON'T HAVE ANY OF HER MEMORIES OR ANYTHING.
I DON'T ACT LIKE HER AT ALL, EITHER.

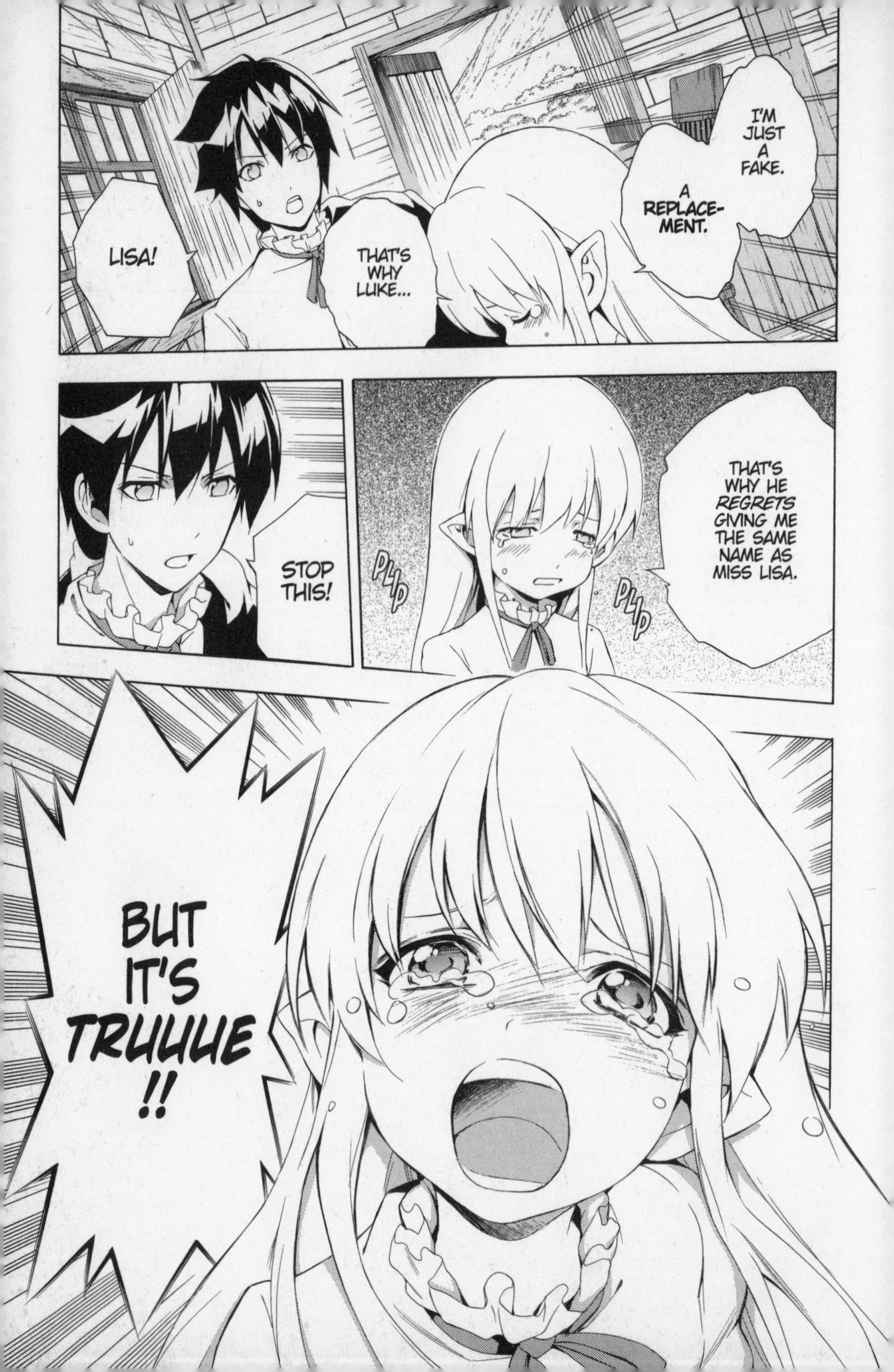
I'M JUST A FAKE.
A REPLACEMENT.
THAT'S WHY LUKE...
LISA!
THAT'S WHY HE REGRETS GIVING ME THE SAME NAME AS MISS LISA.
PLIP
PLIP
STOP THIS!
BUT IT'S TRUUUE!!

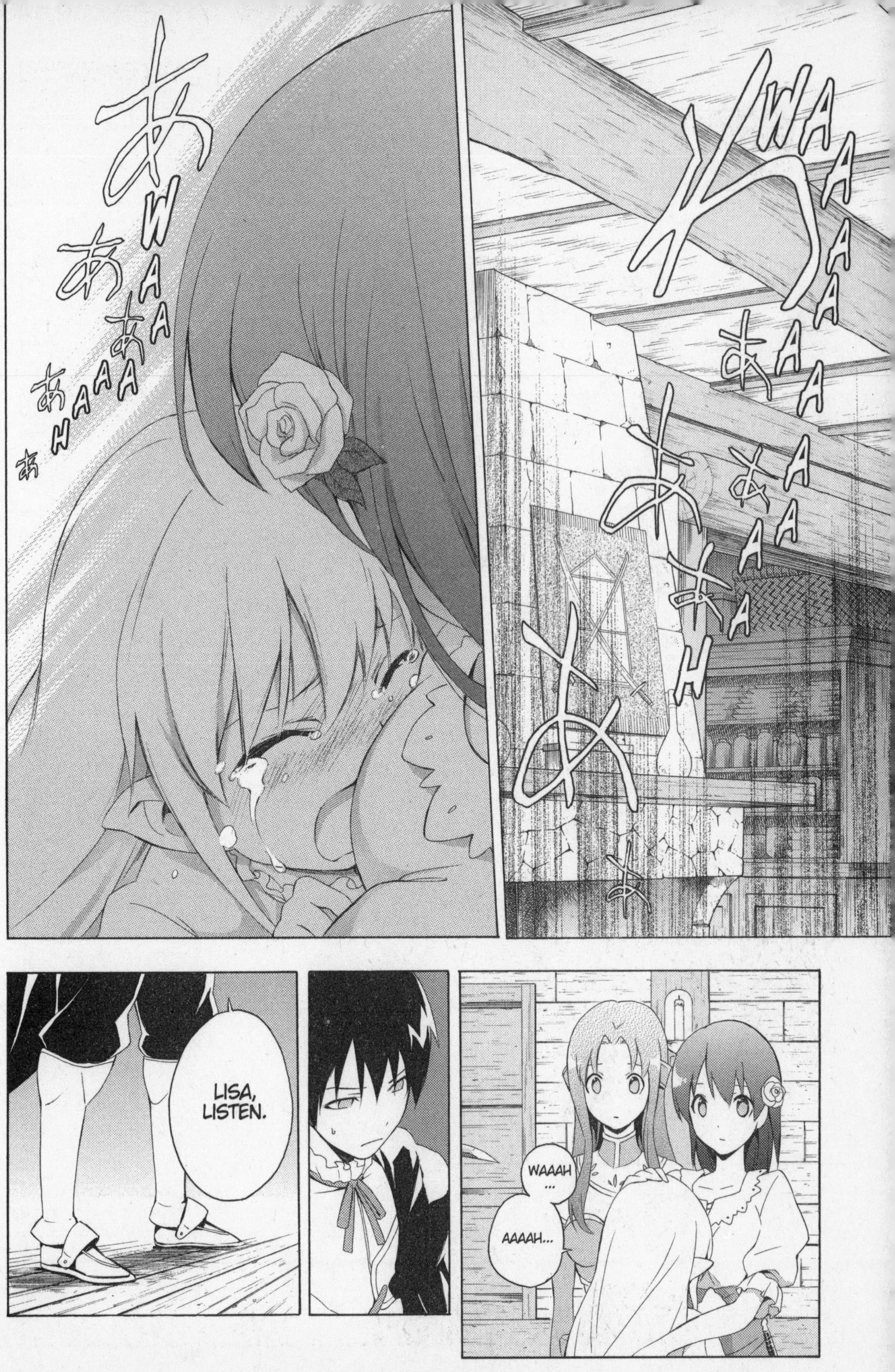
WAAAAAAAAAAAH
ああああ
WAAAAAAH
ああああ
WAAAH
...
AAAAH...
LISA, LISTEN.

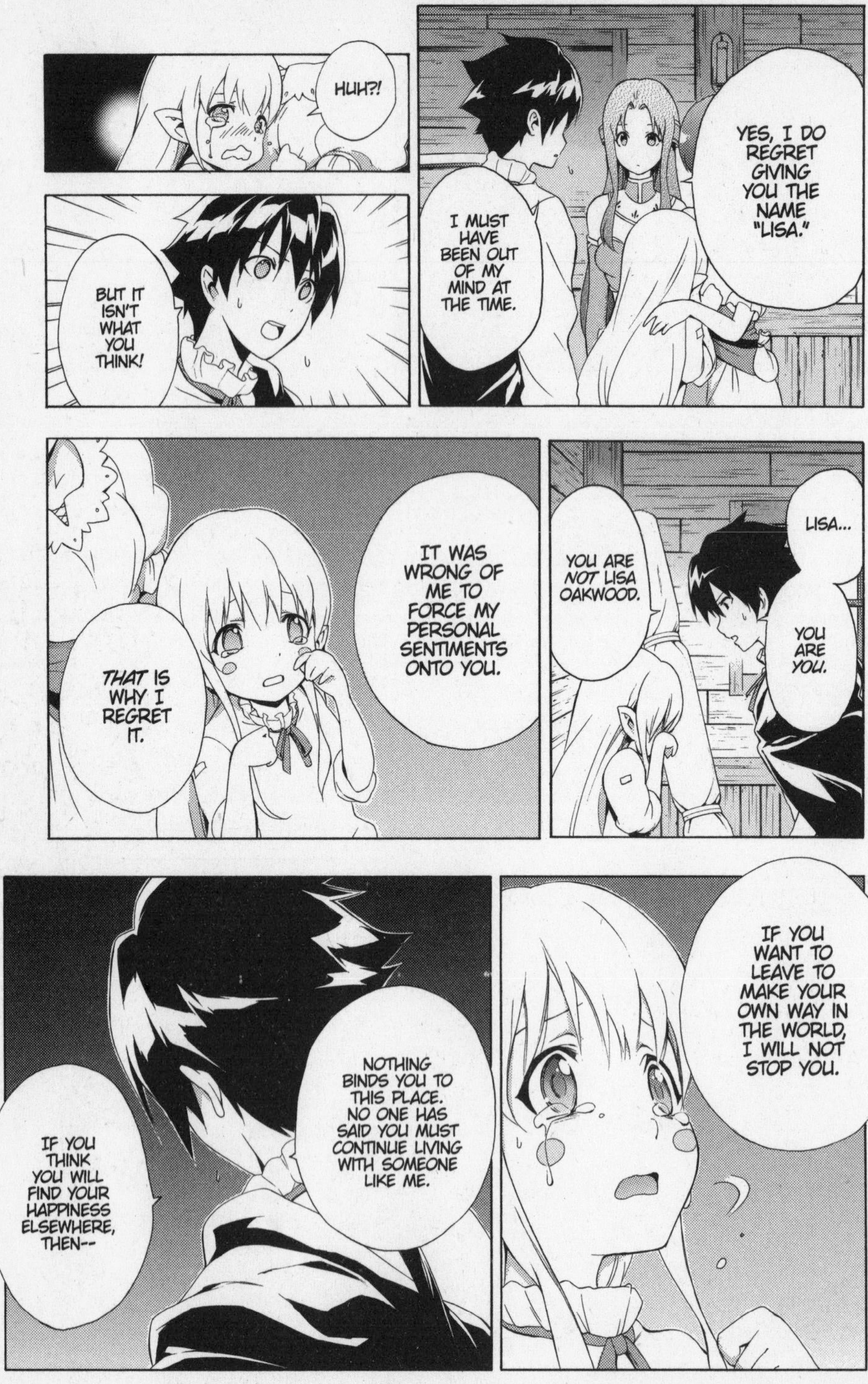
YES, I DO REGRET GIVING YOU THE NAME "LISA."
I MUST HAVE BEEN OUT OF MY MIND AT THE TIME.
HUH?!
BUT IT ISN'T WHAT YOU THINK!
LISA...
YOU ARE YOU.
YOU ARE NOT LISA OAKWOOD.
IT WAS WRONG OF ME TO FORCE MY PERSONAL SENTIMENTS ONTO YOU.
THAT IS WHY I REGRET IT.
IF YOU WANT TO LEAVE TO MAKE YOUR OWN WAY IN THE WORLD, I WILL NOT STOP YOU.
NOTHING BINDS YOU TO THIS PLACE. NO ONE HAS SAID YOU MUST CONTINUE LIVING WITH SOMEONE LIKE ME.
IF YOU THINK YOU WILL FIND YOUR HAPPINESS ELSEWHERE, THEN--

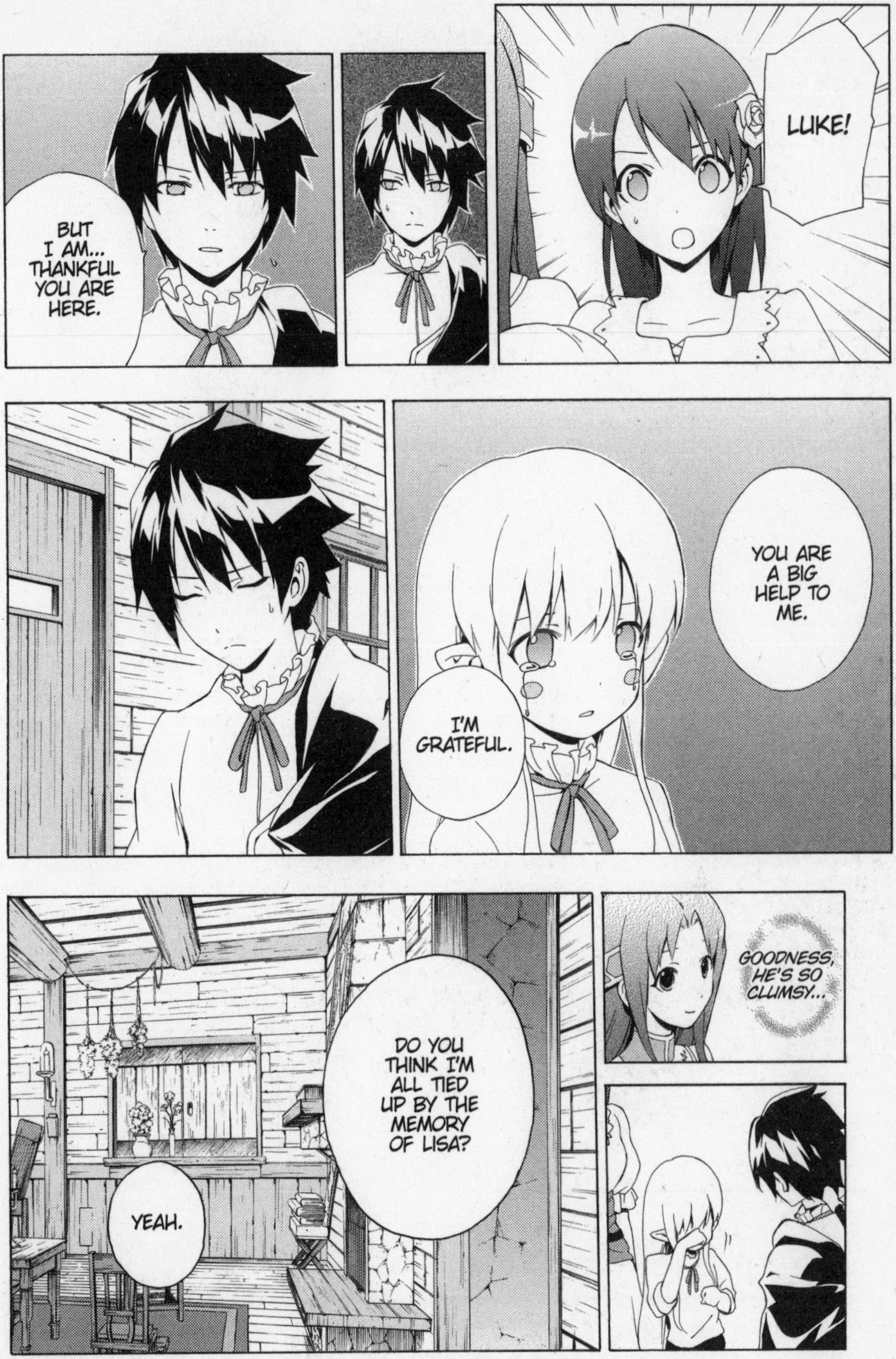
LUKE!
BUT I AM... THANKFUL YOU ARE HERE.
YOU ARE A BIG HELP TO ME.
I'M GRATEFUL.
GOODNESS, HE'S SO CLUMSY...
DO YOU THINK I'M ALL TIED UP BY THE MEMORY OF LISA?
YEAH.

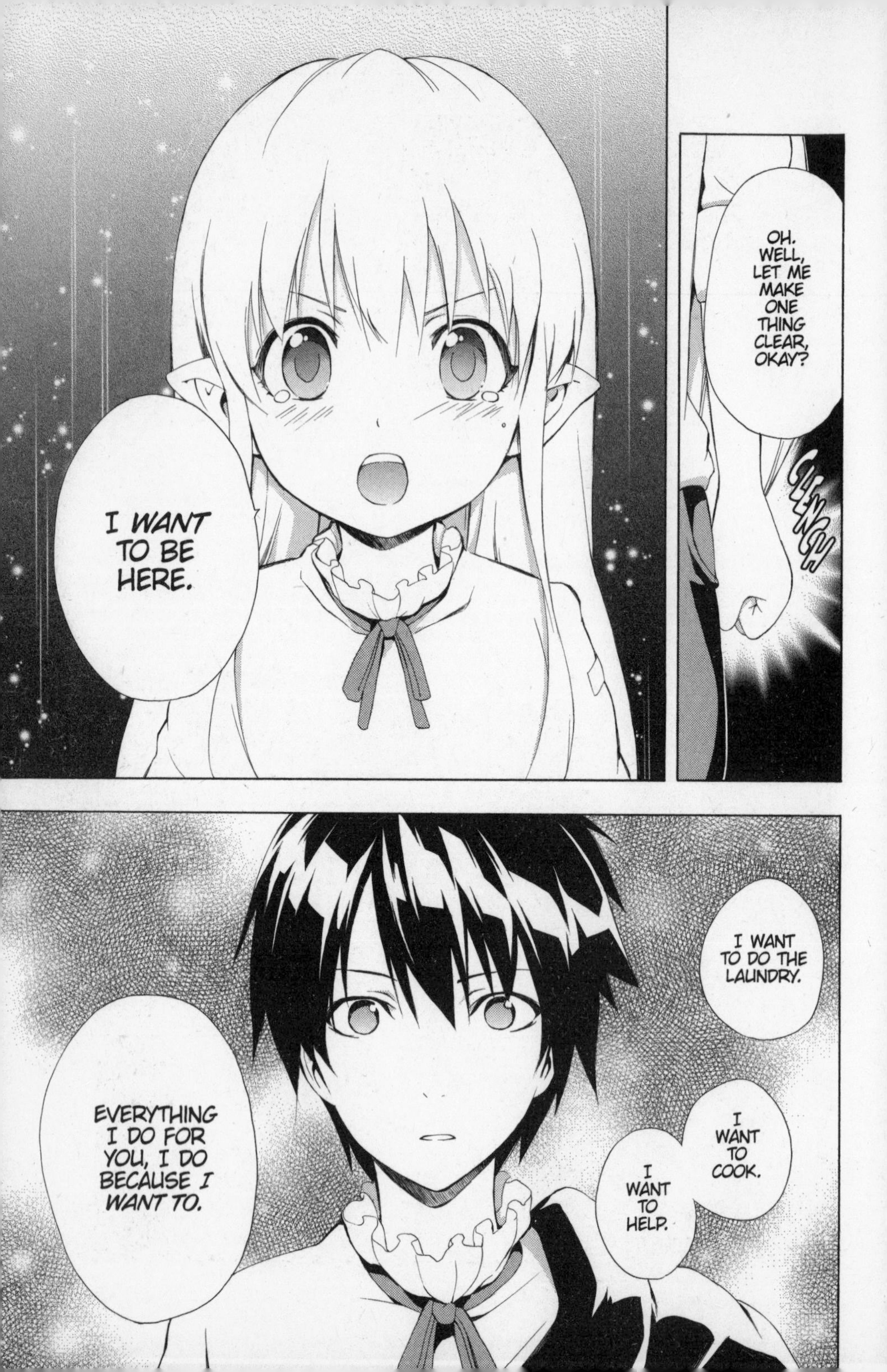
OH. WELL, LET ME MAKE ONE THING CLEAR, OKAY?
CLENCH
I *WANT* TO BE HERE.
I WANT TO DO THE LAUNDRY.
I WANT TO COOK.
I WANT TO HELP.
EVERYTHING I DO FOR YOU, I DO BECAUSE *I* WANT TO.

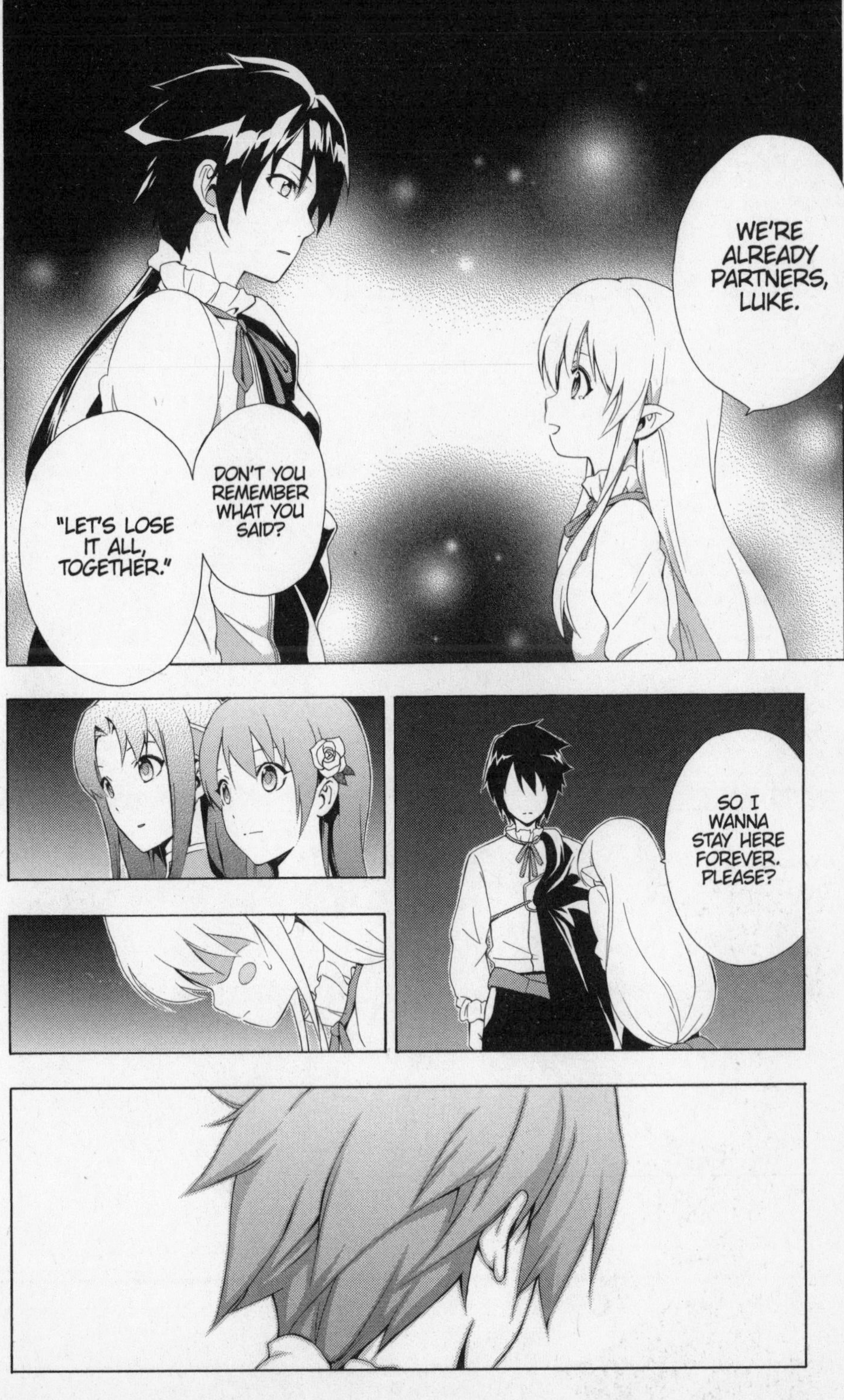
WE'RE ALREADY PARTNERS, LUKE.
DON'T YOU REMEMBER WHAT YOU SAID?
"LET'S LOSE IT ALL, TOGETHER."
SO I WANNA STAY HERE FOREVER. PLEASE?

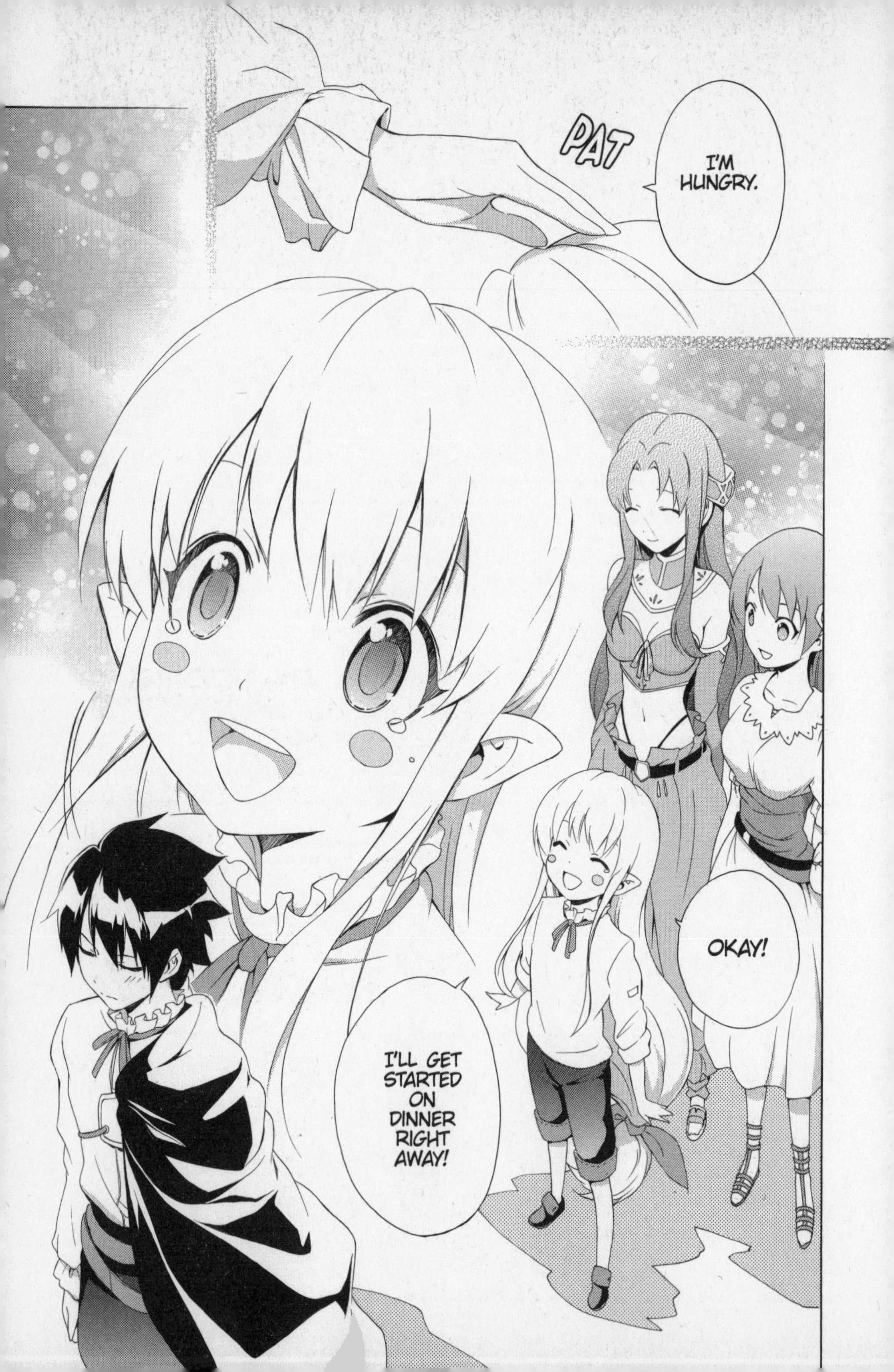
PAT
I'M HUNGRY.
OKAY!
I'LL GET STARTED ON DINNER RIGHT AWAY!

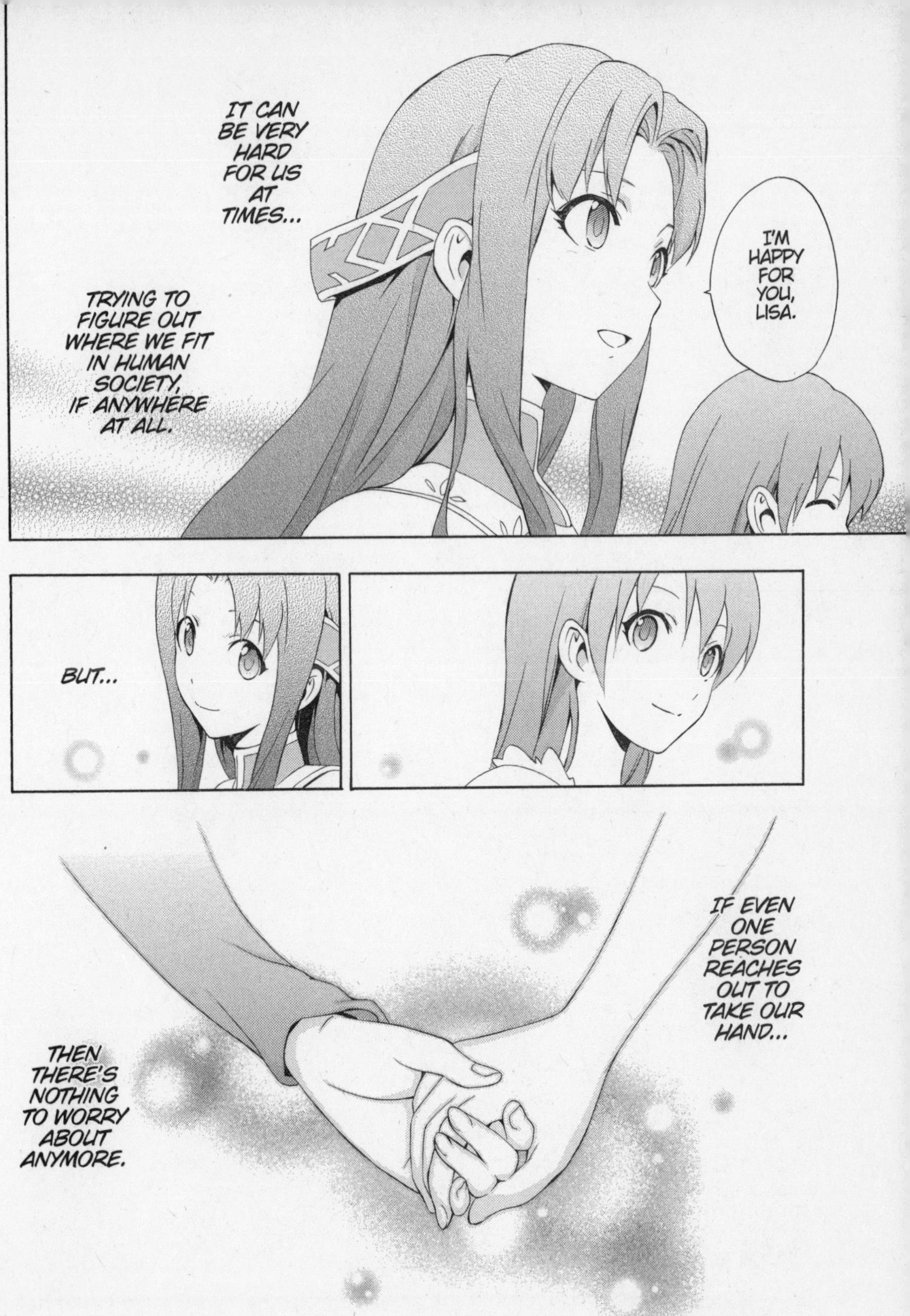
I'M HAPPY FOR YOU, LISA.
IT CAN BE VERY HARD FOR US AT TIMES...
TRYING TO FIGURE OUT WHERE WE FIT IN HUMAN SOCIETY, IF ANYWHERE AT ALL.
BUT...
IF EVEN ONE PERSON REACHES OUT TO TAKE OUR HAND...
THEN THERE'S NOTHING TO WORRY ABOUT ANYMORE.

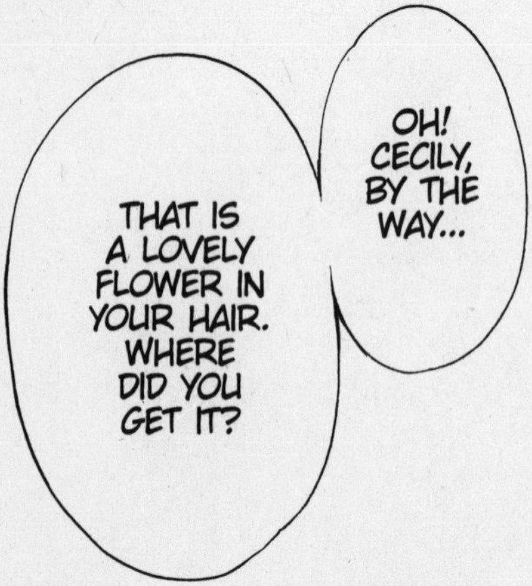
OH! CECILY, BY THE WAY...
THAT IS A LOVELY FLOWER IN YOUR HAIR. WHERE DID YOU GET IT?

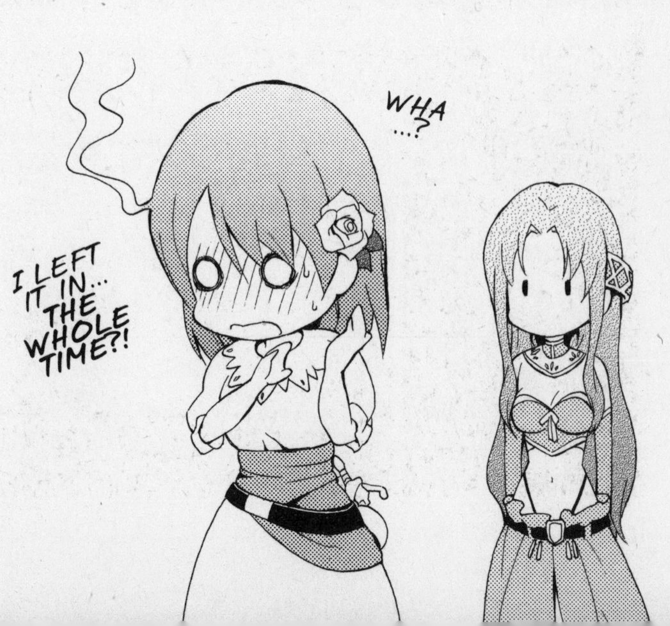
WHA...?
I LEFT IT IN... THE WHOLE TIME?!

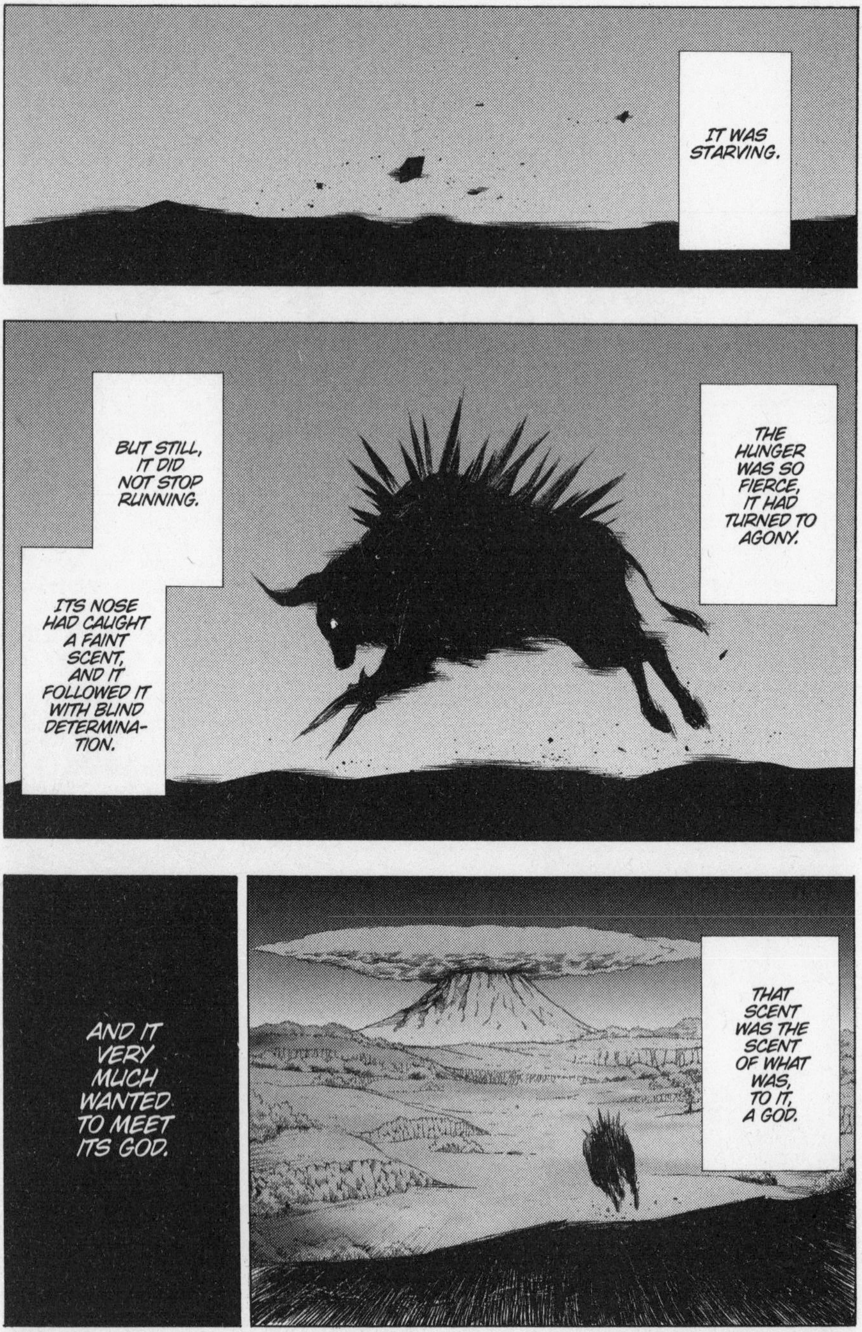
IT WAS STARVING.
THE HUNGER WAS SO FIERCE, IT HAD TURNED TO AGONY.
BUT STILL, IT DID NOT STOP RUNNING.
ITS NOSE HAD CAUGHT A FAINT SCENT, AND IT FOLLOWED IT WITH BLIND DETERMINA-TION.
THAT SCENT WAS THE SCENT OF WHAT WAS, TO IT, A GOD.
AND IT VERY MUCH WANTED TO MEET ITS GOD.

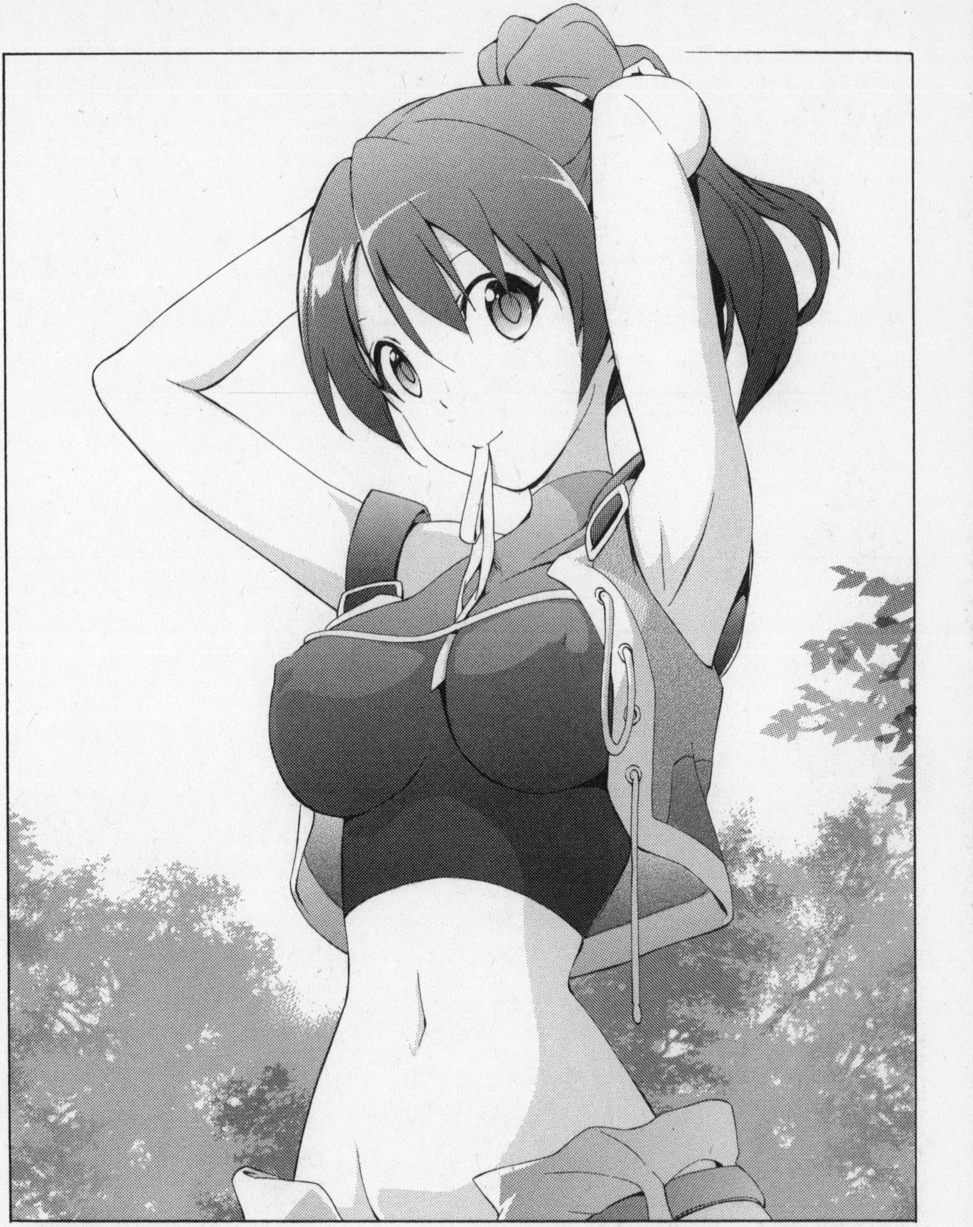

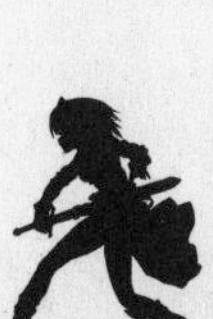

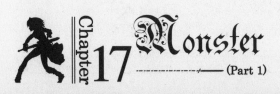

Chapter 17 Monster

(Part 1)

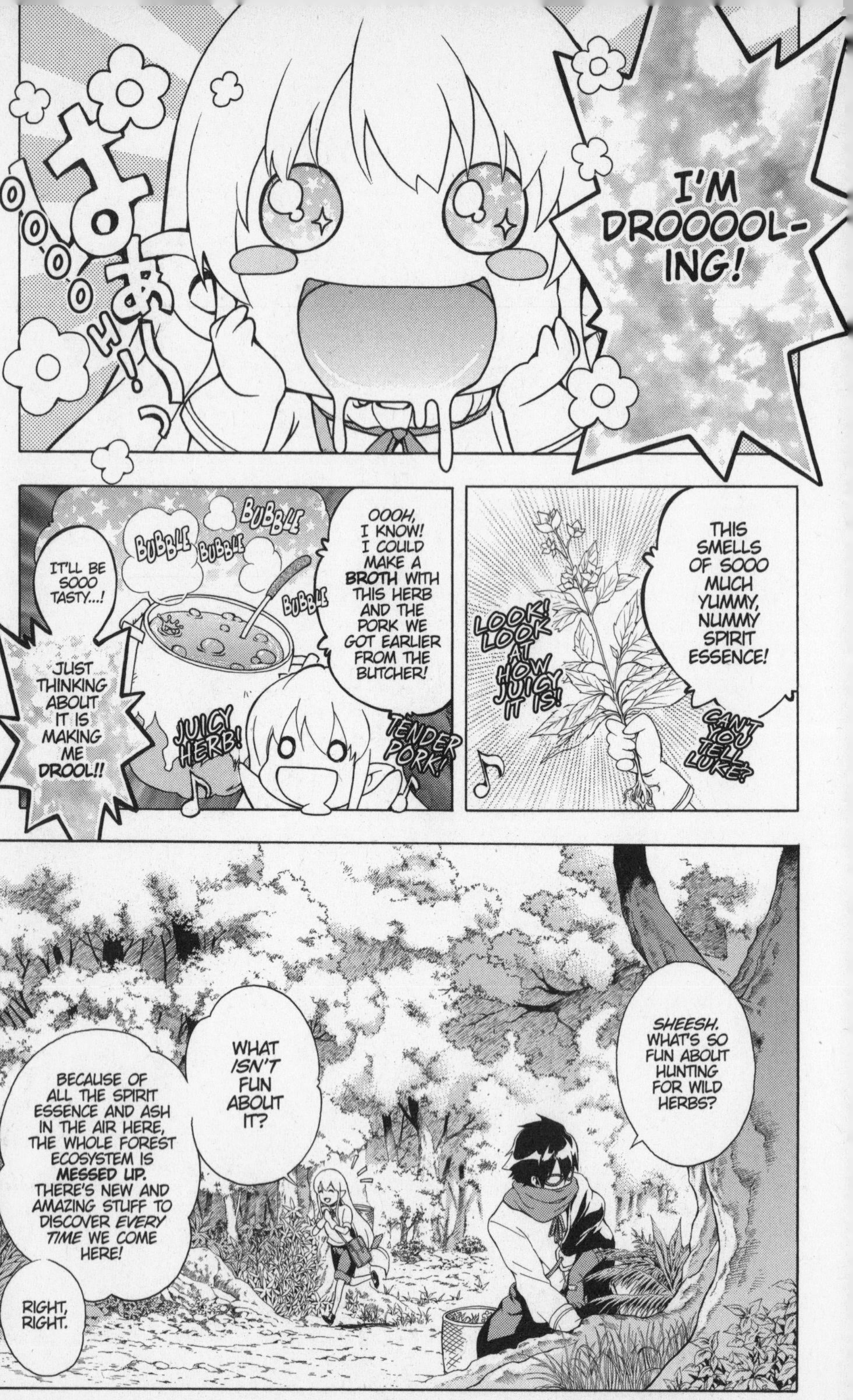
I'M DROOOOOL-ING!
はあっ
OOOOOOH!
THIS SMELLS OF SOOO MUCH YUMMY, NUMMY SPIRIT ESSENCE!
CAN'T YOU TELL, LUKE?
LOOK! LOOK AT HOW JUICY IT IS!
OOOH, I KNOW! I COULD MAKE A BROTH WITH THIS HERB AND THE PORK WE GOT EARLIER FROM THE BUTCHER!
BUBBLE
BUBBLE
BUBBLE
BUBBLE
TENDER PORK!
JUICY HERB!
IT'LL BE SOOO TASTY...!
JUST THINKING ABOUT IT IS MAKING ME DROOL!!
SHEESH. WHAT'S SO FUN ABOUT HUNTING FOR WILD HERBS?
WHAT *ISN'T* FUN ABOUT IT?
BECAUSE OF ALL THE SPIRIT ESSENCE AND ASH IN THE AIR HERE, THE WHOLE FOREST ECOSYSTEM IS **MESSED UP.** THERE'S NEW AND AMAZING STUFF TO DISCOVER *EVERY TIME* WE COME HERE!
RIGHT, RIGHT.

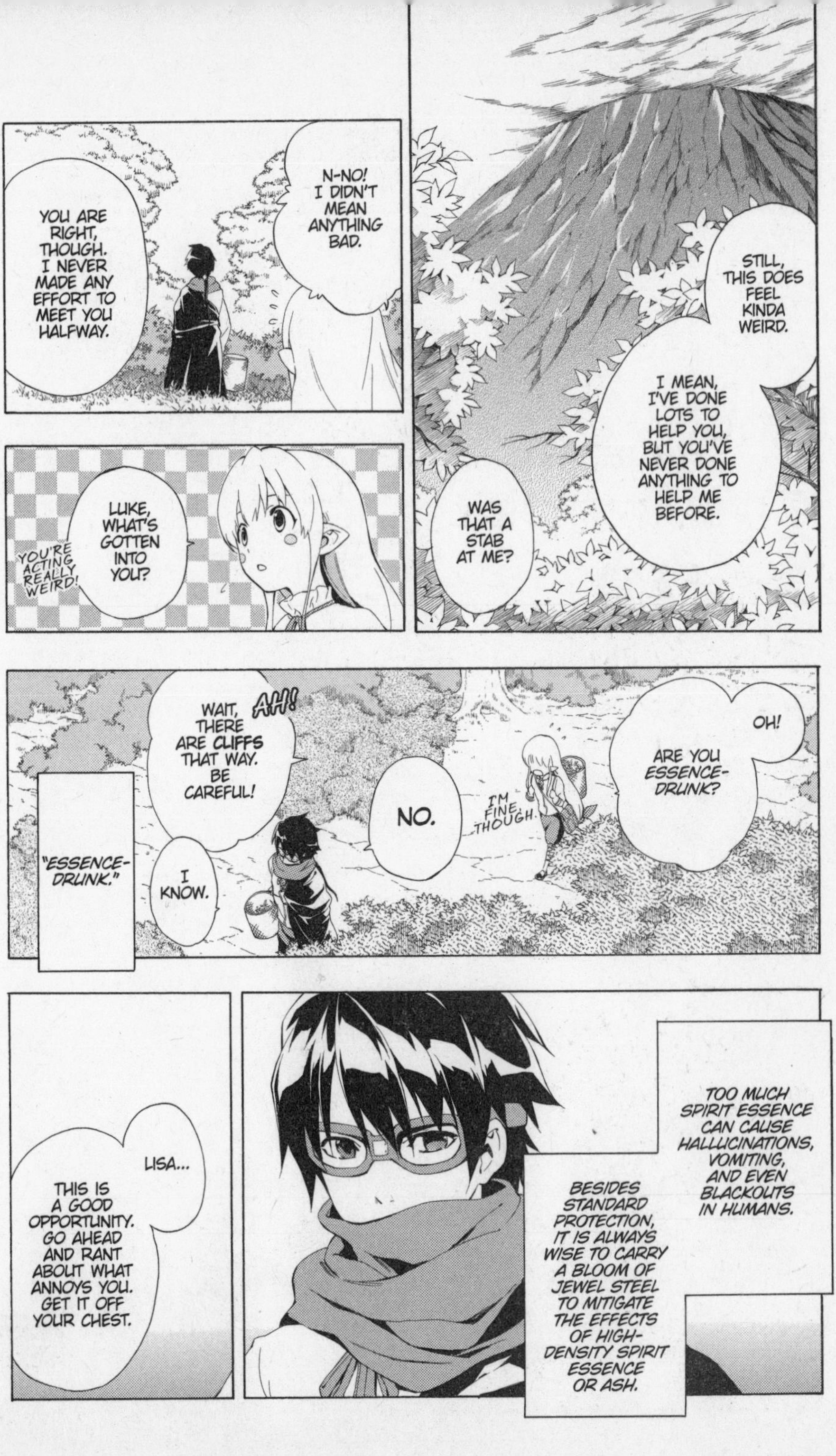
STILL, THIS DOES FEEL KINDA WEIRD.
I MEAN, I'VE DONE LOTS TO HELP YOU, BUT YOU'VE NEVER DONE ANYTHING TO HELP ME BEFORE.
WAS THAT A STAB AT ME?
N-NO! I DIDN'T MEAN ANYTHING BAD.
YOU ARE RIGHT, THOUGH. I NEVER MADE ANY EFFORT TO MEET YOU HALFWAY.
LUKE, WHAT'S GOTTEN INTO YOU?
YOU'RE ACTING REALLY WEIRD!
OH!
ARE YOU ESSENCE-DRUNK?
I'M FINE THOUGH.
NO.
AH!
WAIT, THERE ARE CLIFFS THAT WAY. BE CAREFUL!
I KNOW.
"ESSENCE-DRUNK."
TOO MUCH SPIRIT ESSENCE CAN CAUSE HALLUCINATIONS, VOMITING, AND EVEN BLACKOUTS IN HUMANS.
BESIDES STANDARD PROTECTION, IT IS ALWAYS WISE TO CARRY A BLOOM OF JEWEL STEEL TO MITIGATE THE EFFECTS OF HIGH-DENSITY SPIRIT ESSENCE OR ASH.
LISA...
THIS IS A GOOD OPPORTUNITY. GO AHEAD AND RANT ABOUT WHAT ANNOYS YOU. GET IT OFF YOUR CHEST.

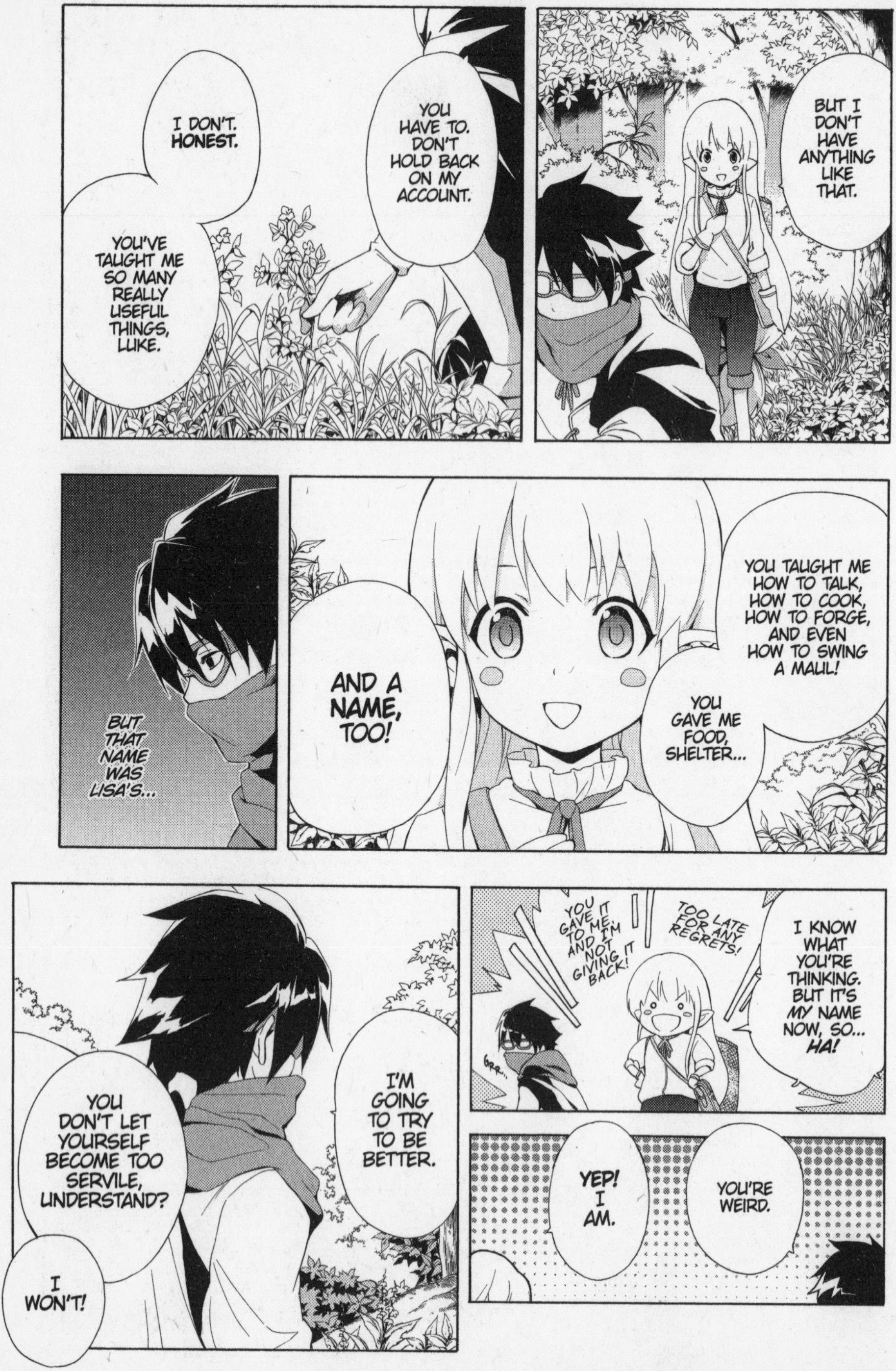
BUT I DON'T HAVE ANYTHING LIKE THAT.
YOU HAVE TO. DON'T HOLD BACK ON MY ACCOUNT.
I DON'T. HONEST.
YOU'VE TAUGHT ME SO MANY REALLY USEFUL THINGS, LUKE.
YOU TAUGHT ME HOW TO TALK, HOW TO COOK, HOW TO FORGE, AND EVEN HOW TO SWING A MAUL!
YOU GAVE ME FOOD, SHELTER...
AND A NAME, TOO!
BUT THAT NAME WAS LISA'S...
I KNOW WHAT YOU'RE THINKING. BUT IT'S *MY* NAME NOW, SO... *HA!*
TOO LATE FOR ANY REGRETS!
YOU GAVE IT TO ME, AND I'M NOT GIVING IT BACK!
GRR...
YOU'RE WEIRD.
YEP! I AM.
I'M GOING TO TRY TO BE BETTER.
YOU DON'T LET YOURSELF BECOME TOO SERVILE, UNDERSTAND?
I WON'T!

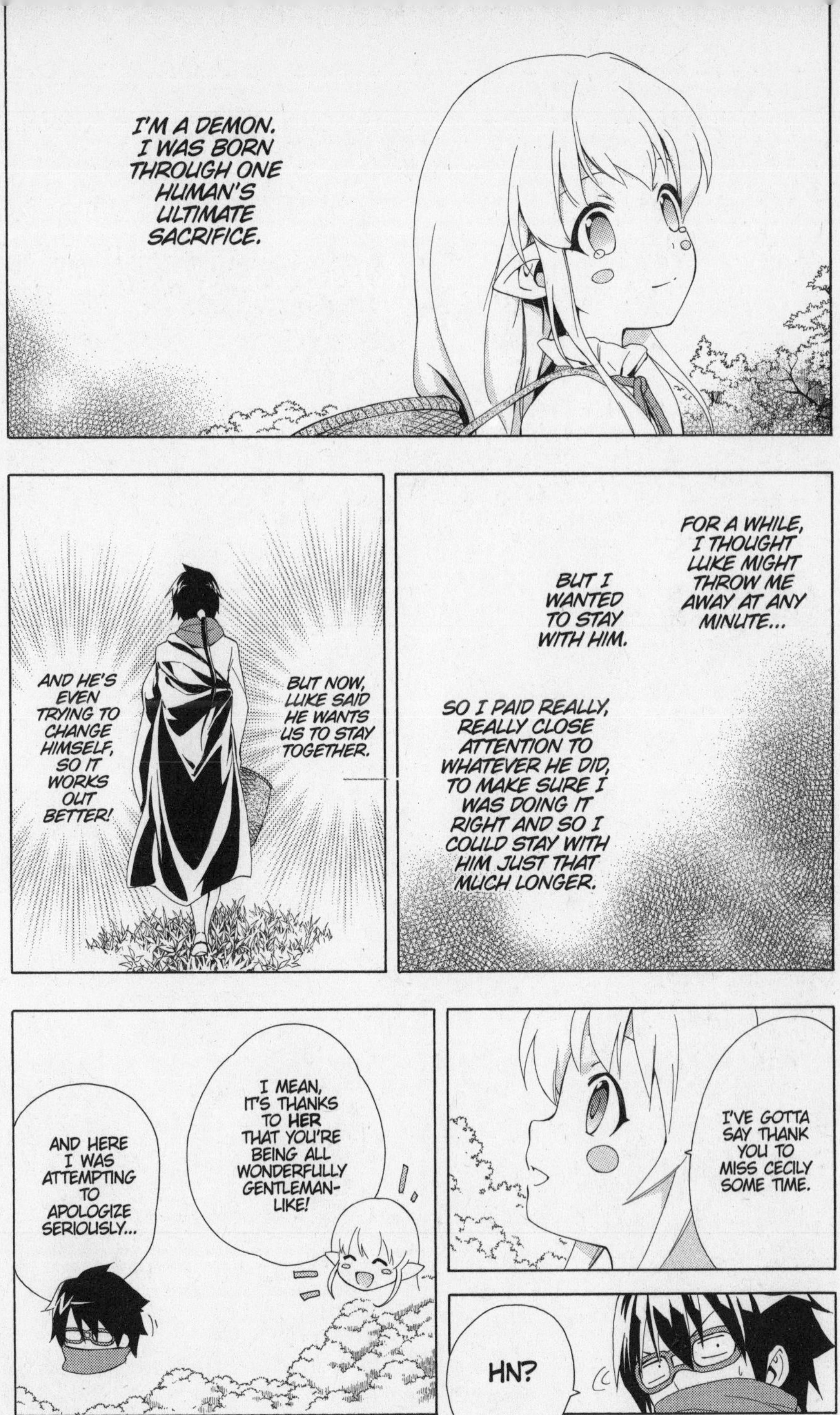
I'M A DEMON. I WAS BORN THROUGH ONE HUMAN'S ULTIMATE SACRIFICE.
FOR A WHILE, I THOUGHT LUKE MIGHT THROW ME AWAY AT ANY MINUTE...
BUT I WANTED TO STAY WITH HIM.
SO I PAID REALLY, REALLY CLOSE ATTENTION TO WHATEVER HE DID, TO MAKE SURE I WAS DOING IT RIGHT AND SO I COULD STAY WITH HIM JUST THAT MUCH LONGER.
BUT NOW, LUKE SAID HE WANTS US TO STAY TOGETHER.
AND HE'S EVEN TRYING TO CHANGE HIMSELF, SO IT WORKS OUT BETTER!
I'VE GOTTA SAY THANK YOU TO MISS CECILY SOME TIME.
HN?
I MEAN, IT'S THANKS TO HER THAT YOU'RE BEING ALL WONDERFULLY GENTLEMAN-LIKE!
AND HERE I WAS ATTEMPTING TO APOLOGIZE SERIOUSLY...

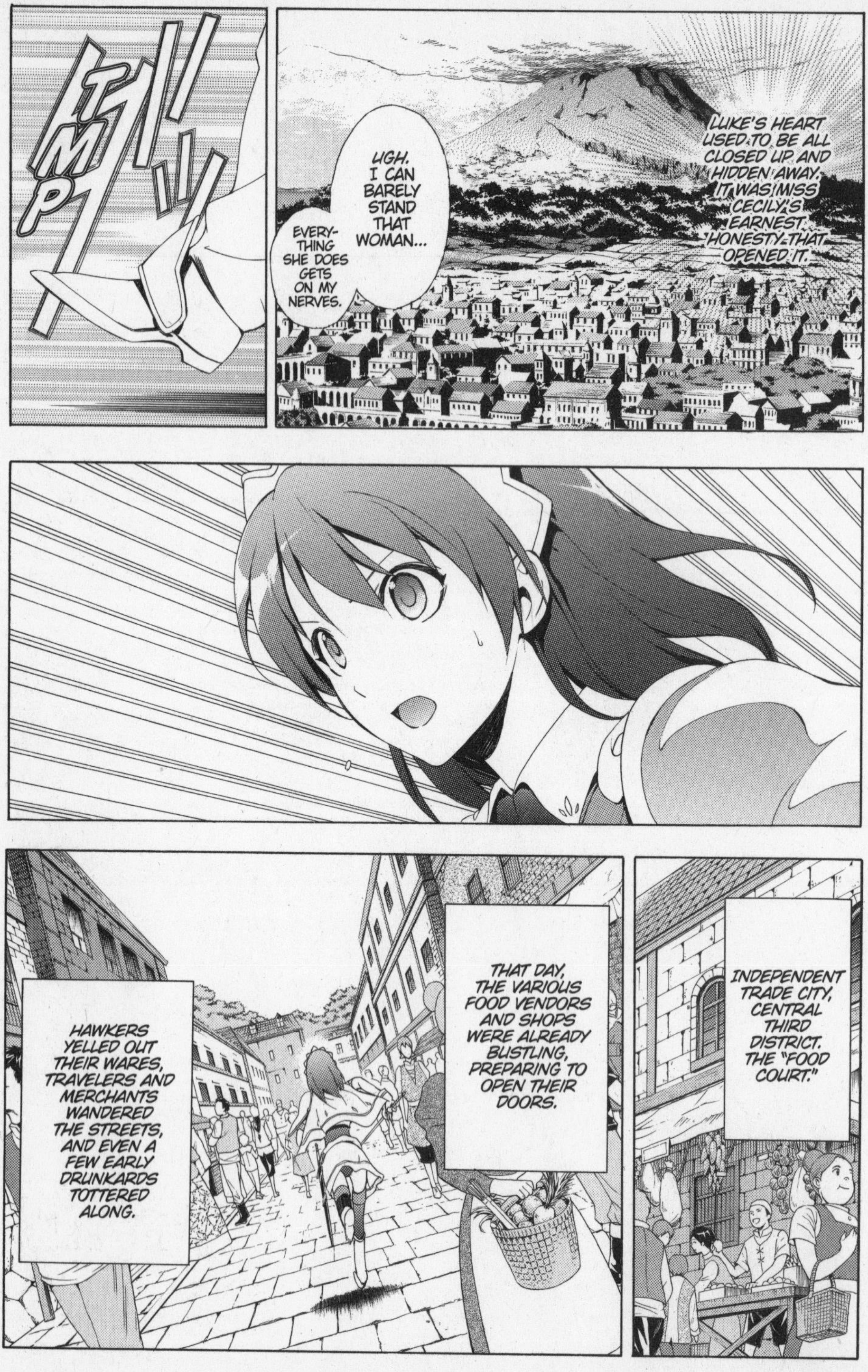
LUKE'S HEART USED TO BE ALL CLOSED UP AND HIDDEN AWAY. IT WAS MISS CECILY'S EARNEST HONESTY THAT OPENED IT.
UGH. I CAN BARELY STAND THAT WOMAN...
EVERY-THING SHE DOES GETS ON MY NERVES.
TMP
INDEPENDENT TRADE CITY, CENTRAL THIRD DISTRICT. THE "FOOD COURT."
THAT DAY, THE VARIOUS FOOD VENDORS AND SHOPS WERE ALREADY BUSTLING, PREPARING TO OPEN THEIR DOORS.
HAWKERS YELLED OUT THEIR WARES, TRAVELERS AND MERCHANTS WANDERED THE STREETS, AND EVEN A FEW EARLY DRUNKARDS TOTTERED ALONG.

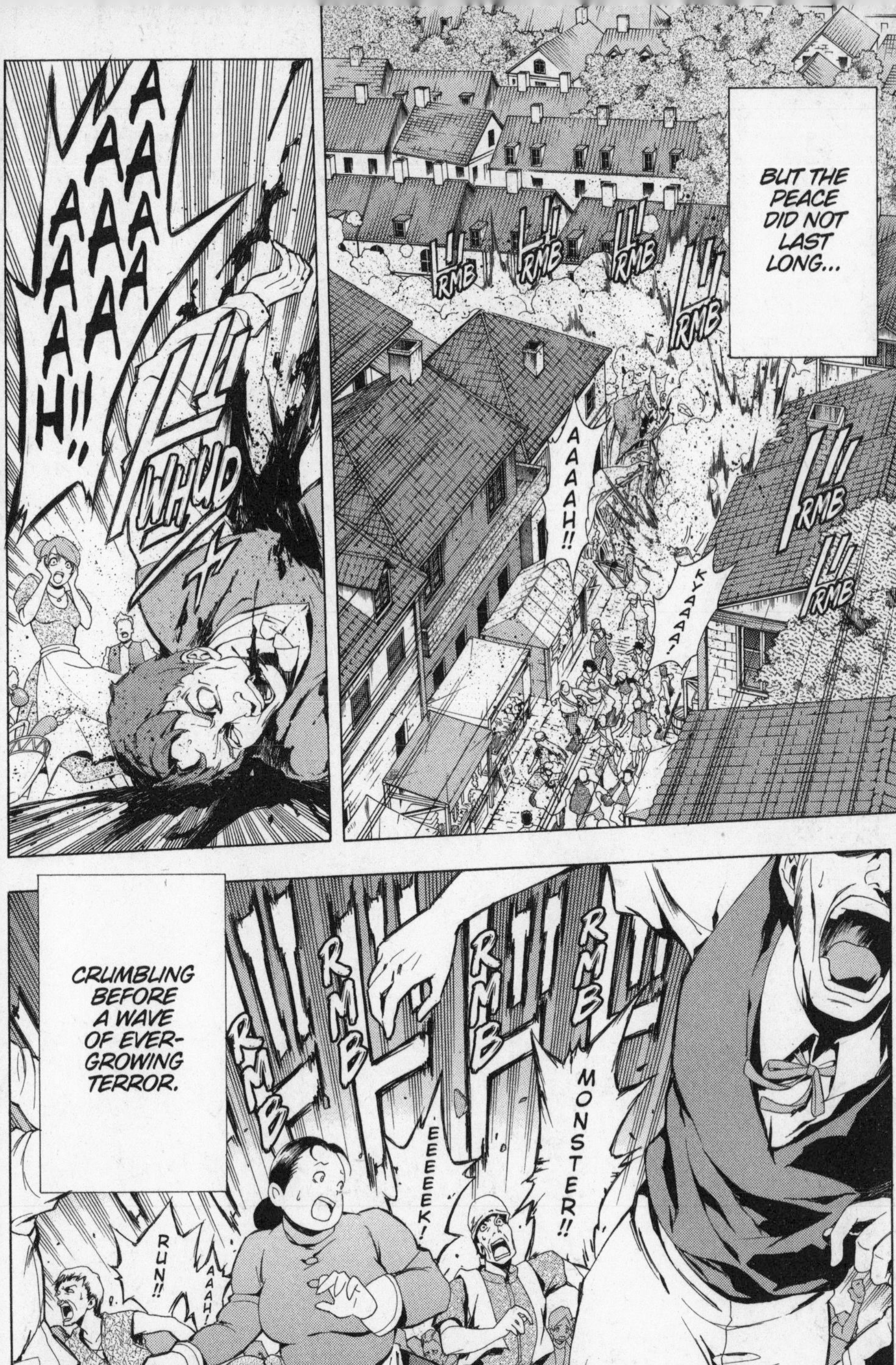
BUT THE PEACE DID NOT LAST LONG...
RMB
RMB
RMB
RMB
RMB
RMB
AAAAAH!!
KYAAAAA!
WAAAAAAAAAAAH!!
WHUD
CRUMBLING BEFORE A WAVE OF EVER-GROWING TERROR.
RMB
RMB
RMB
RMB
MONSTER!!
EEEEEK!
AAAH!
RUN!!

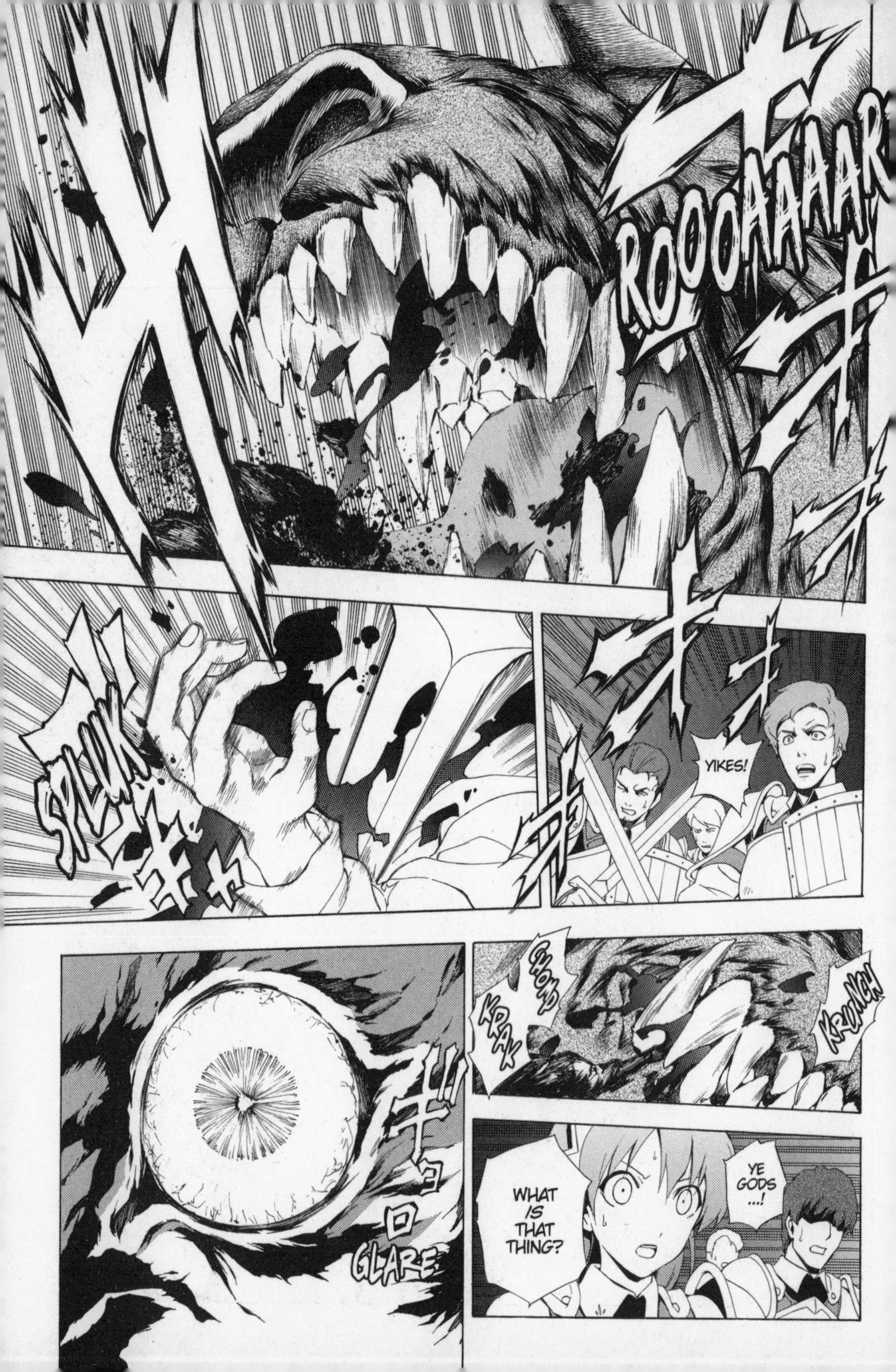
ROOOAAAAR
YIKES!
SPLUK
KRUNCH
CHOMP
KRAK
YE GODS ...!
WHAT IS THAT THING?
GLARE

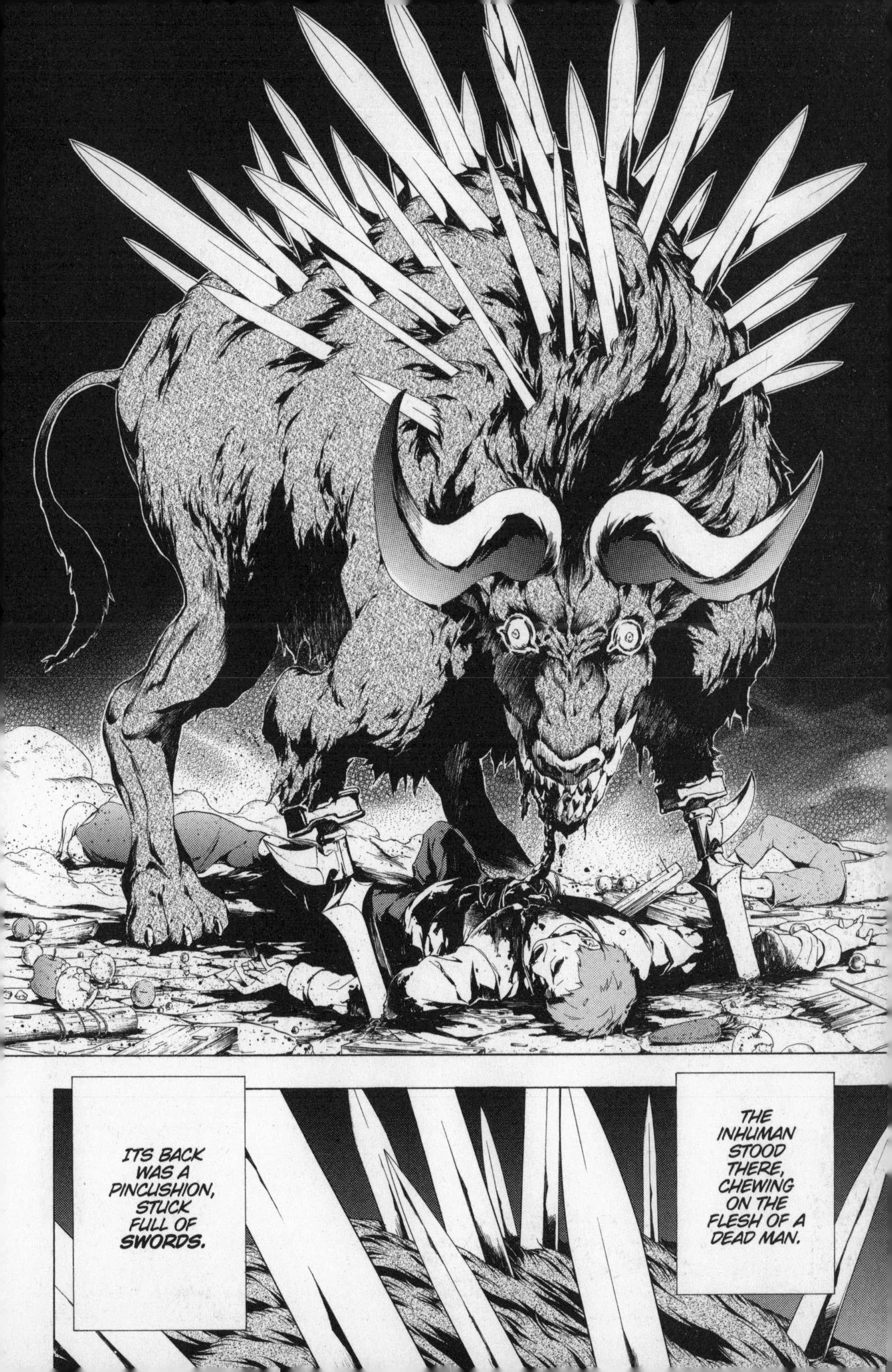
THE INHUMAN STOOD THERE, CHEWING ON THE FLESH OF A DEAD MAN.
ITS BACK WAS A PINCUSHION, STUCK FULL OF SWORDS.

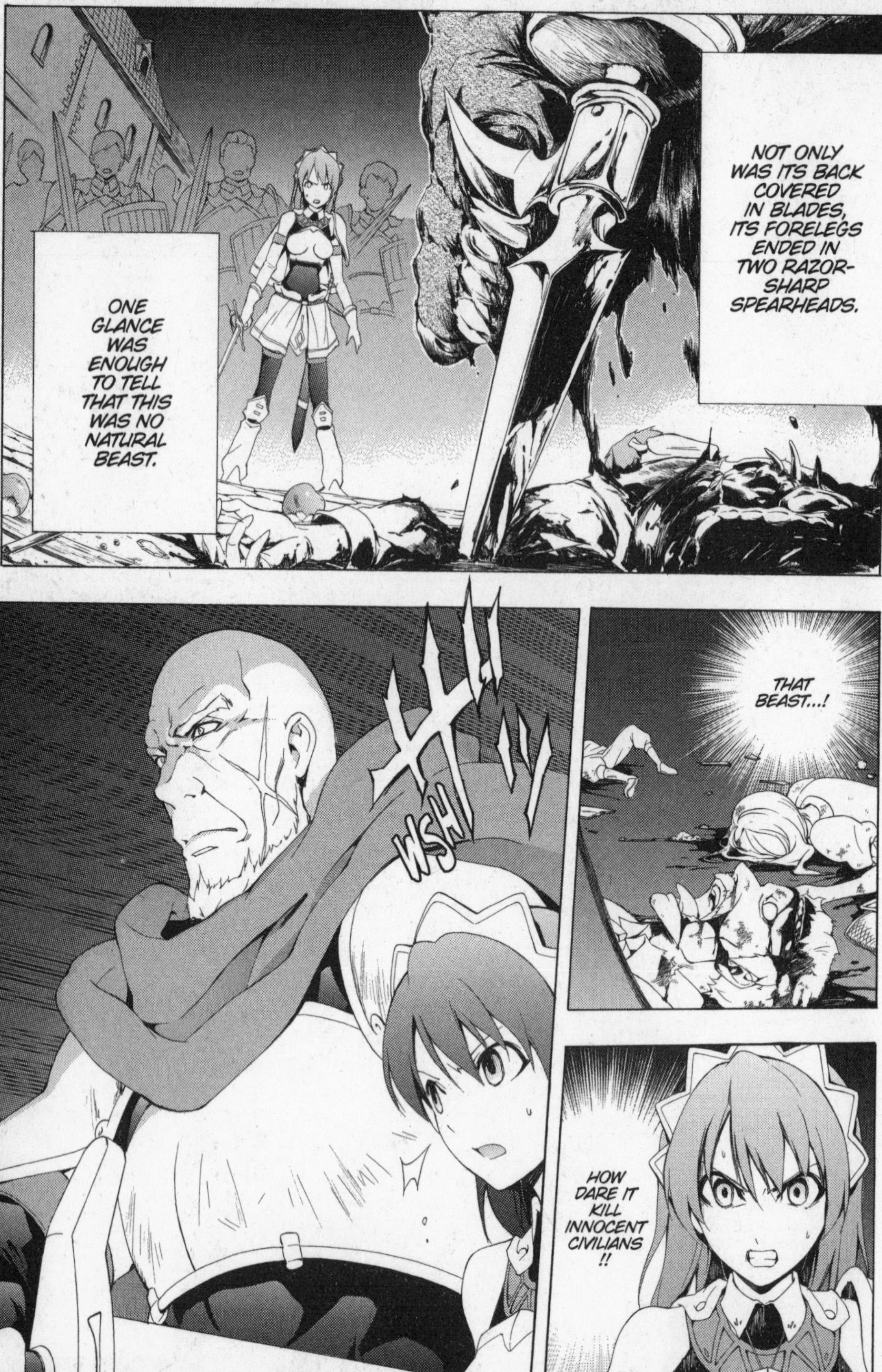
NOT ONLY WAS ITS BACK COVERED IN BLADES, ITS FORELEGS ENDED IN TWO RAZOR-SHARP SPEARHEADS.
ONE GLANCE WAS ENOUGH TO TELL THAT THIS WAS NO NATURAL BEAST.
THAT BEAST...!
HOW DARE IT KILL INNOCENT CIVILIANS !!
WSH

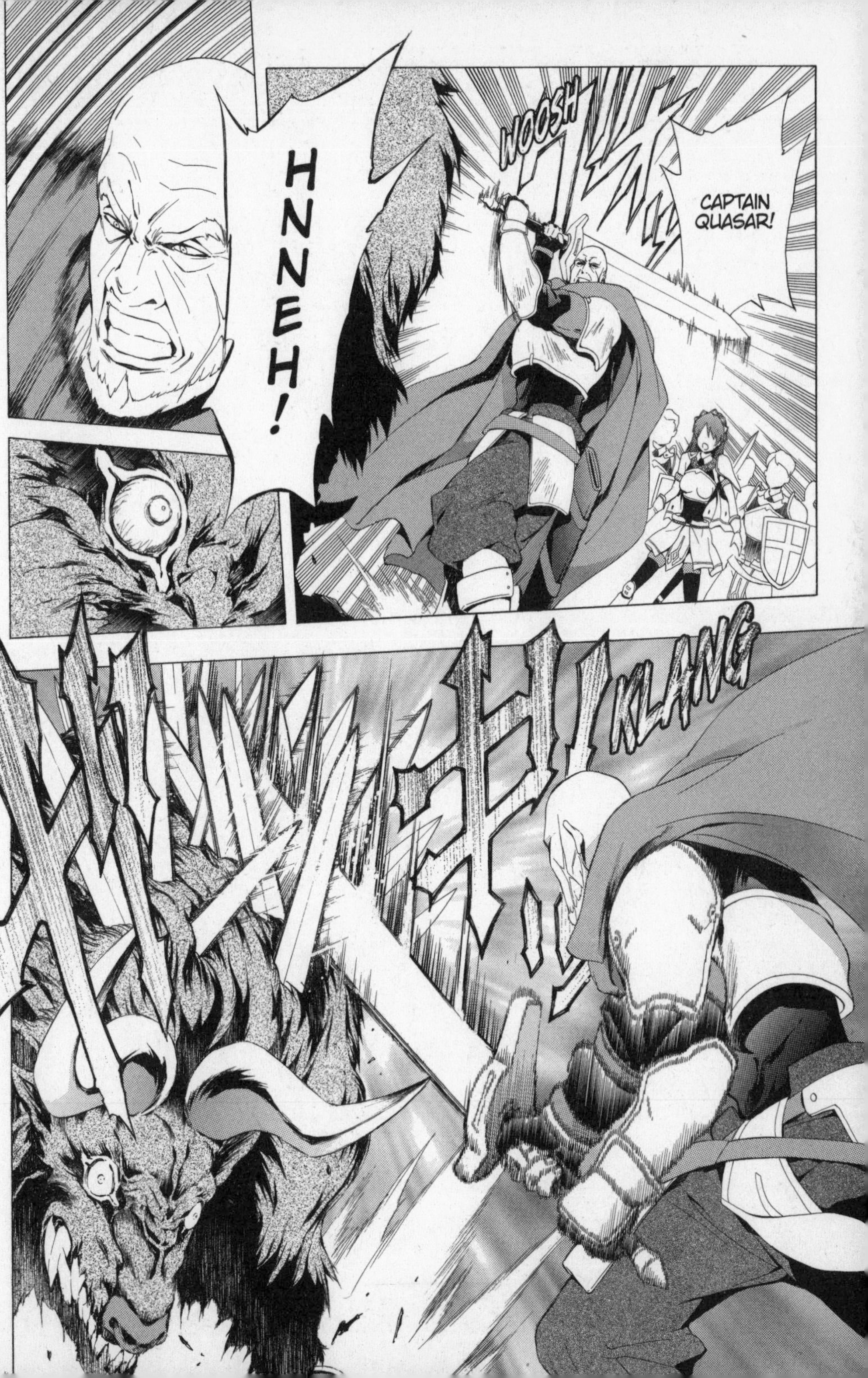
WOOSH
CAPTAIN QUASAR!
HNNEH!
KLANG

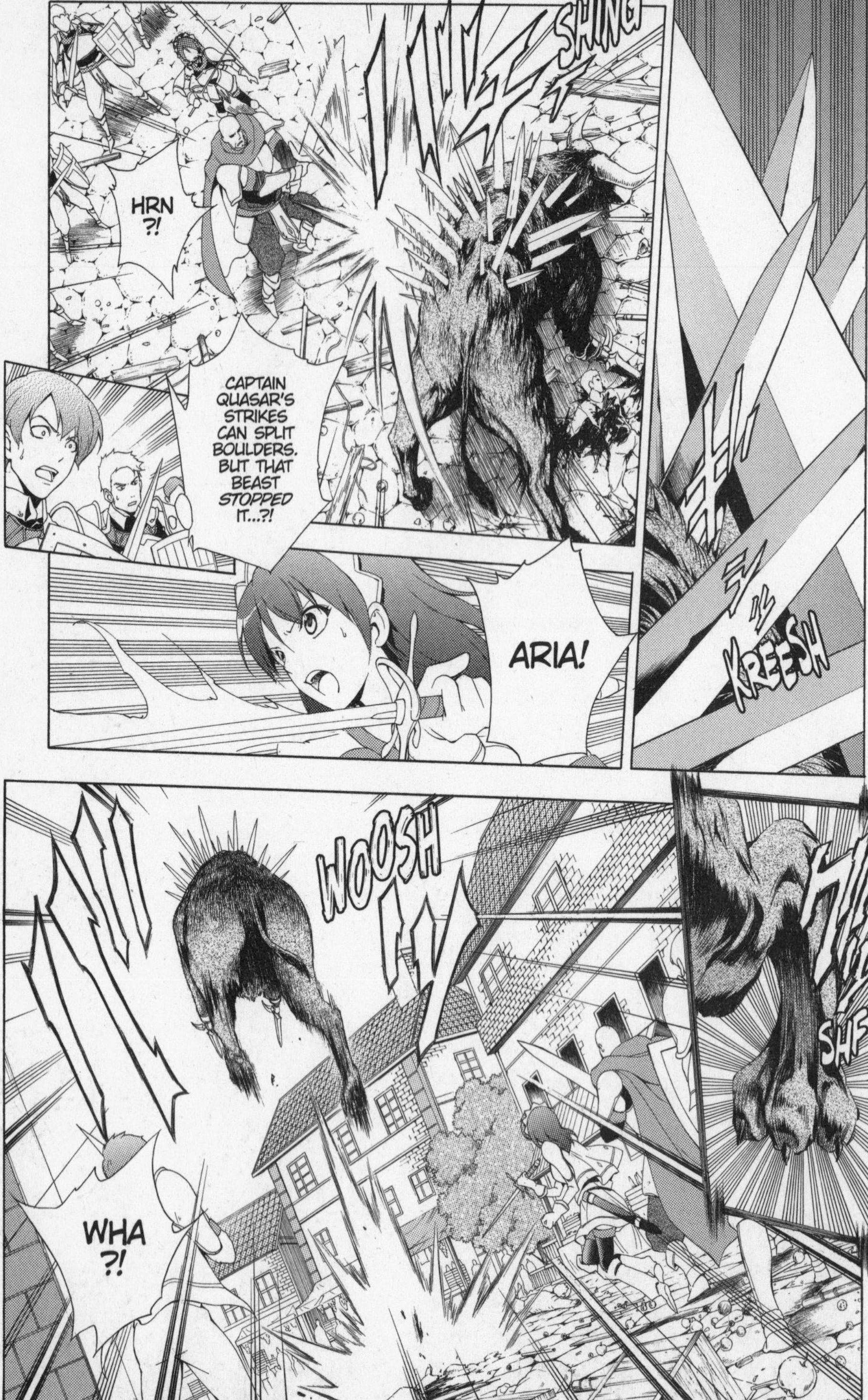

KREESH
SHING
HRN ?!
CAPTAIN QUASAR'S STRIKES CAN SPLIT BOULDERS. BUT THAT BEAST STOPPED IT...?!
ARIA!
SHF
WOOSH
WHA ?!

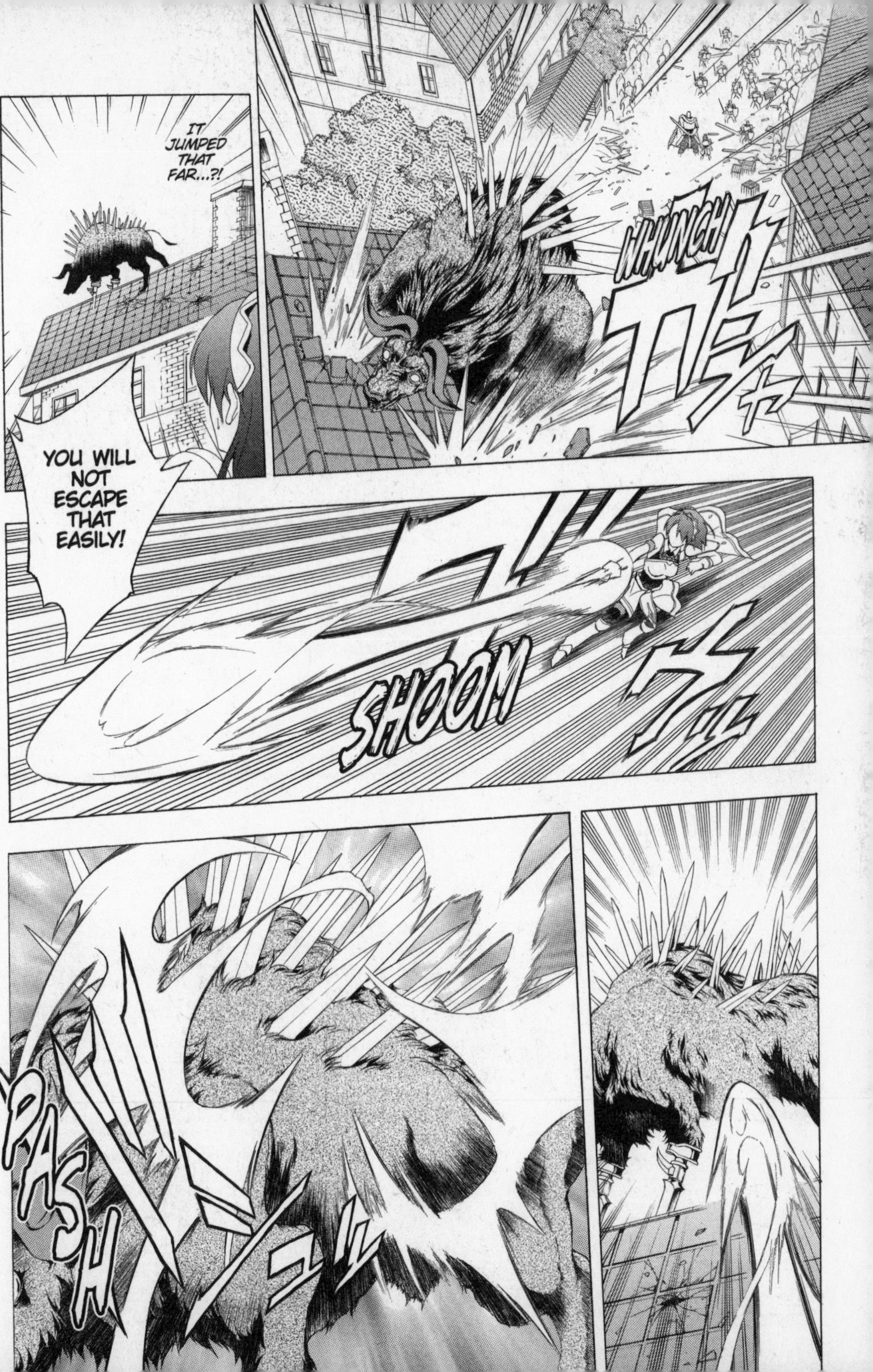
WHUNCH
IT JUMPED THAT FAR...?!
YOU WILL NOT ESCAPE THAT EASILY!
SHOOM
PASH

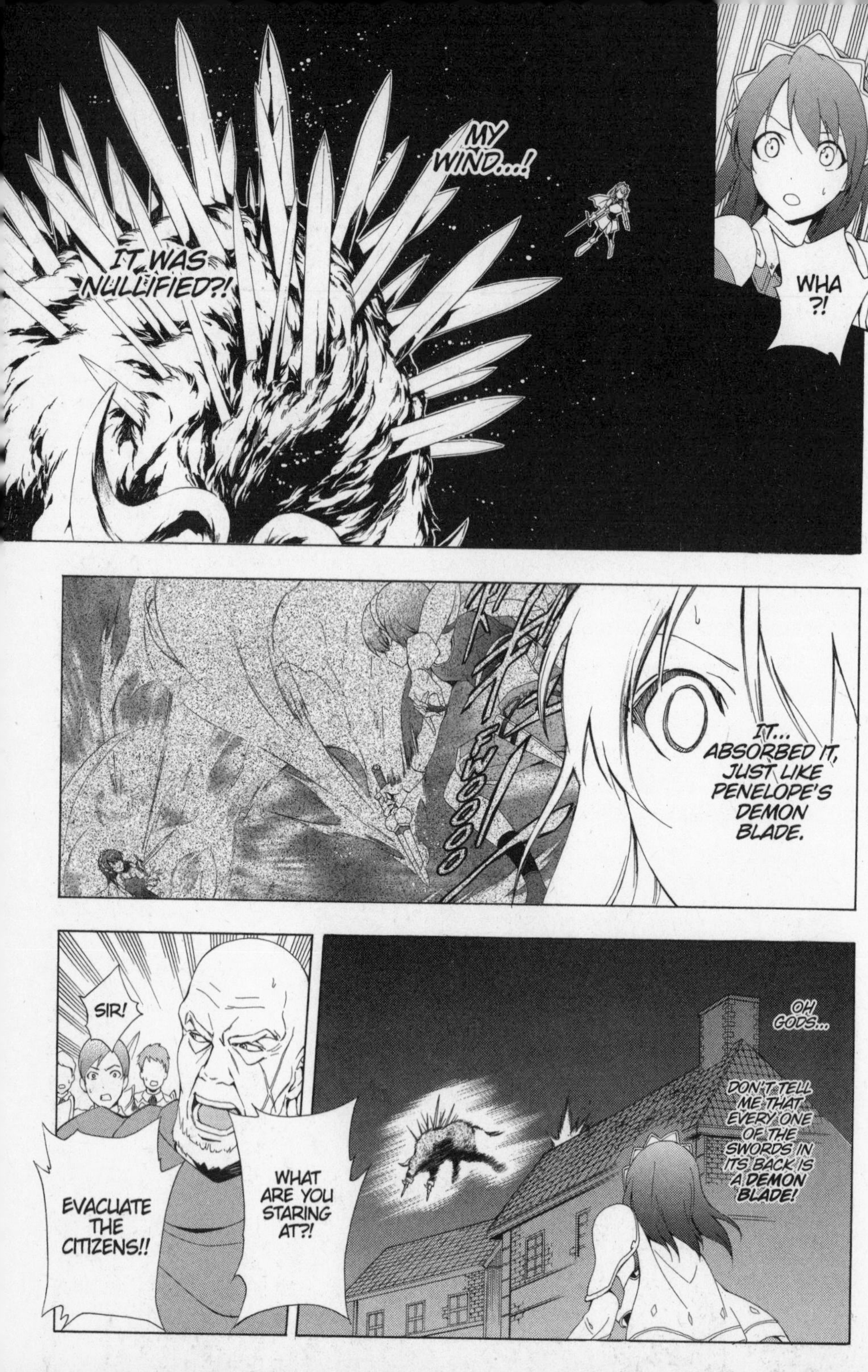
WHA ?!
MY WIND...!
IT WAS NULLIFIED?!
IT... ABSORBED IT, JUST LIKE PENELOPE'S DEMON BLADE.
OH GODS...
DON'T TELL ME THAT EVERY ONE OF THE SWORDS IN ITS BACK IS A DEMON BLADE!
SIR!
WHAT ARE YOU STARING AT?!
EVACUATE THE CITIZENS!!

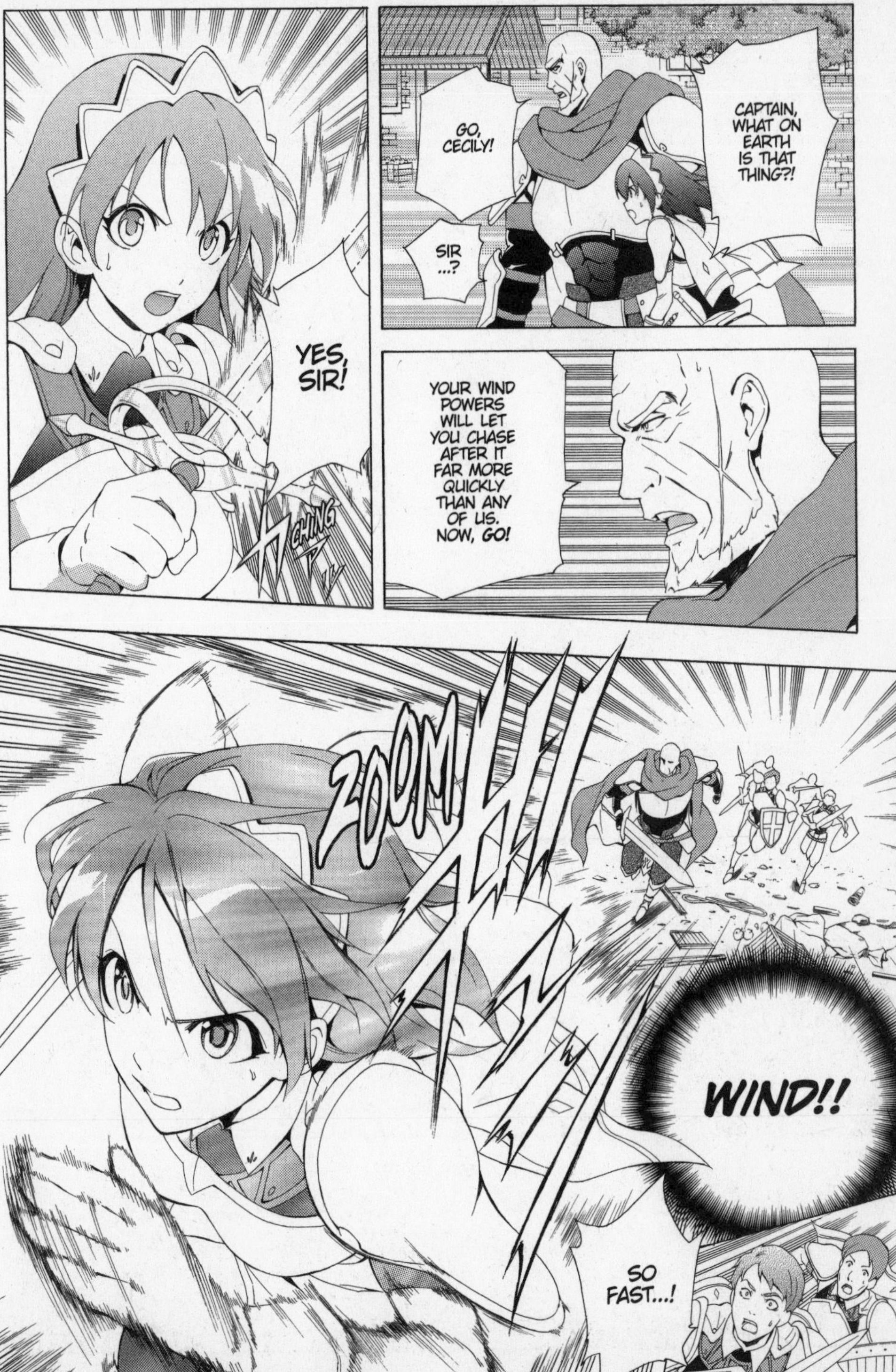
CAPTAIN, WHAT ON EARTH IS THAT THING?!
GO, CECILY!
SIR ...?
YOUR WIND POWERS WILL LET YOU CHASE AFTER IT FAR MORE QUICKLY THAN ANY OF US. NOW, GO!
YES, SIR!
CHING
ZOOM
WIND!!
SO FAST...!

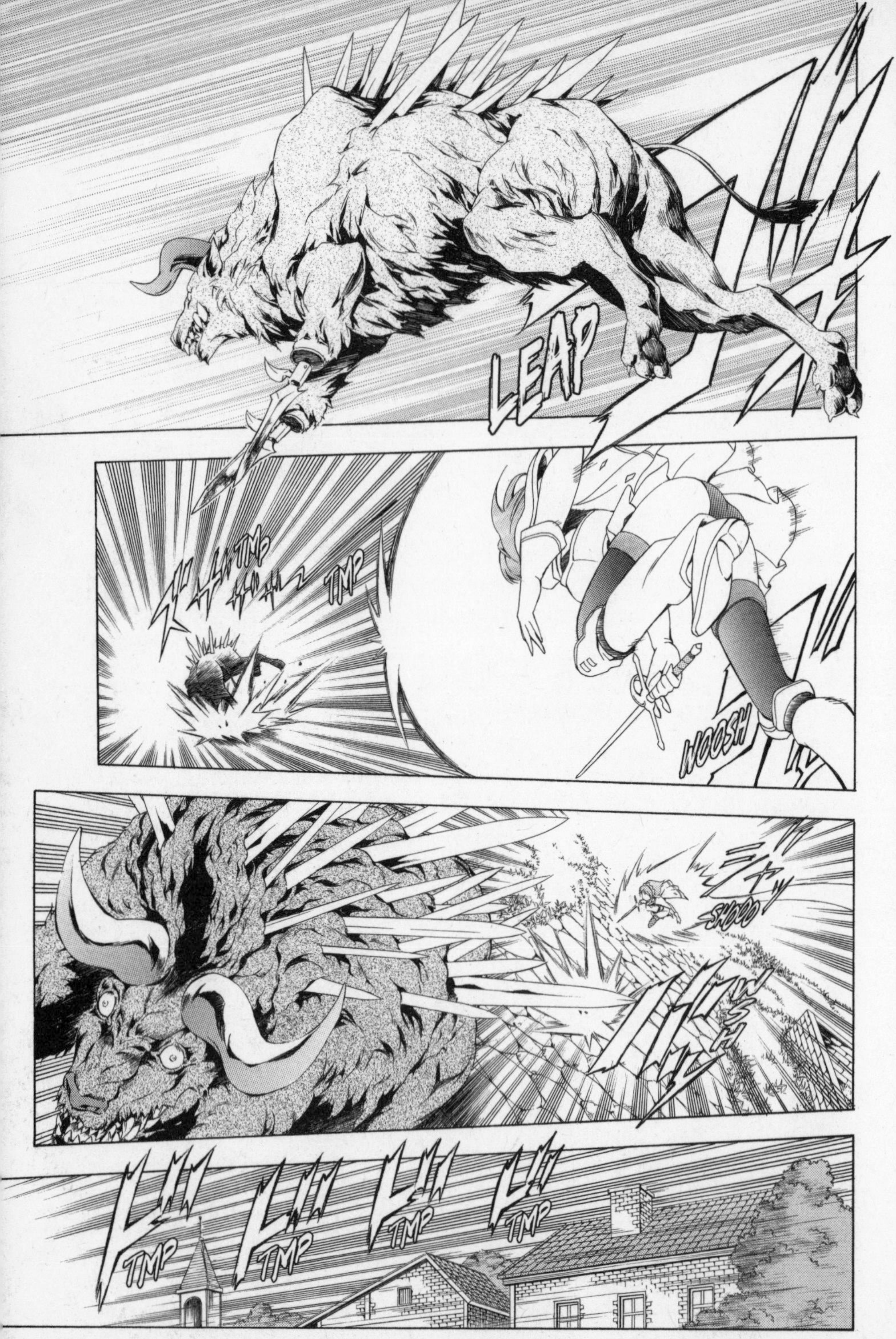
LEAP
WOOSH
TMP
TMP
シャッ
SHOOO
WSH
TMP
TMP
TMP
TMP

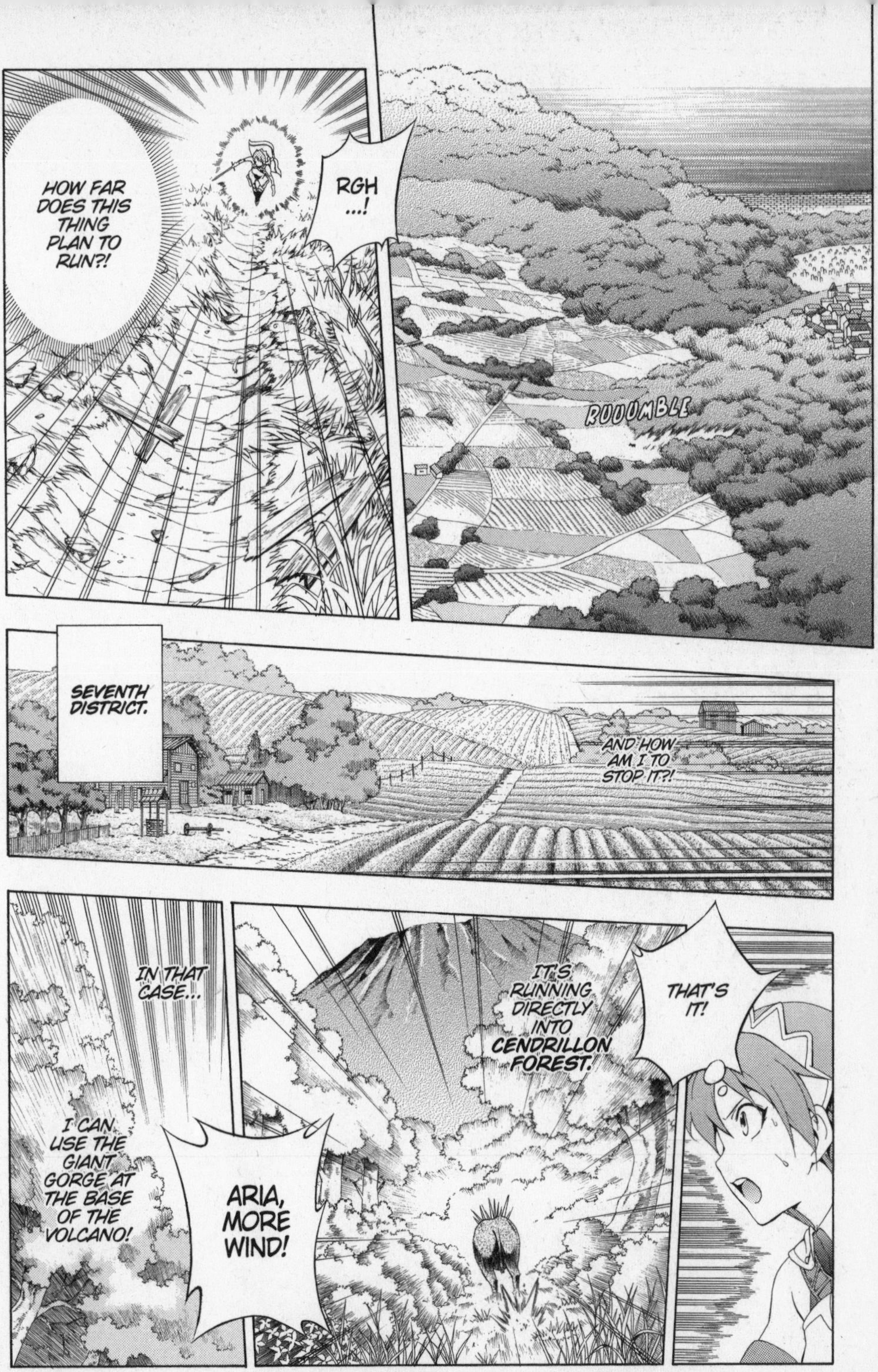
RUUUMBLE
RGH ...!
HOW FAR DOES THIS THING PLAN TO RUN?!
SEVENTH DISTRICT.
AND HOW AM I TO STOP IT?!
IT'S RUNNING DIRECTLY INTO CENDRILLON FOREST.
THAT'S IT!
IN THAT CASE...
I CAN USE THE GIANT GORGE AT THE BASE OF THE VOLCANO!
ARIA, MORE WIND!

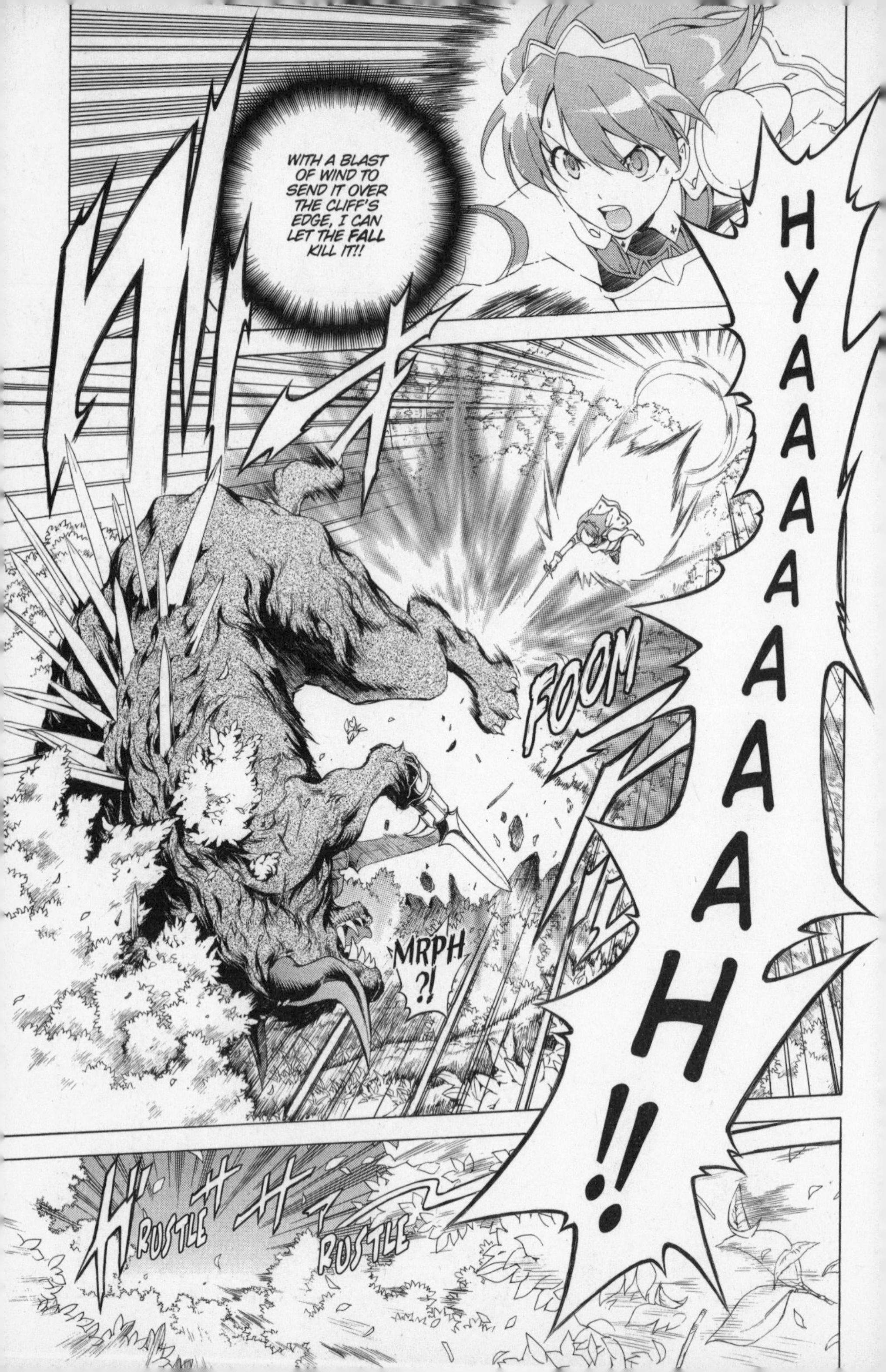
WITH A BLAST OF WIND TO SEND IT OVER THE CLIFF'S EDGE, I CAN LET THE FALL KILL IT!!
HYAAAAAAAAH!!
FOOM
MRPH ?!
RUSTLE
RUSTLE

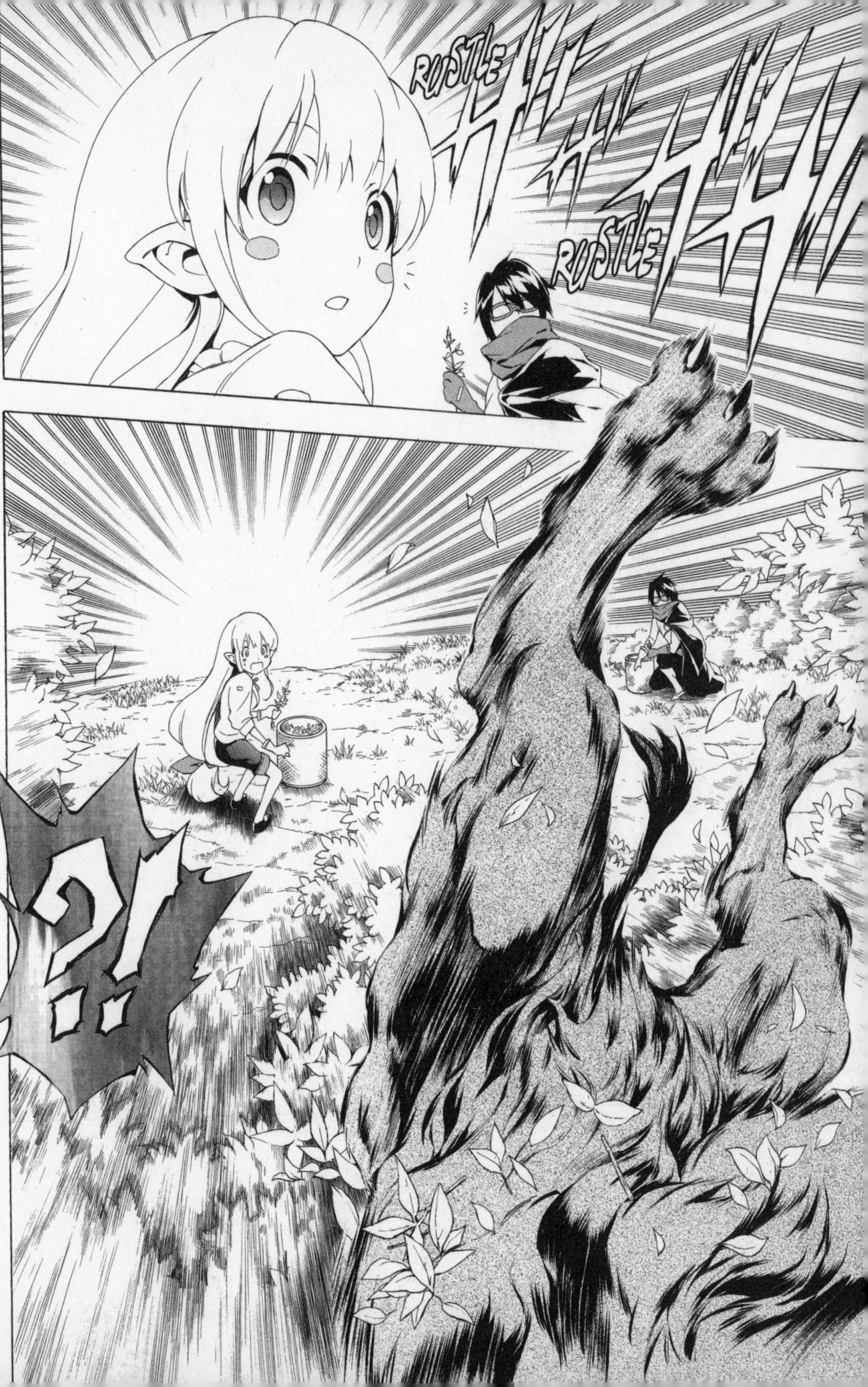
RUSTLE
RUSTLE
?!

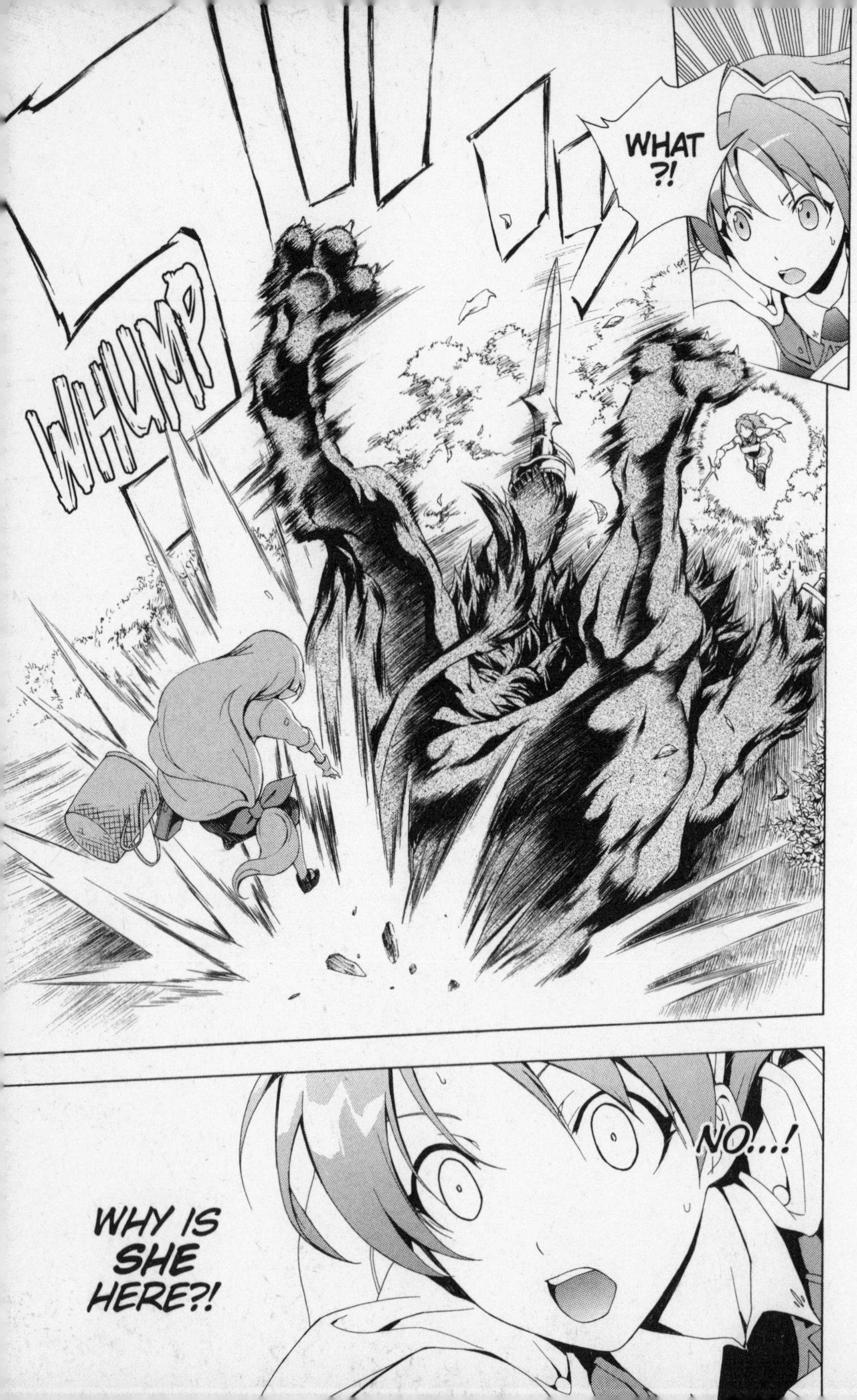
WHAT ?!
WHUMP
NO...!
WHY IS SHE HERE?!

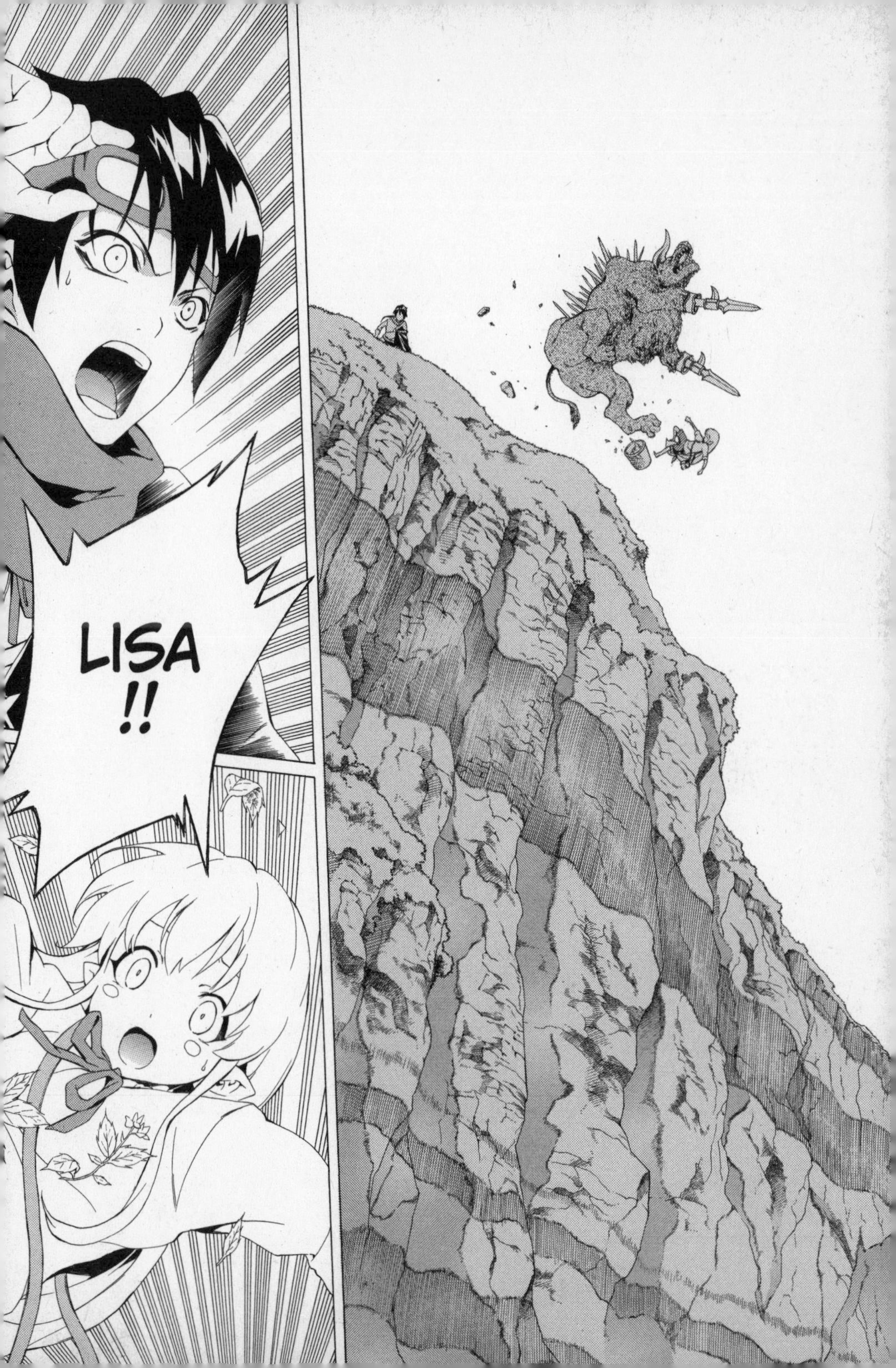
LISA !!

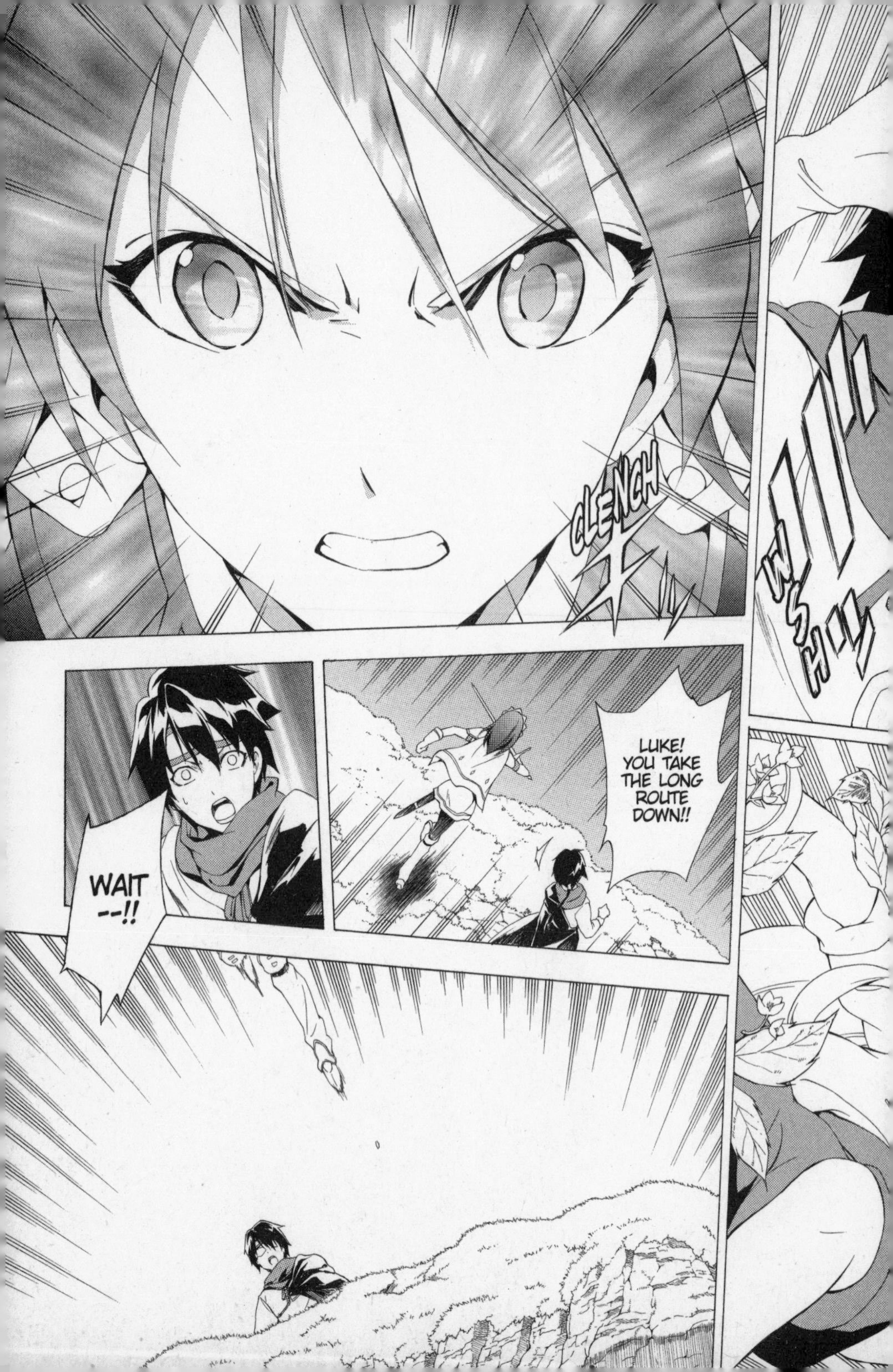
WHSH
CLENCH
LUKE! YOU TAKE THE LONG ROUTE DOWN!!
WAIT --!!

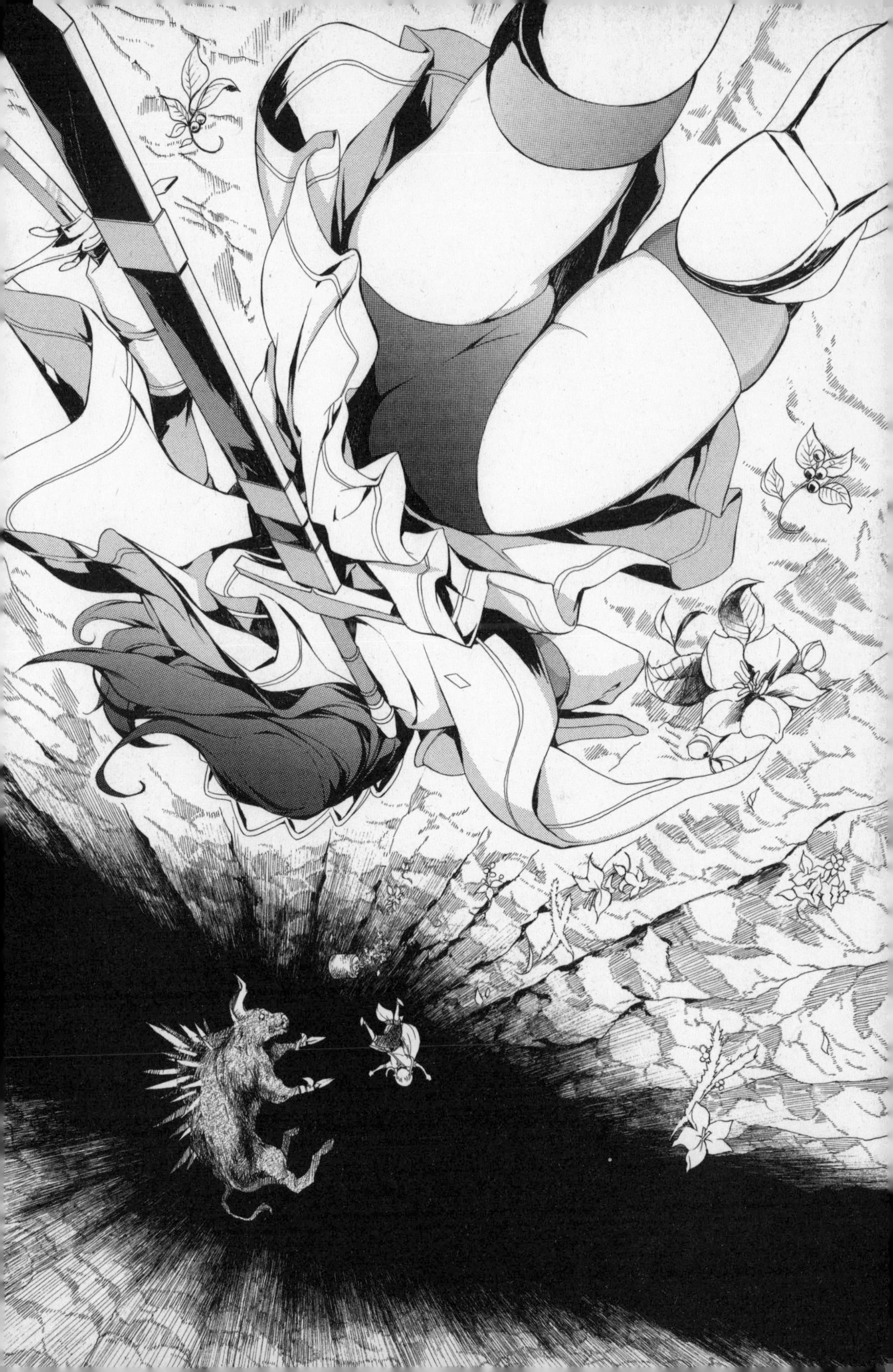

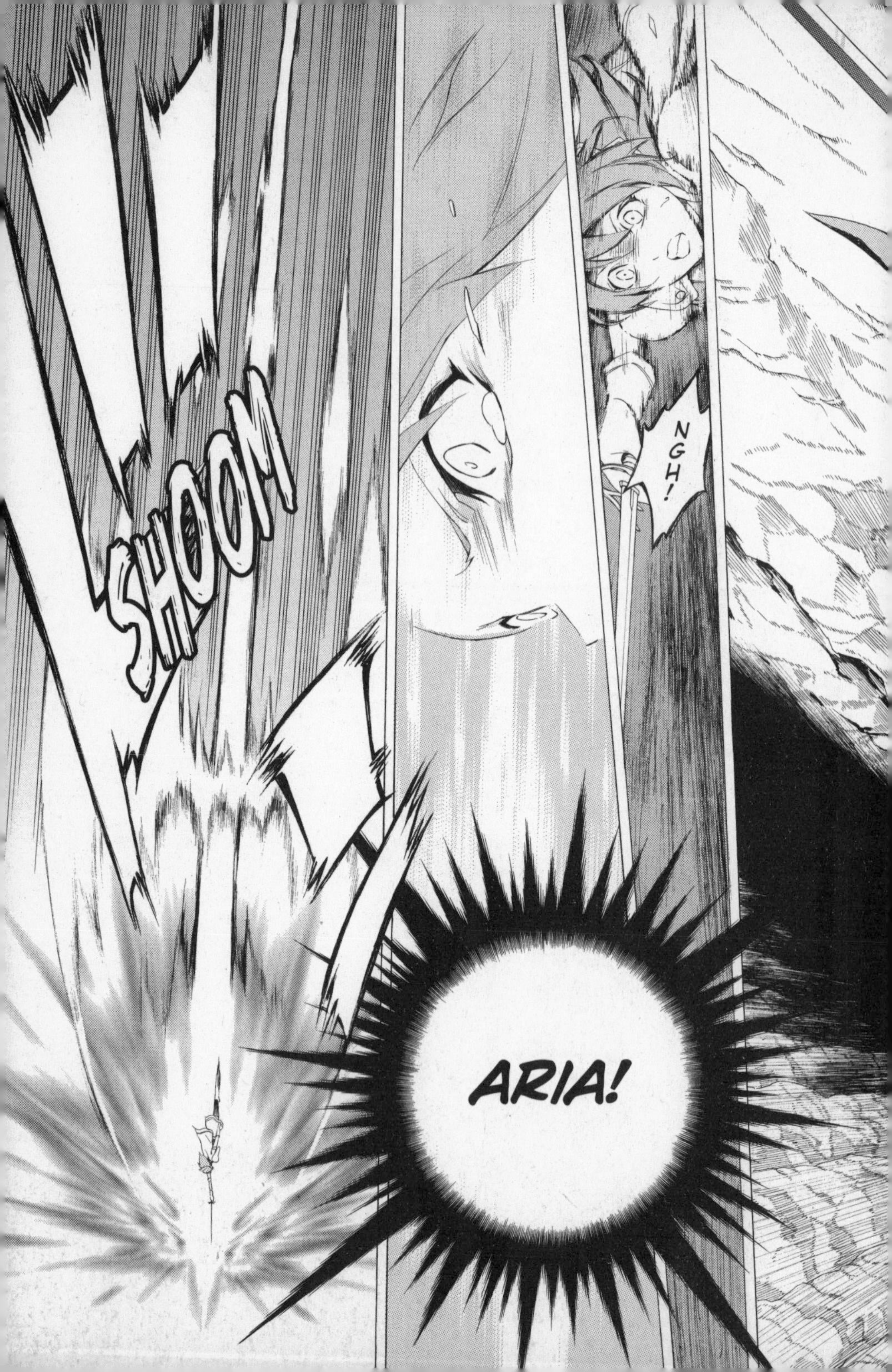
NGH!
SHOOM
ARIA!

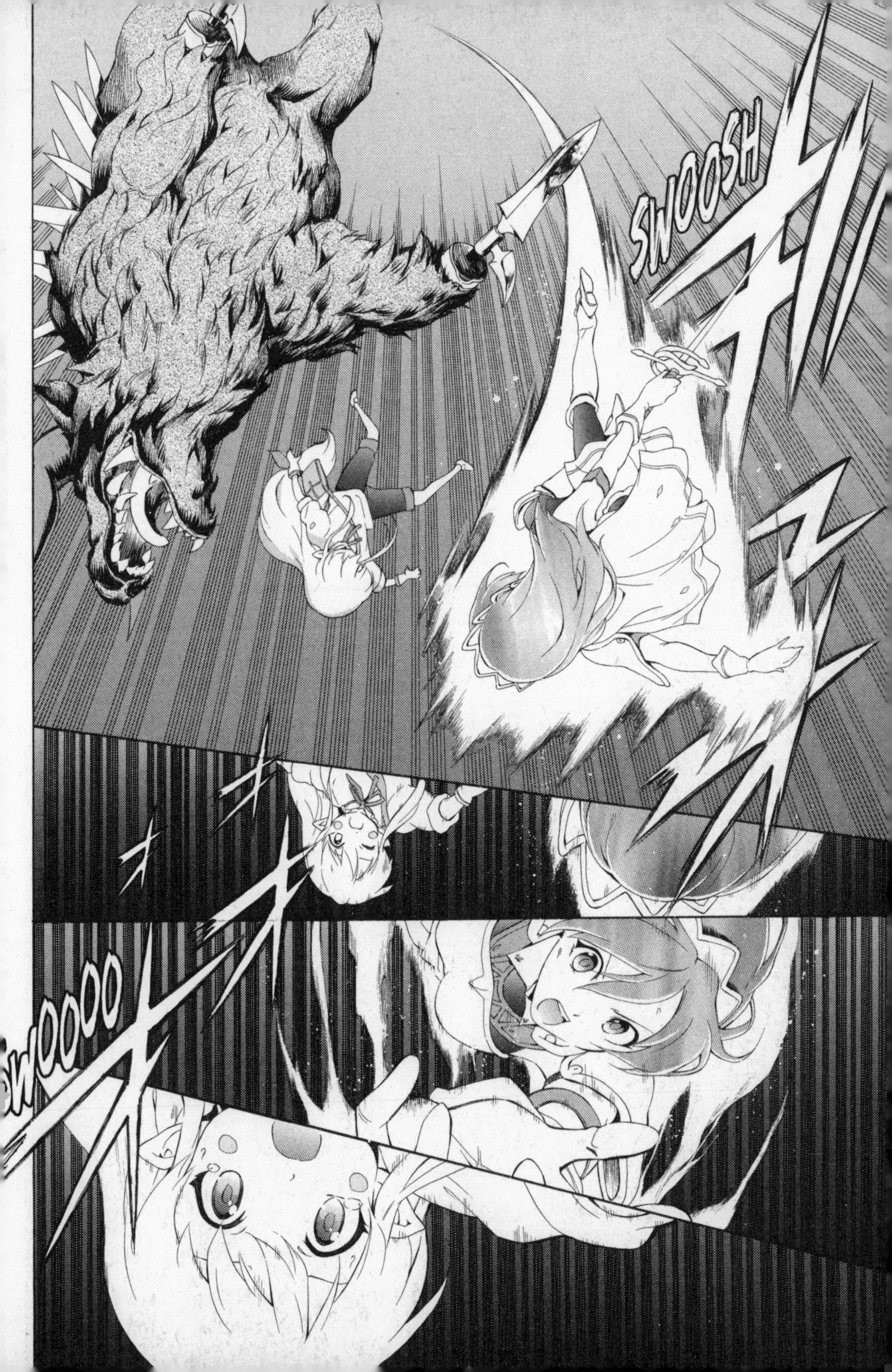
SWOOSH
SWOOOO

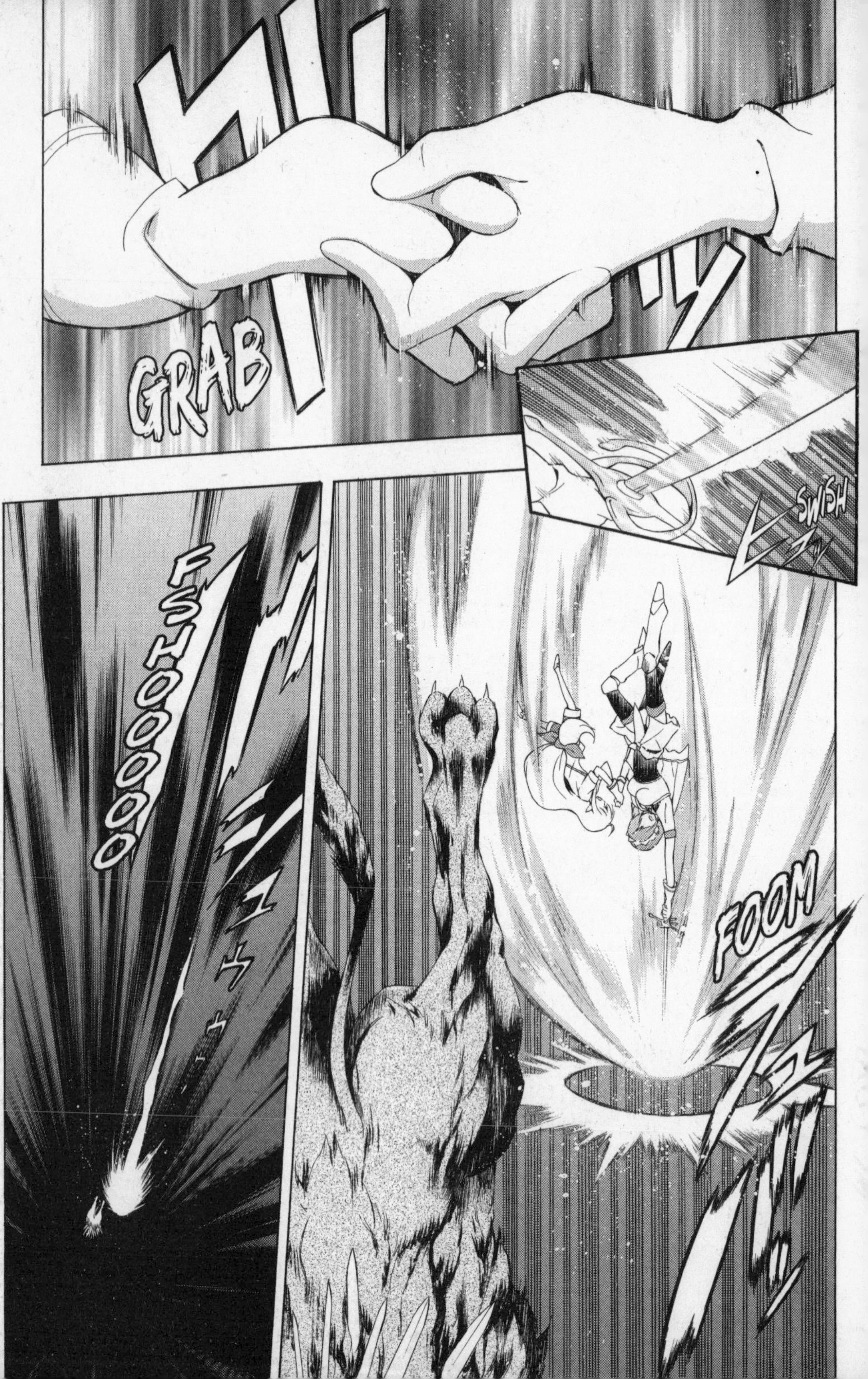
GRAB
SWISH
FOOM
FSHOOOOOOO

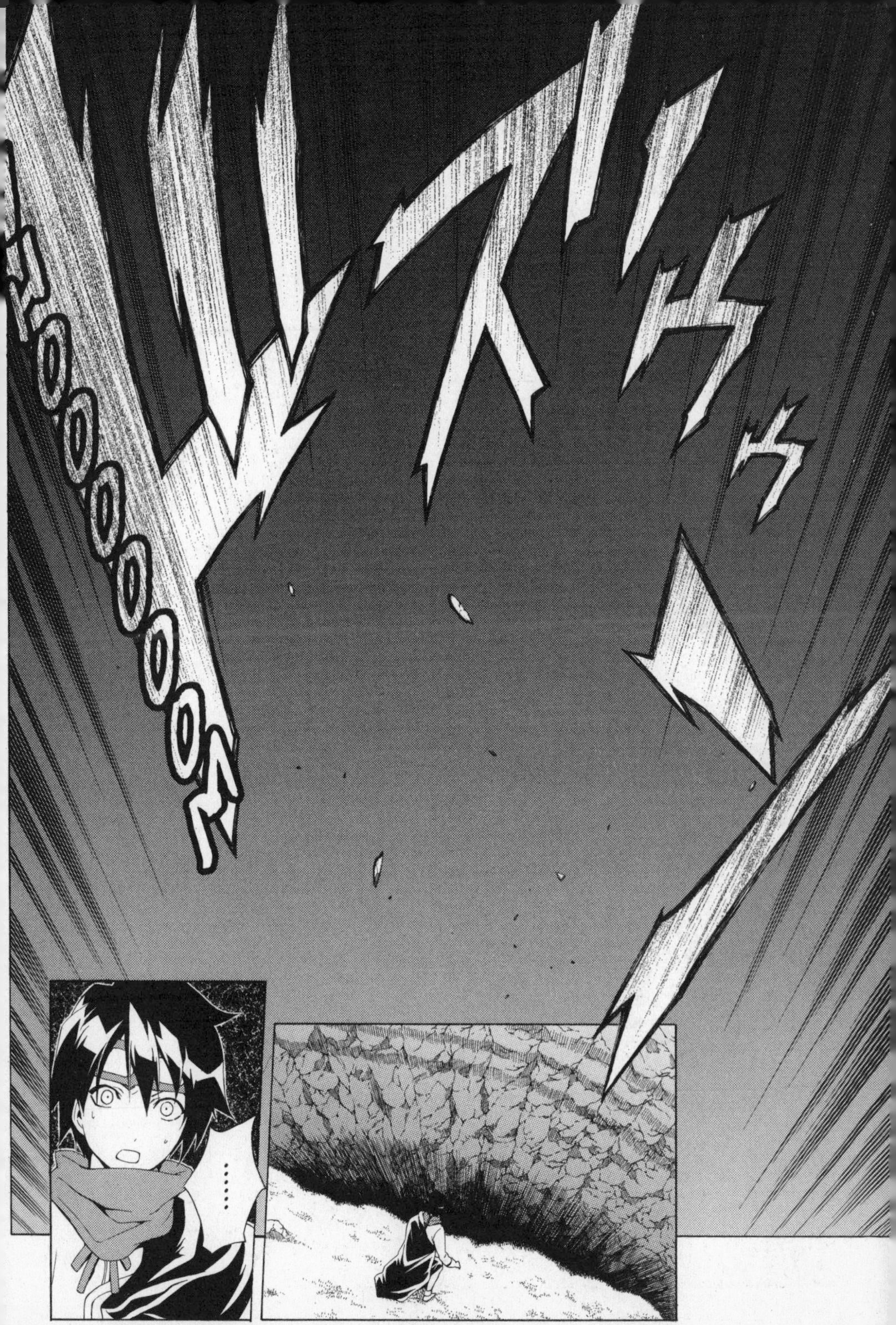
OOOOOOOM

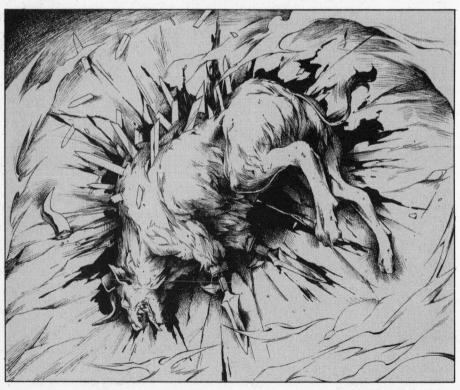

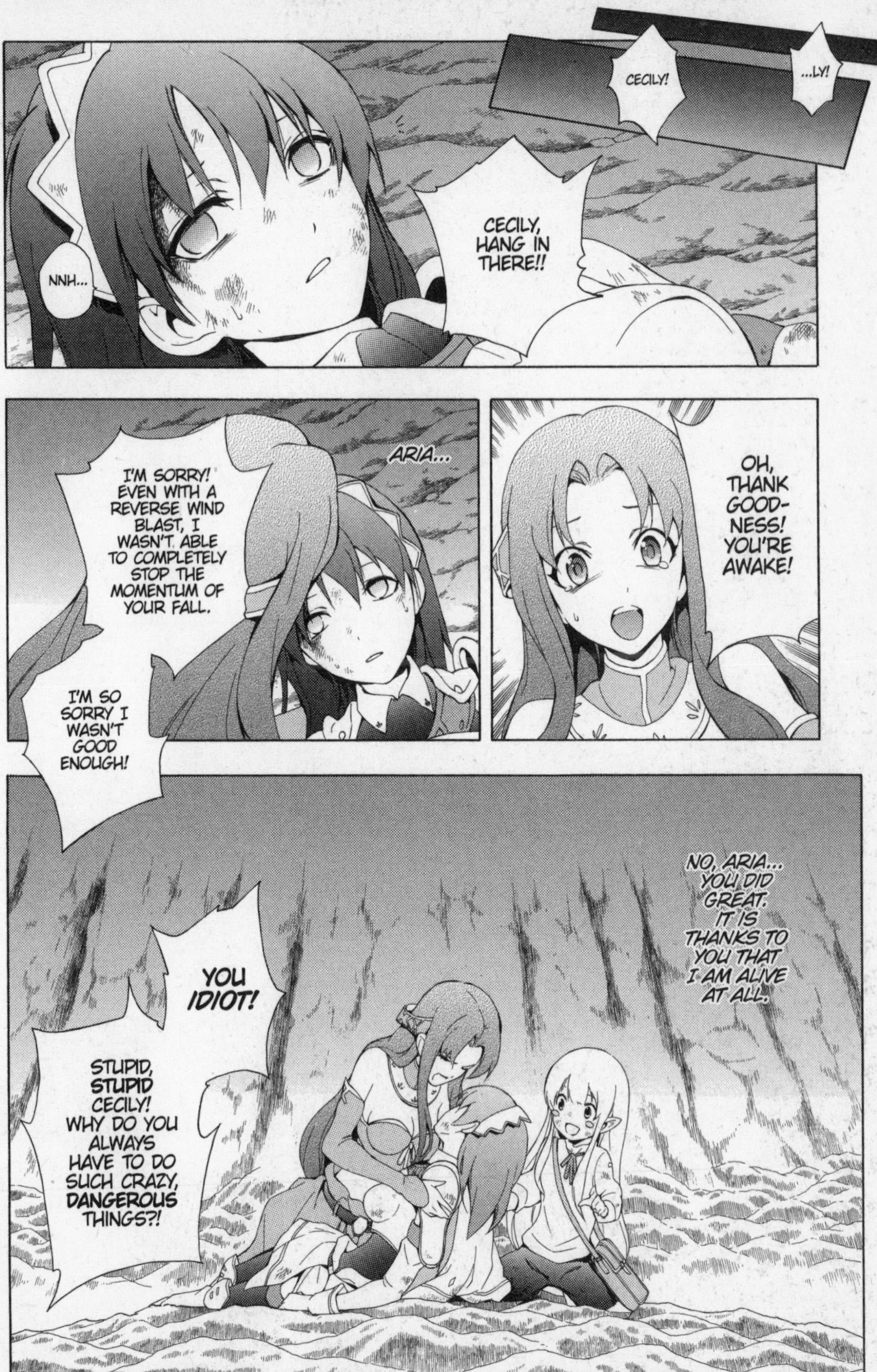
...LY!
CECILY!
CECILY, HANG IN THERE!!
NNH...
OH, THANK GOODNESS! YOU'RE AWAKE!
ARIA...
I'M SORRY! EVEN WITH A REVERSE WIND BLAST, I WASN'T ABLE TO COMPLETELY STOP THE MOMENTUM OF YOUR FALL.
I'M SO SORRY I WASN'T GOOD ENOUGH!
NO, ARIA... YOU DID GREAT. IT IS THANKS TO YOU THAT I AM ALIVE AT ALL.
YOU IDIOT!
STUPID, STUPID CECILY! WHY DO YOU ALWAYS HAVE TO DO SUCH CRAZY, DANGEROUS THINGS?!

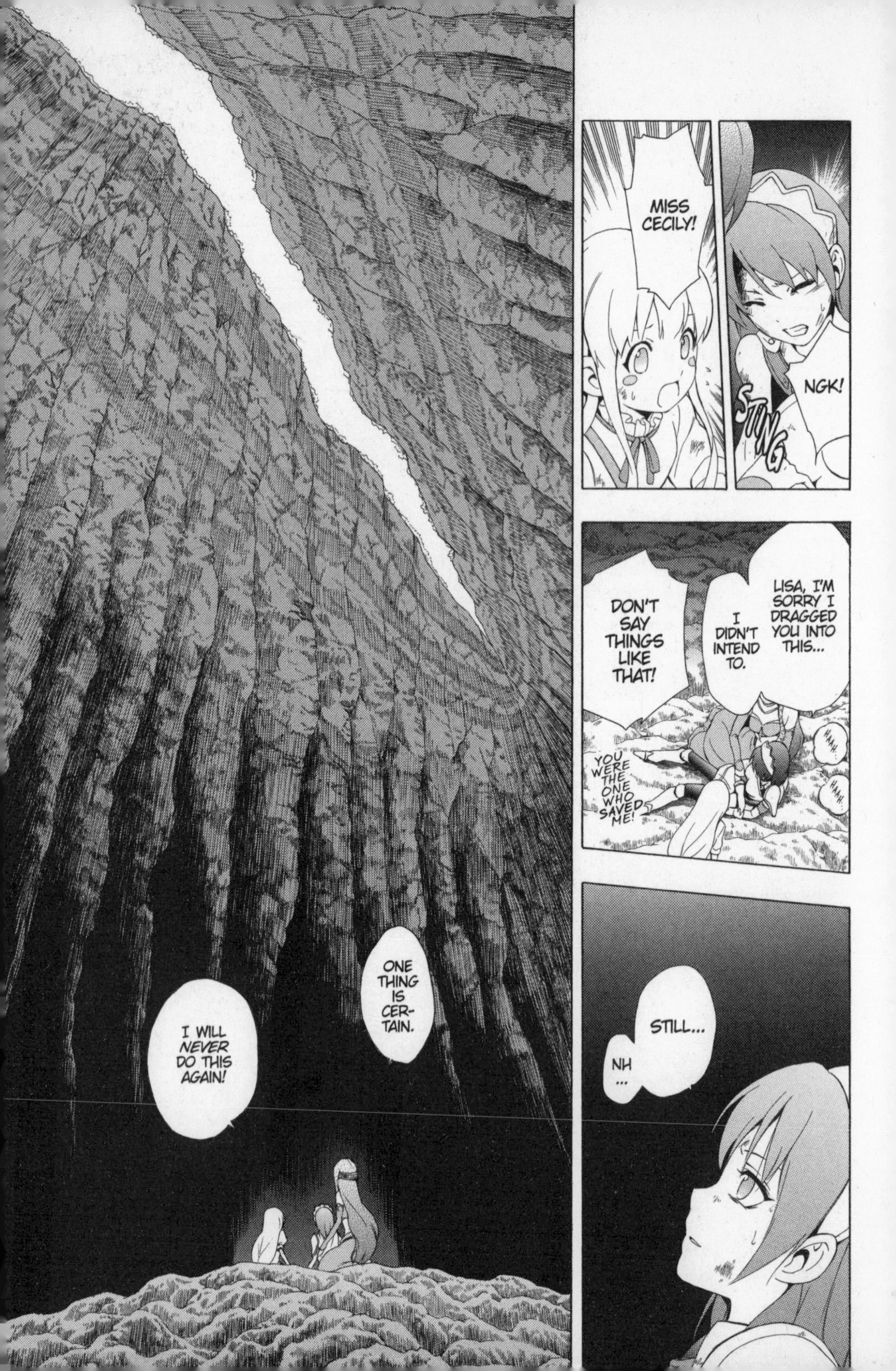
NGK!
STING
MISS CECILY!
LISA, I'M SORRY I DRAGGED YOU INTO THIS...
I DIDN'T INTEND TO.
DON'T SAY THINGS LIKE THAT!
HAAH
HAAH
YOU WERE THE ONE WHO SAVED ME!
STILL...
NH...
ONE THING IS CER-TAIN.
I WILL NEVER DO THIS AGAIN!

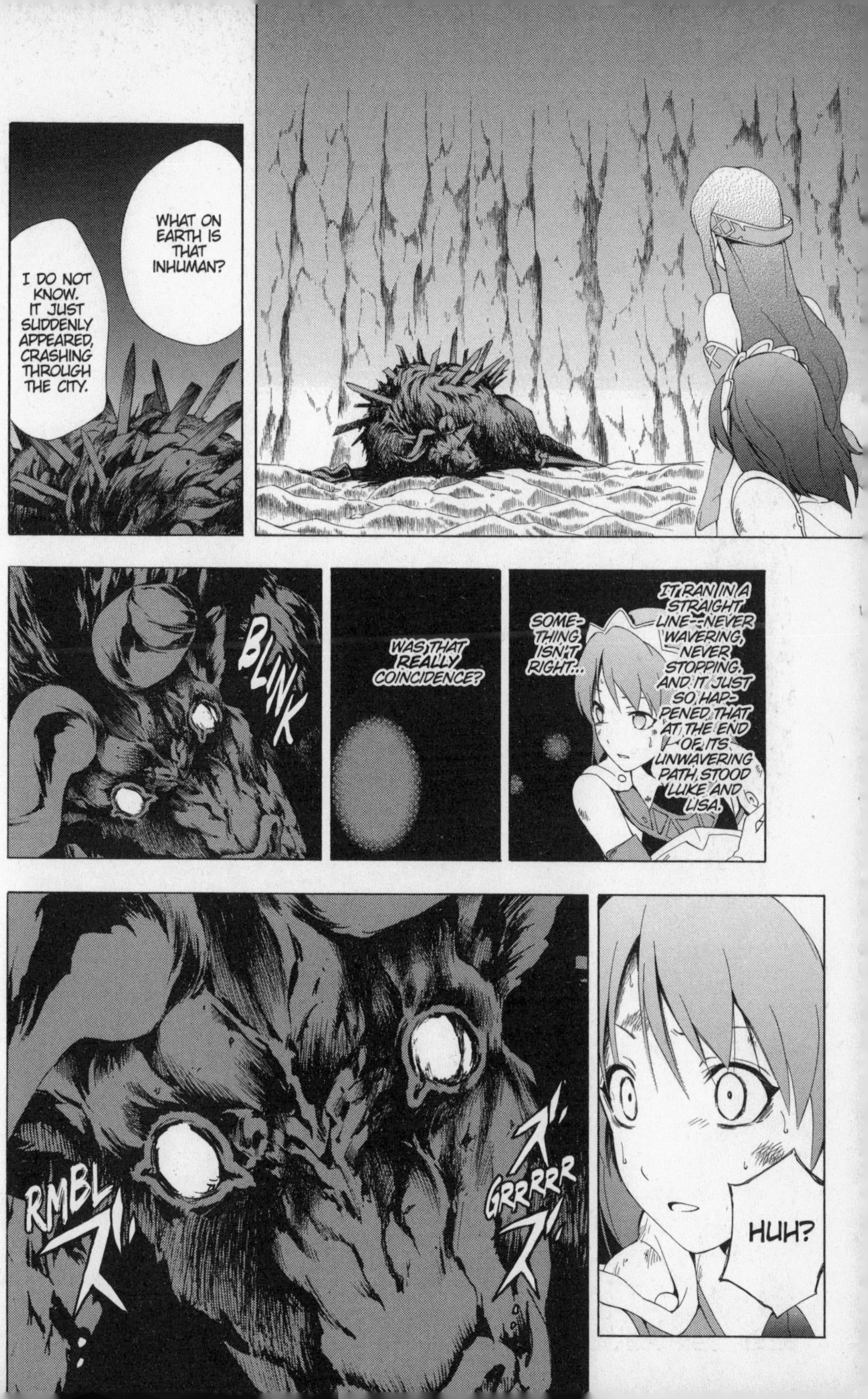
WHAT ON EARTH IS THAT INHUMAN?
I DO NOT KNOW. IT JUST SUDDENLY APPEARED, CRASHING THROUGH THE CITY.
IT RAN IN A STRAIGHT LINE--NEVER WAVERING, NEVER STOPPING. AND IT JUST SO HAPPENED THAT AT THE END OF ITS UNWAVERING PATH STOOD LUKE AND LISA.
SOMETHING ISN'T RIGHT...
WAS THAT REALLY COINCIDENCE?
BLINK
HUH?
GRRRRR
RMBL

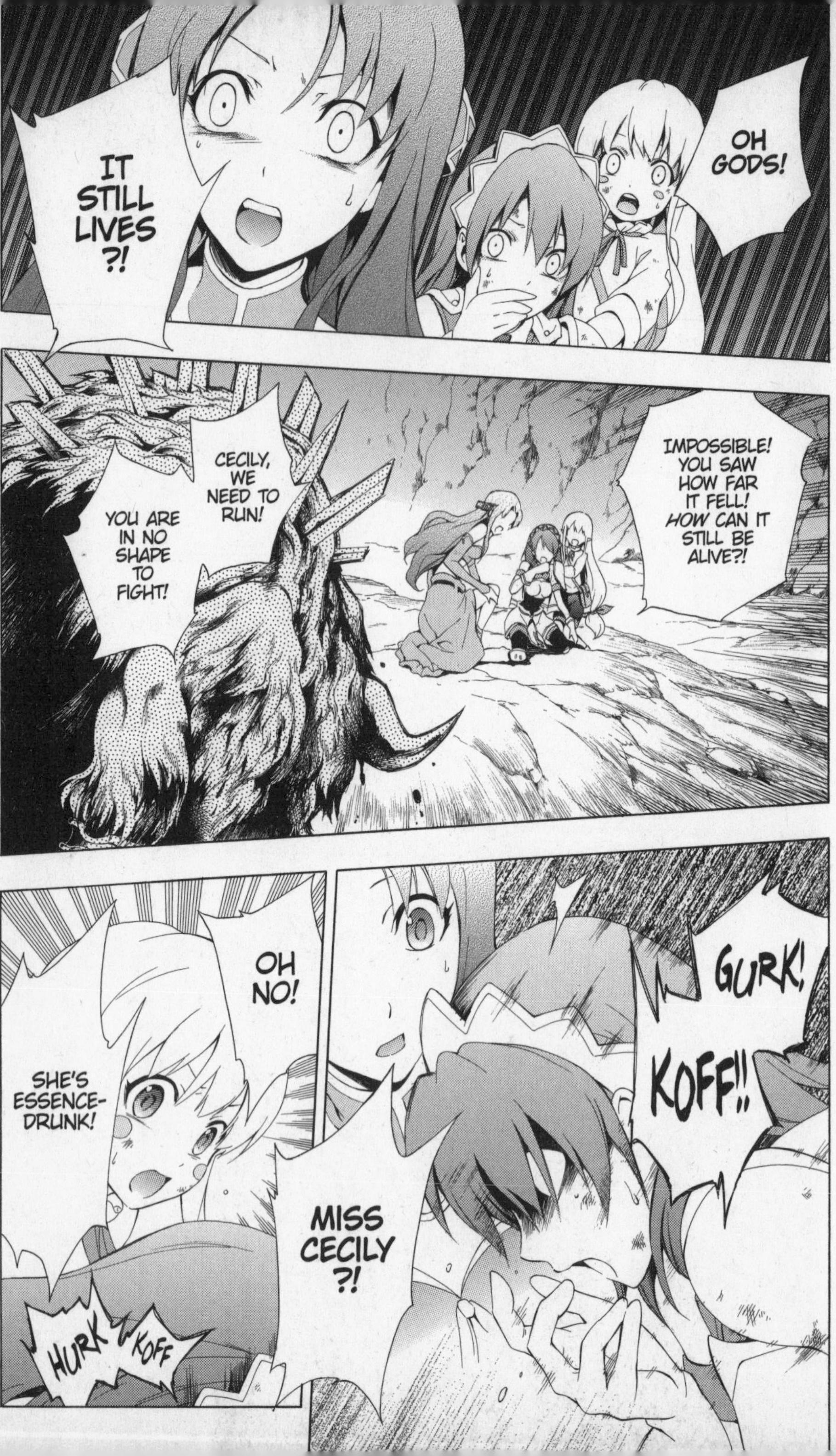
OH GODS!
IT STILL LIVES?!
IMPOSSIBLE! YOU SAW HOW FAR IT FELL! *HOW* CAN IT STILL BE ALIVE?!
CECILY, WE NEED TO RUN!
YOU ARE IN NO SHAPE TO FIGHT!
GURK!
KOFF!!
OH NO!
SHE'S ESSENCE-DRUNK!
MISS CECILY?!
HURK
KOFF

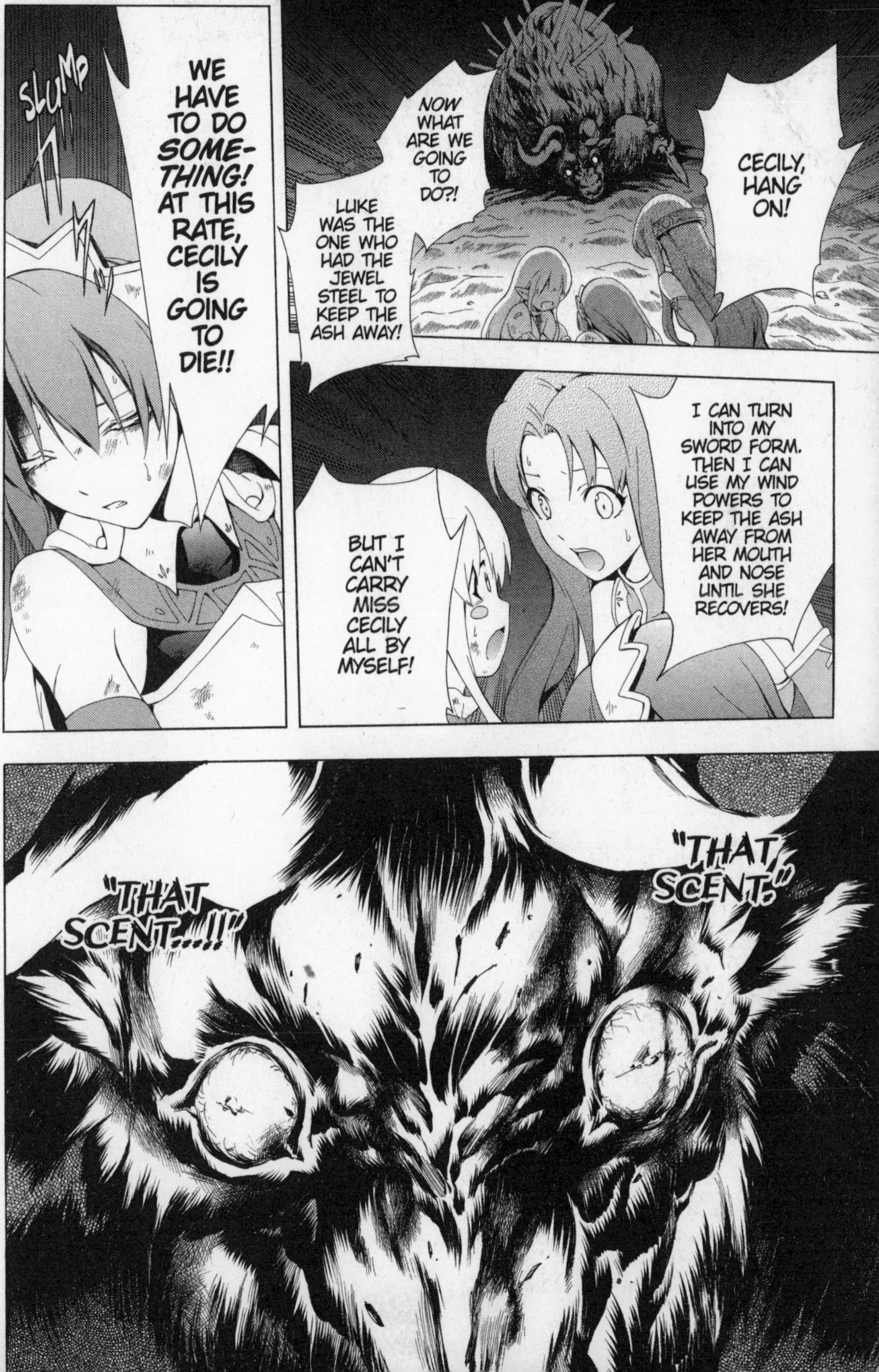
CECILY, HANG ON!
NOW WHAT ARE WE GOING TO DO?!
LUKE WAS THE ONE WHO HAD THE JEWEL STEEL TO KEEP THE ASH AWAY!
I CAN TURN INTO MY SWORD FORM. THEN I CAN USE MY WIND POWERS TO KEEP THE ASH AWAY FROM HER MOUTH AND NOSE UNTIL SHE RECOVERS!
BUT I CAN'T CARRY MISS CECILY ALL BY MYSELF!
WE HAVE TO DO SOMETHING! AT THIS RATE, CECILY IS GOING TO DIE!!
SLUMP
"THAT SCENT."
"THAT SCENT...!!"

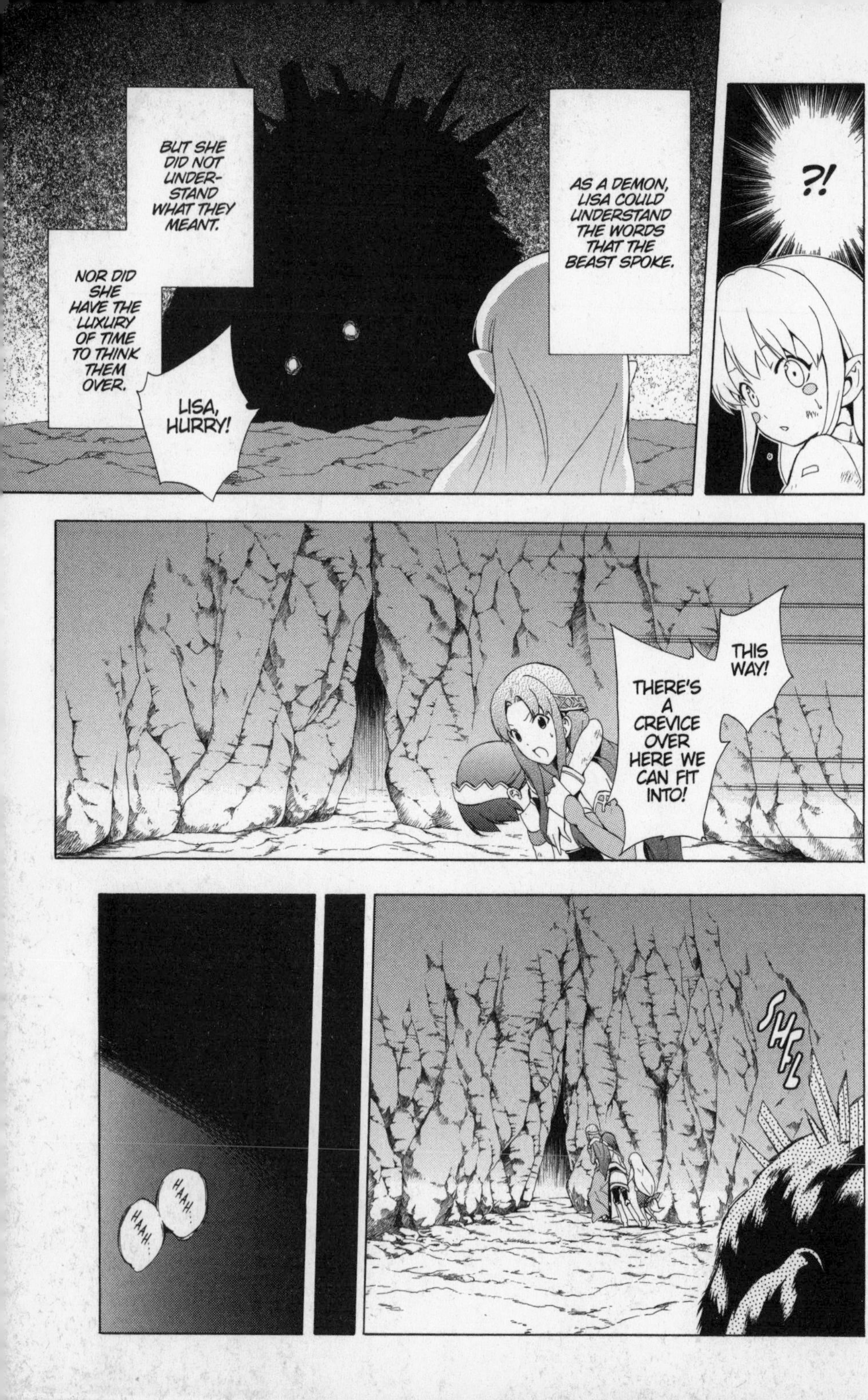
?!
AS A DEMON, LISA COULD UNDERSTAND THE WORDS THAT THE BEAST SPOKE.
BUT SHE DID NOT UNDER-STAND WHAT THEY MEANT.
NOR DID SHE HAVE THE LUXURY OF TIME TO THINK THEM OVER.
LISA, HURRY!
THIS WAY!
THERE'S A CREVICE OVER HERE WE CAN FIT INTO!
SHFL
HAAH...
HAAH...

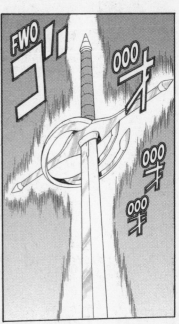

FWO
ゴ"

ооо
オ

ооо
オ

ооо
オ

GOOD.

AS LONG AS WE'RE HIDDEN IN HERE...

LOOM

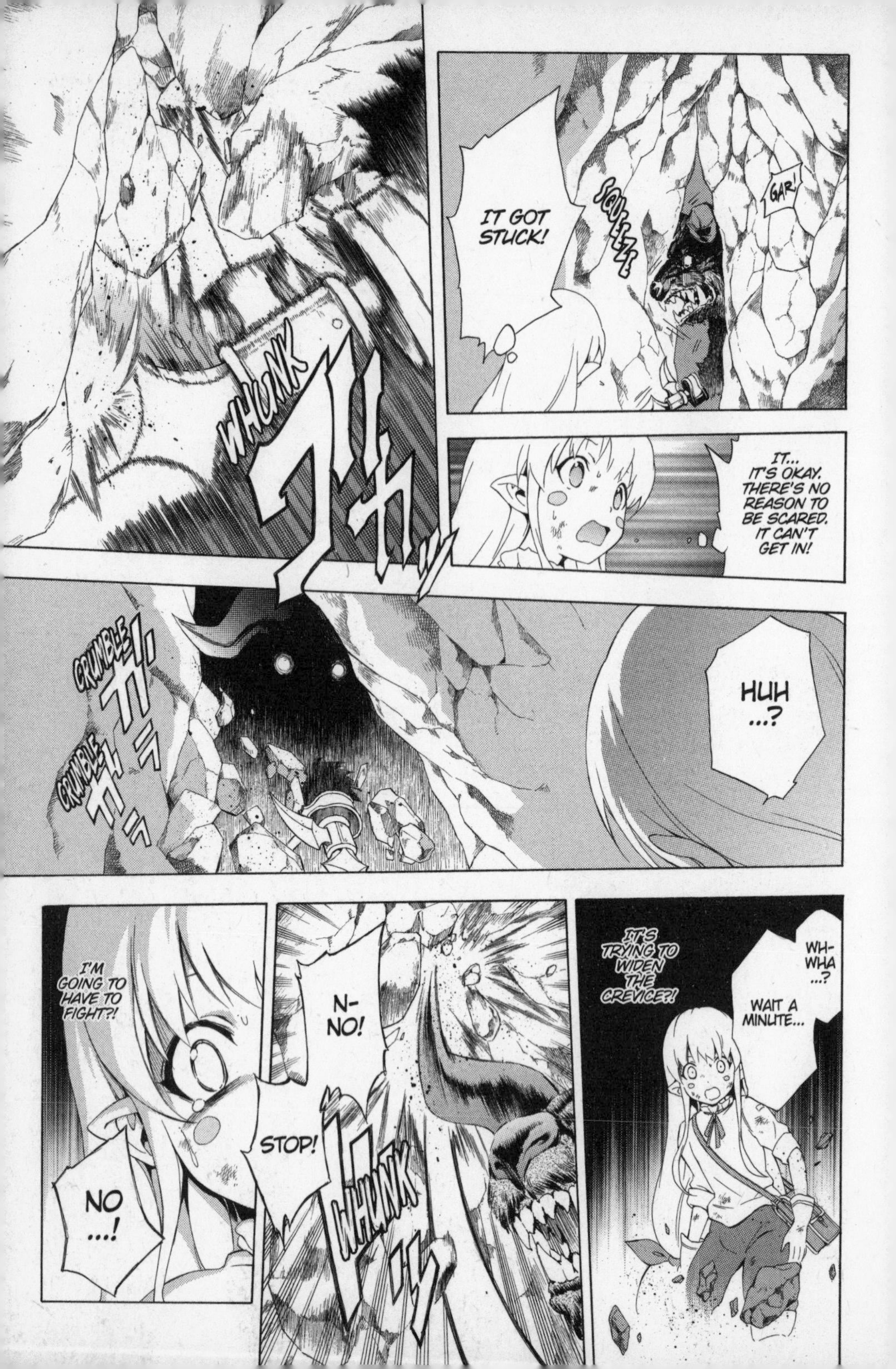
GAR!
SQUEEZE
IT GOT STUCK!
IT... IT'S OKAY. THERE'S NO REASON TO BE SCARED. IT CAN'T GET IN!
WHUNK
HUH ...?
CRUMBLE
CRUMBLE
WH- WHA ...?
WAIT A MINUTE...
IT'S TRYING TO WIDEN THE CREVICE?!
N- NO!
STOP!
WHUNK
I'M GOING TO HAVE TO FIGHT?!
NO ...!

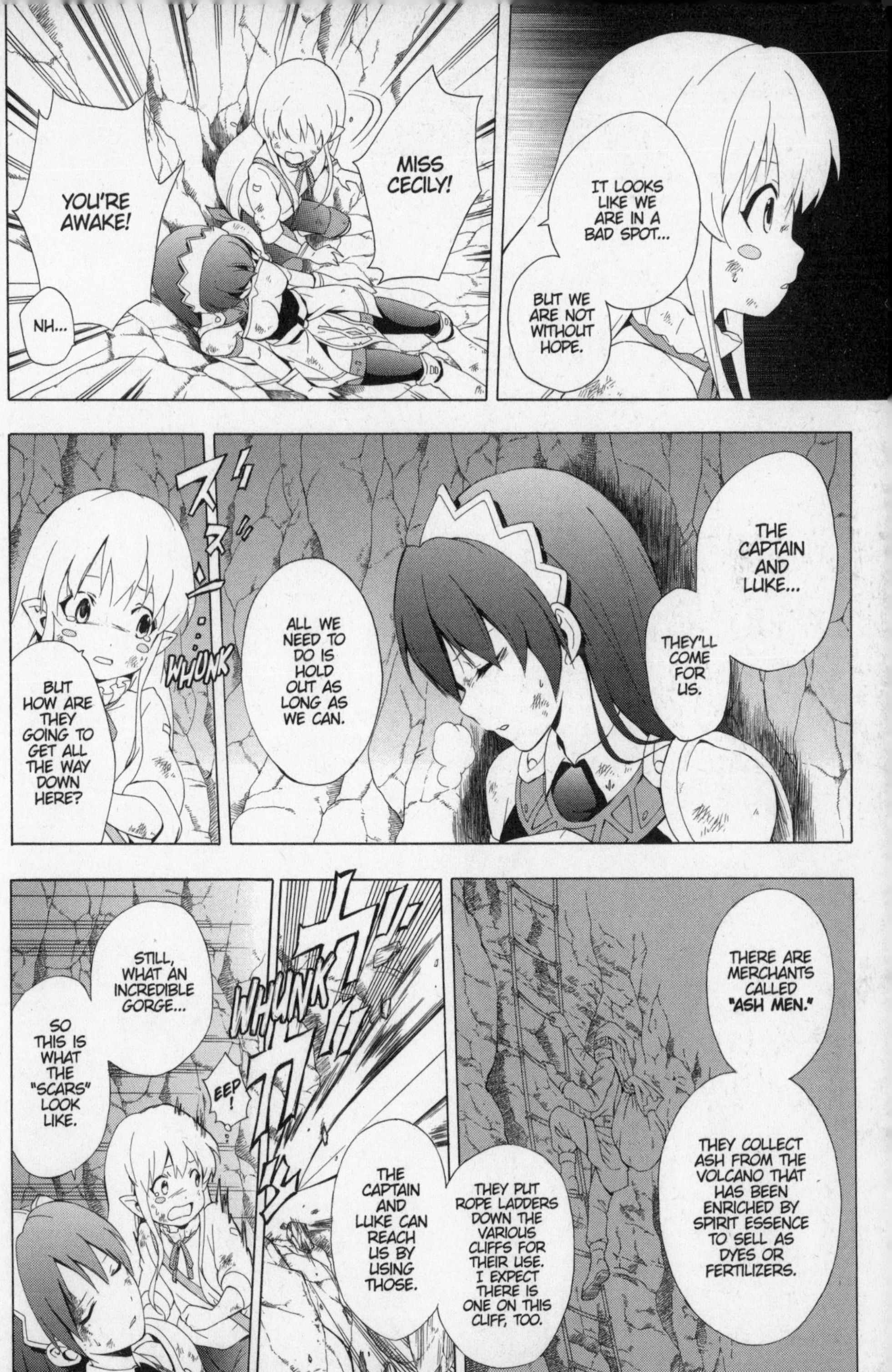
IT LOOKS LIKE WE ARE IN A BAD SPOT...
BUT WE ARE NOT WITHOUT HOPE.
MISS CECILY!
YOU'RE AWAKE!
NH...
THE CAPTAIN AND LUKE...
THEY'LL COME FOR US.
ALL WE NEED TO DO IS HOLD OUT AS LONG AS WE CAN.
WHUNK
BUT HOW ARE THEY GOING TO GET ALL THE WAY DOWN HERE?
THERE ARE MERCHANTS CALLED **"ASH MEN."**
THEY COLLECT ASH FROM THE VOLCANO THAT HAS BEEN ENRICHED BY SPIRIT ESSENCE TO SELL AS DYES OR FERTILIZERS.
THEY PUT ROPE LADDERS DOWN THE VARIOUS CLIFFS FOR THEIR USE. I EXPECT THERE IS ONE ON THIS CLIFF, TOO.
THE CAPTAIN AND LUKE CAN REACH US BY USING THOSE.
WHUNK
STILL, WHAT AN INCREDIBLE GORGE...
SO THIS IS WHAT THE "SCARS" LOOK LIKE.
EEP!

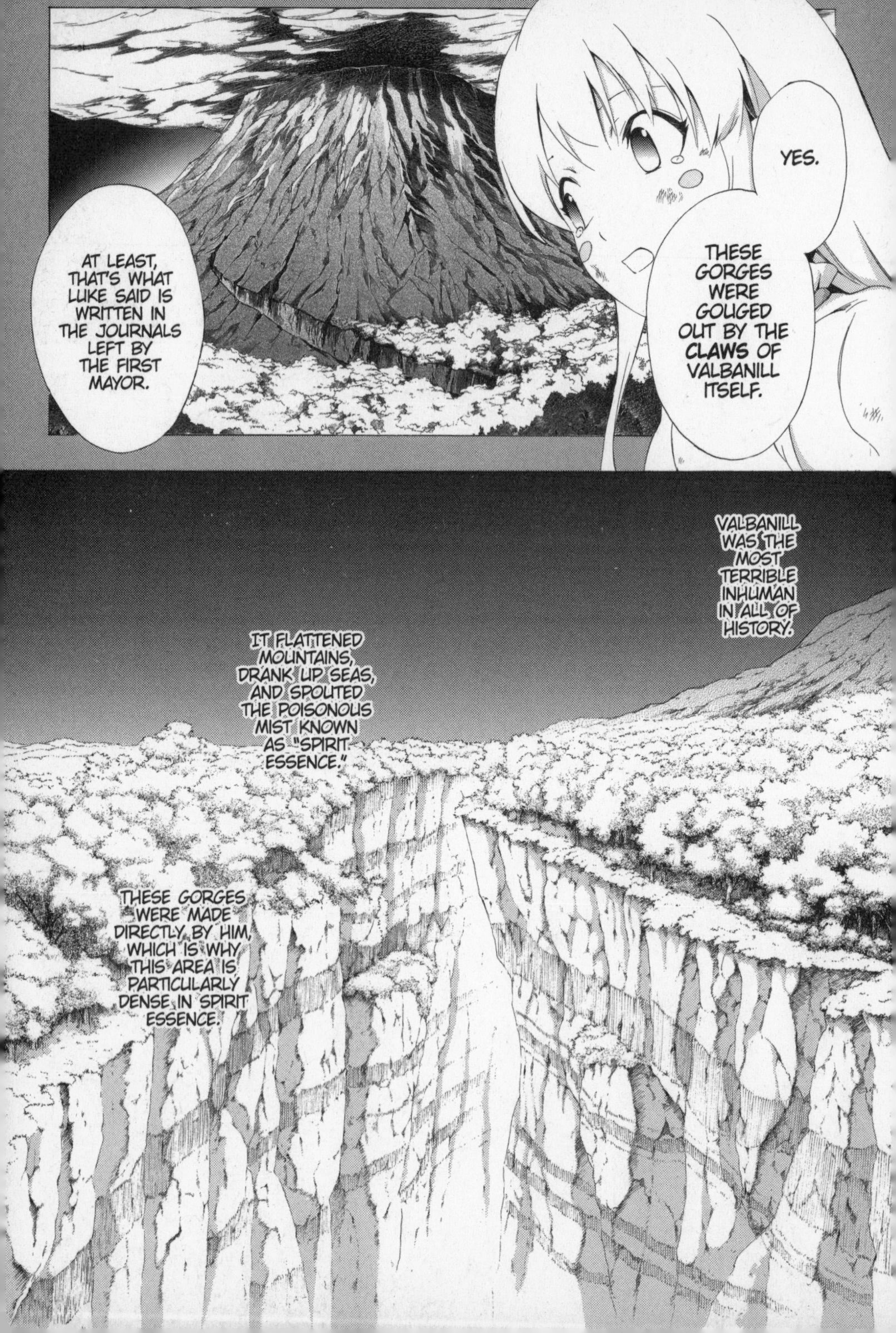
YES.
THESE GORGES WERE GOUGED OUT BY THE **CLAWS** OF VALBANILL ITSELF.
AT LEAST, THAT'S WHAT LUKE SAID IS WRITTEN IN THE JOURNALS LEFT BY THE FIRST MAYOR.
VALBANILL WAS THE MOST TERRIBLE INHUMAN IN ALL OF HISTORY.
IT FLATTENED MOUNTAINS, DRANK UP SEAS, AND SPOUTED THE POISONOUS MIST KNOWN AS "SPIRIT ESSENCE."
THESE GORGES WERE MADE DIRECTLY BY HIM, WHICH IS WHY THIS AREA IS PARTICULARLY DENSE IN SPIRIT ESSENCE.

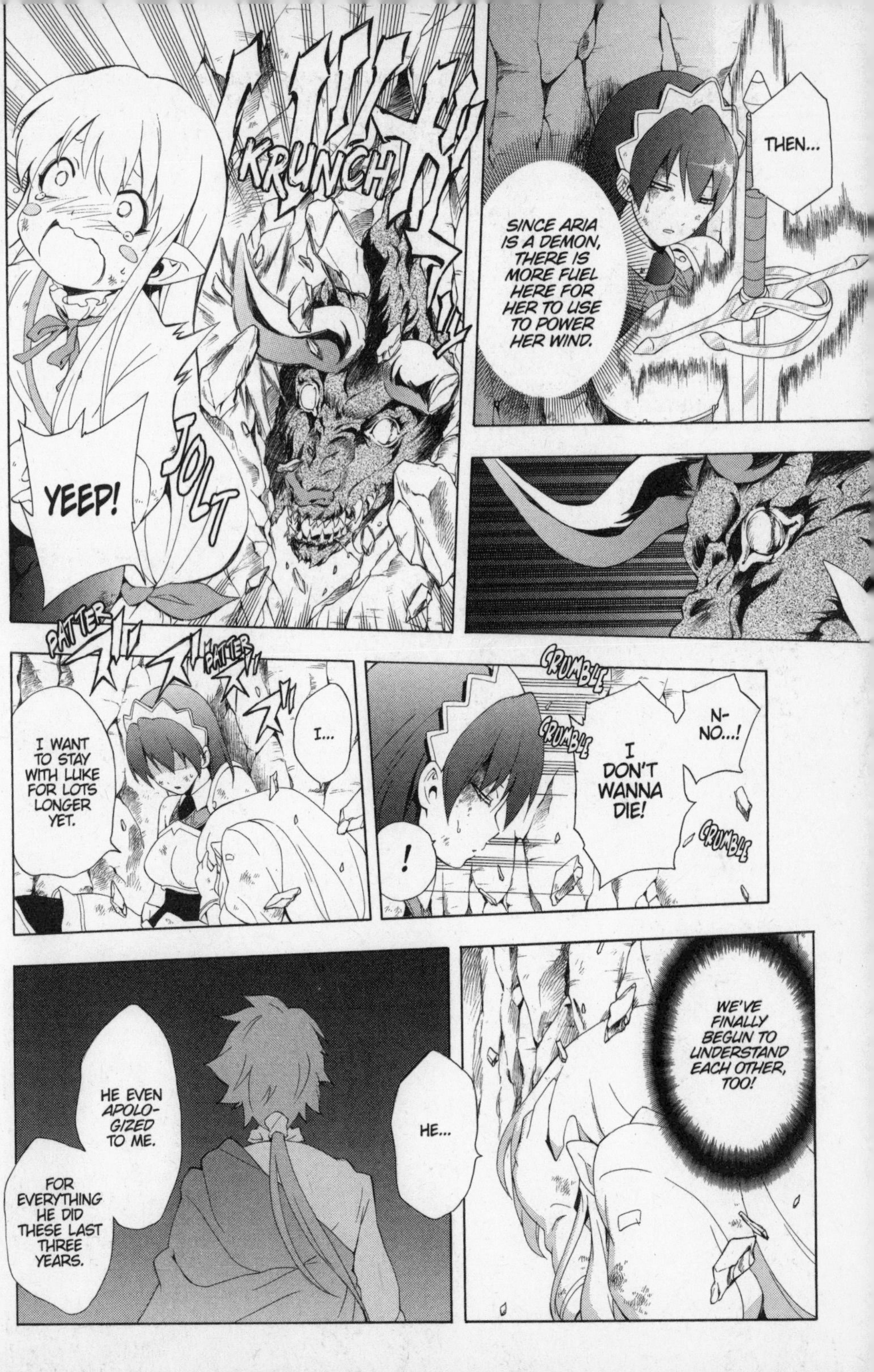
THEN...
SINCE ARIA IS A DEMON, THERE IS MORE FUEL HERE FOR HER TO USE TO POWER HER WIND.
KRUNCH
JOLT
YEEP!
CRUMBLE
CRUMBLE
N- NO...!
I DON'T WANNA DIE!
CRUMBLE
!
PATTER
PATTER
I...
I WANT TO STAY WITH LUKE FOR LOTS LONGER YET.
WE'VE FINALLY BEGUN TO UNDERSTAND EACH OTHER, TOO!
HE...
HE EVEN APOLO-GIZED TO ME.
FOR EVERYTHING HE DID THESE LAST THREE YEARS.

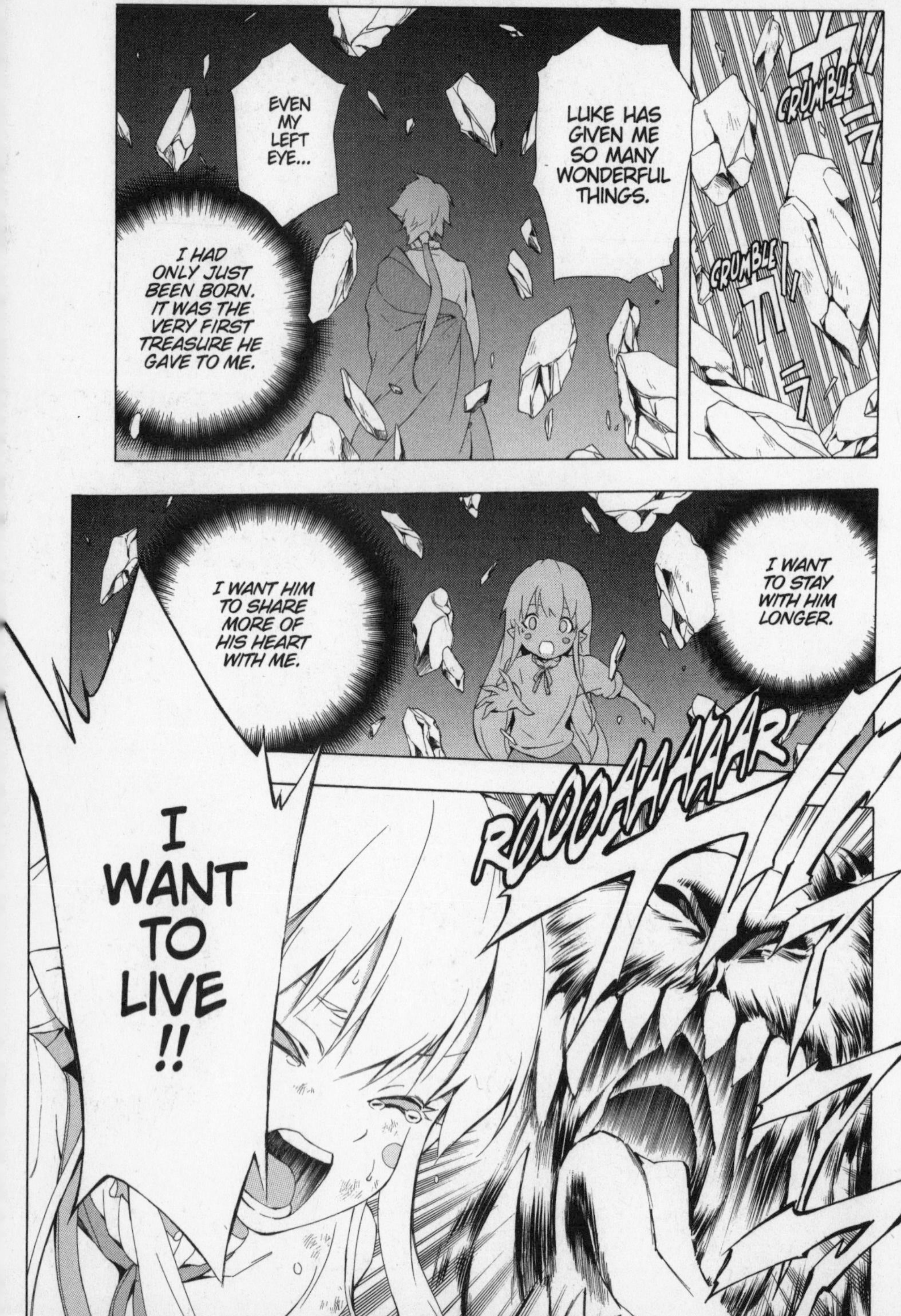
CRUMBLE
CRUMBLE
LUKE HAS GIVEN ME SO MANY WONDERFUL THINGS.
EVEN MY LEFT EYE...
I HAD ONLY JUST BEEN BORN. IT WAS THE VERY FIRST TREASURE HE GAVE TO ME.
I WANT TO STAY WITH HIM LONGER.
I WANT HIM TO SHARE MORE OF HIS HEART WITH ME.
ROOOAAAAAAR
I WANT TO LIVE!!

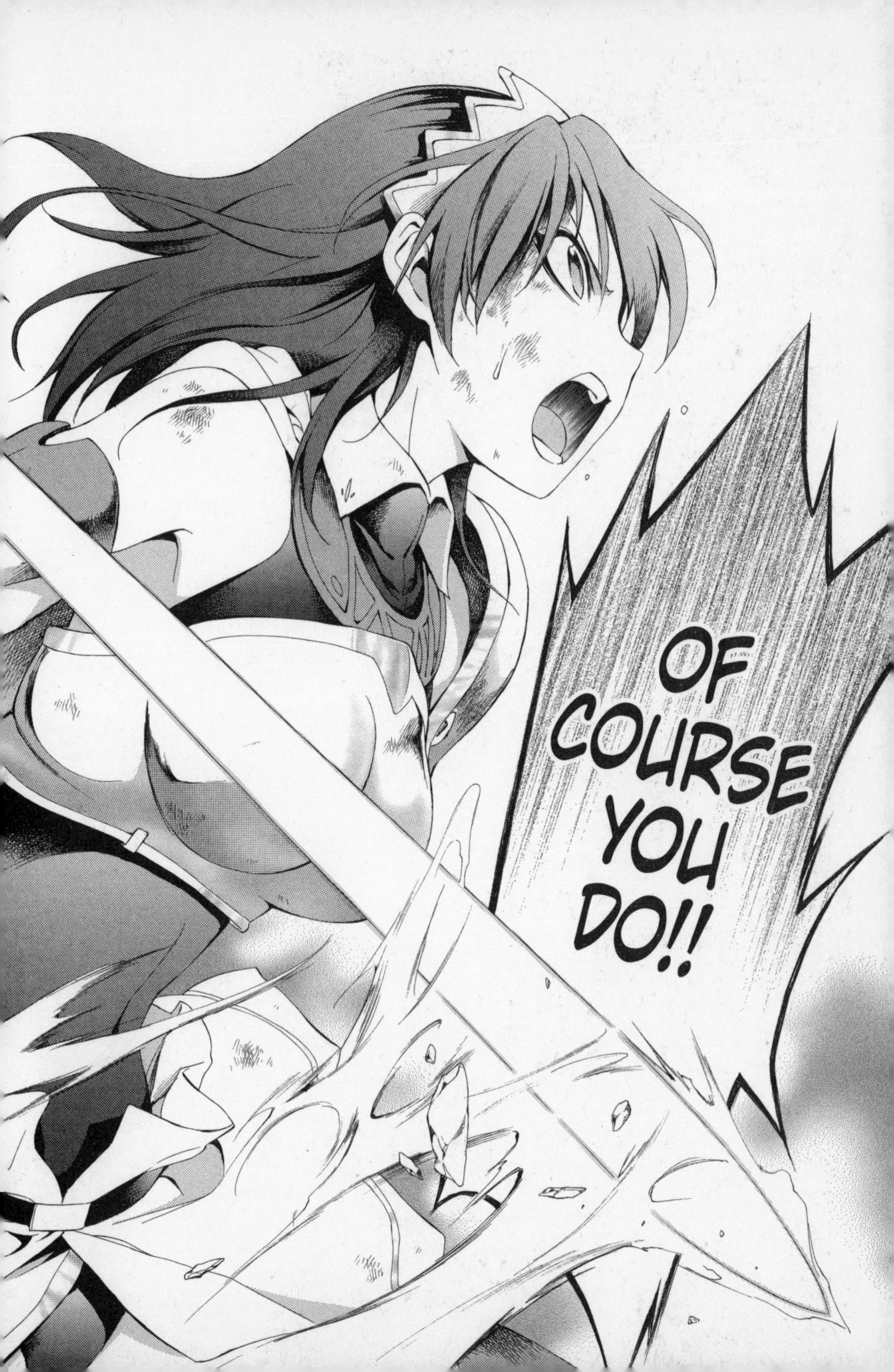
OF COURSE YOU DO!!

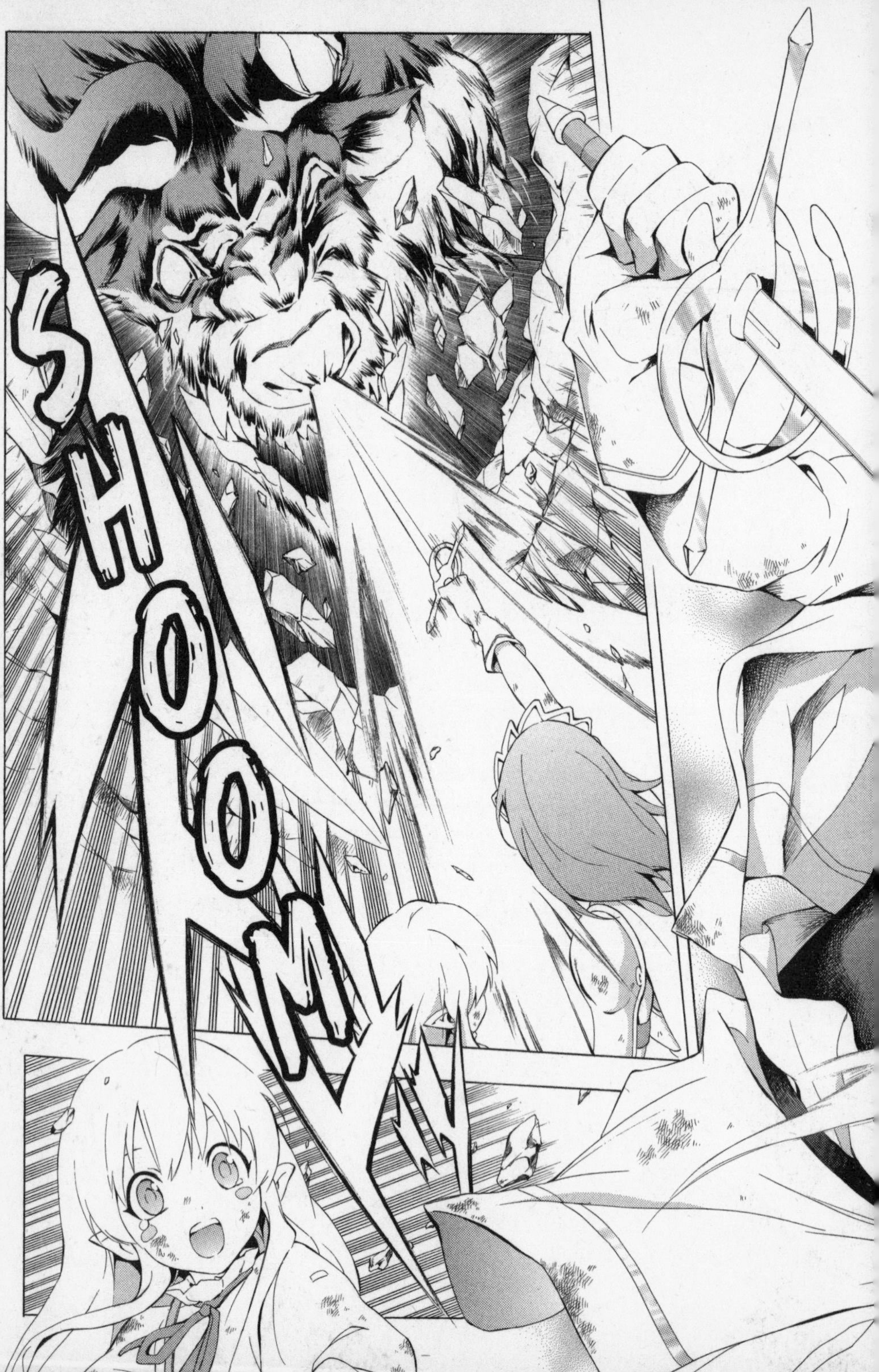
SHOOM

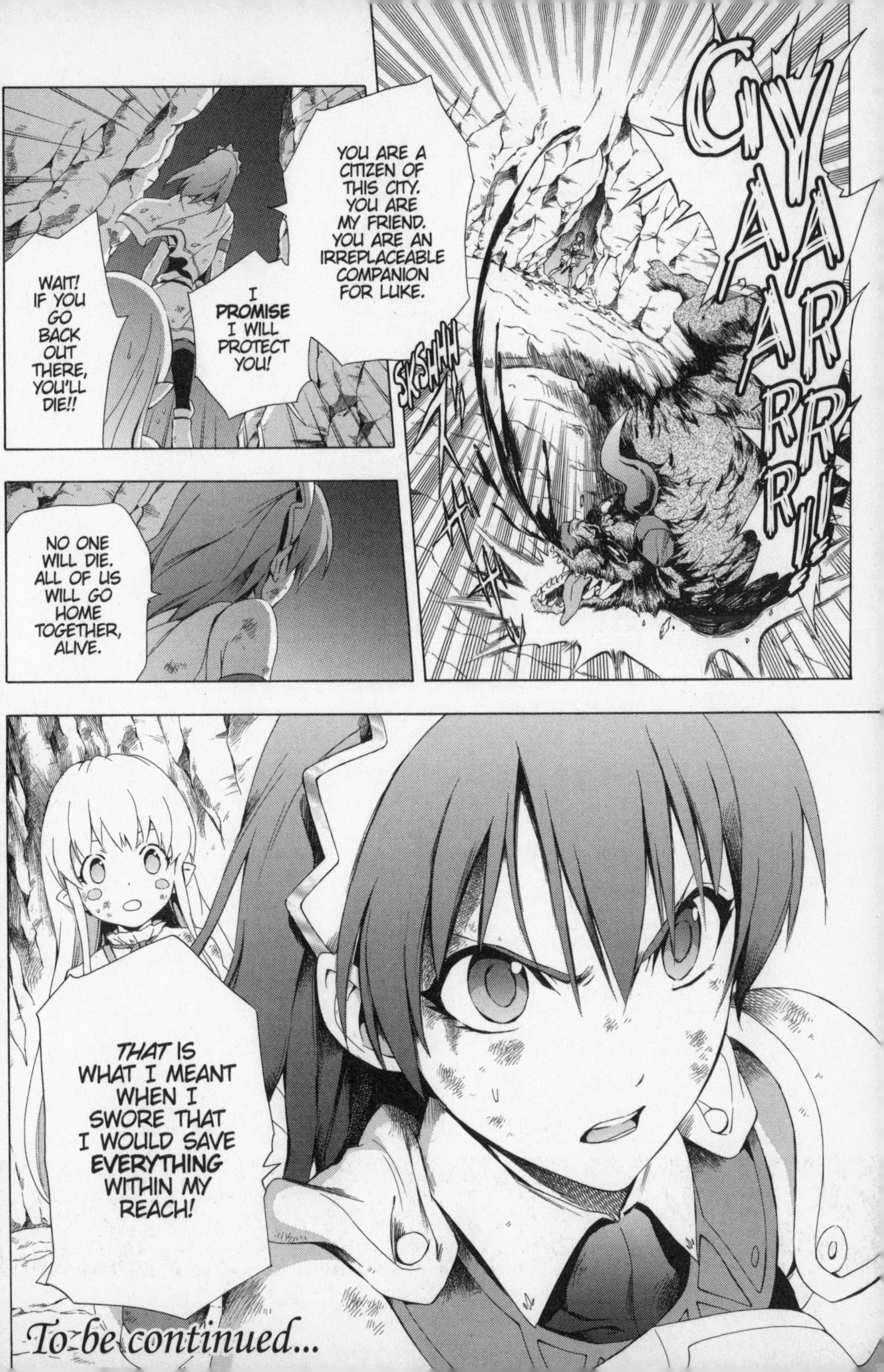
GYAAARRRR!!
SKSHHH
YOU ARE A CITIZEN OF THIS CITY. YOU ARE MY FRIEND. YOU ARE AN IRREPLACEABLE COMPANION FOR LUKE.
I **PROMISE** I WILL PROTECT YOU!
WAIT! IF YOU GO BACK OUT THERE, YOU'LL DIE!!
NO ONE WILL DIE. ALL OF US WILL GO HOME TOGETHER, ALIVE.
THAT IS WHAT I MEANT WHEN I SWORE THAT I WOULD SAVE **EVERYTHING** WITHIN MY REACH!
To be continued...

The Sacred Blacksmith

聖剣の刀鍛冶

工房リーザ
atelier Liza BRANCH OFFICE IV

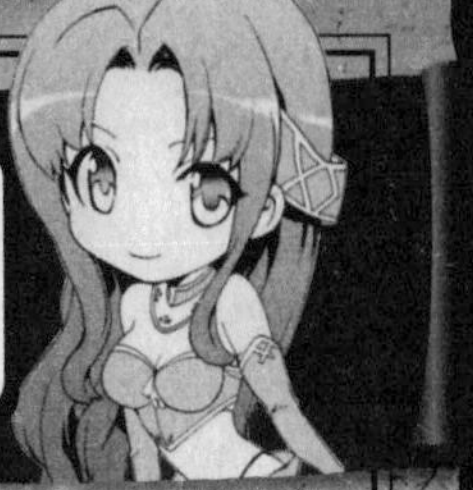
These are so amazing! I wonder if I could ever draw this well...?

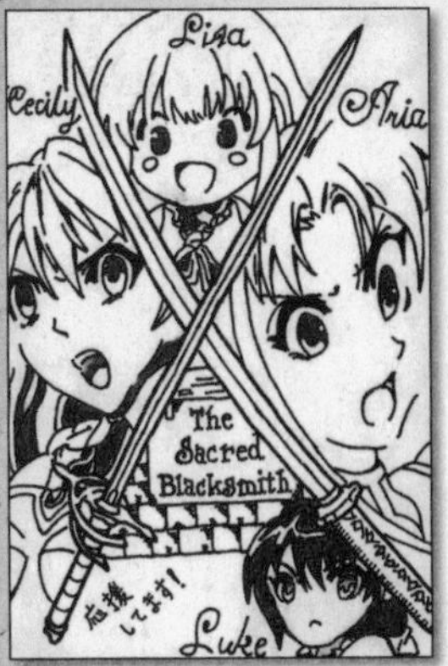
Lisa
Cecily
Aria
The Sacred Blacksmith
応援してます!
Luke

↑Tokyo, Hijiri Kawamoto

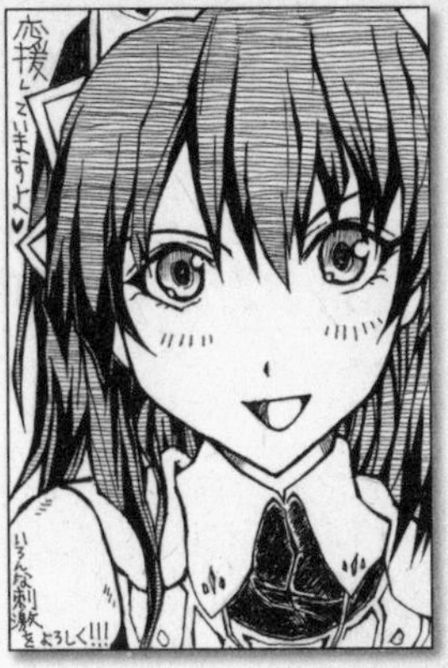
応援しています!

↑Fukuoka, Kyosuke

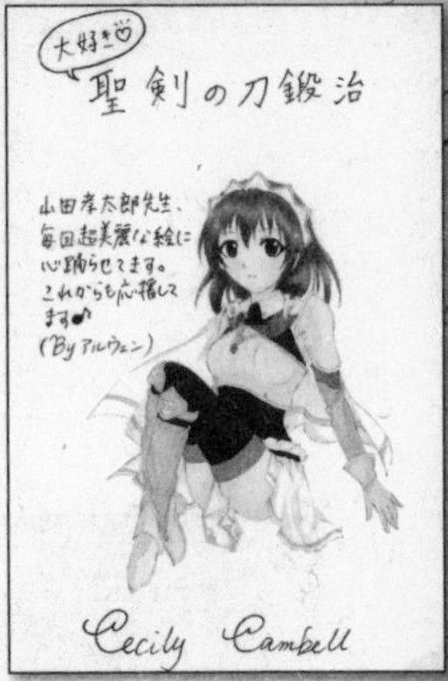
大好き♡
聖剣の刀鍛冶
山田孝太郎先生、
毎回超美麗な絵に
心躍らせてます。
これからも応援して
ます♪
(By アルウェン)
Cecily Cambell

↑Shiga, Yuuki Tamura

Aichi, Excalibur

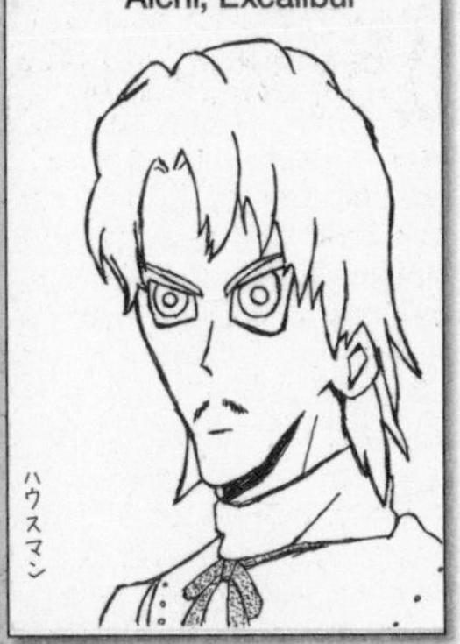
ハウスマン

↑Aichi, Hitoshi

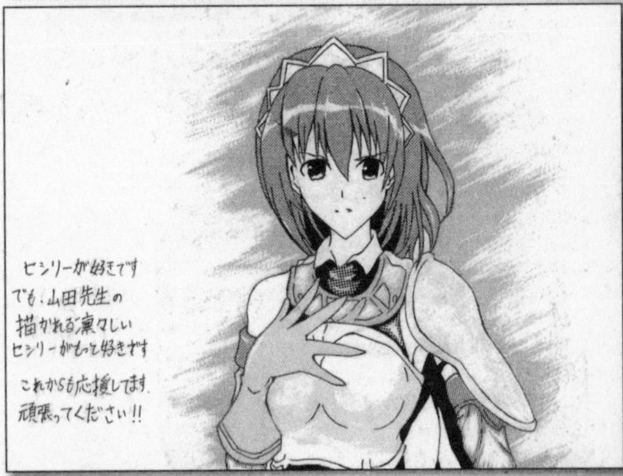
セシリーが好きです
でも、山田先生の
描かれる凛々しい
セシリーがもっと好きです
これからも応援してます.
頑張ってください!!

Okuyama, Masa Kuboki↑

It's because of this kind of wonderful support that we're able to try as hard as we do. I hope you keep sending in this amazing work for me and Cecily!

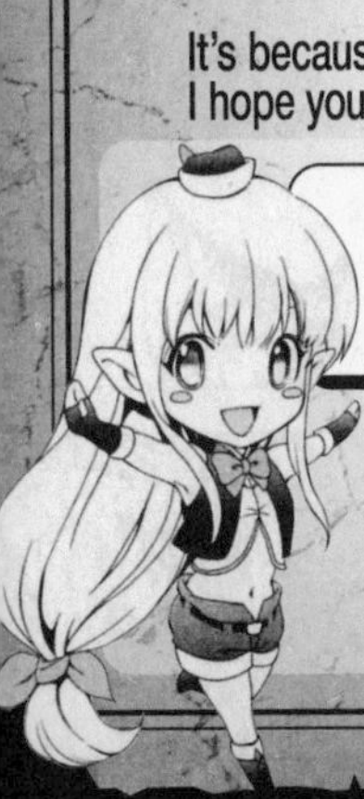
Thank you for all the great postcards! Everyone who was displayed here will receive a personalized sketch from Yamada-sensei himself! We're still accepting submissions, so keep on sending them in!

Note: Fan Art contest only open to residents in Japan.

The Sacred Blacksmith

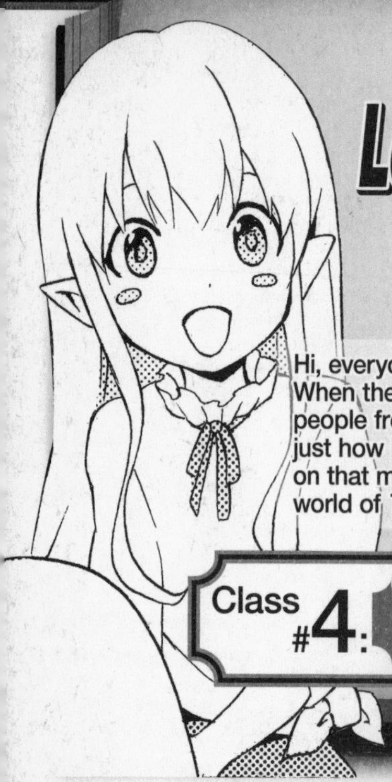

Lisa's Let's Learn Blacksmithing Corner!

Hi, everyone, I'm Lisa! It's been a while.
When the Valbanill Meetings were opened and all of the important people from the various nations showed up, it gives you an idea of just how big Cecily's world is, doesn't it? To shed a little more light on that meeting, in this Corner, I'm going to tell you all about the world of *The Sacred Blacksmith!*

Class #4: The World of The Sacred Blacksmith ~The Continent~

The Precarious Political Balance

Forty-four years after the Valbanill War—

This volume delved into Luke's past. I also got to understand a little of what he's feeling, which is a big relief to me!

Now, the big meeting Luke was summoned to was one of the "Valbanill Meetings," where all the most powerful people of the continent get together. Way back during the Valbanill Wars, every nation was so desperate for victory, they forced not just their soldiers, but even peasants they dragged off the streets to make Demon Pacts. Battles were fought more by demons than by people. And since demons didn't wear any identifying banners or tabards, nobody knew which one was fighting for which nation, so it was all one big bloody brawl that destroyed towns and villages everywhere.

After the war, Demon Pacts were outlawed, and everybody concentrated more on rebuilding than anything else. But the real root cause of that war was the inhuman Valbanill—and the seal keeping him in check was beginning to break! The day would come soon when the seal would vanish completely, so the three major nations and one independent trade city got together and formed what is now called the "Valbanill Meetings" to plan what to do about it. Though from what it looks like now, each nation is spending more time figuring out how they're going to get their hands on the Sacred Blade than anything else.

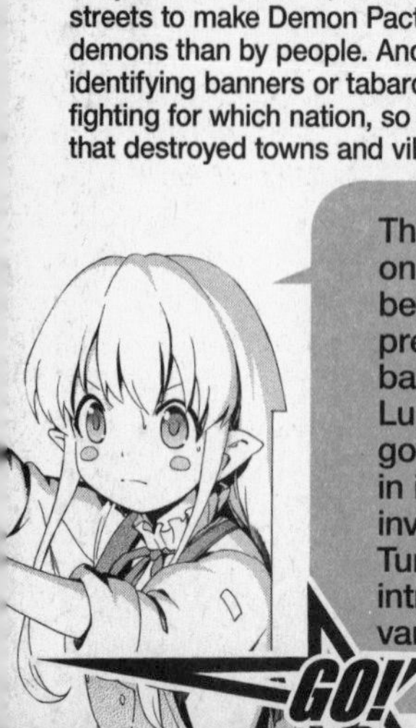

The current peace on the continent is because of a really precarious political balance. How are Luke and Miss Cecily going to get involved in it? What will their involvement do? Turn the page for an introduction to the various nations!

GO!

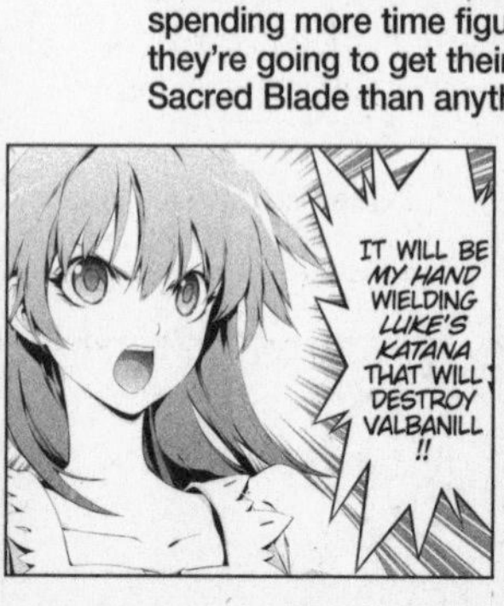
IT WILL BE *MY HAND* WIELDING *LUKE'S KATANA* THAT WILL DESTROY VALBANILL !!

But before we dig any deeper into that, what are the three major nations? And what kind of place is the "Independent" Trade City? Let's take a look!

In-Depth Look! The Nations of The Sacred Blacksmith

Though continental law forbids the publication of world maps, I managed to find one just for you!♪ Let's take a look at the major nations of the world!

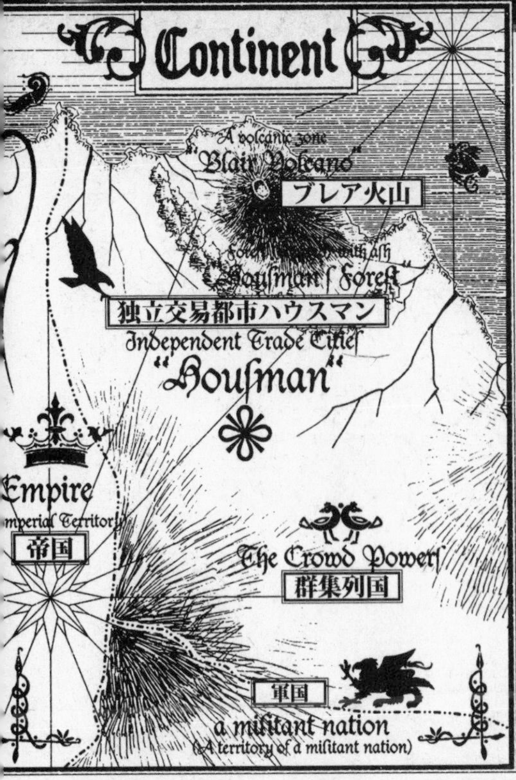
Continent
A volcanic zone
"Blair Volcano"
ブレア火山
Housman's Forest
独立交易都市ハウスマン
Independent Trade Cities
"Housman"
Empire
Imperial Territory
帝国
The Crowd Powers
群集列国
軍国
a militant nation
(A territory of a militant nation)

No one knows exactly how many people died during the Valbanill War, but it was surely an astronomical number. At the end of the war, the territories of the Empire, the Militant Nation, the Crowd Powers and the Independent Trade City were set as you see them on the map to the left. While the general areas of each nation are known, continental law forbids exact figures like size, population and town locations from being disclosed. This law, along with many others, was created by the Continental Legal Council, which was formed at the end of the War. Only a few of the most powerful people on the entire continent are allowed to know the full scope of the land.

Also strongly influencing the continent after the War were the secret documents left behind by the first Housman. He was the one who invented Prayer Pacts, a way to use spirit essence without the terrible results of Demon Pacts. His papers also divulged the existence of Valbanill and the Sacred Blade. Learning of that, the three major nations, along with the Independent Trade City, created regular meetings on the subject, called the "Valbanill Meetings."

Militant Nation

As its name suggests, it is a militant nation where all children, boy or girl, begin military service at age 10.

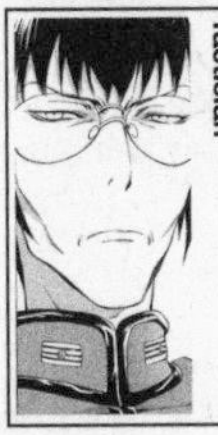

AREVIY IRVING
Tactician

The Empire

A nation ruled by the Emperor and his bloodline, each of whom has the initial "E" as a sign of their rank.

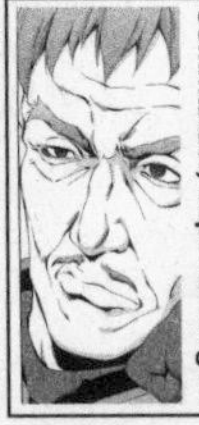

AUGUSTUS ARTHUR
Commander, Imperial Knights

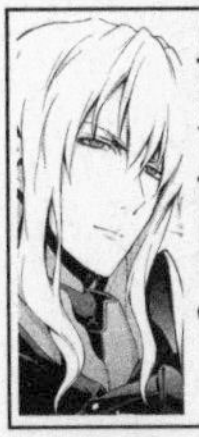

SIEGFRIED
Captain, Imperial Knights

The Crowd Powers

Not a single entity, the Crowd Powers is a collection of small, independent states. They still skirmish with each other for power.

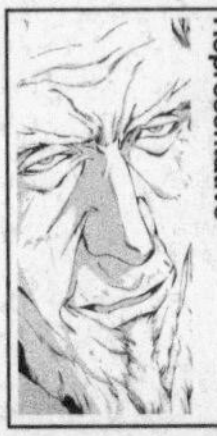

LANCELOT DOUGLAS
Representative

Independent Trade City

Several towns banded together to form the City. Each town is labeled as one of seven "districts." Each district has its own residential, market, and municipal quarters.

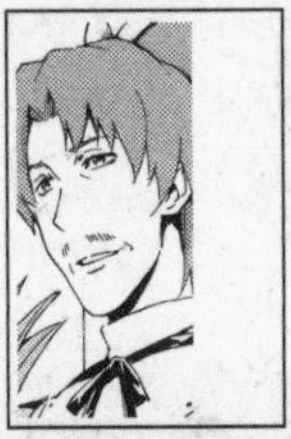

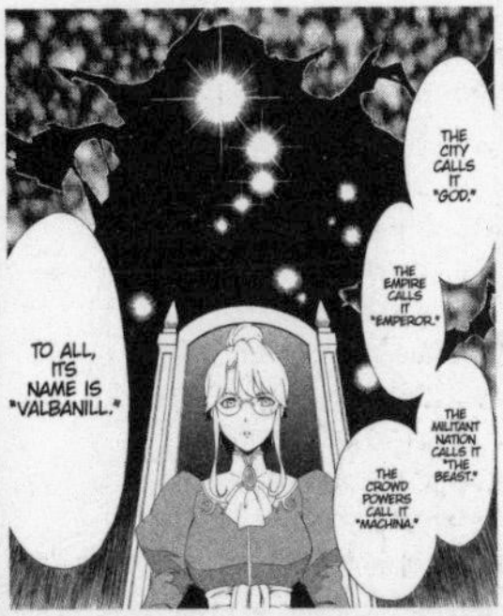
THE CITY CALLS IT "GOD."
THE EMPIRE CALLS IT "EMPEROR."
THE MILITANT NATION CALLS IT "THE BEAST."
THE CROWD POWERS CALL IT "MACHINA."
TO ALL, ITS NAME IS "VALBANILL."

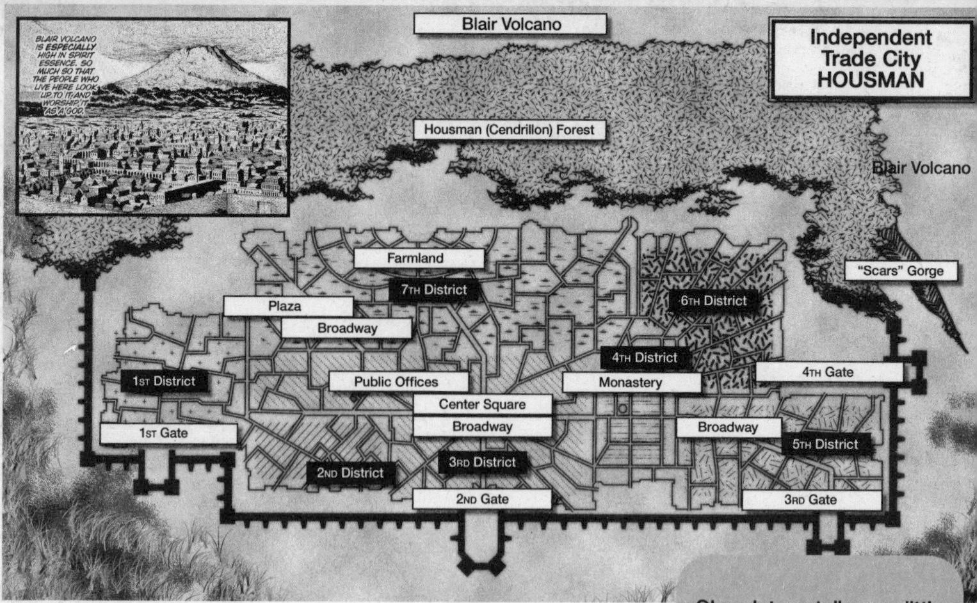
BLAIR VOLCANO IS ESPECIALLY HIGH IN SPIRIT ESSENCE. SO MUCH SO THAT THE PEOPLE WHO LIVE HERE LOOK UP TO IT AND WORSHIP IT AS A GOD.
Blair Volcano
Independent Trade City HOUSMAN
Housman (Cendrillon) Forest
Blair Volcano
"Scars" Gorge
Farmland
7th District
6th District
Plaza
Broadway
4th District
4th Gate
1st District
Public Offices
Monastery
Center Square
Broadway
Broadway
5th District
1st Gate
3rd District
2nd District
2nd Gate
3rd Gate

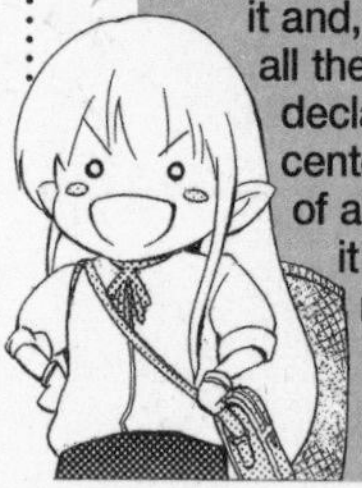

Okay, let me tell you a little about the Independent Trade City of Housman, where we live. It's the only independent city-state on the whole continent! The first Housman founded it and, to keep it out of all the pointless wars, declared it a trading center, independent of all nations. Today, it's peaceful and more prosperous than ever!

[The Market]

The Market is a festival that happens once every three months. Each district—except the 7th, which is only farmland—gets to host it in turn. The biggest attraction is always the Auction! Even Aria was put on sale there once.

[Public Offices]

Each district has its own municipal buildings, but the Mayor has his public offices in the 3rd District, in the middle of the city.

[Common Cemetery]

The city's graveyard is in the 6th district. Jack Strader and Lisa Oakwood were laid to rest there.

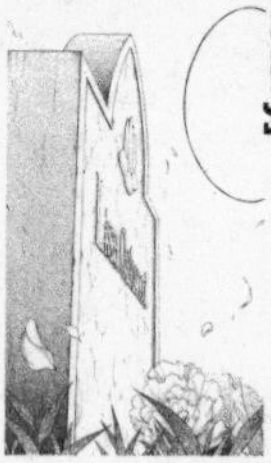

[Atelier Liza]

That's where I work! It's on the edge of the 7th District, near the Cendrillon Forest.

[Housman Forest]

That's the official name for what everybody calls the Cendrillon Forest, which is sandwiched between the city and Blair Volcano. The air there is always full of ash from the volcano, but because of all the spirit essence, the forest survives without being smothered. I'm a demon, so I can go in there just fine, but regular people like Luke and Miss Cecily can't breathe the air in it for too long without getting "essence-drunk." Also, the high level of spirit essence in the forest keeps all the ash from the volcano inside and above it, preventing it from spreading over the city.

Don't forget, continental law forbids spreading this kind of map around, so don't show it to anybody else, okay?

First, we find out the seal on Valbanill is weakening. Next, there's the Empire's Siegfried and what he's up to... so many mysteries! I can hardly wait to read what happens next!

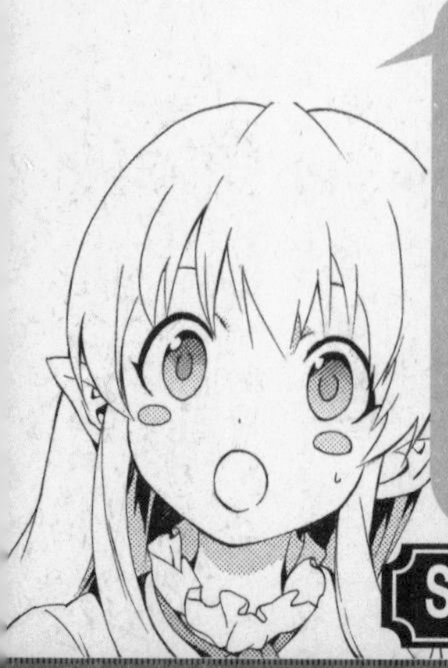

See You Next Time!

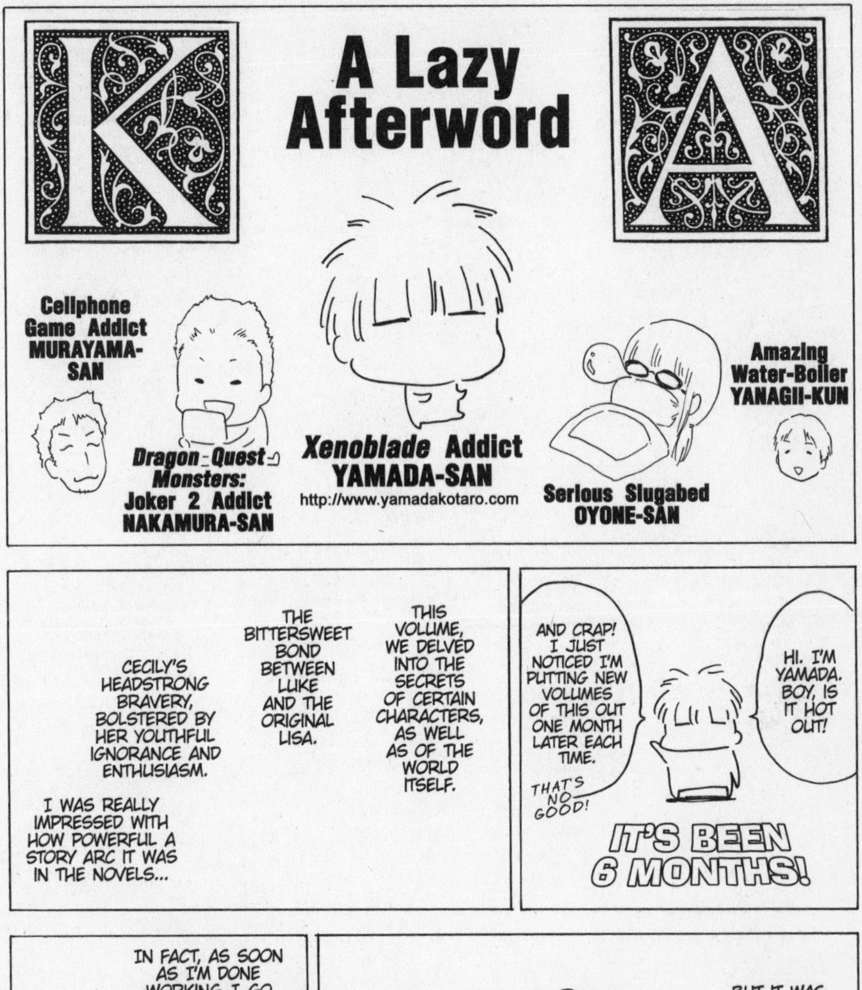
K
A
A Lazy Afterword
Amazing Water-Boiler YANAGII-KUN
Serious Slugabed OYONE-SAN
Xenoblade Addict YAMADA-SAN
http://www.yamadakotaro.com
Cellphone Game Addict MURAYAMA-SAN
Dragon Quest Monsters: Joker 2 Addict NAKAMURA-SAN
HI. I'M YAMADA. BOY, IS IT HOT OUT!
AND CRAP! I JUST NOTICED I'M PUTTING NEW VOLUMES OF THIS OUT ONE MONTH LATER EACH TIME.
THAT'S NO GOOD!
IT'S BEEN 6 MONTHS!
THIS VOLUME, WE DELVED INTO THE SECRETS OF CERTAIN CHARACTERS, AS WELL AS OF THE WORLD ITSELF.
THE BITTERSWEET BOND BETWEEN LUKE AND THE ORIGINAL LISA.
CECILY'S HEADSTRONG BRAVERY, BOLSTERED BY HER YOUTHFUL IGNORANCE AND ENTHUSIASM.
I WAS REALLY IMPRESSED WITH HOW POWERFUL A STORY ARC IT WAS IN THE NOVELS...
BUT IT WAS ALSO ONE REEEALLY LONG MEETING SCENE. I KINDA WANT A LITTLE MORE MOTION GOING ON WHEN I'M DRAWING A MANGA.
FIDGET
FIDGET
FIDGET
FIDGET
SO IN CHAPTER 17, I BROUGHT IN SOME MONSTERS AND SOME ACTION FOR A REFRESHING CHANGE OF PACE! BOY, DID IT FEEL GOOD!
IN FACT, AS SOON AS I'M DONE WORKING, I GO OUT AND RUN AROUND A BIG, GRASSY PLAIN FOR A WHILE. FOR MORE ACTION! IT'S ALWAYS INCREDIBLY REFRESHING!
BAAAAN
AH, SO YOU MEAN RUN AROUND INSIDE OF A VIDEO GAME.

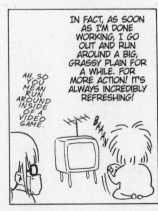

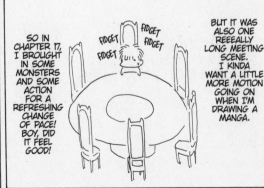

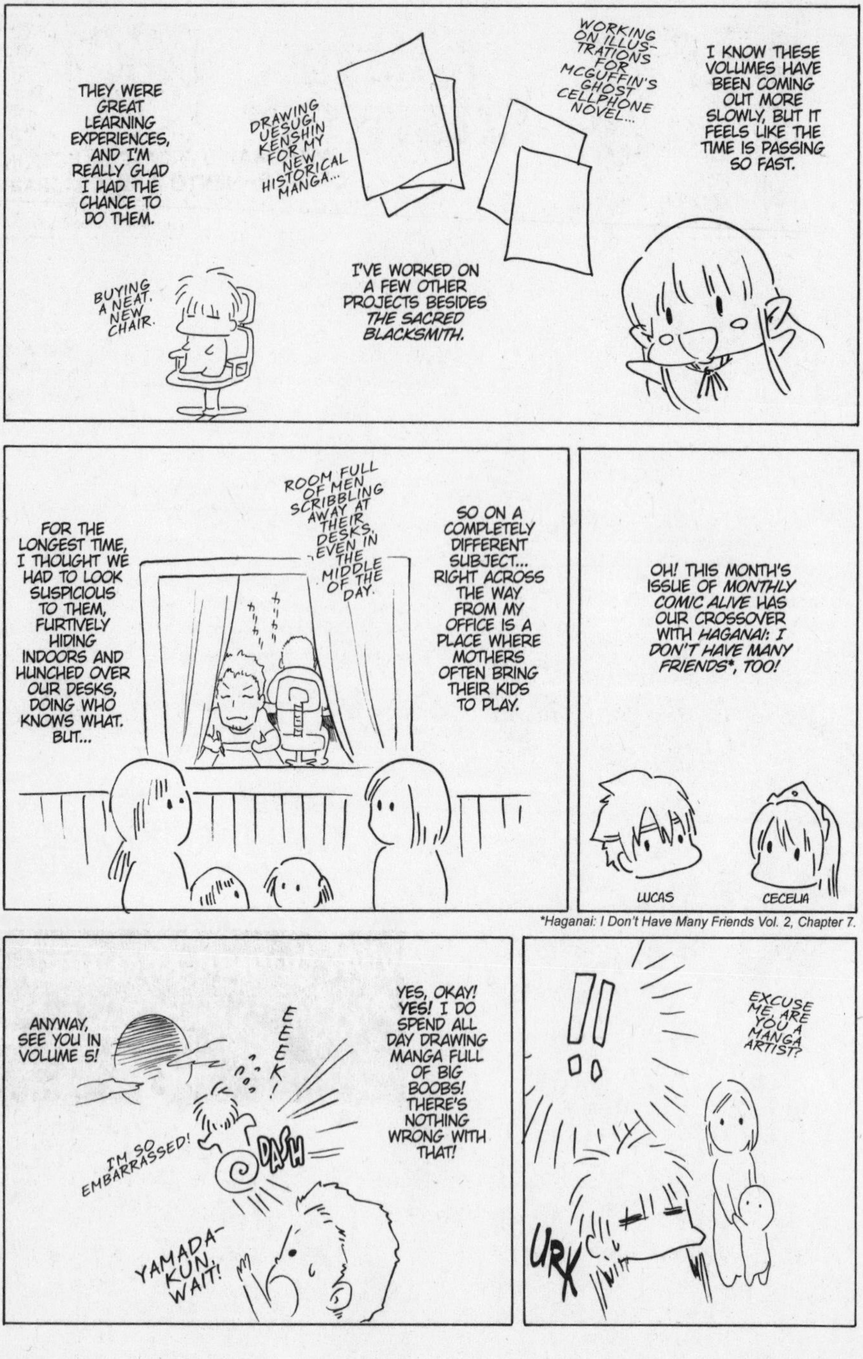
I KNOW THESE VOLUMES HAVE BEEN COMING OUT MORE SLOWLY, BUT IT FEELS LIKE THE TIME IS PASSING SO FAST.
I'VE WORKED ON A FEW OTHER PROJECTS BESIDES THE SACRED BLACKSMITH.
WORKING ON ILLUSTRATIONS FOR MCGUFFIN'S GHOST CELLPHONE NOVEL...
DRAWING UESUGI KENSHIN FOR MY NEW HISTORICAL MANGA...
BUYING A NEAT NEW CHAIR.
THEY WERE GREAT LEARNING EXPERIENCES, AND I'M REALLY GLAD I HAD THE CHANCE TO DO THEM.
OH! THIS MONTH'S ISSUE OF MONTHLY COMIC ALIVE HAS OUR CROSSOVER WITH HAGANAI: I DON'T HAVE MANY FRIENDS*, TOO!
CECELIA
LUCAS
SO ON A COMPLETELY DIFFERENT SUBJECT... RIGHT ACROSS THE WAY FROM MY OFFICE IS A PLACE WHERE MOTHERS OFTEN BRING THEIR KIDS TO PLAY.
ROOM FULL OF MEN SCRIBBLING AWAY AT THEIR DESKS, EVEN IN THE MIDDLE OF THE DAY.
FOR THE LONGEST TIME, I THOUGHT WE HAD TO LOOK SUSPICIOUS TO THEM, FURTIVELY HIDING INDOORS AND HUNCHED OVER OUR DESKS, DOING WHO KNOWS WHAT. BUT...
EXCUSE ME, ARE YOU A MANGA ARTIST?
!!
URK
YES, OKAY! YES! I DO SPEND ALL DAY DRAWING MANGA FULL OF BIG BOOBS! THERE'S NOTHING WRONG WITH THAT!
EEEK!
DASH
I'M SO EMBARRASSED!
YAMADA-KUN, WAIT!
ANYWAY, SEE YOU IN VOLUME 5!

**Haganai: I Don't Have Many Friends Vol. 2, Chapter 7.*

SEVEN SEAS ENTERTAINMENT PRESENTS

THE SACRED BLACKSMITH

art by **KOTARO YAMADA** / story by **ISAO MIURA** **VOLUME 4**

TRANSLATION
Adrienne Beck

ADAPTATION
Janet Houck

LETTERING
Roland Amago

LAYOUT
Bambi Eloriaga-Amago

COVER DESIGN
Nicky Lim

PROOFREADER
Shanti Whitesides

MANAGING EDITOR
Adam Arnold

PUBLISHER
Jason DeAngelis

Seven Seas books may be purchased in bulk for educational, business, or promotional use. For information on bulk purchases, please contact Macmillan Corporate & Premium Sales Department at 1-800-221-7945 (ext 5442) or write specialmarkets@macmillan.com.

ISBN: 978-1-626920-08-8

Printed in Canada

First Printing: March 2014

10 9 8 7 6 5 4 3 2 1

FOLLOW US ONLINE:

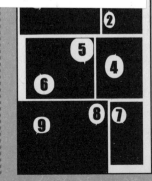

READING DIRECTIONS

This book reads from ***right to left***, Japanese style. If this is your first time reading manga, you start reading from the top right panel on each page and take it from there. If you get lost, just follow the numbered diagram here. It may seem backwards at first, but you'll get the hang of it! Have fun!!

2
5
4
6
8
7
9